THE PRIMEVAL FLOOD CA

Previous research on Mesopotamian Flood traditions tended to focus on a few textual sources. How the traditions originated and developed as a whole has not been seriously investigated. By systematically examining a large body of relevant cuneiform sources of diverse genres from the Early Dynastic III period (*c.*2600–2350 BC) to the end of the first millennium BC, Y. S. Chen observes that it is during the Old Babylonian period (*c.*2000–1600 BC) that the first and classical attestations of the Flood traditions are found. On linguistic, conceptual, and literary-historical grounds, Chen argues that the Flood traditions emerged relatively late in Sumerian traditions. He traces different evolutionary stages of the Flood traditions, from the emergence of the Flood motif within the socio-political and cultural contexts of the early Isin dynasty (*c.*2017–1896 BC), to the diverse mythological representations of the motif in literary traditions, to the historicization of the motif in chronography, and finally to the interactions between various strands of the Flood traditions and other Mesopotamian literary traditions, such as Sumerian and Babylonian compositions about Gilgameš.

By uncovering the processes through which the Flood traditions were constructed, Chen offers a valuable case study on the complex and dynamic relationship between myth-making, the development of literature, the rise of historical consciousness and historiography, and socio-political circumstances in the ancient world. The origins and development of the Flood traditions examined in the book, furthermore, represents one of the best documented examples illustrating the continuities and changes in Mesopotamian intellectual, linguistic, literary, socio-political, and religious history over the course of two and a half millennia.

Y. S. Chen is Research Fellow at the University of Oxford where he is also Associate Faculty Member of the Oxford Oriental Institute.

OXFORD ORIENTAL MONOGRAPHS

This series of monographs from the Faculty of Oriental Studies, University of Oxford, makes available the results of recent research by scholars connected with the Faculty. Its range of subject matter includes language, literature, thought, history, and art; its geographical scope extends from the Mediterranean and Caucasus to East Asia. The emphasis is more on specialist studies than on works of a general nature.

The Primeval Flood Catastrophe

Origins and Early Development in Mesopotamian Traditions

Y. S. CHEN

OXFORD
UNIVERSITY PRESS

OXFORD
UNIVERSITY PRESS

Great Clarendon Street, Oxford, OX2 6DP,
United Kingdom

Oxford University Press is a department of the University of Oxford.
It furthers the University's objective of excellence in research, scholarship, and education by publishing worldwide. Oxford is a registered trade mark of Oxford University Press in the UK and in certain other countries

First published 2013
First published in paperback 2019

Published in the United States of America by Oxford University Press
198 Madison Avenue, New York, NY 10016, United States of America

British Library Cataloguing in Publication Data
Data available

Library of Congress Cataloging in Publication Data
Data available

ISBN 978–0–19–967620–0 (Hbk.)
ISBN 978–0–19–884341–2 (Pbk.)

To my wife, parents and parents-in-law, children,
and our American families

Preface

This book is a revised edition of the first volume of my D.Phil. thesis which was submitted to the Faculty of Oriental Studies at the University of Oxford on 7 October 2009. It aims to trace the origins and development of Mesopotamian Flood traditions. It tackles not just the composition and transmission history of individual Flood traditions, such as the *Atra-hasīs Epic*, but investigates the process through which these traditions evolved as a whole and in relation with one another and other literary traditions. To this end, a large body of relevant cuneiform sources of diverse genres from the Early Dynastic III period to the end of the first millennium BC has been examined. The book has systematically investigated different aspects of the history of the Flood traditions, especially the orthographic and semantic evolution of flood terminology in Sumerian and Akkadian, the development of mythological and historiographical representations of the Flood motif, and the conceptual and literary processes involved in the development of the Flood traditions. It has also explored the socio-political circumstances in which the above linguistic, conceptual, and literary developments occurred in ancient Mesopotamia. It is hoped that the book will not only provide a fresh and overarching view on the history of the Flood traditions, but also assist our interpretation of individual traditions involved and contribute to our understanding of Mesopotamian intellectual, cultural and socio-political history at large. Furthermore, the findings in this study will be useful to scholars working on, or readers interested in, comparative literature, historiography, and mythology in ancient Near Eastern and other cultural traditions. As pointed out by Tigay (1985), the well-documented history of Mesopotamian literary traditions can shed new light on the composition and transmission history of other ancient traditions which are less well documented.

Though I intended to examine all the extant textual sources from ancient Mesopotamia related to the Flood which we now have available, several recently discovered cuneiform sources were made known to me too late to be included in the detailed study of this book: the Schøyen Collection MS 3026, a Neo-Sumerian source of the *Sumerian Flood Story*, as noted by Alster (2005: 33); RS 94.2953, published by Arnaud (2007: 201–2 and pl. 29), which is recognized by Andrew George and Antoine Cavigneaux as a Middle Babylonian source of the Flood episode in the *Gilgameš Epic* or 'a fragment belonging with RS 22.421 (Ugaritica V 167, Lambert and Millard 131–3)' (George 2007: 254); RS 94.2006, a Middle Babylonian source of the opening lines of the *Gilgameš epic*, as published by Arnaud (2007: 130–4 and pls. 19–20) and George (2007: 237–54); the Schøyen Collection MS 5108 and MS 2950, two Old Babylonian sources of the *Atra-hasīs Epic*, as published by George (2009: 16–27 and pls. 5–8, 9–10); and an Old Babylonian source of the *Atra-hasīs Epic* in a private collection which was discovered by Irving Finkel (Kennedy 2010) who is writing a book on the tablet as well as Mesopotamian Flood traditions in general. It is hoped that these sources will be examined in a future study. The recent report in the *New York Times* of a Sumerian tablet in the University of Pennsylvania Museum which allegedly 'dates from about 2700 B.C.' and 'is the world's first known written account of the biblical flood' (Hurdle 2012) turns out to be a mistake. This is the same tablet (CBS 10673 + CBS 10867) from the late Old Babylonian period (*c*.1600 BC) which the museum has had for many years.

Y. S. Chen

Oxford
22 May 2013

Acknowledgements

Throughout the process of researching, writing, and preparing this book, I have received guidance, assistance, and support from my doctoral research supervisors, teachers, colleagues, institutions, friends, and family. I would like to thank them for all their help and encouragement.

I wish to express my gratitude and indebtedness to Professor H. G. M. Williamson at the Oriental Institute, University of Oxford, and Dr Alasdair Livingstone at the Institute of Archaeology and Antiquity, University of Birmingham, who supervised the research and writing of the original thesis. It was under Professor Williamson's supervision that I moved into the historical research of the Flood traditions, initially proposing to pursue a comparative study of biblical and Mesopotamian traditions. As my research gradually shifted to focus on Mesopotamian materials, he made painstaking efforts to ensure that I received proper supervision from an established and suitable Assyriologist while continuing to provide all the advice and assistance needed in my research. Had it not been for his skilful and patient guidance, I could not have completed the project. The current book was also made possible because of his suggestion in 2009 that I propose my thesis for publication in the Oxford Oriental Monographs. It has been the privilege of a lifetime to be able to work with him as an eminent scholar and an unfailing teacher who always does what is best for his students.

I am equally grateful to Dr Livingstone, who became the primary supervisor of my thesis. I benefited immensely from the wealth of his knowledge and experience in Assyriological research, especially his expertise on Mesopotamian mythology and scholarship, and from his unsparing investment of time and effort in discussing numerous details involved. His constant availability and encouragement substantially eased the burden of research and writing. And his great sense of humour also kept many long hours of philological discussions and research lively and enjoyable. I could not expect a better supervisor for my research. I am also indebted to him for his unabated support for the development of my scholarly career beyond my doctoral research.

Special thanks are due to Dr Jacob Dahl at the Oriental Institute, University of Oxford, and Professor Kevin Cathcart at University College, Dublin, as my examiners who gave detailed comments on my thesis. Dr Dahl brought to my attention the new antediluvian king list MS 2855 from the Schøyen Collection, which was published by Professor Jöran Friberg (2007), and Professor Piotr Michalowski's recent publication on the correspondence of the kings of Ur (2011). Dr Dahl has also been instrumental in the development of my postdoctoral career, facilitating my publication of this book and several journal articles, coaching my presentations at different international conferences, involving me in teaching at the Oriental Faculty and in a research project studying the cuneiform collection in the Ashmolean Museum, and encouraging me in my applications for research fellowships. I am immensely grateful for his mentorship and friendship.

I would also like to acknowledge the following scholars at Oxford who provided assistance and constructive criticisms through teaching, examinations, and discussions at different stages of my research and preparation of this book: Dr Graham Cunningham, Dr Stephanie Dalley, Dr Frances Reynolds, and Dr Eleanor Robson. Special thanks should go to Professor Marc Van De Mieroop, who helped me make significant progress in research while he was teaching at Oxford between 2007 and 2008.

The academic skills required for the research and writing of this book were gained not just during my doctoral and postdoctoral training in the UK but also in the US where I did my undergraduate and postgraduate studies. I would like to thank my former teachers Professors Gary Anderson, Michael Bauman, John Currid, Peter Enns, Jo Ann Hackett, John Huehnergard, James Juroe, Michael M. Jordan, James Kugel, Jon D. Levenson, Enoch Wan, and Donald Westblade. Special tribute must be paid to my former supervisor Professor Peter Machinist at Harvard for the profound impact of his teaching and scholarship on my academic development and for his ongoing support. The graduate seminars he taught, especially 'Myth and Myth-Making in the Biblical and Ancient Near Eastern World' and 'History and Historiography in the Ancient Near East', together with his seminal research (e.g., Machinist 1976: 455–82; 1983a: 221–26; 1983b: 719–37; 1986: 183–202; 1993: 77–104; 1994: 35–60; 1995a: 159–75; 1995b: 105–20; 1995c: 179–95; 2003: 117–37; 2005: 31–61) helped lay the theoretical, methodological, and philological foundations for my doctoral research. I am also particularly indebted to my Akkadian teacher at Harvard Professor Paul-Alain Beaulieu for introducing me to Assyriology, for providing stimulating suggestions for the research of this book, and for kindly sending me his article on Babylonian wisdom literature before its publication. I must also thank Professor Huehnergard for responding to my query on the grammatical construction of *(w)atram-ḫasīs* during the final stage of my preparation for this book.

Certain portions of my doctoral thesis were presented as conference papers or seminar lectures at the following international scholarly conferences and academic institutions: the 56th Rencontre Assyriologique Internationale 'Time and History in the Ancient Near East' held at the University of Barcelona on 28 July 2010; the 'Assyriology and the Bible' Section and the 'Bible, Myth, and Myth Theory' Section at the Annual Society of Biblical Literature Meeting in Atlanta, Georgia on 20 and 21 November 2010; the Research Fellow Seminar

Series at Wolfson College, University of Oxford on 1 March 2011; and the 'Signs and Symbols' Research Seminar Series at the London Centre for the Ancient Near East, School of Oriental and African Studies, University of London on 12 December 2011. I am grateful to the following scholars whose critical and stimulating feedback on my presentations during the conferences and seminars contributed to the revision of my thesis for this publication: Dr Nick Allen, Professor Dominique Charpin, Professor Jerrold Cooper, Professor Andrew George, Dr Dina Katz, Professor Jacob Klein, Professor Stefan Maul, Professor Jared Miller, Professor Michael Roaf, Professor Michael Tanret, Dr Mark Weeden, Dr Joan Goodnick Westenholz†, Dr Magnus Widell, Dr Martin Worthington, and Dr Ilya Yakubovich. Professor George also alerted me to the new textual sources of the *Gilgameš Epic* RS 94.2006 and RS 94.2953 and the new textual source of the *Atra-hasīs Epic* which was recently discovered by Dr Irving Finkel.

I must also thank Dr Bendt Alster† for the responses he provided for my thesis, Professor Robert Englund for the technical assistance he lent for the revision of my thesis, Dr Nili Samet for sending me a copy of her doctoral thesis (2009) submitted to Bar-Ilan University which presents a revised edition of the *Lamentation over the Destruction of Ur*, Dr Christopher Metcalf at the University of Oxford and the School of Oriental and African Studies, University of London, who brought to my attention Dr Catherine Mittermayer's recent edition of *Enmerkar and the Lord of Aratta*. Dr Irving Finkel, who kindly responded to my queries on the new tablet concerning the *Atra-hasīs Epic* he discovered, likewise deserves to be acknowledged here. Right before I submitted the manuscript of this book for publication, Professor Daniel Fleming kindly referred me to Dr Sara J. Milstein's doctoral dissertation (2010) submitted to New York University. I am delighted that Dr Milstein and I independently reached some similar observations and conclusions with regard to the *Instructions of Šuruppak* and the *Sumerian King List*.

Several institutions at Oxford should be acknowledged for enabling me to complete my thesis and this book: The Oriental Institute provided all the academic support for my doctoral research and granted me the Associate Faculty Membership for my postdoctoral research. I am particularly indebted to the former Chair of the Faculty Board Dr Luke Treadwell for helping me at a crucial stage in my research programme, and the former Faculty Board Secretary Ms Charlotte Vinnicombe for her excellent administrative support. Worcester College provided much practical support for me and my family while I was pursuing my doctoral research. My college adviser Dr Susan Gillingham, the former Provost Mr Richard Smethurst, and the College Graduate Officer Ms Cath Fraser were of particular help to me.

That this book can be completed is largely due to a Research Fellowship offered by Wolfson College, Oxford, since 2010. I am grateful to the President Professor Dame Hermione Lee, Fellows, and the entire community of Wolfson for all the privileges and enjoyable experience, including research funding, residential, research and teaching facilities, and a stimulating and supportive environment, provided through the Fellowship.

It is important to acknowledge other funding sources for the research of my thesis and this book: Harvey Fellowship, Langham Research Scholarship, the Pusey and Ellerton Fund, and Scholar Leaders International. I am also indebted to several individual friends who made financial contributions to support my research: Leon and Lynn Hsiao, Jason and May Lok, and James and Betty Roberson.

I am grateful to the Delegates of Oxford University Press (OUP) for accepting this book for publication, and to the readers appointed by OUP for the detailed comments they provided for different drafts of this book. Special thanks should go to Professor Geert Jan van Gelder, Former Chair of the Editorial Board of the Oxford Oriental Monographs, my Commissioning Editor Ms Elizabeth Robottom and Production Editors Mr David Tomlinson and Ms Caroline Hawley at OUP, my Copy-editor Ms Heather Watson, and my proofreader Mr Clifford Willis for their first-rate editorial services.

I am also particularly indebted to Ms Maria Giannuzzi who has faithfully provided excellent editorial support for many drafts of my thesis and book in the past ten years.

Dr Michael Athanson, Deputy Map Librarian and Geospatial Data Specialist at the Bodleian Library, University of Oxford, helped produce the fine maps in this book. The following people assisted me with my requests for the photographs and drawings included in this book and the reproduction permissions needed: Mr Kevin Cooney at the American Schools of Oriental Research; Ms Amy Taylor and Ms Hannah Kendall at the Ashmolean Museum, University of Oxford; Professor Jacob Klein at Bar-Ilan University; Ms Gaby van Rietschoten at Brill; Ms Allyson Carless at the British Museum Company Limited; Mr Christopher Sutherns at the British Museum Images; Mr Perry Cartwright at the University of Chicago Press; Ms Monica G. Velez at theriental Institute Museum, University of Chicago; Professor Gershon Galil at the University of Haifa; Mr Perry Harel at the Hecht Museum, University of Haifa; Ms Nicole Centmayer at Harrassowitz Verlag; Professor Piotr Steinkeller at Harvard; Professor Wilfred van Soldt at Leiden University; Professor Marten Stol in the Netherlands; Professor Piotr Michalowski at the University of Michigan; Ms Katherine Blanchard, Ms Chrisso Boulis, and Ms Maureen Goldsmith at the University of Pennsylvania Museum; and Mr Martin Schøyen from the Schøyen Collection. To all of them I express my sincere thanks.

Many friends in the US and UK stood by me and my family during the long and tortuous process of my research in Oxford: Peter and Grace Lee Baughan, Revd Dr Grant and Liang-Shwu Chen, Revd Dr Tsu-Kung and Marie Chuang, Dr Hywel Clifford, Dr Hang Gao and Hui Guo, the Very Revd Dr Chris Hancock, Revd Dr Jerrard Heard, Dr Jill Howard, Dr Michele Hu and Dr Simon Cudlip, Dr Judith Jacobson, David and Gwyneth Johnson, Charles Ko and Sharon Lin, Revd Joe Martin, Professor Rana Mitter, Darren and Joanna Oliveiro-Priestnall, Ian† and Cath Peedle, Revd Vaughan Roberts, Dr Ian J. Shaw, Larry and Victoria Smith, Professor Anh and Chia Ling Tran, Dr Jeffrey and Carmen Tseng, Paul and Nancy Tsou, Revd Peter and Julia Wilkinson, and Revd Dr Chi-Hok Wong. To them I owe much gratitude.

I reserve my deepest appreciations to my families: to my wife Annie for her loving patience and support; to our children Gabriel and Juliana for the great enjoyment they brought to our life in the midst of my long and tedious academic work; to my parents Junjie Chen and Biru Zeng and my parents-in-law Zichang Nie and Maoqiong Liu for the tremendous sacrifice they have made due to many years of our absence in pursuit of higher learning overseas; to James and Ellen Juroe and their family who not only helped me start my academic journey in the West twenty-two years ago but also have cared for my family as their own; and to Frank and Wilma Huyser and their family who likewise have helped sustain my family as their own. Without the above family support, I could not have started and completed this project.

Contents

List of Plates

List of Abbreviations

Abbreviations follow the conventions set forth by the Cuneiform Digital Library Initiative (http://cdli.ucla.edu/wiki/doku.php/abbreviations_for_assyriology) except for what are listed below:

adn.	Adad-nīrārī
AN	Antiquities
ARG	*Archiv für Religionsgeschichte*
ASOR	American Schools of Oriental Research
Borger Esarh.	R. Borger, Die Inschriften Asarhaddons, Königs von Assyrien (= *AfO* Beiheft 9)
CBAA	Catholic Biblical Association of America
CBQ	*Catholic Biblical Quarterly*
CDL	Capital Decisions Ltd
CDOG	Colloquien der Deutschen Orient-Gesellschaft
CRRA	Compte Rendu de la Rencontre Assyriologique Internationale
CSA	Copenhagen Studies in Assyriology
Dur.	Durative
GAAL	Göttinger Arbeitshefte zur altorientalischen Literatur
JANER	*Journal of Ancient Near Eastern Religions*
LE	*Lamentation over the Destruction of Eridu*
LU	*Lamentation over the Destruction of Ur*
LW	*Lamentation over the Destruction of Uruk*
MMA	tablets in the collections of the Metropolitan Museum of Art
MS(S)	Manuscript(s)
NATCP	Neo-Assyrian Text Corpus Project
NL	*Lamentation over the Destruction of Nippur*
OBC	Orientalia Biblica et Christiana
PIP-TraCS	Papers in Intercultural Philosophy and Transcontinental Comparative Studies
SAAS	State Archives of Assyria Studies
Sar.	Sargon II

segm.	segment
Senn.	Sennacherib
SSHMP	Sources and Studies in the History of Mathematics and Physical Sciences
TL	Tell Leilān version of the *SKL*
TSBA	*Transactions of the Society of Biblical Archaeology*
UCBC	tablets in the collections of the Museum of Anthropology at the University of California, Berkeley
Ukg.	Urukagina
UMB	*University Museum Bulletin*
USKL	Ur III copy of the *SKL*
Vol.	Volume
W-B	H. Weld-Blundell collection in the Ashmolean Museum

Note on Transliteration and Translation

Though this book relies primarily on scholarly editions for the cuneiform texts involved, efforts have been made to consult hand or photo copies of the texts when it comes to crucial philological and textual issues, and to check variants in the manuscript traditions of texts (if they have more than one exemplar) as appropriate. Transliteration and translation provided in this study are adapted from the scholarly editions or electronic sources. Unless stated otherwise, citations of most of the Sumerian sources follow the Electronic Text Corpus of Sumerian Literature (http://etcsl.orinst.ox.ac.uk), the canonical lamentations after Cohen (1988), the *Atra-hasīs Epic* and its recensions after Lambert and Millard (1969), and the *Gilgameš Epic* after George (2003). Transliteration of cuneiform signs follows the preferred sign readings of the Cuneiform Digital Library Initiative (http://cdli.ucla.edu/methods/signreading.html) and those of Borger's *Zeichenlexikon* (2003). Critical philological notes and commentaries of the cited sources, though not being included in this book, can be found in Vol. 2 of Chen (2009).

Brief remarks should be made with regard to the use of scholarly editions in this study. By quoting Michalowski's candid statement in his edition of *LSU* that the composite text he presents never existed in history, Black (1998: 32–8) emphasizes the precariousness of relying on such scholarly 'constructs' for literary analysis. Such limitations of the composite text may be counterbalanced by the so-called score presentation of all extant manuscripts in scholarly editions of relevant cuneiform texts, from which the reader can observe how the composite text is put together and to what extent it represents different manuscripts.

Relevant Dates of Ancient Mesopotamia

Late Uruk Period (*c.*3400–3000 BC)
Early Dynastic I–II Periods (*c.*3000–2700 BC)
Early Dynastic III Period (*c.*2600–2350 BC)
Old Akkadian or Sargonic Period (*c.*2350–2200 BC)
Lagaš II Period (*c.*2200–2100 BC)
Ur III Period (*c.*2100–2000 BC)
Old Assyrian Period (*c.*2000–1900 BC)
Old Babylonian Period (*c.*2000–1600 BC)
Middle Babylonian Period (*c.*1500–1000 BC)
Middle Assyrian Period (*c.*1500–1000 BC)
Neo-Assyrian Period (*c.*900–612 BC)
Neo-Babylonian Period (*c.*620–540 BC)
Achaemenid Period (*c.*540–330 BC)
Hellenistic Period (*c.*330–141 BC)
Parthian Period (*c.*141 BC–AD 224)

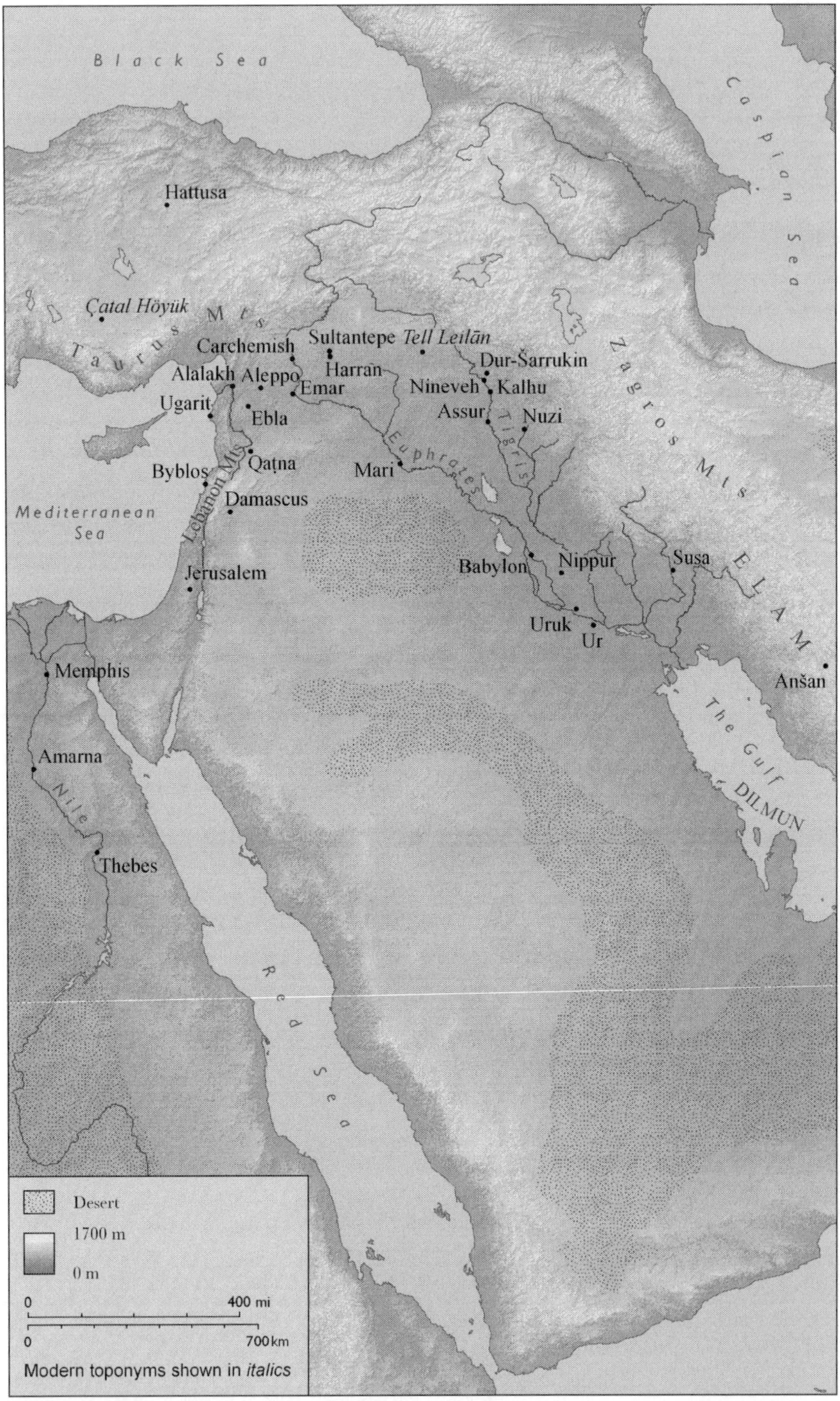

Map 1. Ancient Near East, showing major historical places. (Made with Natural Earth and the Global 30 Arc-Second Elevation Data Set.)

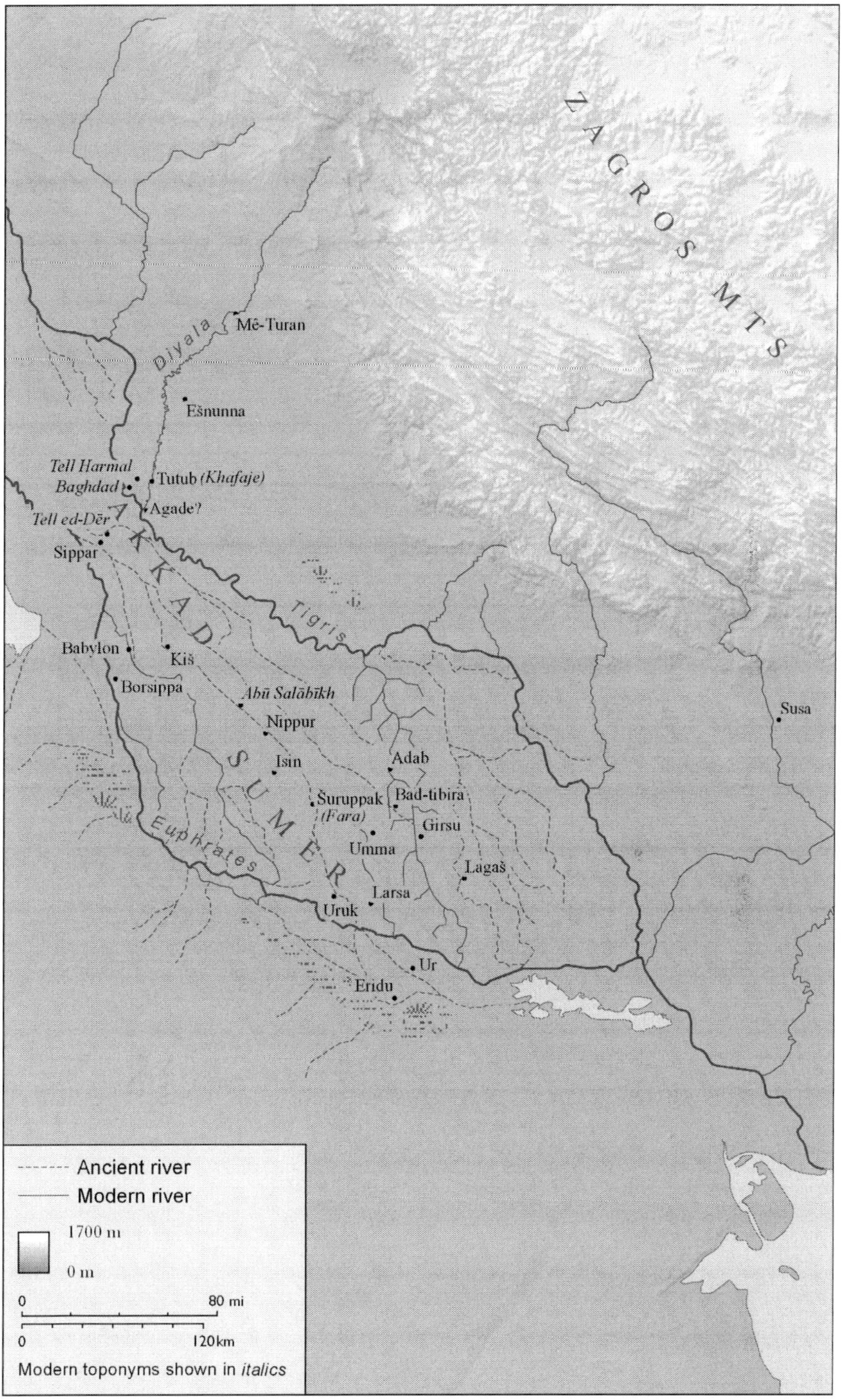

Map 2. Ancient Mesopotamia, showing the major places mentioned in the book. (Made with Natural Earth and the Global 30 Arc-Second Elevation Data Set. Ancient watercourses adapted from Verhoeven 1998: 162.)

Introduction

The flood myth and narrative, it is said, have received more popular or scholarly attentions than any other myths or traditional narratives (Dundes 1988: 1).[1] Among all the flood myths surveyed by Lewis (1992: 798), it is the biblical Flood tradition that has been most widely known in the last two millennia. But since the time of George Smith (1840–76), who galvanized the public and scholarly circles on 3 December 1872 through the announcement of his sensational discovery of the 'Chaldean Account of the Deluge' from the library of Neo-Assyrian king Ashurbanipal, attention has been given increasingly to Mesopotamian Flood traditions. This momentous discovery gave rise to the modern historical and comparative study of the Flood traditions, and led to the birth of the field of Assyriology (Michalowski 2000: 177). The 'Chaldean Account' is part of Tablet XI of the Standard Babylonian version of the *Gilgameš Epic* (Plate 1), which Smith ingeniously reconstructed among several thousands of tablet fragments.[2] Together with excerpts from another version of the Babylonian Flood story—later known as the *Atra-hasīs Epic* (Lambert and Millard 1969: 3)—which Smith subsequently published in 1876, the Flood account from the *Gilgameš Epic* proves invaluable for comparative studies as it contains 'numerous and precise' parallels with the biblical Flood account (Liverani 2005: 234).

Given that the Babylonian accounts are regarded by most scholars to be more ancient than their biblical counterpart and that the Flood story fits the geo-hydrological conditions of Mesopotamia more than those of Palestine,[3] it is generally believed by scholars that the Flood story originated in Mesopotamia and was transmitted into Syro-Palestine, as early as the Amarna Period in the latter half of the second millennium BC. The recension of the *Atra-hasīs Epic*

[1] Throughout this book 'flood' is used to convey the generic sense of the word, while 'Flood' or 'Deluge' is used to denote the primeval flood catastrophe. Not all flood stories or myths deal with the primeval flood.

[2] See Dundes 1988: 29–31; Cathcart 1997: 81; George 2003: 411–15.

[3] See Buringh 1957: 30–46; Adams 1981: 1–26; Postgate 1992: 1–21, 173–90; Cole 1994: 81–109; Cole and Gasche 1999: 87–110; Van De Mieroop 2004: 7–10.

discovered in Ras Shamra, Ugaritica V 167 = RS 22.421 (𝕳), which is dated to around the fourteenth century BC, supports this view (Lambert and Millard 1969: 131–3).

Innumerable comparative and historical studies of the biblical and Mesopotamian Flood traditions have been produced since the time of Smith. Most of these studies tended to focus on the Flood stories and primeval history in the biblical account and a few well-known Mesopotamian mythological narratives (e.g. the *Atra-hasīs Epic* and the Standard Babylonian version of the *Gilgameš Epic*) and chronographical texts (e.g. the Weld-Blundell 444 version of *the Sumerian King List*) available at the time. Towards the end of the twentieth century, interest in the Flood stories seemed to wane, as scholars began to turn to other, fresh areas of research. There was an impression that comparative and historical studies of the Flood traditions had been exhausted.

But with the increasing, even overwhelming, amount of relevant Mesopotamian sources that have come down to us from the Early Dynastic III period (*c.*2600–2350 BC) to the first century BC,[4] studies on the Flood traditions continue to represent a promising and fertile field of research. Sumerian and Akkadian flood terms are found not only in mythological narratives and chronographical texts, but also in divine and royal hymns, royal inscriptions, didactic literature, disputations, administrative documents, administrative and literary letters, astrological and astronomical texts, incantations and magical texts, lexical texts, and literary catalogues. The increase in the amount of relevant fresh evidence, however, makes the task of comparative and historical studies more challenging with more data to collate and more complex historical relationships to sort out.

The abundance, diversity, complexity, and particularity of the textual evidence from a wide historical span on the Mesopotamian side necessitate that the Mesopotamian flood traditions must be studied in their own right before they may be used for comparison with the biblical and other cultural traditions (Jacobsen 1946: 147). Given the vast amount of relevant Mesopotamian sources, even to tackle the Mesopotamian sources alone in a book such as this seems too daunting a task.

Therefore, this book primarily focuses on the textual sources from the Early Dynastic III period to the Old Babylonian period (*c.*2000–1600 BC), though still covering several major textual sources (e.g. the Standard Babylonian version of the *Gilgameš Epic* and Berossos' *Babyloniaca*) from the later periods. The aim of research is to trace the origins and early development of the motif of the primeval flood catastrophe (alternatively, Flood or Deluge) and its diverse mythological and chronographical representations. This book argues

[4] See Chen 2009 (Vol. 2) for compilation of relevant textual sources with philological and textual commentaries.

that though rooted in earlier Mesopotamian cultural and literary history, the Flood motif and its mythological and historiographical representations as found in the *Atra-hasīs Epic* and the W-B 444 version of *SKL* only began to emerge and flourish from the Old Babylonian period.

REVIEW OF LITERATURE

As mentioned above, part of the value of the Babylonian Flood accounts discovered by Smith is their high antiquity. Before these discoveries in the nineteenth century, all the other parallel stories to the biblical account, including those from Berossos' *Babyloniaca*, were assumed to be later than, or even to derive from, the biblical sources. Smith (1873: 214) estimated that the original composition of the Flood account in the Standard Babylonian version of the *Gilgameš Epic* 'cannot be placed later than the seventeenth century before the Christian era'. This estimate is fairly accurate, given that the Flood story in the late version of the *Gilgameš Epic* is an excerpt from the *Atra-hasīs Epic* (Tigay 1982), whose earliest surviving copies are dated back to the reign of king Ammisaduqa (*c*.1646–1626 BC). The antiquity of the Mesopotamian accounts by far pre-dates the biblical traditions. The question is how far back these traditions about the Flood can be traced in history? Because the traditions related to the Flood deal with an event which allegedly took place in the earliest phase of the world's history, they give the facile impression that they came from the deep past. It is no surprise that there is a long-standing and prevailing scholarly assumption that these traditions originated from a very early time in Mesopotamian and human cultural history.[5]

But after nearly a century since Smith's discoveries, Lambert and Millard (1969: 16) observed that there was no evidence for such traditions about the Flood from the Sumerians in the third millennium BC. Lambert and Millard remained hopeful that such traditions would be found as more copies of Sumerian literature from the third millennium BC were to be discovered:

> It is not unlikely that the Sumerians did have traditions of destructive floods, since the country is notoriously liable to them, indeed there is some flooding of the rivers every year. Several ancient sites have revealed flood layers separating

[5] The current author (see also Lambert and Millard 1969: 17) does not belong to the school which holds that all flood or Flood traditions descended from a single oral source. While some traditions may be related historically, others seem to have developed independently at different times given the common experience with flooding among human societies worldwide. Even in ancient Mesopotamia there were different flood myths which developed from different locations during the Old Babylonian period, though it was the mythological tradition presumably from Eridu that became dominant in literary traditions (see Chen 2012: 168–83).

strata of different civilizations. Presumably at various sites and on several occasions floods did wipe out the existing culture.

As more cuneiform sources became available in the ensuing years, indeed numerous references or allusions to destructive floods are found in both Sumerian and Akkadian sources (see PSD A, Vol. 1, Part I, 109–115; CAD A, Vol. 1, Part I, 76–81). Quite a number of relevant Sumerian textual sources are from the third millennium BC. But the flood terminology found in most of these earlier sources is used figuratively as similes or metaphors for the depiction of the invincible and overwhelming power of mythical and human figures, which are presumably based on the common ecological phenomenon of regular flooding in southern Mesopotamia. None of the representations of destructive floods from the third-millennium sources can be identified with the primeval flood catastrophe that was believed to have wiped out the whole world except for a few survivors in the primeval time of origins, as portrayed in the mythological traditions such as the *Atra-hasīs Epic*, or to have divided early world history into the antediluvian and postdiluvian eras, as seen in the chronographical traditions such as the W-B 444 version of *SKL*. The primeval flood catastrophe is distinguished from other destructive floods in Mesopotamian literary traditions by its unique literary, mythological, and historiographical manifestations. All the earliest attestations of a-ma-ru and *abūbu* being used to convey this specialized meaning only go back to the Old Babylonian period.

Since the middle of the last century, several scholars, especially those who work on Sumerian literary and chronographical sources, have suggested that the Flood motif and its literary representations may have emerged and developed comparatively late in Sumerian literary traditions. These suggestions raise doubts about the long-standing and still prevalent scholarly assumption that the literary traditions related to the Flood came from high antiquity in Sumerian culture.

Based on the existing textual evidence, Civil (1969: 139) points out that 'the oldest datable occurrences' of the temporal clause eĝir a-ma-ru ba-ur$_3$-ra-ta 'After the flood/Flood had swept over' and its variants are found in *Išme-Dagan A* 120 and the *Instructions of Ur-Ninurta* 4. Civil further concludes that the theme or motif of the primeval flood catastrophe was a late development in Sumerian literary tradition:

> The theme of a flood which destroys mankind does not seem to belong to the main body of Sumerian traditions. Allusions to it are lacking in the texts which are presumed to go back to older originals, and so best represent Sumerian literary themes. . . . Judging from the information available at the present, the theme of the flood which wiped out all but a handful of the human race became popular during the Isin Dynasty.

In his study of Mesopotamian chronicles, Glassner (2004: 108–9) also observes that the Flood myth, which was 'not an ancient narrative motif' in

Mesopotamian literature, 'suddenly entered the chronicle', i.e. the *SKL*, 'at the very end of the nineteenth or at the beginning of the eighteenth century' during the reign of the last ruler of the Isin dynasty Damiq-ilišu (*c.*1816–1794 BC). Glassner suggests that the entry of the Flood motif in the chronicle was a result of a slightly earlier historiographical development during the Isin dynasty.

> It was thus at the very end of the twentieth century and at the beginning of the nineteenth century that theologians and mythographers of Isin agreed to locate in mythic time, that is, at the beginning, the phenomenon referred to as amaru, at the same time giving it a universal reference. . . . About a century later, at the transition from the nineteenth to the eighteenth century, historians in turn introduced the flood into the fabric of history. The long and detailed introduction of the Babylonian Royal Chronicle (no. 3) shows that this was definitely achieved by the end of the Old Babylonian period. (Glassner 2004: 109)

More recently, Alster likewise notes that the Flood myth seems to be a relatively late development in Sumerian literature:

> The specific details of the mythology connected with the Flood story as we know them were probably relatively late phenomena in Sumerian literature, presumably not older than the Isin-Larsa period. (Alster 2005: 32 n. 8)
>
> the concept in the *Sumerian Flood Story* that Ziusudra was transferred to Dilmun as a sort of Paradise certainly makes best sense in the Isin-Larsa period, when trade with Dilmun flourished. If the notion of an all-destructive flood had been known much earlier, it would be remarkable that it was not incorporated into *Inanna and Šukalletuda*, in which all the 'plagues' tradionally associated with Inanna were included. (Alster 2005: 33 n. 9)

On the basis of his interpretation of the *Instructions of Šuruppak*, however, Alster postulates that though the Flood story in its current form as found in the *Atra-hasīs Epic* emerged only in the Isin-Larsa period, the motif of the primeval flood catastrophe had existed as early as the Early Dynastic III period:

> the mythological connotations associated with the Flood, as an all devouring disaster that separated the antediluvian times from the postdiluvian period, went back in time at least to ED III, ca. 2400 B.C. The absence of the name zi-u_4-sud-rá in the Early Dynastic period seems, however, to indicate that the specific role he plays later, as the only mortal who was transferred to Dilmun to live happily there forever, was a later mythological elaboration, dating probably from the Isin-Larsa period. (Alster 2005: 32)

The assumption that some sketchy form of the primeval flood story might have existed in the third millennium BC or even earlier in Mesopotamia is in fact widely held among scholars. Support for this view is often based on interpretations of certain strands of Mesopotamian literary traditions known for their close associations with the Flood motif or story from the Old Babylonian period onwards. Surely, if the motif or story had indeed existed prior to the second millennium BC, one would normally expect to find evidence not in random sources, but in literary traditions such as the *SKL*, the *Instructions of Šuruppak*, and Gilgameš traditions. In the following, we shall examine some of the major arguments in support of the early existence of the Flood motif or story on the basis of interpretations of these literary traditions.

The *SKL*

One argument in support of the idea of the early existence of Flood traditions derives from the conjecture that since some of the Old Babylonian copies of *SKL*, especially the main version W-B 444 (Plate 2), contain references to the Flood or the antediluvian section, therefore the copies of *SKL* yet to be discovered from the earlier historical periods may also have similar references. The antiquity of *SKL* and its widespread popularity in ancient Mesopotamia have long been established among scholars. Traces of the ideological tenet and phraseology of *SKL* can be found, for instance, in other major Mesopotamian literary traditions, such as the *Curse of Agade* (*Curse Agade*; Cooper 1983), the *Lamentation over the Destruction of Sumer and Ur* (*LSU*; Michalowski 1983, 1989), *Ur-Namma C* (Flückiger-Hawker 1999), and *Enmerka and the Lord of Aratta* (*ELA*; Mittermayer 2009).

Flückiger-Hawker (1999: 41–2, 224) postulates, on the basis of the similarities between *Ur-Namma C* 57–8[6] and 114,[7] the W-B 444 version of *SKL* 40–1,[8] and *Išme-Dagan A* 118–21,[9] that the concept of the Flood can already be found in the term a-ma-ru in *Ur-Namma C* 57. But a close analysis indicates that *Ur-Namma C* 57 should not be counted as equivalent to line 40 in W-B 444, though *Ur-Namma C* 114 may be a genuine allusion to the king list ideology and phraseology (Chen 2009 [Vol. 2]: 41–4). As Civil (1969: 139) has noted, the oldest attestations of the Flood motif are the temporal clause eĝir a-ma-ru ba-ur$_3$-ra-ta and its variants, as found first in *Išme-Dagan A* 120 and then in the *Instructions of Ur-Ninurta* 4. The notion of the Flood is not even explicit in the usage of a-ma-ru in *Išme-Dagan A* 120 where the term seems to refer rather to

[6] ⌜a$^?$⌝-ma-ru [g]i$_4^?$-ba i-ti ma-gi$_4$ ⌜x x⌝-a-ba$^?$ | ^{d}en-lil$_2$-le ⌜u$_4$⌝ du$_{10}$-du$_{10}$-ga-na maš$_2$-e ⌜bi$_2$-in⌝-pa$_3$-de$_3$-en 'When the flood$^?$ had returned$^?$, the moon(light)/month returned for me. Enlil chose me on his most favourable day through extispicy' (Flückiger-Hawker 1999: 214–15).

[7] [an]-ta nam-lugal ma-ra-e$_{11}$ 'Kingship has come down from heaven to me' (Flückiger-Hawker 1999: 218–19).

[8] eĝir a-ma-ru ba-ur$_3$-ra-ta | nam-lugal an-ta e$_{11}$-de$_3$-a-ba 'After the Flood had swept over, when kingship had come down from heaven'.

[9] ^{d}iš-me-^{d}da-gan dumu ^{d}da-gan-na-me-en | ^{d}en-lil$_2$ lugal kur-kur-ra-ke$_4$ | [eĝir a]-⌜ma⌝-ru ur$_3$-ra-ta | [u$_4$ du$_{10}$-du$_{10}$-ga]-ni-še$_3$ maš$_2$-e ḫe$_2$-bi$_2$-in-pa$_3$-de$_3$ 'I am Išme-Dagan, son of Dagan, whom Enlil, the lord of all lands, after the flood had swept over, chose by extispicy on his most favourable day' (TCL 15 9 obv. iii 25′–8′ // PBS 10/2 9 rev. i 21–4; see Flückiger-Hawker 1999: 66–7).

the catastrophic demise of the Ur III dynasty and its aftermath, as depicted with the flood metaphor by the city laments. In short, a-ma-ru in *Ur-Namma C* 57 most likely does not refer to the Flood, but carries a metaphorical sense to symbolize the conspicuous occasion on which Ur-Namma was chosen by Enlil (see *Gudea Cylinder B* iii 5–v 15; *Ur-Namma F* 48–9).

When dating the reference to the Flood and the antediluvian section as a whole in the king list tradition one must not forget that the *SKL* had gone through many revisions or updating processes.[10] That the antediluvian section may be originally independent of, and only secondarily added to, the king list proper has long been suggested by Jacobsen (1939: 55–68). He observed that the stylistic formulae of the antediluvian section in the major version of *SKL*, W-B 444, are evidently distinct from those of the king list proper, though some of the formulae of the antediluvian section seem to have been adapted to correlate with the formulae of the king list proper. Furthermore, Hallo (1963*b*: 56–7; 1991: 174) argues, on the basis of all the extant Nippur exemplars of *SKL* (except for P_5) and the incipit of *SKL* in a literary catalogue from Ur, that the king list originally began with the line nam-lugal an-ta e_{11}-de_3-a-ba to be followed immediately by the dynasty of Kiš, i.e. without the antediluvian section. Hallo further suggested that the antediluvian section was only secondarily added with the insertion of the original opening line of the king list (nam-lugal an-ta e_{11}-de_3-a-ba; line 1 of W-B 444) and the transitional phrase between the antediluvian and postdiluvian eras (eĝir a-ma-ru ba-ur_3-ra-ta; line 40 of W-B 444). Indeed, W-B 62, another Old Babylonian version of *SKL*, represents an independent antediluvian section apart from the king list proper. It has neither the introductory line nam-lugal an-ta e_{11}-de_3-a-ba nor the descriptive formulae for summarizing each dynasty, indicating a change of dynasty, and introducing single rulers and the first ruler of each dynasty. On the other hand, the Ur III copy of *SKL* (*USKL*; Steinkeller 2003: 269; Plate 3) and the Brockmon Collection duplicate of *SKL* (BT 14; Klein 1991: 123–9; 2008: 80; Plates 4 and 5) evidently show that the king list proper had once existed independently

[10] So far at least seventeen copies have been found that date to the Ur III period and the Old Babylonian period from different regions of ancient Mesopotamia and its periphery, including Nippur, Isin, Kiš, Larsa?, and Susa. The text's widespread and prolonged transmission suggests that the *SKL* has gone through different stages of editing to meet the needs of different political entities: (1) the Dynasty of Akkad, as early as the reign of Sargon (*c.*2334–2279 BC), or the reign of Naram-Suen (*c.*2254–2218 BC); (2) the time of Utu-hegal from Uruk towards the end of the third millennium BC; (3) the Ur III Dynasty, principally under the reigns of Ur-Namma (*c.*2112–2095 BC) and Šulgi (*c.*2094–2047 BC); (4) the First Isin Dynasty (*c.*2017–1794 BC); and (5) the First Dynasty of Babylon (*c.*1894–1595 BC). Towards the latter half of the Old Babylonian period, only copies were being made with no new editions produced. The above delineation of the transmission history of *SKL* is based on Vincente (1995: 267–8); Steinkeller (2003: 283–4); and Glassner (2004: 110–14). All the Mesopotamian chronographical sources with the references or allusions to the Flood are dated to the Old Babylonian or post-Old Babylonian periods (see Chapter 3).

without the reference to the Flood and antediluvian section. Both versions of *SKL* start with the introductory line nam-lugal an-ta e_{11}-da-ba to be followed immediately by the first dynasty of Kiš.

Given the evidence above, we can be confident that the antediluvian section and the reference to the Flood in the Old Babylonian copies of *SKL*, principally W-B 444, are secondary developments during the Old Babylonian period as the *SKL* went through revision or updating (see also Milstein 2010: 49–57). The fact that the Flood motif does not feature in the Ur III copy of *SKL* and that the earliest chronographical sources related to this motif are all attested in the Old Babylonian period suggests that the Flood as a watershed in early world history may be a new historiographical concept emerging from the Old Babylonian period in Mesopotamian literary traditions.

The *Instructions of Šuruppak*

Another major argument in support of the belief in the early existence of Flood traditions in Mesopotamia has to do with the discoveries and publications of the third-millennium BC copies of literary works which prior to the 1960s were mostly attested through copies from the Old Babylonian period. These discoveries, particularly the literary texts from Fara (modern site of Šuruppak) and Abū Ṣalābīkh,[11] helped revise the earlier conceptions among Assyriologists about the literary history of Mesopotamia, proving that the first creative period of Sumerian literature could be traced back to the Early Dynastic III period (Hallo 1963*a*: 167–76; 1975: 181–203).[12]

More specifically, it is on the basis of the Early Dynastic III versions of the *Instructions of Šuruppak* from Adab and Abū Ṣalābīkh that some scholars presume or argue for the early existence of the primeval flood story and antediluvian traditions. But these presumptions and arguments must be examined carefully. Though the toponym Šuruppak does occur and the didactic scenario remains the same as in the Old Babylonian version, the name Ziusudra, the hero in the *Sumerian Flood Story* but the son receiving the instructions in the Old Babylonian version of this didactic text, is nowhere to be found in the Early Dynastic III versions. Conceding the absence of the name Ziusudra in the Early Dynastic versions, Alster (2005: 32, 104–5) suggests that UR_2.AŠ, a name or epithet in the Early Dynastic versions which he translates 'Father-in-Law' (compare 'weaver' by Steinkeller as quoted in Davila 1995: 202), is the Early Dynastic name of the son who is later called Ziusudra in the Old Babylonian version. Based on this interpretation, Alster (2005: 32) concludes that some

11 See Biggs 1966: 78–82; 1971: 193–207; 1974: 28–42; Krebernik 1998: 317–24.

12 Now we know that the earliest literary text from Mesopotamia dates to archaic Ur, i.e. ED I period (*c*.2900 BC). The text is 'so far largely incomprehensible' (Alster 2008: 47).

sketchy form of the Flood story as known in the *Sumerian Flood Story* or the *Atra-hasīs Epic* had already existed in the Early Dynastic III period.

To assess Alster's argument, one must tackle the interpretation of the Sumerian phrase šuruppak UR_2.AŠ (AbS-T 2) or šuruppak^{ki} UR_2.AŠ (Adab segm. 1.3, 6) in the Early Dynastic versions. As will be discussed in detail in Chapter 3, though there are evident ambiguities in the syntax of the opening lines of the Early Dynastic versions (primarily the Adab version), in neither version should UR_2.AŠ be treated as the epithet of the son (or the grandson) receiving the instructions of the man from Šuruppak. The syntax of the opening lines of both Early Dynastic III versions rules out the possibility that the son receiving the instructions can be referred to as early as in AbS-T 2 or Adab segm. 1.3–5, by UR_2.AŠ. The designation most likely represents the personal name or epithet of the father, the man from Šuruppak, who gives the instructions.[13] Ancient interpretive traditions of the *Instructions of Šuruppak* since the Old Babylonian period tend to treat UR_2.AŠ as the personal name/epithet of either the father giving the instructions,[14] or the grandfather,[15] provided that these later traditions may have treated the archaic UR_2.AŠ = ušbar$_x$ as ubur/ubar in the name ubūr-tutu/ubār-tutu.[16]

In short, the son receiving the instructions in the Early Dynastic versions is never identified (Biggs 1966: 78), as expected in the didactic context. Only in the Old Babylonian version is he given the name Ziusudra. Thus both of Alster's interpretations, that UR_2.AŠ in the Early Dynastic III versions is the name or epithet of the son receiving the instructions and that the same Sumerian designation is later replaced by Ziusudra in the Old Babylonian version, must be rejected. If UR_2.AŠ indeed means 'father-in-law', it is only odd for the son receiving the instructions to bear such an epithet or name. Lambert and Millard (1969: 19) and Krebernik (1998: 319 n. 779) have also pointed out that UR_2.AŠ can in no way be identified with Ziusudra. The assumption, that because the city Šuruppak figures in the Early Dynastic III versions of the didactic text the name of the Flood hero Ziusudra and the notion of the antediluvian era or dynasties should also have been known in the Early Dynastic III period (see Mallowan 1964: 69), proves untenable. Therefore, one must accept that the name of Ziusudra as the Flood hero and the idea of the Flood as hinted by the name Ziusudra in the Old Babylonian version of the *Instructions of Šuruppak* are only developments of the Old Babylonian period (see also Milstein 2010: 46–8). During this period, the didactic text was updated with the information from the burgeoning antediluvian traditions.

[13] See Alster 1974: 25; Steinkeller quoted in Davila 1995: 202 n. 21; Krebernik 1998: 319 n. 779.

[14] See UCBC 9-1819 14; the *Dynastic Chronicle* 11–12; *SB Gilgameš* IX 6; X 208; XI 23; Babyloniaca.

[15] See line 15 of the W-B 62 version of *SKL* and line 7 of the Old Babylonian version of the *Instructions of Šuruppak*.

[16] See Steinkeller quoted in Davila 1995: 202 n. 21; Alster 2005: 104.

Gilgameš Traditions

A third major argument in support of the belief in the early existence of Flood traditions has to do with the historical association between the Ziusudra tradition and the Gilgameš tradition. The Standard Babylonian version of the *Gilgameš Epic* makes an unmistakable identification of the long-lived hero called ^{m}UD-*napišti*(zi) *rūqu* (UD-napištim the Distant) in the epic and the Flood hero Ziusudra as the same literary figure. Such identification, as far as the textual evidence is concerned, had already started in the Old Babylonian version of the *Ballade of Early Rulers* (George 2003: 98–9). The identification can also be seen in the Middle Assyrian copy (Akk_1) of the *Instructions of Šurrupak*, where UD-*napušte* represents Ziusudra (Alster 2005: 57), in the Neo-Assyrian copy of a group vocabulary, zi-sud_3-da = UD-*na-puš*$_2$-*te* (George 2003: 96, 152). Due to the prolonged historical association of the two names and the respective literary figures, modern scholars almost unanimously accept that ^{m}UD-*napišti*(zi) *rūqu* is the Akkadian interpretation or even direct translation of zi-u_4-su_3-ra_2: UD parallels with u_4 'day, or days', *napištu* with zi 'life', and *rūqu* with su_3-ra_2 'distant, far-away'.[17] In addition, according to scholarly consensus, the identification of the two names goes as far back as to the Old Babylonian version of the *Gilgameš Epic*, despite the fact that no reference or allusion to the Flood is made concerning *ūta-na'ištim rūqu* (Ūta-na'ištim the Distant), the name of the long-lived hero from whom Gilgameš sought eternal life, in the Old Babylonian tablet (OB VA + BM) of the *Gilgameš Epic* from Sippar. Given that the Babylonian *Gilgameš Epic* is to a certain extent based on Sumerian stories or poems about Bilgames,[18] one may argue that the long-lived hero in the Old Babylonian version of the *Gilgameš epic* who is thought to be the Flood hero could have his antecedent in Sumerian literary traditions from before the second millennium BC (e.g. Mallowan 1964: 70).

To respond to the above arguments for the early existence of the Flood traditions on account of the long-standing association between the traditions about Gilgameš and the Flood hero, one needs to examine the philological equation of the Sumerian name zi-u_4-su_3-ra_2 and the Akkadian name Ūta-na'ištim/UD-napišti the Distant, and the conceptual and literary identification of the Flood hero with the long-lived hero in the Babylonian *Gilgameš Epic*. As will be discussed in detail in Chapter 3, there are philological problems in equating the Sumerian and Akkadian names. Furthermore, the legendary hero Ūta-na'ištim the Distant in the Old Babylonian *Gilgameš Epic* (OB VA + BM) and the Flood hero Ziusudra were at one time two distinct literary figures who were characterized rather differently in the literary contexts to which they

[17] See Tigay 1982: 229–30; Durand 1988: 423; Alster 2005: 32.
[18] See Kramer 1944*a*: 7–23; Tigay 1982: 52–4; George 2003: 8–17.

belonged and were associated with different conceptual frameworks and plots. The two names and the respective literary figures were only syncretized starting from the Old Babylonian period in certain textual sources. OB VA + BM in its extant form, however, contains little evidence supporting the identification of these two figures with each other, except that Ūta-na'ištim the Distant like Ziusudra from the *Sumerian Flood Story* had achieved immortality and resided in a remote part of the world.

The above observations are also correlated with the fact that the legend surrounding the hero in the Babylonian Gilgameš tradition is in many respects alien to the Flood traditions. For example, the ale-wife, who was later named Šiduri in the Standard Babylonian version, and Sursunabu (OB VA + BM) or Ur-šanabi (the Standard Babylonian version), the boatman of Ūta-na'ištim/ UD-napišti the Distant, through whose help Gilgameš finally reached the legendary hero, are not part of the Flood epic. Moreover, it has already been established that the Flood story had originally existed independently of Gilgameš traditions (Tigay 1982: 19, 214–50; George 2003: 18). The story was first alluded to in the Sumerian composition called the *Death of Bilgames* in the Old Babylonian period and later on was borrowed extensively in the Standard Babylonian version of the *Gilgameš Epic* probably around the Middle Babylonian period. In its extant state the Old Babylonian *Gilgameš Epic* (OB VA + BM) shows no indication of connection with either the Flood hero or the Flood story.

In all three textual cases examined above, the *SKL*, the *Instructions of Šuruppak*, and Gilgameš traditions, references or allusions to the Flood story or the Flood hero were only inserted secondarily. The insertions were made as these literary traditions underwent considerable adaptations in the light of the Flood traditions which emerged in the Old Babylonian period.

If the traditions about the Flood only began to emerge and develop from the Old Babylonian period onwards, is it possible to trace the process of their emergence and early development? To do so will require systematically combing through a large body of relevant textual data of diverse kinds from the Early Dynastic III period, in which the first substantial corpus of literary texts in Sumerian is discovered, to the Old Babylonian period, from which the first and classical attestations of the Flood motif and its mythological and historiographical representations are found. This is the task of the current book.

STRUCTURE OF THE BOOK

This book contains four chapters. Chapter 1 is a lexicological study, analysing first the orthography and semantics of Sumerian and Akkadian flood terms, and then the use of the terms in their literary contexts, in order to trace the emergence of the specialized meaning 'the primeval flood catastrophe' in the use of the terms. Chapter 2 examines the emergence and development of the Flood motif in a broader context of the conceptual and stylistic development of representations of the primeval time of origins chiefly among Sumerian literary sources. Chapter 3 focuses on the development of antediluvian traditions in chronographical, didactic, and mythological sources that provide specific information about the names or epithets of the Flood hero; the names, kinship structure, and number of rulers from the last antediluvian dynasty; and antediluvian dynasties as a whole. Chapter 4 is devoted to analysing the contributions of the Sumerian compositions dealing with catastrophe to the development of the Flood epic, especially in terms of the depictions of destruction and restoration.

THEORETICAL CONSIDERATIONS

Because this study investigates the emergence and development of the Flood traditions primarily in Mesopotamian literary sources, it is important here to give some thought to theoretical issues related to the study of Mesopotamian literature and literary history.[19] As the world's oldest literature with a history that stretches at least from 2900 BC to 100 BC, Mesopotamian literature has its own particularities and problems that the literary historian must reckon with. Black (1998: 20–49) has laid out in detail some of the critical problems that confront specialists and non-specialists alike in their study and appreciation of Sumerian literature: 'limitations of linguistic knowledge', 'problems with chronology and phonology', 'absence of ancient literary theory', 'lack of integrity of the text', 'fragmentary state of preservation', 'critical theory and missing information'. Veldhuis (2004: 1–113) also points out problems with some of our modern concepts, such as 'literature', 'genre', 'authorship', and 'audience', when they are applied to Sumerian literature, which is substantially different from our modern literary traditions in terms of composition, consumption, and transmission. Thus, both the temporal, social, and conceptual differences between the literary traditions then and the literary (especially scholarly) traditions now, and our incomplete information about and understanding of the ancient traditions, pose challenges and limitations for literary and historical research.

Given all these challenges and limitations, we must acknowledge that any interpretation or historical reconstruction is only tentative at best, and that caution is needed either when we approach Mesopotamian literature from the

[19] Primarily Sumerian, given that the majority of textual sources involved in this study are Sumerian.

perspective of our modern concepts unconsciously or when we intentionally apply modern literary theories and classifications in the study of the ancient literary traditions. These challenges, however, should not discourage us from pursuing literary-historical study. As noted by several historians (Hallo 1975: 182; Tigay 1982: 2–3, 19, 22; Veldhuis 2004: 10), such study is facilitated by comparatively rich and well-documented sources from different historical periods (with some periods represented better than others) over the course of more than two millennia. Given its 'antiquity, longevity, and continuity' (Hallo 1975: 182), Mesopotamian literature is better suited for the study of literary evolution than most other ancient literatures. The emergence and development of Mesopotamian flood traditions especially, according to Hallo (1990: 194–9), represent a paradigmatic case for the study of not just the literary, but also linguistic, political, and religious history of the ancient Near East.

The issue in fact is not whether literary-historical study should be done, but how it should be done. Literary-historical study can be meaningfully and fruitfully carried out if we continuously improve our theoretical frameworks, modify our research questions or aims, and refine our research tools or methods to overcome or compensate for the limitations in order to more effectively ferret out historical information from the growing body of cuneiform sources that are being made available.

Not only the current state of knowledge of ancient Mesopotamian literary phenomena, but also complexities in the composition and transmission of Mesopotamian literature, pose challenges and limitations for literary-historical studies. Scholars have noted that the composition of literary works, whether they originate in oral or written format, was often done in the form of patchwork with blocks of motifs, themes, or narratives (Lambert and Millard 1969: 14–27; Alster 1992: 53; Black 1992: 86) being freely borrowed and adapted from previous traditions. It is difficult for the literary historian to discern to what extent the ancient authors relied on previous traditions and to what extent their compositions can be attributed to their own creative artistry.

Another important but elusive issue is the complex relationship between oral and written traditions in the composition and transmission process. Oral traditions, in Sumerian for example, must have existed long before the rise of writing towards the end of the fourth millennium BC. Early writing was neither designed for nor capable of transmitting literature. The first substantial corpus of written literature from Mesopotamia is from Fara and Abū Ṣalābīkh texts. Some of the oral literature must have been committed to writing for preservation or scribal training, after which process the same oral tradition could still have gone on either to exist independently of, or to interact closely with, written traditions.[20] Despite the various roles they might have played in

[20] See Michalowski 1989: 23–4; Vogelzang and Vanstiphout 1992; Black 1998: 29.

the development of Mesopotamian literature, oral traditions are never recoverable due to lack of living informants. The literary historian now can only depend on written documents produced by ancient scribes. Nor can one ever find out 'the extent to which the written and oral traditions overlapped, and the ways in which they influenced each other' (Cooper 1992: 109).

How literature, oral or written, was transmitted in ancient Mesopotamia is also uncertain. The transmission process could have varied from case to case: dictation (Alster 1992: 24), memory (Black 1998: 29), and copying directly from older tablets, all of which could have played a role in scribal training in schools (Alster 1992: 24; Veldhuis 2004: 44–5). The last mode of transmission is indicated by the colophons of some of the literary tablets that acknowledge the previous written sources they copied from. At least by the first millennium BC, Babylonian scholars 'were already editing texts on the basis of multiple exemplars from different sources' (Black 1998: 30; see also Michalowski 1989: 21).

Both the complex modes and styles of composition and transmission of Mesopotamian literature seem to make it virtually impossible to reconstruct the historical relationship between one manuscript and another (Black 1998: 30–1), as traditional literary-historical scholarship has attempted to do. Many earlier scholarly attempts to reconstruct the transmission or composition history tended to be built on the assumption that ancient authors or redactors knew the same texts we have. For example, by comparing *Enūma eliš*, Tablet XI of the Standard Babylonian version of the *Gilgameš Epic*, and the *Sumerian Flood Story*, Langdon (1915) and King (1918) drew their conclusions about the borrowing from and adaptation of the Sumerian composition by the Babylonian compositions. The conclusions assume that the authors or redactors of the Babylonian compositions had access to the Sumerian composition. Though no one would deny some of the obvious intertextual relationships among the written sources used for comparison, such methodologies, assumptions, and conclusions with regard to the transmission history of the ancient texts may reflect more of the limited repertoire of Mesopotamian written sources we have available than of the corpora of traditional compositions the ancient author or redactor had access to.

Investigations into ancient Mesopotamian scribal curricula (e.g. Tinney 1999: 159–72) can potentially help answer what specific corpora of traditional texts ancient scribes might have trained with, have had access to, and thus have been influenced by in different historical periods and at different scribal schools. Such investigations, however, are beyond the scope of the current study. So for the time being, it may be preferable to investigate historical relationships among traditions (be they oral or written originally) represented by the texts or the manuscripts of texts that are used for comparison, rather than to draw direct historical relationships between the texts or the manuscripts of texts. Even with two strands of tradition that share similar motifs and themes, one can still argue that historical relationships may not be established because the motifs could have derived from a common literary repertoire. For this reason, as will be discussed in the following section on methodology, a combination of criteria or approaches, as suggested and exemplified in Tigay's studies (1982, 1985), is adopted for the current study.

The complexities in the history of composition and transmission of Mesopotamian literature also suggest that the traditional literary-historical emphasis on reconstructing the 'original text' or the 'original context or original use' of a literary composition is problematic (Black 1998: 31; Tinney 1996: 7; Veldhuis 2004: 59, also 41–3), especially given the variations in the manuscript traditions of certain literary compositions (Black 1998: 44) and the diverse contexts and uses of literary works in the process of transmission (Veldhuis 2004: 44).

One may not, nevertheless, be convinced that, however idealistic or difficult, the tasks of reconstructing the 'original text' or the 'original context or original use' of a literary composition such as the *Atra-hasīs Epic*, the *Sumerian Flood Story*, or the Babylonian *Gilgameš Epic* ought to be abandoned. Such tasks or exercises may still be carried out as long as there is enough supporting evidence. Though the final goal may never be achieved, the process of sorting through the relationships among relevant manuscripts is helpful in tracing various lines of transmission. And the view can be defended that regardless of the pre-composition or transmission history of these anonymous compositions, it is very likely that some of these texts had been composed by single authors. The fact that 'many texts may have been molded in the process of transmission by various generations of scribes' (Veldhuis 2004: 72) does not diminish the monumental contributions of individual scribes or scholars who initiated new stages of literary development through their ingenious and creative use of traditions (Lambert 1965: 297). This is a point which even Veldhuis (2004: 108) would concede. On the authorship of the *Atra-hasīs Epic*, Lambert and Millard (1969: 23) write:

> The plot was traditional though the author had to choose from variant forms of the tradition, and to blend his selection into a dramatic whole. The careful build-up of the material used, and the interest shown in human life and society clearly compels belief in one author rather than in a traditional story that was worked up over a period of time by successive generations of story-tellers. The freedom of individual scribes to make their own versions does not conflict with this conclusion.

George (2003: 22) too has taken a similar position with regard to the authorship of the Old Babylonian *Gilgameš Epic*, which, though currently only preserved in fragments, 'was originally the work of a single poetic genius, whether he sang it or wrote it'.

The criticisms offered by Black and Veldhuis on the traditional literary-historical approach can properly serve to remind us that we should not privilege the original composition and its functions over the subsequent stages of development of the composition (Hallo 1962: 13–26; Tinney 1996: 8). Each stage in the composition and transmission process contains its own originality and special functions,[21] thus deserving to be studied as a piece of literature and a historical document in its own right. Ideally, literary-historical study ought to take into consideration the pre-composition, composition, and transmission stages of literature so as to more accurately identify continuities and innovations.

In addition to the current state of knowledge of Mesopotamian literary phenomena and the complexities of composition and transmission history of Mesopotamian texts, the recent emphasis of scribal training as the social origin and context of some of the Sumerian compositions from the Ur III and Isin-Larsa period may also call into question the methods of traditional literary-historical research. The tendency to date the royal hymns praising the Ur III rulers such as Šulgi to the Old Babylonian period and to attribute the origin of the hymnic compositions to the Old Babylonian scribal and educational settings (Brisch 2007: 28–31) implies that the emphasis on the political functions of the hymns in traditional historical studies may be wrong-headed. But the theory that 'all these hymns were written about kings who were long dead at the time of the school curriculum' (Brisch 2007: 30, see also 31 n. 35) does not seem credible. And clarifications are needed as to whether the hymns were copied or composed in the Nippur school during the Old Babylonian period.[22] Even if it turns out to be true that some of the Sumerian compositions relevant to this study, though allegedly having come from the Ur III period, were actually written in the Old Babylonian period, it would only strengthen the main argument of this book that the Old Babylonian period should be regarded as the most formative period for the developments of the Flood traditions. Again, research into the school curricula during the Old Babylonian period,[23] albeit beyond the scope of the present study, would undoubtedly help define more precisely the traditional corpora used for scribal training from which the authors of the texts related to the Flood, such as the *Atra-hasīs Epic* or the *Sumerian Flood Story*, might have drawn inspiration or source materials for their works.

[21] e.g. compare the Early Dynastic III and Old Babylonian versions of the *Instructions of Šuruppak*, or the Old Babylonian and Standard Babylonian versions of the *Gilgameš Epic*.

[22] Note how Brisch (2007: 30) moves from the statement 'it is remarkable that the majority of royal praise poetry at Nippur was *copied* at a time when most of these kings had long been dead. Consequently, the authenticity of the poems may be unclear, and, as was pointed out above (p. 16), in addition to this we know that not all of the original poetic works of king were transmitted into the Old Babylonian school curriculum' to 'However, in this connection the fact that all these hymns were *written* about kings who were long dead at the time of the school curriculum may be important. One could speculate that the Sumerian royal hymns that present us with super-human images of kings were only *written* about kings of the past' (*italics* added).

[23] See Michalowski 1995; Veldhuis 1997; Tinney 1999, 2011; Robson 2001, 2002, 2011; Brisch 2007; Charpin 2010.

METHODOLOGY

Both Black (1998: 6–7, 43–6) and Veldhuis (2004: 39–45) have summarized the three main approaches to Mesopotamian literature: (1) the literary-historical approach (the 'positivist approach' or 'author-centred approach' in Black's terms, but 'the documentary approach' for Veldhuis), which focuses on, according to Black's apt summary, 'the genesis of the text, the social and historical *Sitz im Leben* of the composition, the recovery of the intentions of the author (where appropriate), and the use of linguistic history to invest the words of the text with meaning' (Black 1998: 6); (2) the literary approach ('the poetic approach' in Veldhuis's words), which employs stylistic criteria and structuralism to study literature (Veldhuis 2004: 41–3); and (3) the social–functional approach, according to Veldhuis (the 'historical context' approach according to Black), which attempts to understand literature 'in the social and institutional context in which it was used' (Veldhuis 2004: 43). A methodological shift from the first approach to the last two is perhaps discernible in Assyriological research. Though some scholars tend to prefer one approach to another out of theoretical or practical concerns, it is important to maintain a balanced view that regards these approaches as complementary and applies them wherever they are appropriate.

To trace the historical developments of the Flood traditions, it is important not to restrict research to the study of a few well-known textual sources such as the *Atra-hasīs Epic*, the Standard Babylonian version of the *Gilgameš Epic*, the *Sumerian Flood Story*, and the W-B 444 version of *SKL*. One needs to collect and analyse a wide spectrum of pertinent data (lexicological, literary, chronographical, and conceptual) from diverse textual sources (narrative and mythological compositions, chronographies, didactic compositions, disputations, divine and royal hymns, and royal inscriptions) in which flood terms or references to the Flood occur. This comprehensive approach to data collection and analysis for the reconstruction of literary history can be observed in the directives set forth in Lambert and Millard (1969: 14) in their study of the literary history of the *Atra-hasīs Epic*:

> The fullest understanding of, say, Shakespeare's Julius Caesar is only possible when the various sources for Roman history available to Shakespeare have been compared, so that one may see how he selected and modified his material, so imparting to it his own stamp. This kind of critical dissection is all the more important with an ancient text from a milieu that knew no literary rights and had no aversion to plagiarism. The wide divergences between the Old Babylonian copies illustrate how the scribes and editors could take a free hand in rewriting the text. Was the author of *Atra-hasīs* merely retelling a tradition story, or was he a creative artist?

According to Hallo (1962: 13–26), the literary historian should investigate not only the composition stage, but also various stages of literary history. It is important therefore to trace the growth of a literary composition from its conception, selection of source materials, and creative composition when it was first set down in writing to its subsequent stages of adaptation in new forms and even new languages. It is this methodical approach that led the current study to trace the growth of Mesopotamian Flood traditions from the emergence of the Flood motif to its succeeding stages of literary and chronographical development in antediluvian traditions and the Flood epic.

Tracing the evolution of one Mesopotamian tradition inevitably involves tackling the evolution of related literary traditions and the complex web of historical and intertextual relationships among the traditions. This is particularly true for the study of Mesopotamian flood traditions, which frequently converged and intertwined with different major strands of literary traditions, such as those dealing with Gilgameš or the primeval time of origins. The complex relationships of these traditions have to be wrestled with and disentangled simultaneously so that the development of each tradition may be clarified.

The historical and intertextual relationships among relevant textual sources in this study are mostly established through comparing these sources by a combination of criteria (e.g. stylistic, formal, structural, conceptual, ideological). As already observed in previous research, especially in Tigay's study (1982), the role of the comparative method is more than just comparing or contrasting several texts of related motifs or themes in order to observe their similarities and differences, or commonalities and distinctiveness. The method has been used by philologists and literary historians as a crucial part of the procedure through which the complex mechanisms and particularities in the composition and transmission of ancient texts may be revealed, and the traditions behind the texts may be recovered.

It is also clear that Mesopotamian literary phenomena did not develop in isolation, but resulted from various intellectual and social factors. Thus deliberate efforts are made in this book to go beyond the immediately relevant data so as to explore the broader linguistic, literary, intellectual, and social contexts in which the Flood motif and its mythological and historiographical representations emerged and developed.

Though using textual sources as historical documents, this book also makes serious attempts to understand each source in its own right and in its unique literary context. Such approach is exemplified especially in the scholarly works of Black and Vanstiphout. Because ancient Mesopotamian texts were often composed by relying on, responding to, and adapting previous sources, sorting out the intertextual and historical relationships among the relevant textual sources can facilitate and enrich the understanding of each individual text involved.[24]

[24] Black (1998: 120–56) clearly understood this when he noted the intertextual and historical relationship between the two Sumerian compositions dealing with Lugalbanda: *Lugalbanda and the Anzu Bird*, and *Lugalbanda in the Mountain Cave*.

To better understand ancient texts and traditions, one also ought to make use of ancient interpretive or scholarly traditions that had already wrestled with some of the same philological, historical, and literary issues that confront modern scholars (see Livingstone 1986). The perspective of interpretive history can be quite illuminating for the literary-historical study of the texts involved. The divergent representations of the Flood hero and the last antediluvian rulers in the textual sources, for example, seem to be a result of various attempts by ancient scribes or scholars at making sense of the opening lines in the Early Dynastic III versions of the *Instructions of Šuruppak* (see Chapter 3).

Given that each chapter of this book approaches Mesopotamian flood traditions from different angles, various methodologies are developed from previous scholarship. In the first part of Chapter 1, analysis of the textual evidence is designed on the basis of the orthographic and semantic study of Eichler (1993: 90–4). The methodology of the rest of the chapter that examines flood terms in the context of figurative language or imagery in Sumerian and Akkadian literature is developed on the basis of the studies by Heimpel (1968), Westenholz (1996), Black (1998), and Streck (1999). Specifically, Heimpel's comprehensive collection of the relevant data, Westenholz's attention to different levels of meaning of imagery, Black's emphasis on the literary context, and Streck's systematic analysis of imagery have contributed to the design and presentation of the chapter.

In Chapter 2 the approaches used for the study of Sumerian and Akkadian representations of the primeval time of origins are developed on the basis of van Dijk's study (1964) on diverse Sumerian cosmological and cosmogonic traditions; Michalowski's study (1991) on negative descriptions in Mesopotamian literature as a stylistic and dynamic device; the studies of Castellino (1957), Wilcke (1975, 1977), Black (1992), and Streck (2002) on the form and content of Sumerian and Akkadian mythological prologues; and Ferrara's narratological study (2006) on representations of the primeval events and temporal sequence in Sumerian literature.

In Chapter 3 the study on the development of antediluvian traditions follows the methodological models of historical studies done by Jacobsen (1939), Lambert and Millard (1969: 1–28), Tigay (1982), and George (2003: 1–155).

In Chapter 4 the comparative and historical study on the Flood epic and the Sumerian compositions dealing with catastrophe is inspired by the works of Cooper (1983), Michalowski (1983, 1989), Klein (1985, 1990), Ferrara (1995), Tinney (1996), Flückiger-Hawker (1999), and Brisch (2007) on literary conventions and innovations during the Ur III and Isin-Larsa periods.

1

Flood Terminology

The study of Eichler (1993: 90–4) represents the most important treatment of the orthography of flood terminology. Based on an extensive study of the textual evidence from literary and lexical sources, he analyses the orthographic relationships between a-ma-ru (generally rendered 'flood or deluge'), e$_2$-mar-uru$_5$/e$_2$-mar-ru$_{10}$ (generally rendered 'quiver'), and mar-uru$_5$/mar-ru$_{10}$ (generally rendered 'tempest, stormwind'). He argues that in the Neo-Sumerian and early Old Babylonian periods, the orthographic differences between these terms were observed. But starting from the Old Babylonian period confusion began to occur between a-ma-ru and (e$_2$-)mar-ru$_{10}$ 'in the context of weaponry'. At the same time, confusion between a-ma-ru and mar-ru$_{10}$ also emerged because of the close literary association between winds/storms and floods, 'the use of the same verb zi(-g) in describing their common action of rising up', and the occasional interchangeability of the two terms (Eichler 1993: 93). 'This orthographic confusion', Eichler (1993: 94) further notes, 'seems to have increased in the post-Old Babylonian periods when mar-ru$_{10}$ "tempest" and "quiver" began to be written as ma$_2$-ru$_{10}$ and subsequently a-ma-ru began to be written as a-ma$_2$-ru$_{10}$, as attested in the bilingual versions of Lugale and Angim.'

After a close examination of the textual evidence which Eichler uses in support of his argument concerning the orthographic differentiation between a-ma-ru 'flood' and mar-uru$_5$/mar-ru$_{10}$ 'tempest' in the Neo-Sumerian and early Old Babylonian periods, it becomes clear that there is only one indisputable piece of evidence: rev. 2′ (saĝ-kal a-ma-ru mar-uru$_5$ [. . .]) from a fragment housed in the University of Pennsylvania Museum which represents line 237 of *Ur-Namma A*. Eichler refers to this piece of evidence three times in his article. Another passage Eichler (1993: 92) adduces, *Angim* 142 (MS Q) mir lu$_2$-ra te-a ^{ĝeš}pan mar-uru$_5$-ĝu$_{10}$ mu-da-an-ĝal$_2$-la-a[m$_3$], can also be used as a piece of supporting evidence.[1] The other two passages used by Eichler in

[1] However, the Old Babylonian witness MS P of *Angim* for the same line, which has ⌜a-ma-ru⌝-ĝu$_{10}$ instead of mar-uru$_{10}$-ĝu$_{10}$, should probably not be so easily dismissed as an error (Eichler 1993: 92), because the weapon referred to in this passage can be 'my deluge-bow' instead of 'my bow (and) quiver'. See Cooper (1978: 81), who follows MS P in his edition of *Angim*.

support of his argument, *Gudea Cylinder B* ix 22 mar-uru$_5$-gin$_7$ zi-ga and *Lugale* 114 nu-kuš$_2$-u$_3$ la-ba-tuš-u$_3$ a$_2$-be$_2$ mar-uru$_5$ DU, are ambiguous or uncertain as to whether mar-uru$_5$ functions as an orthographic variant of a-ma-ru 'flood', or stands for 'tempest, stormwind'.[2] Thus the orthographic and literary coalescence (or confusion) between a-ma-ru and mar-uru$_5$ seems to have occurred already in the Neo-Sumerian period, earlier than what Eichler argues.

For the usage of flood terminology, CAD A I and PSD A I are two major treatments so far. They contain extensive compilations and documentations of the extant sources. Some of the salient features of the usage are highlighted: the mythical aspect in which flood terms are used to describe divine and mythical figures, the close association of flood terms with battle and weaponry terms, and the primeval flood catastrophe as a cosmic and chronographical event. PSD A I also pays attention to the orthographic variants of a-ma-ru. In several respects, though, these treatments by CAD and PSD are in need of improvement. Overall, the prevalent use of flood terminology in figurative language is not emphasized. Often only similes are noted because of the obvious formal features: the equative case marker -gin$_7$ in Sumerian (PSD A I 110) and the preposition *kīma* and the ending *-iš* or *-āniš* in Akkadian (CAD A I 76–7). But metaphors are not at all openly acknowledged or stressed as such, which may risk them being read literally.[3] Semantically, further clarification and refinement are needed for categorizing the use of flood terminology, especially regarding what type of flood the terminology might refer to in a particular literary context: a local and regular flood, a cosmic flood, or the primeval flood catastrophe.[4] The choice of the designation 'Deluge' by CAD A I 77 to refer

[2] For *Gudea Cylinder B* ix 22, Falkenstein (1949: 41) renders 'flood', while Eichler translates 'tempest'; compare 'floodstorm' by Edzard (1997: 94). The ambiguity in how to render mar-uru$_5$ in *Lugale* 114 is even noted by Eichler himself (1993: 92–3).

[3] Mistaking metaphors based on a common and regular flood as literal allusions to the primeval flood catastrophe is not uncommon in Assyriological publications. For example, a-ma-ru in *Lugale* 229 is interpreted by van Dijk (1983: 31, 33, 79) as referring to the primeval flood catastrophe when in reality the term is used metaphorically as Ninurta's epithet (Black 1992: 81–4).

[4] Most likely, none of the following examples from the Neo-Assyrian period which CAD A I 78 lists under the same category 'the Deluge as cosmic event' as that of the examples from the *Atra-hasīs Epic*, Tablet XI of the Standard Babylonian version of the *Gilgameš Epic*, the *Cuthean Legend of Naram-Suen, Erra and Išum* seems to refer to the primeval flood catastrophe: '*kīma a-bu-be asappan* I cast down like the Deluge KAH 2 84: 18 (Adn. II); *eli ša a-bu-bu nalbantašu ušattir* I tore its brickwork down worse than had the Deluge done it OIP 2 84: 53 (Senn.); *mīlu kaššu tamšīl a-bu-bu* (var. *-bi*) a huge flood, a very Deluge Borger Esarh. 14 Ep. 7: 41; *kīma ša a-bu-bu u'abbitu tillāniš ukammer* I heaped them up in ruin hills as if the Deluge had devastated them TCL 3 90 (Sar.), *kīma ša a-bu-bu u'abbitu qirbissa ušēpišma* ibid. 183.' The term *abūbu* is used figuratively as a topos in these passages, evoking only normal and localized destructive flooding. For the passage from *Adad-nīrārī II*, see now Grayson (1991: 148) who seems to treat the *abūbu* as referring to normal flooding (thus the translation 'deluge' rather than 'Deluge'), RIMA 2 A.0.99.2 18 [*k*]*i*-⌜*ma*⌝ ^{d}GIŠ.BAR *a-ḫa-maṭ* GIM *a-bu-bu a-sa-pan* 'I scorch like the god Girru (fire god), I overwhelm like the deluge.' For the passage from Sennacherib, Luckenbill

to different concepts ('1. the Deluge as cosmic event, 2. The Deluge personified as the ultimate of wrath, aggressiveness, and destructiveness, 3. the Deluge mythologized as a monster with the definite features') further complicates the matter. By contrast, PSD A I reserves the capitalized designation 'Flood' only for the primeval flood catastrophe, while using the lower-case designation 'flood' for all other cases. In terms of the historical development of flood terminology, neither CAD nor PSD offers any more remarks than a few brief observations on the different 'representations of the mythological figures called *abūbu*' 'according to period and region' (CAD A I 81) and on the orthographic variants of a-ma-ru (PSD A I 109).

Though far less extensive than CAD and PSD in their treatments of the use of flood terminology, the studies of Hallo (1990: 194–9; 1991: 173–81), Westenholz (1996: 194–200), and Streck (1999: 59, 106, 113, 132, 211) have advanced the subject in terms of historical studies and figurative language. Two aspects of Hallo's study are especially relevant for the current discussion. First, he observes that the flood topos that occurs frequently in Mesopotamian traditions is used in most cases as figurative language, or 'in a purely metaphoric sense' (1990: 195; 1991: 173), either to signify 'divine displeasure' or 'cataclysms'. The second relevant aspect of Hallo's study is his provocative attempt to reconstruct the historical development of the Flood motif in the use

(1924: 84) in OIP 2 also treats the *abūbu*, correctly, as referring to a normal flood in his translation *eli ša a-bu-bu* 'than that by a flood'. The translation of the passage from Esarhaddon in CAD A I seems to be influenced by Borger (1956: 14) 'ein geschwelltes Hochwasser, ein Ebenbild der Sintflut'. But note that *tamšīl abūbi* is taken as a form of simile 'like a flood' in CDA 397. Lastly, there is nothing in the context of the passages from the Eighth Campaign of Sargon II that suggests the *abūbu* is used to refer to the primeval flood catastrophe. The formulaic expression *kīma ša a-bu-bu u'abbitu*, as pointed out by Thureau-Dangin (1912: 16), is associated with the idiom *kīma til abūbi*, which is translated without any reference to flooding 'like hills of ruins'; see CAD A I 78; compare the rendering 'ruins of (as left by) a flood' for *til abūbim* in Driver and Miles (1955: 105).

It is unclear whether the flood topos in the form of a simile in *Angim* 72 lugal a-ma-ru b[a$^{!?}$-ur$_3$-ta] (MS J); [lugal a-ma$_2$-ru an-ur$_3$-ru-da]: EN *a-bu-ba-ni-iš i-ba-'* (MS bB) (see also lines 73, 117; and in the form of a metaphor in *Angim* 141, 160, 207) is treated by Cooper (1978: 66–101) as referring to the primeval flood catastrophe when he uses 'Deluge' in the translation 'As the sovereign swept on like the Deluge'. On the one hand, Cooper (1978: 112) compares the flood term here with the occurrence of the flood terms in similar syntactical constructions in lines 39–40 of the W-B 444 version of *SKL* and the *Sumerian Flood Story* 202, 204. On the other hand, in his commentary on *Angim* 72, Cooper (1978: 112) instead uses 'deluge': 'In Ninurta texts, Ninurta is (like) the deluge, brings the deluge, and uses the deluge as a weapon.' The switch between the capitalized style and the lower-case style indicates Cooper's ambiguity concerning the identification of the flood involved. To the current author, the flood topos in *Angim* again refers simply to a normal (or cosmic at best) flood, albeit in a heightened form of poetic language.

A more recent example of confusion in flood typology can be found in the interpretation of *abūbu* in SB *Gilgameš* II 221 ^{d}*ḫum-ba-ba rig-ma-šu a-bu-bu*, which is clearly a metaphorical construction, as referring to the primeval flood catastrophe by Keetman (2008: 172): 'Ḫumbaba brüllt so laut wie die Sintflut, Utnapištim erzählt von der Sintflut und wie er sie mit Hilfe des Weisheitsgottes Ea überlebt hat.'

of flood terminology. He argues that the motif as a literal meaning of flood terminology in Sumerian 'uru or maru or amaru or even amarru' grew out of their metaphorical usage. In this usage, the flood symbolizes the invading semi-nomadic Semitic-speaking hordes, designated by 'the Sumerian ethnicon marru or mardru, Akkadian *amurru*',[5] 'who descended on the urban centers of Mesopotamia from a presumed home in the Syrian desert in the successive waves starting at the beginning of the third millennium' (1990: 197). The historical circumstance for the transformation from 'metaphor to reality', according to Hallo (1990: 199), is the abandonment of the 'metaphor' that makes 'the not altogether flattering equation of Amorites and the Flood' by the Babylonian rulers and scribes who were of Amorite origin.

Hallo's treatment of flood imagery, however, requires further theoretical and methodological reflections. Not only has no attention been given to the form of imagery, the assessment that flood terminology is 'frequently employed in a purely metaphoric sense' also ignores the fact that a simile or metaphor (except in a cliché or dead image) can hardly be functional without evoking the literal meaning of the symbol or signifier. For a complex image such as the flood, even when the figurative meaning is dominant, it is important not to concentrate on this level of meaning to the exclusion of the literal and mythical meanings (see Westenholz 1996: 190, 192, 194). Hallo's reconstruction of the development of the Flood motif has also oversimplified the historical process through which the motif emerged. The reconstruction fails to take into account the persistence of the figurative usage of the flood even in Babylonian traditions. Furthermore, it has not explained the development of the Flood as a primeval event. Granted that the flood catastrophe symbolizing the recent destruction of lower Mesopotamia as a result of the foreign invasion was transformed into a real event of meteorological catastrophe, how did such a recent catastrophe become a primeval event? The process of development of the Flood motif, it seems, involves much more than just a shift from 'metaphor to reality', though the shift may indeed have been a critical step in the process.

The study of Westenholz (1996: 194–200) represents the first serious attempt at approaching the use of flood terminology from the perspective of figurative language. The study is conducted within the context of an investigation into the figurative process in Akkadian literature, and to some extent, its Sumerian precursor. The theoretical and methodological issues which Westenholz has

[5] See Eichler (1993: 91): 'Since some of the winds with which mar-ru$_{10}$ has been associated are also identified in lexical lists with directional winds, namely IM-u$_{18}$-lu with *šūtu* "the southwind" and IM-mir with *ištānu* "the northwind," it is tempting to associate the mar-ru$_{10}$ with IM-mar-TU = *amurru* "the westwind." This seemingly attractive suggestion, however, cannot be maintained with certainty because of the orthographic evidence. While mar-ru$_{10}$ "tempest" is usually written with either the URU$_5$ (= TE-*gunû*)-sign or the TE-sign, none of the references to IM-mar-du$_2$(TU): *amurru* "westwind," to mar-du$_2$(TU): *amurru* as an ethnic or geographic designation, or to ^{d}mar-du$_2$(TU) "the god Mardu" are written with the URU$_5$-sign.'

wrestled with, in particular, the typology and formal indicators of the figurative process as well as the morphological, semantic, and literary problems involved in identification of imagery (1996: 183–91), become instrumental for her ensuing analyses of simple and complex multi-layered images. The flood image is treated as the latter type. Westenholz repeatedly emphasizes that to understand imagery, one must attend to all levels—literal, mythical, and figurative—of meaning (1996: 190–1, 192–4). In her treatment of 'complex multi-layered images', she writes:

> The most noteworthy feature of these symbols and metaphors is their extreme flexibility and their capability to refer to several levels of perception at the same time. A metaphor may have several meanings at the same time in the same text. It is difficult to read love lyrics without sensing that the distinction between the metaphorical and the literal meanings of the words vanishes like smoke. (Westenholz 1996: 193)

In her treatment of the use of flood terminology, which is based on the thematic categorization in CAD A I, Westenholz notes the close figurative and literary association between flood and battle in both Sumerian and Akkadian literature. In the 'congruence' type (i.e. simile), 'battle can be likened to flood or flood to battle' (1996: 196); and in the type of 'semantic transformation' (i.e. metaphor), '(A) flood can be substituted for (B) battle and (B) battle can be substituted for (A) flood' (1996: 197). Interestingly, these figurative constructions are found by Westenholz in the depiction of the Flood in the Flood epic: OB *Atra-hasīs* III iii 11–12; viii 12–13; SB *Gilgameš* XI 122.

The above passages from the *Atra-hasīs Epic* may be viewed as evidence supporting Hallo's hypothesis that the Flood motif developed on the basis of flood imagery. While the motif has shifted to a literal use of flood terminology in the Flood epic, vestiges of the figurative (as well as mythical) use of the terminology still remain. Though Westenholz does not pursue historical implications of the figurative depiction of the Flood in these lines, she does touch upon another crucial aspect of the historical development of the Flood motif. In her examination of the literary development of the 'expanded metaphor' of the flood catastrophe in Sumerian and Akkadian literature, especially during the Old Babylonian period (1996: 198–200), she argues that the Flood epic represented by the Old Babylonian version of the *Atra-hasīs Epic* has reused and transformed some of the older, expanded metaphorical depictions of the flood catastrophe as found in the Sumerian and Akkadian compositions dealing with catastrophe, such as *Curse Agade* and the *Cuthean Legend of Naram-Suen*. The motif of the human noise, the suppression of which is represented as the initial stage of catastrophe in *Curse Agade* and the *Cuthean Legend*, for example, is changed into the cause of divine punishment in the *Atra-hasīs Epic*.

Streck's study (1999) is undoubtedly by far the most systematic and comprehensive investigation into figurative language in Akkadian literature, focusing primarily on ten epics including the *Atra-hasīs Epic* and the Standard Babylonian version of the *Gilgameš Epic*. Most of the theoretical and methodological issues concerning figurative language, such as the differentiation between simile and metaphor (and other types of imagery), the identification and relationship between the signified (*Bildempfänger*) and the signifier (*Bildspender*), formal features, the frequency of imagery, and the historical development of Sumerian and Akkadian imagery, have been treated at length. His observations on the usage of *abūbu* in the Flood epic are particularly relevant to the current discussion. In addition to listing the cases of figurative usage of flood terminology in the Flood epic which have already been pointed out by Westenholz, Streck has identified the following additional examples: OB *Atra-hasīs* III iii 15; SB *Gilgameš* XI 110–11, 130–1 (Streck 1999: 59, 106, 107, 113, 132). Many other images, though not directly associated with the Flood, have also been identified in the *Atra-hasīs Epic* and SB *Gilgameš* XI 15–206 (see the indices in Streck 1999: 251–4).

The above review of previous scholarship suggests that to trace when and how Flood traditions emerged and developed in ancient Mesopotamia, one needs to first examine the use of flood terminology in available Mesopotamian sources. Such examination is to analyse how flood terms are used lexicologically (in terms of orthography, grammar, style, and semantics) and literarily (in terms of the functions or roles of the terms in literary contexts where they are found). And these linguistic and literary examinations are also to be done from a historical perspective, so as to track important changes in the use of flood terms and to explore various factors that may have led to these changes.

ORTHOGRAPHY

Orthographic Variations

Sumerian

a-MAR 'flood'

This writing, attested only once, is found in the *Stele of the Vultures* obv. x 4 from the Early Dynastic III period,[6] representing the earliest orthography for 'flood' in Sumerian. Note that MAR is the emesal form for ĝar or $ĝa_2$ 'to put, place, lay down' (Thomsen 2001: 289); see a-mar-ra = a-ĝar-ra = A.MEŠ *ra-ḫa-ṣu*; a-ma-ma⁻ $a\text{-}ĝa_2\text{-}ĝa_2$ = A.MEŠ *ra-ḫa-ṣu* 'to flood with water' (MSL IV 33 67, 68).

[6] All the textual data referred to in this chapter are collected in Chen 2009 (Vol. 2) with philological and textual commentaries.

a-ma-ru

1 'flood'

This is the most prevalent orthography of the Sumerian term for 'flood', which refers to either the regular/local or cosmic flood, and can be used literally, mythically, and figuratively. Its occurrence and distribution in textual sources until the Old Babylonian period can be seen from the following.

Sargonic Period: *Temple Hymns* 338

Lagaš II Period: *Gudea Cylinder A* iv 18 (a-ma-ru-kam); *A* x 2 = *A* xxiii 14; *A* xv 24 (^{tukul}a-ma-ru/tukul a-ma-ru); *B* x 21 (a-ma-ru-gin$_7$); *B* vii 14 (^{ĝeš}a-ma-ru/ĝeš-a-ma-ru); *Gudea Statue B* v 37 (a-ma-ru-me$_3$-ka-ni)

Ur III Period: *Ur-Namma A* 236; *Ur-Namma C* 57$^?$; *Šulgi C*, segm. A 88 (a-ma-ru-kam); *Šulgi M* 5–6; *Šulgi S* 4 (a-ma-ru-gin$_7$); CBS 11553 (a royal hymn to Šulgi) obv. 14 (a-ma-ru-gin$_7$); *Letter from Šulgi to Puzur-Šulgi about work on the fortress Igi-hursaĝa*, version A, segm. B 21 (a-ma-ru-kam); *Šu-Suen D* 6; UM 29-16-42 (a commemorative inscription of Šu-Suen) i 17; *Šu-Suen Historical Inscription B* iii 20; *Letter from Ibbi-Suen to Puzur-Šulgi hoping for Išbi-Erra's downfall*, version A 38 (a-ma-ru-kam); *Year Name 22 of Ibbi-Suen; Curse Agade* 149–50

Old Babylonian Period: *Letter from Išbi-Erra to Ibbi-Suen about the purchase of Grain* 57 (a-ma-ru-kam); CBS 7849 iii 16′; *Šu-ilīšu A* 15; *Iddin-Dagan D* 59; *Išme-Dagan A* 120; *Išme-Dagan S* 13; *LW* 3.3, 4.4; *Lipit-Eštar D* 46–7; *Ur-Ninurta F* segm. A 4; *Būr-Suen A* 30–1; *ELUM GUSUN (Honoured One, Wild Ox)* B+93–B+96, B+101; *AGALGAL BUR SUSU (Flood Which Drowns the Harvest)* 44; CBS 15120 rev. 5′; *LSU* 76, 107–8; *LU* 198; *ELA* 571–2; *Eršemma 163.1* 7; *Angim* 72–3, 117 (a-ma-ru-gin$_7$), 141, 207; *Inana B* 11, 78; *Eršemma 168* 41 (a-ma-ru-gin$_7$); *Nergal B* 18; *Eršemma 45* 1; *Ninurta C* 59; *Lugalbanda in the Mountain Cave*, segm. A 28 (a-ma-ru-kam); *Death of Bilgames*, the Mê-Turan Version 243 (a-ma-ru-kam); *Lugale* 3, 229, 660; VAT 6481 16; TuM NF 3 53 i 20 (a-ma-ru-am$_3$); PRAK 1, pl. 38 B472 ii 4′ (a-ma-ru-gin$_7$)

2 'the primeval flood catastrophe' (or 'Flood/Deluge')

The same orthography a-ma-ru is also used for 'the primeval flood catastrophe'. But all the attestations of this usage are from the Old Babylonian period (and onwards): the *Instructions of Ur-Ninurta* 4; *Death of Bilgames*, N_1 iv 10; *Death of Bilgamas*, STVC 87 B 6″; *Death of Bilgames*, the Mê-Turan Version 72, 152, 162; the *Sumerian Flood Story* 137, 156, 202, 204; *Inana and the Numun-Grass* 9, 19; W-B 62 version of *SKL* 18; W-B 444 version of *SKL* 39, 40; *Rulers of Lagaš* 1. The occurrence of the term in the *Instructions of Ur-Ninurta* represents the first attestations to a-ma-ru being used in the sense of the Flood. It needs to be pointed out that not all of the above passages, but only the ones from the *Death of Bilgames* and the *Sumerian Flood Story*, are clearly associated with the Flood story as embedded in the *Atra-hasīs Epic*. The passage from *Inana and the Numun-Grass* represents a different literary and mythological tradition about the Flood. The textual witnesses from the versions of *SKL* and from the *Rulers of Lagaš* belong to the chronographical traditions, which also seem to have existed independently of the Babylonian Flood epic (Lambert and Millard 1969: 20–1).

3 'quiver' (= e_2-mar-uru_5)
Only in one instance does a-ma-ru function as an orthographic variant for e_2-mar-uru_5 'quiver': the *Debate between Grain and Sheep* 101 as attested in CBS 15161 rev. 11 and CBS 13941 + UM 29-15-973 obv. 30; compare a-mar-uru_5 in UM 29-16-461 + UM 29-16-662 rev. 5 and $^{ĝeš}e_2^{!?}$-ma-uru_5 in the Philadelphia Free Library prism FLP 2628 (see Eichler 1993: 93 n. 53).

a-ma-ru_{12} 'flood'

Lagaš II Period: *Gudea Cylinder A* viii 26 (a-ma-ru_{12}-gin_7)

Ur III Period: CBS 11553 (a royal hymn to Šulgi) obv. 14 (a-ma-ru_{12}-gin_7)

a-ma_2-ru 'flood'

This orthography is attested in the Middle Assyrian MS bM of *Angim* 72 and the Late Middle Assyrian MSS aA and cC of *Angim* 207 (see Cooper 1978: 66, 100).

a-ma_2-uru_5 'flood'

As pointed out by Eichler (1993: 94 n. 60), this orthography is generally attested in the post-Old Babylonian periods (e.g. the Neo-Babylonian sources x and n_2 of *Lugale* 229; the Neo-Assyrian source e of *Angim* 141, 142), except for one possible textual witness from the Ur III period, *Šulgi E* 153, which is only attested in TCL 15, 14 (pl. 41) rev. iv 5′ (a-$ma_2^?$-$uru_5^?$).

e-ma-ru 'flood'

Ur III Period$^?$: *Letter from Šulgi to Išbi-Erra about the purchase of Grain* 14 (e-ma-ru-uk-ka 'it is urgent!' see Michalowski 2011: 385, 389)

ma_2-uru_5 'flood/tempest'

Old Babylonian Period: *Ninurta D* 6 (u_4-de_3 ⸢ma_2-uru_5⸣-gin_7 $teš_2$-bi ga-am_3-gu_7 ama-$ĝu_{10}$ ḫu-⸢mu-da-an-zu⸣ 'Like a flood/tempest in a storm, I will devour all. Let my mother know it'; compare *LSU* 2 u_4-de_3 mar-uru_5-gin_7 $teš_2$-bi i_3-gu_7-e 'The storm, like the flood/tempest, devours all')

mar-uru_5

The Sumerian term mar-uru_5 can function as an orthographic variant for a-ma-ru 'flood' (but never for 'Flood') as well as for e_2-mar-uru_5 'quiver', while having a separate meaning 'tempest, stormwind' (Eichler 1993: 90–4). It is also argued that mar-uru$_5$ should be read as mar-ru$_{10}$, on account of the variant ma-ru for mar-uru$_5$ 'quiver' in *Temple Hymns* 63 and the exchange between the variants a-ma-ru, a-mar-uru$_5$ and ^{ĝeš}e$^{!?}$-ma-uru$_5$ 'quiver' in the *Debate between Grain and Sheep* 101 (Eichler 1993: 90 n. 6; 93 n. 53). Furthermore, in *Dumuzi's Dream* 67 and the *Debate between Bird and Fish* 115, one finds the variant mar-TE or ^{im}mar-TE for mar-uru$_5$(TU) 'tempest' (Eichler 1993: 90 nn. 8, 9).

Eichler (1993: 90–4) argues that at least in the Neo-Sumerian period and the early Old Babylonian period the orthographic differentiation between mar-uru$_5$ standing for 'tempest, stormwind' and a-ma-ru 'flood' was observed, and that this differentiation had already begun to break down in the Old Babylonian period with mar-uru$_5$ functioning as an orthographic variant for a-ma-ru. This collapsed differentiation is either due to the orthographic confusion between the two Sumerian terms or because of their close literary association and interchangeability. But as pointed out earlier, the semantic ambiguity of mar-uru$_5$ in relation to its orthographic confusion with a-ma-ru seems to have taken place earlier than the Old Babylonian period. Attempts have been made in the following to demonstrate the semantic field of this term in its textual witnesses. In several cases, it is reasonably certain that mar-uru$_5$ functions as an orthographic variant for either a-ma-ru 'flood' or e$_2$-mar-uru$_5$ 'quiver', or denotes 'tempest'. But in other cases, it remains unclear as to whether mar-uru$_5$ means 'tempest' or 'flood'.

1 'flood' (= a-ma-ru)

Ur III Period: *Šu-Suen D* 2$^?$

Old Babylonian Period: *Inana I* 13; *Lugale* 689; *Ninĝišzida B* 17 (mar-uru$_5$-am$_3$; in parallel with a-ĝi$_6$-am$_3$ 'like a flood-wave' in line 16)

2 'flood/tempest'

Lagaš II Period: *Gudea Cylinder B* ix 22 (mar-uru$_5$-gin$_7$)

Ur III Period: *Ur-Namma 46* 1 (mar-uru$_5$-an-ki-ra)

Old Babylonian Period: *LSU* 2$^?$, 113$^?$ (mar-uru$_5$-gin$_7$); *Inana C* 19, 29; *Inana D* 84; *Eršemma 185* rev. i 36 (mar-uru$_5$-gin$_7$); *Nergal B* 3, 10$^?$; *Ninurta D* 6 (⸢mar-uru$_5$⸣-gin$_7$)

3 'tempest'

Early Dynastic III Period: *Za$_3$-mi$_2$ Hymns* 53$^?$

Sargonic Period: *Inana and Ebih* 4, 136$^?$

Ur III Period: *Ur-Namma A* 237; *Šulgi A* 62; *Šulgi V* 13

Old Babylonian Period: *Inana F* 9; *Eršemma 184* rev. ii 97; *Inana and Šu-kale-tuda* 188; *Lugale* 82$^?$, 114; *Dumuzi's Dream* 67

4 'quiver' (= e_2-mar-uru_5)
Sargonic Period: *Inana and Ebih* 135

Ur III Period: *Šu-Suen Historical Inscription B* i 32

Old Babylonian Period: *Angim* 142 (thus MS Q = Ni 4297 rev. 11; while MS P = CBS 14012 + UM 29-16-64 has the variant ⸢a-ma-ru⸣-$\hat{g}u_{10}$); the *Debate between Tree and Reed* 186 (mar-uru_5-da)

uru_2 (URU×UD) 'flood'

Sargonic Period: *Temple Hymns* 488

Old Babylonian Period: *LU* 98 (uru_2-gin_7); 184 ($^{\hat{g}e\check{s}}$tukul uru_2-ke_2); *Enki's Journey to Nippur* 56; *Nergal C* 22 (uru_2-gin_7), 27 (uru_2-gin_7); *Lugale* 83; *Proverb* 13.34 (a uru_2-ke_4)

uru_5 'flood'

Old Babylonian Period: *Asarluhi A* 21

uru_{18} (URU×A) 'flood'

Early Dynastic III Period: UET 2 supp. 02 (= IM 049839) obv. i 1

Ur III Period: *Šu-Suen Historical Inscription B* i 43 (uru_{18}-maḫ 'great flood'); *Ibbi-Suen 1* ii 4

Akkadian

abūbu

1 '(devastating) flood'
Old Babylonian Period: *CH* 27b 79 (*til_2*[DU_6] *a-bu-bi-im*); OB *Gilgameš* III (YBC 2178) iii 110

2 'the primeval flood catastrophe' (or 'Flood/Deluge')
Old Babylonian Period: OB *Cuthean Legend of Naram-Suen* iv 17′; OB *Atra-hasīs* II vii 44, 46 (restored); III i 37, ii 11, 15, 20, 23, 53, iv 29, v 42, vi 21, viii 9, 18

***biblu* '(devastating) flood'**

Old Babylonian Period: UET 5 212 9; YOS 9 34 7; 10 16 5; 10 17 59; 10 18 62; 10 35 17 (CAD B 222)

bibbulu

1 '(devastating) flood'
Old Babylonian Period: *CH* 45 43; 48 5 (*bi-ib-bu-lum*); CT 6 2 28 (OB liver model)(*bi-bu-lum*); IM 49532 7 (Tell ed-Dēr, courtesy D. O. Edzard) (CAD B 298)

2 'day of the disappearance of the moon'
Old Babylonian Period: *ZA* 43 309 6; 43 310 8 (OB astrol.) (CAD B 298)

Orthographic Confusion/Alternation, Literary Association, and Semantic Ambiguity

As already observed by Eichler (1993: 93–4) and from the analysis above, orthographic confusion clearly exists between a-ma-ru, mar-uru$_5$, and e$_2$-mar-uru$_5$. The confusion between either a-ma-ru or mar-uru$_5$ with e$_2$-mar-uru$_5$ can be identified and resolved with little difficulty. But the confusion between a-ma-ru and mar-uru$_5$ is not so easy to disentangle. The problem lies in mar-uru$_5$, which can either represent an orthographic variant of a-ma-ru 'flood' or stand for 'tempest, stormwind'. Context and syntax are not always helpful when one tries to decide which of these two meanings is intended in a particular occurrence of mar-uru$_5$. (Note that the following examples listed on the opposite sides of the comparative chart are not literary parallels.)

	a-ma-ru	mar-uru$_5$
association with u$_4$ 'storm'	*Gudea Cylinder A* viii 26–7 CBS 11553 obv. 13–14 *Curse Agade* 149–50 *Būr-Suen A* 30–1 *LSU* 76–81, 107–8 *LU* 198 *Angim* 72–5 *Lugale* 1–3, 688–94 PRAK 1 pl. 38 B472 ii 4′	*Za$_3$-mi$_2$ Hymns* 53 *Inana and Ebih* 4, 133–6 *Šulgi A* 62 *Šulgi V* 13 *LSU* 2 *Inana C* 28–9 *Eršemma 184* 94–7 *Nergal B* 2–3
association with u$_{18}$-lu 'southwind/storm'	*Temple Hymns* 338–9 *Eršemma 45* 1 *Ur-Ninurta F* segm. A 4 *Ninurta C* 59 *Išme-Dagan S* 13 *Eršemma 45* 1–2	*Inana and Šu-kale-tuda* 188 *Lugale* 81–2
association with ^{im}mir or mir 'northwind/storm'	*Temple Hymns* 338–40 *Šu-ilīšu A* 15 *Iddin-Dagan D* 59–60 *Ur-Ninurta F*, segm. A 4	*Šulgi A* 62–3
association with uru$_2$ 'flood'	CBS 15120 rev. 5′	*Lugale* 82–3

association with me$_3$ or ĝeš-la$_2$ 'battle'	*Gudea Cylinder B* viii 2 *Šulgi C*, segm. A 88 CBS 11553 obv. 13–14 *Šu-Suen D* 2 UM 29-16-42 i 17–20 *LW* 3.3–4 *Būr-Suen A* 30–1 *Eršemma 163.1* 5–7 (MS C) *Angim* 116–19, 141 *Lugale* 3–4, 688–9	*Inana and Ebih* 3–4, 133–6 *Gudea Statue B* 37 *Šu-Suen Historical Inscription B* i 42–3 LIH 60 = CT 21 42 iv 9 *Inana C* 19–20 *Inana F* 8–9 *Inana I* 8–14
association with weaponry	*Gudea Cylinder A* xv 24 *Gudea Cylinder B* vii 14 *Šulgi E* 153 CBS 11553 obv. 10–14 UM 29-16-42 i 17–19 *Angim* 141–2 *Lugale* 3–5, 689	*Inana and Ebih* 2–4, 131–6 *Gudea Statue B* 37 *Inana I* 13
association with piriĝ or ug 'lion'	*Gudea Cylinder A* iv 18–19 *Šu-Suen D* 2	*Gudea Cylinder B* ix 21–2
employment of zi 'to rise'	*Curse Agade* 150 *Būr-Suen A* 30 *UDAM KI AMUS* 15 *AGALGAL BUR SUSU* 44 (restored), a+80 *Eršemma 185* rev. i 36 *Eršemma 168* 41	*Gudea Cylinder B* ix 22 *Šu-Suen Historical Inscription B* i 43–4 *E TUGIN NIGINAM* a+39 *Nergal B* 3 *Ninĝišzida B* 17

Similiar associations with other meteorological images and the images of battle, weaponry, and lion, as well as the use of the same Sumerian verb zi for both a-ma-ru and mar-uru$_5$ indicate that these two terms may be used interchangeably, as already pointed out by Eichler (1993: 93), possibly for stylistic reasons, such as variety. Atmospheric phenomena, such as 'wind' and 'storm', are often closely associated with 'floodwater' (Eichler 1993: 93) in Sumerian literary traditions, which must have been based on the ancient Mesopotamian's knowledge of *realia*. Etymologically, Eichler (1993: 94 n. 63) suggests that 'If one understands a-ma-ru as a cataclysmic phenomenon comprised of devastating floodwaters and hurricane winds, one is tempted to see both aspects of water and wind in the etymology of the term, a + mar-ru$_{10}$ > a-ma-ru.'

In short, it seems that at least up to the Old Babylonian period, seldom had conscious attempts been made to differentiate semantically between mar-uru$_5$ meaning 'tempest, stormwind' and mar-uru$_5$ meaning 'flood', or to differentiate orthographically between mar-uru$_5$ 'tempest, stormwind' and a-ma-ru/

mar-uru$_5$ 'flood'. *Ur-Namma A* 237 saĝ-kal a-ma-ru mar-uru$_5$ [. . .] (attested by the Nippur version, MS G rev. 3′) represents the only clear example of such attempts at differentiation. Even this case, it must be noted, attests to the close literary association of 'flood' and 'tempest, stormwind'. Ambiguity remains in many other cases.

Diachronic Observations

The use of a-ma-ru and its variants and related terms for 'flood' can be traced from the Early Dynastic III period to the Old Babylonian period. The choice of the orthography a-ma-ru alone to convey the specialized meaning 'the primeval flood catastrophe' only began in the Old Babylonian period, more specifically during the reign of Ur-Ninurta (1923–1896 BC), as far as the textual evidence is concerned. Contrary to the opinion that there are too few data available from before the second millennium BC to trace the development of the Flood motif, the above examination demonstrates that sufficient textual and orthographic evidence exists in Sumerian tradition from the Early Dynastic III period to the early Isin-Larsa period for us to reach the conclusion concerning the comparatively late development of the motif. On the Akkadian side, though the textual and orthographic evidence is rather scanty, all the attestations of *abūbu* meaning 'the Flood' also emerged only from the Old Babylonian period onwards.

USE OF FLOOD TERMINOLOGY

Figurative

Based on the analysis of the textual sources compiled by the current author (Chen 2009 [Vol. 2]), it is clear that in the majority of cases flood terminology is used figuratively. As noted earlier, most previous studies on this subject are limited either by the lack of more rigorous theoretical discussions and methodological control or by the scope of research. Often, it is primarily the exemplars from Akkadian sources that are treated, with occasional comments on the evidence from Sumerian sources. But the neglect of the Sumerian evidence is rather unfortunate, because, as indicated by our above examination, most of the relevant textual witnesses from the Early Dynastic III period to the Old Babylonian period are Sumerian. During these periods, the Sumerian textual witnesses outweigh their Akkadian counterparts not only by number, but also by variety, in terms of orthography, literary representations, and generic distribution.

Form of Imagery

Before moving on to the analysis, it is important to discuss the relationship between simile and metaphor, two main types of figurative language in Aristotelian categorization. This relationship, especially the distinction between simile and metaphor, has often been ignored or avoided in some of the previous studies on Sumerian and Akkadian imagery. As a result, the categories 'simile' and 'metaphor' are sometimes used interchangeably and confusingly. The issue of distinction between the two types of figurative language is only addressed in Heimpel (1968: 12–42), Wilcke (1975: 210–12), Berlin (1979: 29), Black (1998: 15–17, 50–1), and Streck (1999: 30–41, 57–124). Among these scholars, Heimpel, Black, and Streck provide extended discussions on the subject. To tackle the relationship of simile and metaphor, one needs to attend to both the definition of the terms given by literary theorists and the formal indicators of simile and metaphor in the Sumerian and Akkadian languages.

From the perspective of literary theory, strictly defined, simile conveys 'similarity' as indicated by the formula 'A is like B', while metaphor communicates 'identity' as expressed by the formula 'A is B' (Black 1998: 15). But metaphor can be used in a wider sense as a general or 'superordinate' term to 'cover any non-literal (*uneigentlich*) sense of a word' (Black 1998: 15; see also Heimpel 1968: 12 n. 1). In this sense, metaphor 'is a genus of which all the other tropes are species. . . . To speak of metaphor, therefore, means to speak of rhetorical activity in all its complexity' (the Venerable Bede cited in Eco 1986: 87–8). Syntactically speaking, the identification of similes is generally made by the equative postposition -gin$_7$ in Sumerian (Heimpel 1968: 24–42),[7] and the endings *-iš*, *-iša(m)*, and *-āniš*; the prepositions *kīma* and *mala*; the prepositional phrases *kī pî* and *kī ša*; and the verbal forms *mšl*, *mḫr*, *manû*, *šakānu*, and *târu* in Akkadian (Streck 1999: 57–96). Metaphors, on the other hand, are often unmarked grammatically. In Sumerian, metaphors are expressed syntactically 'als Apposition, als nominales (mit und ohne Kopula) oder verbales Prädikat, als dimensionale oder Akkusativobjekt, als Genitivverbindung und schliesslich ohne Nennung eines Beziehungswortes' (Wilcke 1975: 210). In Akkadian, they can be indirectly identified by various syntactical structures, such as 'Apposition', 'Parallelismus', 'Chiasmus', and 'Vokativ' (Streck 1999: 105–8).

But difficulties arise in differentiating similes and metaphors in Sumerian when the enclitic copula -am$_3$ (conveying identity) used in a figurative expression in Sumerian can sometimes be translated with the Akkadian preposition

[7] But not every occurrence of the postposition -gin$_7$ indicates a simile (Berlin 1979: 29). Black (1998: 16 n. 45) refers to *Lugale* 391–2 where the postposition means 'in recognition of the fact that'.

kīma (Heimpel 1968: 34). In lexical traditions, -am$_3$ is equated with *kīma*, as seen in MSL 4, 175, 270 f. (Heimpel 1968: 36). Moreover, within Sumerian tradition itself, the postposition -gin$_7$ (conveying similarity) is occasionally replaced or alternated with the copula -am$_3$ (conveying identity) 'in parallel phrases or even in different manuscripts of the same passage' (Black 1998: 16; see also Heimpel 1968: 33–4). Therefore, strict differentiation between simile and metaphor can be problematic in Sumerian literature (Black 1998: 16–17; Veldhuis 2004: 53 n. 21). Even though one still needs to attend to 'the formal distinction of language or style', it is important to be aware of the problems in applying the stylistic categories or criteria of the Western literary tradition when discussing 'a pre-Western literature' such as that of Sumerian (Black 1998: 16–17, 50).

Simile

Lagaš II Period: *Gudea Cylinder A* viii 26 a-ma-ru$_{12}$-gin$_7$ u$_2$-uru$_{18}$ gul-gul-zu 'your (heart) destroys cities like a flood'; *B* ix 21–3 lu$_2$ ug-gin$_7$ šeg$_{12}$ gi$_4$-a | mar-uru$_5$-gin$_7$ zi-ga | maškim da-ga ^{d}⌜nin-ĝir$_2$⌝-su-ka 'the one who roars like a lion, who rises like a flood/tempest, a hurrying bailiff of Ninĝirsu'; *B* x 21 a-ma-ru-gin$_7$ sa-ga du$_{11}$-<ga>-ni 'which (the heart of the lord) strikes like a flood'

Ur III Period: *Šulgi S* 4 [a-m]a-ru-gin$_7$ ur$_4$-ur$_4$-ra-am$_4$ 'Like a flood, he (Enlil) was engulfing'; CBS 11553 (a royal hymn to Šulgi) obv. 14 [a]-ma-ru-gin$_7$ šu ur$_3$-ur$_3$-zu-u$_3$-še$_3$ 'When you, like a flood, sweep over (the lands)'; *Šu-Suen Historical Inscription B* i 40–5 kur gu$_2$-erim$_2$-ĝal$_2$ | nu-še-ga-na | me$_3$ ĝeš-ĝeš-še$_3$ la$_2$-a-ba | a-ma-ru uru$_{18}^{!}$-maḫ | zi-ga-gin$_7$ | uĝ$_3$-ba ur$_3$-ur$_3$-de$_3$ 'in order to sweep over, like a flood, a rising great flood, its population—(namely) the enemy country which is disobedient to him (Šu-Suen), in its setting in order battle (and) hostilities'

Old Babylonian Period: *E TURGIN NIGINAM* (the *House is Encircled like a Cattle Pen*) a+39 gaba-tuku ša$_3$ ḫur-saĝ-ĝa$_2$-ke$_4$ mar-uru$_5$ im-ma-an-zi '(its) opponent rose up in the midst of the mountains (like) a flood'; *LSU* 2 u$_4$-de$_3$ mar-uru$_5$-gin$_7$ teš$_2$-bi i$_3$-gu$_7$-e 'The storm, like a flood/tempest, devours all'; *LU* 98 u$_4$ uru$_2$-gin$_7$ gul-lu-ba ni$_2$-bi ḫa-ma-la$_2$-la$_2$ 'the storm, destructive like a flood, its terror hangs (heavy) on me'; *LU* 198 u$_4$ a-ma-ru-gin$_7$ uru$_2$ i$_3$-gul-gul-e 'the storm, like a flood, completely destroyed the city'; *Eršemma 168* 41 [a]-ma-ru-gin$_7$ zi-ga-ĝu$_{10}$-ni a-ba saĝ ba-ab-šum$_2$-mu 'When I rise up like a flood, who can oppose (me)?'; *Eršemma 185* rev. i 36 mar-uru$_5$-gin$_7$ zi-ga-ĝu$_{10}$-de$_3$ [a-ba saĝ ba-ab-šum$_2$-mu] 'When I rise up like a flood/tempest, who can oppose (me)?'; *Nergal B* 3 [igi-ni-še$_3$ u$_{18}$]-ru bar-ra-ni-še$_3$ mar-uru$_5$ zi-ga '[whose front] is exalted, who surges (like) a flood/tempest to his side'; *Nergal C* 22 (= 27)[nam-u]r-saĝ-ĝ[a$_2$-na] uru$_2$-gin$_7$ šud$_3^{?}$ du$_{11}^{?}$-[du$_{11}^{?}$] 'who in his heroism like a flood demands

> respect$^{?}$'; *Ninĝišzida B* 17 a-ša$_3$-ga mar-uru$_5$-am$_3$ na-zi-zi 'he (you$^{?}$) rises in the field like a flood'; *Ninurta D* 6 u$_4$-de$_3$ ⸢ma$_2$-uru$_5$⸣-gin$_7$ teš$_2$ ga-am$_3$-gu$_7$ ama-ĝu$_{10}$ ḫu-⸢mu-da-an-zu⸣ 'Like a flood/tempest in a storm$^{?}$, I will devour all. Let my mother know it'; *Dumuzi's Dream* 67 siki-ĝu$_{10}$ mar-uru$_5$-gin$_7$ an-na ma-ra-ni$_{10}$-ni$_{10}$-e 'That my hair will whirl around in the sky like a tempest for you'; OB *Cuthean Legend of Naram-Suen* iv 8′–10′ *ki-ma a-bu-ub me-e ša ib-ba-šu-u$_2$* | *i a ni-ši* [(x)] *ma-aḫ-ri-a-ti* | *ma-at a*[*k-ka*]*-di-i uš-te-mi* 'Like the Flood of water that arose among the first peoples . . . , it has transformed the Land of Akkad'; *Angim* 72–3 lugal a-ma-ru b[a$^{!?}$-ur$_3$-ra-ta] | ^{d}ninurta u$_4$ ki-bal-[a] a-m[a-ru ba-ur$_3$-ra-ta] 'As the sovereign swept over like a flood, As Ninurta, the storm, swept over the rebellious lands (like) a flood';[8] *Angim* 116–17 me$_3$ an-gin$_7$ ⸢keš$_2$$^{?}$-am$_3$$^{?}$⸣ [ ]-ab-sa$_2$-e | a-ma-ru-gin$_7$ [ ] 'Battle arrayed like heaven—[no one can] rival me$^{?}$, like a flood [ ]'; the *Debate between Bird and Fish* 112 ^{im}mar-uru$_5$ an-ša$_3$-ga-še$_3$ bu$_4$-bu$_4$-gin$_7$ (*i-ša-a*) an-na mu-un-ni$_{10}$-ni$_{10}$ (*u$_2$-na-ra-ḫiš$^{?}$*) 'Like a tempest whirling in the midst of heaven, it circled in the sky'; PRAK 1, pl. 38 B472 ii 4′ ki u$_4$ ge$_6$ a-ma-ru-gin$_7$ x x 'the dark storm . . . the place like a flood'

All the above examples can be identified as *Subjektvergleich* (Streck 1999: 57), which means that the flood image is used as a simile for the depiction of the subject of a sentence. One can also see that some of the similes are not marked morphologically in Sumerian: *E TURGIN NIGINAM* (*The House is Encircled like a Cattle Pen*) a+39; *Nergal B* 3; and *Angim* 72–3. But that the flood terms in these passages are used as similes can hardly be missed, as attested by the Akkadian translations of *Angim* 72–3. The use of the enclitic copula -am$_3$ rather than the equative postposition -gin$_7$ in *Ninĝišzida B* 17 a-ša$_3$-ga mar-uru$_5$-am$_3$ na-zi-zi 'he (you$^{?}$) rises in the field like a flood' further suggests that the use of the enclitic copula does not always indicate a metaphor. Finally, one may note that formalistically (Streck 1999: 57–90), while some of the similes noted above are unextended, e.g. *Gudea Cylinder A* viii 26 a-ma-ru$_{12}$-gin$_7$ 'like the flood', others are extended in various ways: (1) apposition: *Šu-Suen Historical Inscription B* i 43–4 a-ma-ru uru$_{18}$$^{!}$-maḫ | zi-ga-gin$_7$ 'like a flood, a rising great flood'; (2) a genitive construction: OB *Cuthean Legend of Naram-Suen* iv 8′–10′ *kīma abūb mê* 'Like the Flood of water . . .'; (3) a subordinate clause: the *Debate between Bird and Fish*

[8] So MS J; cf. MS bB: [lugal a-ma$_2$-ru an-ur$_3$-ru-da]: EN *a-bu-ba-ni-iš i-ba-'* | [^{d}ninurta ki-bal-a] a-⸢ma$_2$⸣-ru an-ur$_3$-ru-da: [^{d}*ninurta māt nu-ku*]*r$_2$-ti a-bu-ba-niš i-ba-'* 'As the sovereign swept over like a flood, as Ninurta swept over the rebellious lands like a flood'; MS c: lugal a-ma$_2$-uru$_5$ ba-ur$_3$-ta: *be-lum a-bu-ba-niš ib-ta-'* | ^{d}⸢nin⸣urta bad$_3$ ki-bal-a gul-gul a-ma$_2$-uru$_5$ ba-ur$_3$-ta: ^{d}MIN *mu-ab-bit* ⸢*du*⸣*-ri* KUR *nu-kur$_2$-tim a-bu-*⸢*ba*⸣*-niš ib-ta-'* 'As the sovereign swept over like a flood, as Ninurta, destroying the fortifications of the rebellious lands, swept over like a flood' (Cooper 1978: 66–7).

112 ^{im}mar-uru$_5$ an-ša$_3$-ga-še$_3$ bu$_4$-bu$_4$-gin$_7$ 'Like a tempest whirling in the midst of heaven'.

Metaphor

1 The predicative construction

Sargonic Period: *Temple Hymns* 488 me ḫe$_2$-aĝ$_2$-e eš$_3$-zu uru$_2$ 'May he measure out the divine power—your shrine (is) a flood.'

Old Babylonian Period: *Šu-ilīšu A* 15 šul zi-ga-ni mir a-ma-ru kur-kur un-tu$_{11}$(ḪUB$_2$)-be$_2$ 'youth whose rising (is) a storm, a flood when it strikes down the lands'; *Išme-Dagan S* 13 zi-ga-ni u$_{18}$-lu a-ma-ru im sumur-ba du-a 'whose (Išme-Dagan's) surge is a storm, a flood, a rain storm blowing in its fury'; *Būr-Suen A* 30 lugal zi-ga-ni a-ma-ru na-me saĝ nu-šum$_2$-mu 'The king, whose rising is a flood which no one can oppose'; *ELUM GUSUN* B+93–B+96 a-ma-ru na-nam kur al-gul-gul | u$_3$-mu-un-e e-ne-eg$_3$-ga$_2$-ni a-ma-[ru na-nam] | ša$_3$-bi e-lum-e a-ma-ru na-[nam] | ša$_3$-bi «e» ^{d}mu-ul-lil$_2$ a-ma-ru na-nam 'He is a flood. The land is devastated. The lord, his word, is a flood. His heart, (of) the honoured one, is a flood. His heart, (of) Enlil, is a flood'; *LSU* 76 DU-bi a-ma-ru ^{d}en-lil$_2$-la$_2$ gaba gi$_4$ nu-tuku-am$_3$ 'Their advance was the flood of Enlil that cannot be withstood'; *Eršemma 45* 1 ur-saĝ u$_4$-u$_{18}$-lu a-ma-ru na-nam 'Warrior, south-storm, he is a flood'; OB *Gilgameš* III (YBC 2178) iii 110 ^{d}[*ḫu-w*]*a-wa ri-ig-ma-šu a-bu-bu* 'Huwawa, his voice is the flood'; VAT 6481 (OB Catalogue possibly from Zimbir) 16 [x] x a-ma-ru na-nam '[. . .] . . . is a flood'; TuM NF 3 53 i 20 [zi]-ga$^{!}$-ni a-ma-ru-am$_3$ 'His rising is a flood'; *Inana I* 13 mar-uru$_5$ tukul il$_2$-la me-e ši-in-[ga-ĝen-na] 'I am a flood, a raised weapon$^{?}$.'

As observed by Wilcke (1975: 211), the predicative construction in Sumerian may or may not have the enclitic copula. Among the above examples, *Temple Hymns* 488 and *Šu-ilīšu A* 15 are without the copula, while *Išme-Dagan S* 13, *Būr-Suen A* 30, *ELUM GUSUN* B+93–B+96, *Eršemma 45* 1, VAT 6481 16, and TuM NF 3 53 i 20 have the copula. In Akkadian, the predicative construction has no enclitic element, with simply the subject and the predicate being in apposition (Streck 1999: 97–8), as seen in OB *Gilgameš* III (YBC 2178) iii 110.

2 The genitive construction

2.1 As regens

Lagaš II Period: *Gudea Statue B* v 37–8 šar-ur$_3$ a-ma-ru-me$_3$-ka-ni | mu-na-du$_3$ 'Šar-ur, his flood of battle, he (Gudea) made for him (Ninĝirsu).'

Old Babylonian Period: a bilingual royal hymnic inscription of Hammurabi (LIH 60 iv 8 = CT 21 42) iv 5–9 ḫa-am-mu-ra-bi | lugal ur-saĝ | kal-ga | erim$_2$ ĝeš-ḫaš ak-ak | mar-uru$_5$ ĝeš-ĝeš-la$_2$: *ḫa-am-mu-ra-bi* | *šar-ru-um qar-ra-du-um* | *da-an-nu-um* | *ša-ki-iš a-a-bi* | *a-bu-ub tu-ku-ma-tim* 'Hammurabi, king, hero of strength, fighting enemies, flood of battles: Hammurabi, king, strong hero, slaughtering enemies, flood of battles'; *LSU* 76 DU-bi a-ma-ru ^{d}en-lil$_2$-la$_2$ gaba gi$_4$ nu-tuku-am$_3$ 'Their advance was the flood of Enlil that cannot be withstood'; *Angim* 141 a-ma-ru me$_3$-a šita$_2$ saĝ-ninnu-ĝu$_{10}$ mu-da-an-ĝal$_2$-la-a[m$_3$] 'I bear the flood of battle, my fifty-headed mace';[9] 160 kal-ga a-ma$_2$-ru ^{d}en-lil$_2$-le kur-ra gaba nu-gi$_4$-me-e[n]: *dan-nu a-bu-ub* ^{d}*en-lil$_2$ ša i-na* KUR-*i la-a im-ma-ḫa-ru a-na-k*[*u*] 'I am the strong one, flood of Enlil, unopposed in the mountains: I am the strong one, flood of Enlil who cannot be opposed in mountains';[10] 207 kal-ga a-ma-ru ^{d}en-lil$_2$-la$_2$ 'The strong one, flood of Enlil'[11]

2.2 As rectum

Old Babylonian Period: *Iddin-Dagan D* 59 gu$_3$ a-ma-ru nu-še-ga dul [. . .] zu 'The voice (of) the flood that covers the disobedient, that knows . . .'; *CH* 27b 76–80 *e-li* URU-*šu* | *ez-zi-iš* | *li-is-si-ma* | *ma-su$_2$ a-na til$_2$*(DU$_6$) | *a-bu-bi-im li-te-er* 'Upon his city may he thunder furiously and may he turn his land into ruins of (as left by) a flood'; *LU* 184 ^{ĝeš}tukul uru$_2$-ke$_2$ saĝ gaz i$_3$-ak-e teš$_2$-bi i$_3$-gu$_7$-e 'The flood weapon (lit. weapon of the flood) smashes heads and devours all.'[12]

3 Combination of the genitive and predicative constructions

This form of metaphor is frequently used in an idiomatic way, to convey urgency or importance, as attested especially in administrative or literary letters.

Lagaš II Period: *Gudea Cylinder A* iv 18 sig-ba-a-ni-še$_3$ a-ma-ru-kam 'As regards his lower body, he was of a flood'

Ur III Period: *Šulgi C* segm. A 88 me$_3$-ĝu$_{10}$ a-ma-ru-kam sag$_2$ nu-um-ši-ib$_2$-en$_3$ 'my battle is of a flood, I will not relent$^{?}$'; *Letter from Šulgi to Puzur-Šulgi about work on the fortress Igi-hursaĝa*, version A, segm. B 21 a-ma-ru-kam 'It is urgent'; *Letter of Šulgi to Išbi-Erra about the purchase of grain* 14 e-ma-ru-uk-ka ša$_3$-ab-bi$_3$ ḫu-un-na-an-gi-ga: *ap-pu-tu* ŠA$_3$-*šu la i-ma-ra-aṣ-ku* 'It is urgent! May he not become angry with

[9] So MSS P Q R S T Aa (Cooper 1978: 80–1).

[10] So MS cC (Cooper 1978: 86–7).

[11] So MSS P′ X Z (Cooper 1978: 100–1).

[12] ^{ĝeš}tukul uru$_2$-ke$_2$ is translated as 'the weapons of the city' with uru$_2$ being taken as the Emesal form of uru/iri 'city' by Samet (2009: 81; see also ETCSL c.2.2.2). The translation provided in the above study assumes uru$_2$ as an orthographic variant of a-ma-ru (see discussion on orthography above); compare tukul a-ma-ru (*Gudea Cylinde A* xv 24); ^{ĝeš}tukul a-ma$_2$$^{?}$-uru$_5$$^{?}$ (*Šulgi E* 153); ^{ĝeš}tukul a-ma-ru (UM 29-16-42 [*a commemorative inscription of Šu-suen*] i 17) listed below.

you' (compare Michalowski 2011: 282–391); *Letter from Ibbi-Suen to Puzur-Šulgi hoping for Išbi-Erra's downfall*, version A 38 a-ma-ru-kam za-e nam-ba-še-be$_2$-en 'It is urgent! Do not be neglectful!'

Old Babylonian Period: *Letter from Išbi-Erra to Ibbi-Suen about the purchase of grain* 57 a-ma-ru-kam nam-ba-e-šub-de$_3$-en-ze$_2$-en 'It is urgent (or it is important)! May you not reject them$^?$'; *Lugalbanda in the Mountain Cave*, segm. A 28–9 unu^{ki} zi-ga-a-bi a-ma-<ru>-kam | kul-aba$_4$^{ki} zi-ga-a-bi an dungu ĝar-ra 'Unug's levy was of a flood, Kulaba's levy was a clouded sky'; *Death of Bilgames*, the Mê-Turan version 243 unu^{ki} zi-ga-a-bi a-ma-ru-kam | kul-aba$_4$ zi-ga-a-bi dungu mu-un-ĝar-ra-am$_3$ 'The levy of Unug was of a flood! The levy of Kulab was a heavy cloud.'

4 Asyndeton

The examples below all deal with mythical weaponry. It is unclear as to what kind of syntactical relationship exists between the noun denoting weaponry and flood terminology. For example, should tukul a-ma-ru be viewed as in apposition 'weapon, flood'; in the genitive construction 'the weapon of flood', or as 'the flood weapon' in which tukul functions as a determinative?

Lagaš II Period: *Gudea Cylinder A* xv 23–5 šar$_2$-ur$_3$ a$_2$ zi-da lagaš^{ki}-a | tukul a-ma-ru lugal-la-na-še$_3$ | tun$_3$ im-ma-bar 'Šar-ur, the right arm of Lagaš—the flood weapon, for his master, he (Gudea) had the axe split (or hew) (the cedar wood so as to shape [it])'; *B* vii 14 eme ĝiri$_2$ mi-tum ^{ĝeš}a-ma-ru 'the blades of daggers, the *mitum* weapon—the flood weapon'

Ur III Period: *Šulgi E* 153 ^{ĝeš}tukul a-ma$_2$$^?$-uru$_5$$^?$ ki-bal [. . .] ⌜gul⌝-gul-lu-de$_3$ [x x] 'the flood weapon, to destroy the rebel land . . .'; UM 29-16-42 (a commemorative inscription of Šu-Suen) i 17–18 ^{ĝeš}tukul a-ma-ru | ni$_2$-gal mu-šub 'the flood weapon—which casts great fear'

5 Apposition

All of the following exemplars function as epithets of deities or human rulers.

5.1 The signified-signifier construction

In this construction, the signified is given first, then the flood or tempest as the signifier.

Sargonic Period: *Temple Hymns* 338 [x (x)] nam-gu$_7$ ^{d}iškur a-ma-ru ur$_3$$^?$-ra 'destruction (of) Iškur, a sweeping$^?$ flood'

Lagaš II Period: *Gudea Cylinder A* x 2 = A xxiii 14 lugal a-ma-ru ^{d}en-lil$_2$-la$_2$ 'King, the flood of Enlil'; *B* viii 2 ^{ĝeš}šar$_2$-ur$_3$ a-ma-ru me$_3$ 'Šar-ur, the flood (of) battle'; *Gudea Statue B* v 37–8 šar-ur$_3$ a-ma-ru-me$_3$-ka-ni | mu-na-du$_3$ 'Šar-ur, his flood of battle, he (Gudea) made for him (Ninĝirsu).'

Ur III Period: *Ur-Namma 46* 1 ^{d}en-ki mar-uru$_5$-an-ki-ra 'For Enki, the flood/tempest of heaven and earth'; *Ur-Namma A* 236–7 [^{d}]⌜en⌝-ki lugal eridu^{ki}-ga-[ke$_4$ . . .]-ta-an-e$_{11}$-da | saĝ-kal a-ma-ru mar-uru$_5$ '[. . .] That Enki, the king of Eridu, brought him$^?$ out of [. . .]. That the foremost, flood (and) tempest [. . .]'; *Šulgi V* 13 dub$_3$-tuku u$_4$ mar-⸢uru$_5$⸣ za$_3$-še-ni nu-til-e 'The (swift) runner, storm, tempest, (the strength of) his loins is never ending'; *Šu-Suen D* 2 ^{d}nin-urta x mar-uru$_5$ ug gal šen-šen-na ru-ru-gu$_2$ 'Ninurta, . . . flood, great lion, fierce opponent in battle'; *Šu-Suen Historical Inscription B* iii 19–21 ⸢lugal⸣ x [x x] | [a-m]a-ru | ki-bal-a ur$_3$-ur$_3$ 'king (Šu-Suen) . . . , [a f]lood which sweeps over the rebel lands'; YBC 3654 (Ur III catalogue at Yale) 20 lugal a-ma-ru 'king, flood'; YBC 3654 40 ur-saĝ piriĝ ḫuš uru$_2$ me gal-gal 'Hero, furious lion, flood, the greatest *me*'

Old Babylonian Period: *Šu-ilīšu A* 14–15 ^{d}nergal ab ḫu-luḫ ni$_2$ ḫuš ri na-me gaba ru-gu$_2$ nu-zu | šul zi-ga-ni mir a-ma-ru kur-kur un-tu$_{11}$(ḪUB$_2$)-be$_2$ 'Nergal, angry sea, inspiring fearsome terror, whom no one knows how to confront, youth whose rising is a storm, a flood when it strikes down the lands'; *Lipit-Eštar D* 46–7 en a-ma-ru maḫ suḫuš erim$_2$-ma bu-re | ^{d}nin-urta en a-ma-ru maḫ suḫuš erim$_2$-<ma> bu-re 'Lord, mighty flood which tears out the foundation of the enemy! Ninurta, lord, mighty flood which tears out the foundation of the enemy'; LIH 60 iv8 = CT 21 42 (a bilingual royal hymnic inscription of Hammurabi) iv 5–9 ḫa-am-mu-ra-bi | lugal ur-saĝ | kal-ga | erim$_2$ ĝeš-ḫaš ak-ak | mar-uru$_5$ ĝeš-ĝeš-la$_2$: *ḫa-am-mu-ra-bi* | *šar-ru-um qar-ra-du-um* | *da-an-nu-um* | *ša-ki-iš a-a-bi* | *a-bu-ub tu-ku-ma-tim* 'Hammurabi, king, strong hero, slaughtering enemies, flood of battles'; *Asarluhi A* (a hymn to Asarluhi) 21–2 ^{d}asar-lu$_2$-ḫi uru$_5$ maḫ nam gal tar-re | šu bar a-ra$_2$ niĝ$_2$-nam nu-zu-zu 'Asarluhi, mighty flood determining great fates, unleashed and knowing no course whatsoever'; *UDAM KI AMUS* (*It Touches the Earth like a Storm*) 15 e-ne-eg$_3$-ga$_2$-ne$_2$ a-ma-ru zi-ga gaba-šu-ĝar nu-un-tuku: *a-bu-bu te-bu-u$_2$ ša$_2$ ma-ḫi-ra la i-šu-u* 'His word, a rising flood, has no rival: A rising flood which has no opponent'; *ELUM GUSUN* (*Honoured One, Wild Ox*) B+101 e-ne-eg$_3$-ga$_2$-ni a-ma-ru zi-ga gaba-šu-ĝar nu-[tuku] 'His word, a rising flood, has no rival'; *AGALGAL BUR SUSU* (*Flood Which Drowns the Harvest*) a+78–a+80 e-ne-eg$_3$ ^{d}a-nun-na in-ge$_{16}$-[le]-em$_3$-ma$_3$-eš-a-ni | a-zu nu-tuku šim-mu$_2$ nu-un-tuku | a-ma-ru-zi-ga gaba-šu-ĝar nu-tuku: *a-ma-at* ^{d}MIN *ša$_2$ ša$_2$-[aḫ-lu]-uq-ti* | *ba-ra-a ul i-ši ša$_2$-i-li ul i-ši* | *a-bu-bu te-bu-u$_2$ ša$_2$ ma-ḫi-ri la i-šu-u$_2$* 'His word, (at) which Anunna-gods stumble, has neither diviner nor interpreter, a rising flood which has no rival'; CBS 15120, rev. 5′ [. . .] nam-gu$_2$ ^{d}iškur a-ma-ru uru$_2$ ⸢ur$_3$$^?$⸣-ra '. . . the destruction (of) Iškur, a flood which sweeps away (like) floodwaters'; *Enki's Journey to Nippur* 56 e$_2$-engur-ra uru$_2$-maḫ ki us$_2$-sa 'E-engura, mighty flood, imposing on the earth'; *Inana C* 29 lipiš bal-a-ni niĝ$_2$ LAGAR-e mar-uru$_5$ šu nu-ru-gu$_2$ 'at her anger is something . . ., a devastating flood/tempest which cannot be opposed'; *Angim* 160, 207 (quoted above,

Section 2.1 'As regens'); *Lugale* 1–3 lugal u$_4$ me-lam$_2$-bi nir-ĝal$_2$ | ^{d}nin-urta saĝ-kal usu-maḫ-tuku kur a-ga-na laḫ$_4$ | a-ma-ru mir-ša$_4$ nu-kuš$_2$-u$_3$ ki-bala ĝa$_2$-ĝa$_2$ 'O King, the storm, whose frightening splendour is majestic; Ninurta, foremost, who possesses majestic strength and pillages the mountains all by himself, the flood, the serpent that is indefatigable, who sets against the rebel land';[13] *Lugale* 660 ur-saĝ a-⸢ma⸣-[ru] gaba šu nu-ĝa$_2$-ĝa$_2$ 'Hero, the flood, whom no one can oppose'; *Lugale* 688–9 lugal-me$_3$ ki-bal-a u$_4$-a[n$^?$-n]a$^?$ saĝ-e-eš ḫe$_2$-rig$_7$ | ^{ĝeš}tukul mar-uru$_5$ kur-re izi šum$_2$-mu 'King (of) battle, I have bestowed (on you) the storm of heaven against the rebel lands, the flood weapon which sets fire in the mountains';[14] *Inana D* 84 ^{d}inana mar-uru$_5$ kuš$_7$-za su$_3$-[su$_3$-da-zu-de$_3^?$] 'when you, Inana, the flood, in your devastation submerges (everything)'; *Ninurta C* 58–9 ^{d}nin-urta-ke$_4$ šeg$_{11}$(KA×BALAG) gi$_4$-a-zu-še$_3$ kur i$_3$-tuku$_4$-tuku$_4$-e | a-ma-ru ^{im}u$_{18}$-lu nim-gin$_7$ ĝir$_2$-ĝir$_2$-e 'Ninurta, before your roaring the mountains tremble, the flood, the southstorm that flashes like lightning'

Some of the above examples are unextended metaphors, e.g. YBC 3654 (Ur III catalogue at Yale) 20 lugal a-ma-ru 'king, flood'. But others are extended in various ways: (1) an attributive adjective or a participle: e.g. *Enki's Journey to Nippur* 56 uru$_2$-maḫ 'mighty flood'; *Temple Hymns* 338 a-ma-ru ur$_3^?$-ra 'a sweeping$^?$ flood'; (2) the genitive construction: e.g. *Gudea Cylinder A* x 2 = A xxiii 14 a-ma-ru ^{d}en-lil$_2$-la$_2$ 'the flood of Enlil'; (3) a subordinate clause: e.g. *Šu-Suen Historical Inscription B* iii 20–1 [a-m]a-ru | ki-bal-a ur$_3$-ur$_3$ '[a f]lood which sweeps over the rebel lands'.

5.2 The signifier-signified construction

In this construction, the flood or tempest is mentioned first as the signifier, to be followed by the signified.

Early Dynastic III Period: *Za$_3$-mi$_2$ Hymns* 53–4 mar-uru$_5$ u$_4$ | am-gal-nun za$_3$-mi$_2$ 'The flood/tempest, the storm, Amgalnum, be praised'

Ur III Period: *Šu-Suen D* 6–7 a-ma-ru ki-bal-še$_3$ ḫu-luḫ-ḫa gaba-šu-ĝar nu-tuku | ^{d}nin-urta i-lim u$_5$ su niĝ$_2$-ĝir$_2$ u$_4$ ĝar A ⸢MUŠ$_3^?$⸣ [. . .] 'A flood which frightens the rebel lands, and has no rival; Ninurta, deathly silence, . . . lightning$^?$ . . .'; *Curse Agade* 149–51 u$_4$ te-eš du$_{11}$-ga kalam teš$_2$-a ĝar-ra | a-ma-ru zi-ga gaba-šu-ĝar nu-tuku | ^{d}en-lil$_2$-le nam e$_2$-kur ki aĝ$_2$-ĝa$_2$-ni ba-ḫul-a-še$_3$ a-na-am$_3$ im-gu-lu-a-ba 'The roaring storm that subjugates the entire land, the rising flood that has no rival, Enlil, (in return) for the wrecking of his beloved Ekur, what should he destroy?'

[13] So MSS A B C F$_3$ D$_4$ (van Dijk 1983: 51).

[14] So MSS T$_2$ I$_4$ J$_4$ S$_4$ (van Dijk 1983: 142).

Old Babylonian Period: *AGALGAL BUR SUSU* (*Flood Which Drowns the Harvest*) 44–6 [a-ma-ru]-zi-ga gaba-šu-[ĝar nu-tuku] | [e-ne]-eg$_3$-zu IGI in-zu-a IGI in-zu nu-[. . .] | [e-ne]-eg$_3$-zu a-maḫ-zi-ga-gin$_7$ kur [. . .] 'a rising flood which has no opponent, when your word is announced, the announcement is not. . . . Your word, like a rising flood . . . the land'; *Eršemma 184* 97 mar-uru$_5$ an-ta zi-zi DI.DI saĝ an-še$_3$ mi-ni-in-il$_2$ 'a flood/tempest rising from above, rushing about, he (Iškur) raised head to heaven'

6 As object

Early Dynastic III Period: *Stele of the Vultures*, obv. x 1–4 e$_2$-an-na-tum$_2$-me | umma^{ki}-a | im-ḫul-im-ma-gin$_7$ | a-MAR mu-ni-tak$_4$ 'Eanatum, in Umma, like the destructive winds, unleashed$^?$ a flood.'

Lagaš II Period: *Gudea Statue B* v 37–8 šar-ur$_3$ a-ma-ru-me$_3$-ka-ni | mu-na-du$_3$ 'Šar-ur, his flood of battle, he (Gudea) made for him (Ninĝirsu).'

Ur III Period: UM 29-16-42 (a commemorative inscription of Šu-Suen) i 17–18 ^{ĝeš}tukul-a-ma-ru | ni$_2$-gal mu-šub '(Ninlil asked from Enlil for Šu-Suen) the flood weapon—which casts great fear'

Old Babylonian Period: *Inana C* 18–19 suḫ$_3$ igi suḫ$_3$-suḫ$_3$-suḫ$_3$ mu-un-sar-re uĝ$_3$ lu$_2$ nu-še-ga-ni-ir | ^{ĝeš}ĝeš-la$_2$ sul-sul mar-uru$_5$ ḫub$_2$ sar-sar-re su-lim ḫuš gu$_2$ e$_3$ 'She stirs confusion and chaos against those who are disobedient to her, hastening battle and making the devastating flood run, clothed in terrifying radiance'; *Inana F* 9 mar-uru$_5$ ma-an-ze$_2$-⸢eĝ$_3$⸣ ⸢dal$^?$⸣-ḫa-mun ma-<an-ze$_2$-eĝ$_3$> 'He gave me the tempest/flood and he gave me the dust cloud'; *Nergal B* 18 a-⸢ma⸣-[ru] kur sig$_{10}$-sig$_{10}$-ge$_5$ mu-ni-du$_{11}$-ga 'you command the flood which flattens the hostile land'; *Angim* 141 (quoted above, Section 2.1 'As regens'); *Lugale* 114 nu-kuš$_2$-u$_3$ la-ba-tuš-u$_3$ a$_2$-be$_2$ mar-uru$_5$ du 'the tireless one, the one who never rests, whose arms (talons$^?$) bear the tempest'

7 As part of a prepositional phrase

Sargonic Period: *Inana and Ebih* 4 u$_4$ mar-uru$_5$-a šu tag du$_{11}$-ga 'who (Inana) is adorned with storm and tempest'; *Inana and Ebih* 136 mar-uru$_5$ zi-ga saḫar ḫul bi$_2$-ib-zi 'In a rising flood/tempest, she raised evil dust.'

8 Difficult and poorly preserved images

Early Dynastic III Period: UET 2 supp 02 (= IM 049839), obv. i 1 1(aš) uru$_{18}$ sukkal '1 uru$_{18}$, the secretary', with uru$_{18}$ as a personal name or epithet

Ur III Period: *Šulgi M* 5–6 [. . .] x KA KA ḫu-luḫ-ḫa-ba a-ma-ru [. . .] | x SI A NE KA KA ḫu-luḫ-ḫa-ba a-ma$^!$-ru 'In its fearsome . . . the flood. . . . In its fearsome . . . the flood', in a broken context

Old Babylonian Period: *Nergal B* 10 [. . .] GAL x x [mar]-⸢uru$_5$⸣ x x x 'great . . . , . . . flood . . .', with mar-uru$_5$ most likely serving as an epithet of Nergal

The Flood or Tempest as the Signifier

This section examines how flood or tempest terminology serves as the signifier in the figurative process. The signified is listed before each textual reference. The exemplars below are organized according to two main categories of what is signified: the concrete and the abstract.

Concrete

Within the concrete category, exemplars are divided into two sub-categories: the animate and the inanimate.

1 Animate
The animate covers both the supernatural world and the human world.

1.1 Supernatural world
This category includes deities and other mythical figures, such as monsters.

1.1.1 Epithets or characterizations

Early Dynastic III Period: Amgalnum (*Za$_2$-mi$_2$ Hymns* 53–4)

Sargonic Period: Iškur (*Temple Hymns* 338)

Lagaš II Period: Ninĝirsu (*Gudea Cylinder A* x 2)

Ur III Period: Enki (*Ur-Namma 46* 1); Enki$^?$ (*Ur-Namma A* 237); Ninurta (*Šu-Suen D* 2); Enlil (*Curse Agade* 150); Ninurta$^?$ (YBC 3654 20, 40)

Old Babylonian Period: Ninurta (*Lipit-Eštar D* 46–7); Iškur (*Ur-Ninurta F*, segm. A 4); Asarluhi (*Asarluhi A* 21); Enlil (*ELUM GUSUN* [*Honoured One, Wild Ox*] B+93); Ninurta (*Eršemma 163.1* 7 [MS C]); Inana (*Inana B* 11; *Inana C* 29; *Inana I* 13); Iškur (*Eršemma 184* 97); Nergal (*Eršemma 45* 1); Ninurta (*Ninurta C* 59; *Ninurta D* 6); Ninurta (*Angim* 160, 207); Ninurta (*Lugale* 3, 229$^?$, 660); the monster invoked by Enlil to destroy Sumer and Akkad (*LW* 3.3); the monster$^?$ that marches in front of Ninurta in battle (*Lugale* 83); the Flood perceived as a monster$^?$ (OB *Atra-hasīs* II vii 44–6)

1.1.2 Body parts or organs

Lagaš II Period: the lower body of Ninĝirsu (*Gudea Cylinder A* iv 18)

Old Babylonian Period: Enlil's heart (*ELUM GUSUN* [*Honoured One, Wild Ox*] B+95, 96)

1.1.3 Action or movement

Sargonic Period: how Inana is adorned/equipped for battle (*Inana and Ebih* 4); how Inana raised evil dust in battle (*Inana and Ebih* 136)

Lagaš II Period: the rising of En-šeg-nun, Ninurta's bailiff (*Gudea Cylinder B* ix 22)

Ur III Period: how Enlil sweeps (*Šulgi S* 4); the sweeping over of the enemy country by Inana[?] for Šu-Suen (*Šu-Suen Historical Inscription B* i 43)

Old Babylonian Period: Nergal's rising (*Šu-ilīšu A* 15); Ninurta's rising (*Būr-Suen A* 30); destruction (by) Iškur (CBS 15120, rev. 5′); Iškur's rising (*Eršemma 168* 41; *Eršemma 185* rev. i 36); Nergal's rising (*Nergal B* 3); Nergal's demanding respect in his heroism (*Nergal C* 22, 27); Ninĝišzida's rising in the field (*Ninĝišzida B* 17); Ninurta's sweeping across (*Angim* 72–3)

From the above attestations, one can see that two of the most frequently used verbs for flood or tempest terminology in Sumerian are zi 'to rise; to stand up' and ur_3 'to wipe clean; to sweep away/over; to drag' (ePSD).

1.1.4 Psychological states or emotions

Second Dynasty of Lagaš: how Ninĝirsu's heart destroys cities (*Gudea Cylinder A* viii 26); how Ninĝirsu's heart strikes the lands (*Gudea Cylinder B* x 21)

1.1.5 Voice or roaring

Old Babylonian Period: of An (*Iddin-Dagan D* 59); of Huwawa (OB *Gilgameš* III [YBC 2178] iii 110)

1.1.6 Words or speeches

Old Babylonian Period: of An and Enlil (*LW* 4.4); of various gods (*UDAM KI AMUS* [*It Touches the Earth like a Storm*] 15); of Enlil (*ELUM GUSUN* [*Honoured One, Wild Ox*] B+93–B+94, 101); of Nergal (*AGALGAL BUR SUSU* [*Flood Which Drowns the Harvest*] a+44, 80)

1.2 Human beings

1.2.1 Epithets

Early Dynastic III Period: of a professional (UET 2 supp 02 = IM 049839, obv. i 1)

Ur III Period: Šulgi as a runner (*Šulgi V* 13); Šū-Suen (*Šū-Suen Historical Inscription B* iii 20)

Old Babylonian Period: Hammurabi (LIH 60 = CT 21 42 [a bilingual royal inscription of Hammurabi] iv 9)

1.2.2 Action or movement

Ur III Period: how Šulgi sweeps over (the lands) (CBS 11553 obv. 14)

Old Babylonian Period: the rising of Išme-Dagan (*Išme-Dagan S* 13); the opponents of Eridu rising up in the midst of the mountains (*E TURGIN NIGINAM* [*The House is Encircled like a Cattle Pen*] a+39); the advance of

Gutium sent by Enlil (*LSU* 76); the whirling around of the hair of Dumuzi's sister as an expression of her lament for him (*Dumuzi's Dream* 67)

1.3 Animals: action or movement
Old Babylonian Period: The circling movement of Bird (The *Debate between Bird and Fish* 112)

2 Inanimate

2.1 Nature: meteorological phenomena
Old Babylonian Period: the storm (*LSU* 2; *LU* 98, 198); the dark storm (PRAK 1, pl. 38 B472 ii 4′)

2.2 Architecture
Sargonic Period: the shrine in Sippar (*Temple Hymns* 488)
Old Babylonian Period: E-engura, Enki's shrine in Eridu (*Enki's Journey to Nippur* 56)

2.3 Mythical weaponry
Note that some of the weaponry listed below can be animate. Šar-ur, Ninurta's weapon, for example, is sometimes portrayed as a warrior (ur-saĝ ^{ĝeš}šar$_2$-ur$_3$ me$_3$-a kur šu-še$_3$ ĝar-ĝar 'Hero Šar-ur, who in battle subdues the enemy land'; *Gudea Cylinder B* vii 19).

Lagaš II Period: Šar-ur, Ninurta's weapon (*Gudea Cylinder A* xv 24; *B* v 37; *B* vii 14); Ninĝirsu's *mitum* weapon (*Gudea Cylinder B* vii 14)

Ur III Period: the flood weapon (*Šulgi E* 153); the flood weapon (UM 29-16-42 [a commemorative inscription of Šu-Suen] i 17)

Old Babylonian Period: the flood weapon (*LU* 184); mythical weaponry (*Inana F* 9); mythical weaponry (*Inana I* 13); Ninurta's fifty-headed mace (*Angim* 141); Ninurta's flood weapon (*Lugale* 689)

2.4 Levy
Old Babylonian Period: Unug's Levy, probably in terms of scale and speed (*Lugalbanda in the Mountain Cave*, segm. A 28; *Death of Bilgames* 243)

Abstract

1 Battle
Ur III Period: of Šulgi (*Šulgi C* segm. A 88)
Old Babylonian Period: of Ninurta (*Angim* 117)

2 Catastrophe, devastation, or ominous occasions
Ur III Period: the receding[?] of the flood upon which Ur-Namma was chosen as king by Enlil (*Ur-Namma C* 57); the stormy and tempestuous day on

which Šulgi ran from Ur to Nippur (*Šulgi A* 62); the catastrophe ordered by the gods against Ur (*Year Name 22 of Ibbi-Suen*)

Old Babylonian Period: the catastrophe after which Išme-Dagan was chosen by Enlil (*Išme-Dagan A* 120); the catastrophe after which Ur-Ninurta was chosen by Ninurta (the *Instructions of Ur-Ninurta* 4); the catastrophe that destroyed Sumer and Ur (*LSU* 107); the devastation caused by Inana (*Inana C* 19); the devastation caused by Nergal (*Nergal B* 18); the devastation caused by Inana (*Inana and Šu-kale-tuda* 188); the catastrophe caused by the enemies of Naram-Suen (OB *Cuthean Legend of Naram-Suen* iv 8′, 17′)

3 Urgency or importance

Ur III Period: *Letter from Šulgi to Puzur-Šulgi about work on the fortress Igi-hursaĝa*, version A, segm. B 21; *Letter from Šulgi to Išbi-Erra about the purchase of grain* 14; *Letter from Ibbi-Suen to Puzur-Šulgi hoping for Išbi-Erra's downfall*, verson A 38

Old Babylonian Period: *Letter from Išbi-Erra to Ibbi-Suen about the purchase of grain* 57

The Flood or Tempest as the Signified

This section examines how flood or tempest terminology serves as the signified in the figurative process. The signifier is listed before each textual reference.

Likened to other meteorological phenomena

Early Dynastic III Period: like the destructive winds (*Stele of the Vultures* obv. x 3–4)

Old Babylonian Period: like a great storm roaring over the earth (*LSU* 107–8)

Likened to animals

Old Babylonian Period: the Flood bellowed like a bull (OB *Atra-hasīs* III iii 15)

Likened to battle

Old Babylonian Period: OB *Atra-hasīs* III iii 11–12; III viii 12–13

Difficult or poorly preserved images

Old Babylonian Period: [. . .] ⌜bu⌝-ra-gin$_7$ a uru$_2$(URU×UD)-ke$_4$ gu$_3$ al-de$_2$-de$_2$-[e] '. . . like a torn out . . . the flood$^?$ waters were gushing' (*Proverb* 13.34)

Different Types of the Flood/Tempest

Normal flood

The majority of the flood/tempest images are based on normal meteorological disasters that devastated restricted or extended areas, e.g. *Stele of the Vultures*, obv. x 1–4 e$_2$-an-na-tum$_2$-me | umma^{ki}-a | im-ḫul-im-ma-gin$_7$ | a-MAR mu-ni-tak$_4$ 'Eanatum unleashed$^?$ a flood, like the destructive winds, in Umma'; *Šu-ilīšu A* 15 šul zi-ga-ni mir a-ma-ru kur-kur un-tu$_{11}$(ḪUB$_2$)-be$_2$ 'youth whose rising (is) a storm, a flood when it strikes down the lands'.

Cosmic flood/tempest

Ur III Period: *Ur-Namma 46* 1 ^{d}en-ki mar-uru$_5$-an-ki-ra 'For Enki, the flood/tempest of heaven (and) earth';[15] *Šulgi A* 62–9 u$_4$-bi-a u$_4$-de$_3$ gu$_3$ ḫe$_2$-eb-be$_2$ mar-uru$_5$ ḫe$_2$-niĝin-niĝin | ^{im}mir mir-ra ^{im}u$_{18}$-lu ur$_5$-bi ni$_2$-bi-a ḫu-mu-un-ša$_4$ | nim ĝir$_2$-ĝir$_2$ im 7-bi-ta an-na teš$_2$ ḫe$_2$-ni-gu$_7$ | u$_4$ te-eš du$_{11}$-ga ki ḫe$_2$-em-tuku$_4$-tuku$_4$ | ^{d}iškur-re an niĝ$_2$-daĝal-la-ba gu$_3$ ḫu-mu-ni-dub$_2$-dub$_2$ | im an-na-ke$_4$ a ki-ta gu$_2$ ḫe$_2$-em-ma-da-ab-la$_2$ | na$_4$ di$_4$-di$_4$-bi na$_4$ gal-gal-bi | murgu-ĝa$_2$ dub-bad ḫe$_2$-em-mi-ib-za '(But), on that day, the storm shrieked, the tempest whirled; the northwind and the southwind howled at each other. Lightning with its seven winds devoured everything in the heavens. Roaring storms made the earth quake. Iškur roared in the vast heavens. The rains of heaven embraced with the waters of the earth. Their small (hail)stones (and) their large (hail)stones, made noise on my back' (Klein 1981: 196–7); *Year Name 22 of Ibbi-Suen* mu ^{d}i-bi$_2$-^{d}suen lugal uri$_2^{ki}$-ma-ke$_4$ a-ma-ru niĝ$_2$-du$_{11}$-ga diĝir-re-ne-ke$_4$ za$_3$ an-ki im-suḫ$_3$-suḫ$_3$-a uri$_2^{ki}$ uru$_2$ (URU×UD)^{ki} tab-ba | bi$_2$-in-ge-en 'Year Ibbi-Suen, king of Ur, held firm the cities of Ur and URU×UD stricken by a flood which had been ordered by the gods and blurred the boundaries of heaven and earth' (Civil 1987: 27–8; Sigrist and Damerow 1991: 13–14; de Maaijer and Jagersma 1997–8: 282; Frayne 1997: 365)

The above cases are indicative of the attempts of the authors to exaggerate or dramatize, in a heightened style, the scale or effect of the flood. The context of *Šulgi A* 62–9 suggests that the author intended to invoke the violent stormy condition at the opening stage of the primeval era, as represented in the *Barton Cylinder* i 1–14 and *Bilgames, Enkidu, and the Netherworld*, version A 16–20 (see discussion in Chapter 2). But this mythologized meteorological event should be distinguished from the primeval flood catastrophe with the former being related to cosmogony and theogony at the opening stage of the primeval era and the latter being the meteorological catastrophe that brought the era to

[15] The expression mar-uru$_5$-an-ki 'flood/tempest of heaven (and) earth' here serves as an epithet of Enki.

an end. The flood in *Year Name 22 of Ibbi-Suen* seems to be an inversion of the traditional image of stormy weather used to portray the separation of heaven and earth during cosmogony.

The primeval flood catastrophe

The flood image in the following passages, all from the Old Babylonian period, is clearly indicative of the primeval flood catastrophe.

Old Babylonian Period: the *Instructions of Ur-Ninurta* 1–4 u_4-ul-li-ta u_4-ub-ba til-la-[a-ta] | gig-re be_2-re $\hat{g}i_6$ ba-su_3-[da-a-ta] | mu-su_3-da mu ba-ši-[su_3-da-a-ta] | eĝir a-ma-ru ba-ĝar-re-[a-ta] 'After the days of yore had come to an end, after nights had become remote from those distant nights, after years had become remote from remote years, after the Flood had swept over'; OB *Cuthean Legend of Naram-Suen* iv 8′–9′ *kīma abūb mê ša ibbašû* | *ina nišî maḫri'āti* 'like the Flood of water that took place among the first peoples . . .'; OB *Atra-hasīs* II vii 44–7 *abūbu ša taqabb* [*âninni*] | *mannu šū anāku* [*ul īdi*] | *anākūma ullada* [*abūba*] | *šipiršu ibašši it*[*ti* ᵈ*enlil*] 'The Flood that you are commanding [me], who is it? I [do not know]. Am I to give birth to [the Flood]? That is the task of [Enlil]'; III iii 15 [*abūb*]*u kīma lî išabbu* '[The Floo]d bellowed like a bull.'

Distribution of the Images within Individual Texts

Immediate contexts

The examination below focuses on the immediate literary contexts (Black 1998: 84–109) in which the flood/tempest image is found. The context may coincide with what the flood/tempest images signify.

1 Illustration of power

1.1 Destructive power or weaponry in battle, especially against foreign lands

1.1.1 With divine protagonists or mythical figures

Sargonic Period: *Inana and Ebih* 1–6, 130–7

Lagaš II Period: *Gudea Cylinder A* x 2 = *A* xxiii 14; *A* xv 23–5; *B* vii 12–viii 6; *B* x 21–3; *Gudea Statue B* v 37–40

Ur III Period: *Šu-Suen D* 2–6; *Šu-Suen Historical Inscription B* i 40–8

Old Babylonian Period: *Lipit-Eštar D* 46–9; *Būr-Suen A* 28–31; *CH* 27b 76–80; LIH 60 = CT 21 42 (a bilingual royal hymnic inscription of Hammurabi) iv 5–12; *LU* 184; *Enki's Journey to Nippur* 56–60; *Eršemma 163.1* 4–9; *Inana B* 11–33; *Inana C* 18–30; *Inana F* 8–9; *Inana I* 8–15; *Nergal B* 1–20; *Eršemma 45* 1–11; *Ninurta D* 1–13; OB *Gilgameš* III (YBC 2178) iii 110–15; *Angim* 71–5, 116–22, 141–2, 202–7; *Lugale* 1–11, 76–95, 106–14, 229–31, 652–61, 688–94; OB *Atra-hasīs* III viii 9–19

1.1.2 With human (royal) protagonists
Early Dynastic III Period: *Stele of the Vultures* obv. x 1–4

Ur III Period: *Šulgi C* segm. A 86–8; *Šulgi E* 152–3; CBS 11553 (a royal hymn to Šulgi) obv. 13–14; UM 29-16-42 (a commemorative inscription of Šu-Suen) i 17; *Šu-Suen Historical Inscription B* iii 19–25

1.2 Power in determining fates: with divine protagonists
Old Babylonian Period: *Asarluhi A* 20–2

1.3 Power in speed or action

1.3.1 With divine protagonists
Second Dynasty of Lagaš: *Gudea Cylinder B* ix 21–x 2

1.3.2 With human (royal) protagonists
Ur III Period: *Šulgi V* 13–14

Old Babylonian Period: *Išme-Dagan S* 13–19

1.4 Power in word/command: with divine protagonists
Old Babylonian Period: *UDAM KI AMUS* (*It Touches the Earth like a Storm*) 15–24; *ELUM GUSUN* (*Honoured One, Wild Ox*) B+93–B+101; *AGALGAL BUR SUSU* (*Flood Which Drowns the Harvest*) 44–6; a+80–a+89

1.5 Unopposed and fearsome power in general, often against foreign lands

The display of destructive power by the divine, mythical, or human protagonists through the flood/tempest may be an expression of anger in all of the textual sources listed below. In a few passages the flood image is used specifically to describe the ruthless and furious emotions of the protagonists involved, e.g. *Gudea Cylinder A* viii 18–ix 4; *B* x 16–23; *Inana and Šu-kale-tuda* 185–9.

Early Dynastic III Period: *Za$_3$-mi$_2$ Hymns* 53–4

Sargonic Period: *Temple Hymns* 338–42

Lagaš II Period: *Gudea Cylinder A* iv 18; viii 23–7; *B* x 16–23b; *B* viii 1–6

Ur III Period: *Ur-Namma 46* 1–8; *Šulgi S* 4; *Curse Agade* 149–50; YBC 3654 20, 40

Old Babylonian Period: *Ur-Namma A* 236; *Šu-ilīšu A* 13–16; *Iddin-Dagan D* 57–60; *Ur-Ninurta F* segm. A 1–9; CBS 15120 (= PBS XIII No. 65), obv. 5′–8′; *Inana B* 77–9; *Inana D* 79–87; *Eršemma 168* 32–41; *Eršemma 184* 68–99; *Eršemma 185* rev. i 10–36; *Nergal C* 21–30; *Ninĝišzida B* 16–19; *Ninurta C* 107–19; *Inana and Šu-kale-tuda* 185–9; *Angim* 159–63; VAT 6481 16; TuM NF 3 53 i 20

2 Illustration of catastrophic or ominous occasions in Sumer and Akkad
Ur III Period: *Ur-Namma C* 57[?]; *Šulgi A* 62–9; *Year Name 22 of Ibbi-Suen* 1–6

Old Babylonian Period: *Išme-Dagan A* 120; *LW* 3.1–25, 4.1–5.20; the *Instructions of Ur-Ninurta* 4; *LSU* 1–21, 58–82, 107–11; *LU* 87–98, 172–211; OB *Cuthean Legend of Naram-Suen* iv 1′–18′; OB *Atra-hasīs* II vii 44–53; III iii 4–24; *Inana and the Numun Grass* 1–20

3 Illustration of lament
Old Babylonian Period: *Dumuzi's Dream* 66–9

4 Illustration of the immense scale of levy (which was raised at a great speed)
Old Babylonian Period: *Lugalbanda in the Mountain Cave*, segm. A 24–38; *Death of Bilgames* 239–50

5 Illustration of the urgency or importance of work to be done
See above, Abstract, Section 3, 'Urgency or importance'.

6 Illustration of motion
Old Babylonian Period: the *Debate between Bird and Fish* 110–12

7 Illustration of the fearsomeness of a shrine
Sargonic Period: *Temple Hymns* 488

8 Illustration of the fearsomeness of opponents
Old Babylonian Period: *E TURGIN NIGINAM* (*The House is Encircled like a Cattle Pen*) a+39

Image clusters

Berlin (1979: 29) is probably the first one who began to pay attention to how frequently imagery is used and how images tend to occur in 'dense clusters' in a piece of Sumerian literature, namely, *Enmerkar and Ensuhkešdanna* (or *Enmerkar and En-suhgir-ana*). By using statistics, Black (1998: 52–5, 73–7, 115–18) demonstrated the frequency and density of imagery in a number of Sumerian literary compositions. The following section investigates how the flood or tempest image occurs in clusters with other images in the textual sources collected in Vol. 2 of Chen (2009). The aim of this investigation is to document the use of meteorological images in the context of the literary conventions from the Early Dynastic III period to the Old Babylonian period. Each entry first gives the textual reference, to be followed by the image in Sumerian with its English translation, with what is signified in brackets. Note that the images listed below may not signify the same things as signified by the flood or tempest image.

1 Concrete
There are two sub-categories under this heading concerning images: the animate and the inanimate.

1.1 Animate

1.1.1 Deities

Old Babylonian Period: *Inana B* 10 ^{d}iškur (how Inana roared at the earth); *Eršemma 184* rev. i 35 an 'An' (Iškur); OB *Atra-hasīs* III iii 40 *tiruru šuāti* 'That Tiruru' (how Enlil brought up the evil/Flood)

1.1.2 Fauna

1.1.2.1 Mammals

ab$_2$ 'cow'

Old Babylonian Period: *LU* 102 (the victimized Ningal)

am; *lī'um* 'wild bull'

Sargonic Period: *Temple Hymns* 333 (the gate tower of Iškur's temple)

Ur III Period: *Šu-Suen D* 4 am gal 'great wild bull' (Ninurta); *Šu-Suen Historical Inscription B* i 29 am (Inana)

Old Babylonian Period: *LW* 5.17 ⌜am⌝ gal 'great wild bull' (the destroyed Uruk); *Inana C* 25 am gal 'great wild bull' (Inana); *Angim* 123 am (the gods who hid away from Ninurta); OB *Atra-hasīs* III iii 15 *lī'um* (the Flood)

gu$_4$ 'bull'

Old Babylonian Period: *LW* 5.10 (Unug to be destroyed)

maš; maš$_2$ 'goat'; u$_8$ 'ewe'; or *imēru* 'sheep'

Old Babylonian Period: *Išme-Dagan S* 18 maš$_2$-dara$_3$ 'young wild goat$^?$' (Išme-Dagan as a runner); *LW* 4.23 maš kar-ra 'stampeding goats' (the Subarians who devastated Sumer and Akkad); *LSU* 103 u$_8$ 'ewe' (the people sold by Nanna); OB *Atra-hasīs* III iv 19 *imērī* 'sheep' (how the gods filled the trough)

piriĝ; piriĝ$_3$(UG); ur; ur-maḫ 'lion'

Lagaš II Period: *Gudea Cylinder B* ix 21 piriĝ$_3$ (the roaring of En-šeg-nun, Ninurta's herdsman)

Ur III Period: CBS 11553 (a royal hymn to Šulgi) obv. 2–3 piriĝ-banda$_3$ 'young lion; panther' (Šulgi), 4 ur-maḫ (Šulgi); *Šu-Suen D* 2 piriĝ$_3$ gal 'a great lion' (Ninurta); YBC 3654 40 piriĝ ḫuš 'furious lion' (Ninurta$^?$)

Old Babylonian Period: *Iddin-Dagan D* 6 šu piriĝ 'paws of a lion' (concerning Ninisina), 8 gir$_2$ piriĝ 'claws of a lion' (concerning Ninisina), 11 piriĝ šeg$_{12}$ gi$_4$-gi$_4$ 'roaring lion' (Ninisina); *Išme-Dagan S* 15 piriĝ ḫuš 'fierce lion' (Išme-Dagan); *LU* 205 piriĝ$_3$ (the storm); *Enki's Journey to Nippur* 57 piriĝ (E-engura [Enki's temple in Eridu]); *Inana C* 24 piriĝ-banda$_3$ 'young lion; panther' (Inana); *Eršemma 184* 92 piriĝ$_3$-banda$_3$ 'young lion' (Iškur); *Eršemma 185* rev. i 22 [piriĝ$_3$-banda$_3$^{da}] '[young lion]'

(Iškur); *ELA* 544 pirig̃$_3$ gal 'great lion' (Iškur); *Angim* 120 su pirig̃ sa pirig̃ 'lion's flesh and sinew' (Ninurta); *Lugale* 11 za$_3$ pirig̃ 'strength [lit. arm] of a lion' (Ninurta); 109 $^{g̃eš}$tukul sag̃-pirig̃$_3$-g̃a 'a lion-headed weapon'; the *Debate between Bird and Fish* 110 igi pirig̃-g̃a$_2$ 'lion's face' (the Bird)

^{anše}si$_2$–si$_2$ 'horse'

Old Babylonian Period: *Išme-Dagan S* 17 (Išme-Dagan as a runner)

sun$_2$ 'wild cow'

Old Babylonian Period: *LW* 5.18 (the destroyed Unug)

ur-bar 'wolf'

Old Babylonian Period: *Lugale* 693 (the flood weapon of Ninurta$^?$)

1.1.2.2 Reptiles

Snakes or dragons

Sargonic Period: *Temple Hymns* 336–8 muš-gir$_2$ 'snakes' (Iškur's temple); *Šulgi V* 3 ušum ni$_2$-gu[r$_3$] 'fearsome snake' (Šulgi$^?$); 7 muš-gal 'dragon' (Enlil$^?$)

Old Babylonian Period: *Šu-ilīšu A* 16 ušumgal 'dragon' (Nergal); *Iddin-Dagan D* 5 ušumgal 'dragon' (Ninisina), 65 ušum dig̃ir-re-e-ne 'viper of the gods' (Enlil); *Inana B* 9 ušumgal 'dragon' (Inana); *Angim* 142 mir 'a mythical snake; a snake-like weapon' (Ninurta's weapon); *Lugale* 3 mir-ša$_4$ 'snake' (Ninurta), 10 ušum 'dragon' (Ninurta$^?$)

1.1.2.3 Birds

Anzu Bird

Lagaš II Period: *Gudea Cylinder A* iv 17 (with regard to Ning̃irsu's arms/wings)

Old Babylonian Period: *LW* 3.7, 10 (with regard to the glint of the eyes of the mythical monster)

mušen 'bird'

Old Babylonian Period: *LU* 105 mušen an-na 'bird of heaven' (the victimized Ningal); *Lugale* 110 (Ninurta's weapon)

buru$_4$-dugud^{mušen} 'flock of crows'

Old Babylonian Period: *Lugalbanda in the Mountain Cave*, segm. A 32 (Unug's huge levy$^?$)

buru$_5$^{mušen} 'sparrow, small birds'

Old Babylonian Period: *Angim* 122 buru$_5$^{mušen} (the gods who fled from Ninurta)

^{d}nin-šara$_2$(LAGA×SIG$_7$)^{mušen} 'hawk'

Ur III Period: *Šulgi A* 60 (Šulgi)

sur$_2$-du$_3$^{mušen}; ^{mušen}sur$_2$-du$_3$ 'falcon'

Lagaš II Period: *Gudea Cylinder B* vii 21 (Šar-ur)

Ur III Period: *Šulgi A* 60 (Šulgi)

u$_{11}$-ri$_2$-in^{mušen}; *arû/erû* 'eagle'

Old Babylonian Period: *LW* 3.14 u$_{11}$-ri$_2$-in^{mušen} '(the talons) of an eagle' (the mythical monster's feet); the *Debate between Bird and Fish* 110 umbin u$_{11}$-ri$_2$-in^{mušen}-na 'eagle's talons' (the talons of Bird); OB *Atra-hasīs* III iii 16–17 *arû/erû* (how the winds roared; after von Soden 1994: 640)

1.1.2.4 Insects

buru$_5$; *arbî* 'locust'

Old Babylonian Period: *Lugale* 94 (the burned animals of the steppe)

kulīlu 'dragonfly'

Old Babylonian Period: OB *Atra-hasīs* III iv 7 (the destroyed human beings)

zubbu(m)/subbu(m) 'flies'

Old Babylonian Period: OB *Atra-hasīs* III iii 19, 44 (the destroyed human beings); III v 35, 46 (the hungry gods); III vi 2 (the hungry gods/the destroyed human beings$^?$)

1.2 Inanimate

1.2.1 Nature

1.2.1.1 Celestial, terrestrial, and subterranean worlds

ab 'sea'

Lagaš II Period: *Gudea Cylinder A* viii 23 (Ninĝirsu's heart)

Old Babylonian Period: *Šu-ilīšu A* 14 ab ḫu-luḫ 'angry sea' (Nergal); *Enki's Journey to Nippur* 53–4 a-ab zi-ga 'rising sea' (Eridu)

an 'Heaven' and/or ki 'Earth'

Second Dynasty of Lagaš: *Gudea Cylinder A* iv 14–15 (Ninĝirsu); *A* ix 2 (Ninĝirsu's heart)

Old Babylonian Period: *Eršemma 45* 10 (Nergal); *Lugalbanda in the Mountain Cave*, segm. A 29 an dungu 'a clouded sky' (Unug's levy); *Angim* 116 an (battle); 124 an (Ninurta's fearsome radiance)

edin daĝal 'broad plain'

Old Babylonian Period: the *Debate between Bird and Fish* 114 (the bird nest)

ḫur-saĝ 'mountain'

Old Babylonian Period: *Eršemma 163.1* 3 (Enlil$^{?}$)

i_7 'river'

Lagaš II Period: *Gudea Cylinder B* x 20 $^{i}{}_{7}$buranun^{ki} 'Euphrates' (the heart of Ninĝirsu)

Ur III Period: CBS 11553 (a royal hymn to Šulgi), obv. 16 i_7 ku$^{?}$-x ḫu-luḫ-ḫa 'a . . . frightening river' (Šulgi)

Old Babylonian Period: *Enki's Journey to Nippur* 55 i_7-maḫ ni_2-$\hat{g}al_2$-la 'mighty awe-inspiring river' (Eridu); 59 i_7-maḫ-zi-⸢ga⸣ 'a rising mighty river' (the battle cry of E-engura, Enki's temple in Eridu); *Lugale* 108 i_7-maḫ 'a mighty river' (how Ninurta roared)

kar 'quay'

Old Babylonian Period: *Šu-ilīšu A* 2 kar gal an ki 'mighty quay of heaven and earth' (Nergal)

kur 'Netherworld'

Old Babylonian Period: *LW* 3.8, 15 (the wide grimace of the mythical monster)

$šita_3$ 'water-channel'

Old Babylonian Period: *Inana C* 30 $šita_3$ maḫ 'a mighty water-channel' (Inana)

apsû 'underground water'

Old Babylonian Period: OB *Atra-hasīs* III i 29 (the roof of the boat which Ea instructed Atra-hasīs to build)

1.2.1.2 Meteorological Phenomena

a 'water'

Lagaš II Period: *Gudea Cylinder A* viii 25, ix 1 a e_3-a 'rushing water' (Ninĝirsu's heart); *B* x 22–3 (Ninĝirsu's heart); *B* vii 18 (how the lands of Enlil's enemies may be inundated)

Ur III Period: CBS 11553 (a royal hymn to Šulgi) obv. 15 a-zi-ga 'a rising water' (Šulgi)

Old Babylonian Period: *Iddin-Dagan D* 70 (how those who disobeyed Iddin-Dagan may be drowned); *LW* 4.22, 5.20 a maḫ e_3-a 'a swelling flood' (the invading Subarians); *UDAM KI AMUS* (*It Touches the Earth like a Storm*) 20 a-zi-ga: *abūbu tebû* 'rising flood' (the word of Asarluhi), 21 a-maḫ 'mighty water/flood' (the word of Asarluhi); *AGALGAL BUR SUSU* (*Flood Which Drowns the Harvest*) 46 a-maḫ-zi-ga 'a rising flood' (the word of Nergal); a+85 a-zi-[ga] 'a rising flood' (the word of a god); a+86 a-maḫ 'a mighty water/flood' (the word of a god); *LU* 183 a maḫ e_3-a 'rushing flood' (the evil wind); *ELA* 565 a maḫ e_3-a 'a rising flood' (Inana); *Angim* 119 a-maḫ e_3-a 'a rising flood' (Ninurta's battle); *Lugale* 658 a-e_3-a 'a rising flood' (Ninurta) a-ĝi$_6$ 'wave, flood'

Old Babylonian Period: *Ninĝišzida B* 16 (Ninĝišzida); *Lugale* 95 (devastation)

bar-šeĝ$_3$ 'fog, haze'

Old Babylonian Period: *LU* 188 an-bar$_7$ bar-šeĝ$_3$ il$_2$-il$_2$-la-gin$_7$ 'like the haze that rises at noon' (how Enlil made fires blaze)

dal-ḫa-mu; ^{im}dalhamu$_5$ 'dust storm; disaster'

Old Babylonian Period: *Inana C* 21 ^{im}dalḫamu$_5$ (Inana's garment); *Inana F* 9 ⌜dal$^?$⌝-ḫa-mun (Inana's weapon)

dungu(IM.SI.A) 'cloud'

Sargonic Period: *Temple Hymns* 335 dungu sir$_2$-ra 'thick cloud' (Iškur's temple$^?$)

Old Babylonian Period: *Lugalbanda in the Mountain Cave*, segm. A 29 (Unug's levy); *Death of Bilgames* 244 (Unug's levy)

im 'wind; rain'

Old Babylonian Period: *Iddin-Dagan D* 61 (An); *Išme-Dagan S* 13 (Išme-Dagan); *Ur-Ninurta F*, segm. A 7 (Iškur); *LSU* 77 im gal edin-na 'great wind of the steppe' (the advance of the Gutians); 193 im-im 'winds' (devastation); *Eršemma 168* 40 IM.MA.A.A. 'rain' (Iškur); *Eršemma 184* rev. ii 88–9 (devastation); *Eršemma 185* rev. i 16–17 (devastation); *Lugalbanda in the Mountain Cave*, segm. A 31 im-peš-peš 'dense rain$^?$' (Unug's levy); *Lugale* 77 im-ussu 'eight winds' (Ninurta)

im-ḫul/im-ḫul-im(-ḫul) 'destructive winds'

Early Dynastic III Period: *Stele of the Vultures* obv. x 3–4 (the flood envoked by Eanatum)

Old Babylonian Period: *LU* 178, 183 (devastation)

iz-zi$_8$ 'wave'

Lagaš II Period: *Gudea Cylinder A* viii 24 (Ninĝirsu's heart)

mir; ^{im}mir 'northwind'

Sargonic Period: *Temple Hymns* 339–400 (Iškur$^?$)

Ur III Period: *Šulgi V* 2 mir-ru-gal-^{d}a-nun-ke$_4$-ne 'giant wind of the Anuna gods' (Enlil)

Old Babylonian Period: *Šu-ilīšu A* 15 (Nergal's rising); *Ur-Ninurta F*, segm. B 2 ^{im}mir mir-ra 'raging northwind' (Iškur)

muru$_9$(IM.DUGUD) 'rainstorm'

Old Babylonian Period: *Lugalbanda in the Mountain Cave*, segm. A 30 muru$_9$ [IM.DUGUD]-dugud 'heavy rainstorm' (Unug's levy)

niĝ$_2$-ĝir$_2$; nim; nim-ĝir$_2$ 'lightning'

Ur III Period: *Šu-Suen D* 7 niĝ$_2$-ĝir$_2$ (Ninurta$^?$)

Old Babylonian Period: *LW* 3.7 nim ĝir$_2$-re (the glint of the eyes of the mythical monster); *Ninurta C* 59 nim (Ninurta)

saḫar 'dust'

Sargonic Period: *Inana and Ebih* 136 saḫar ḫul 'evil dust' (destruction caused by Inana)

Ur III Period: *Šu-Suen D* 3 (complete destruction)

Old Babylonian Period: *LW* 4.26 (destruction of Sumer); *Nergal B* 19–20 (destruction); *Ninurta D* 11 (complete destruction); *Lugale* 84 (destruction); *Inana and the Numun-Grass* 21 (hardship)

šeĝ$_x$(IM.A.A) 'rain'

Sargonic Period: *Temple Hymns* 332 (Iškur's temple$^?$)

tir-an-na 'rainbow'

Old Babylonian Period: *Lugale* 9 (Ninurta)

u$_4$ 'storm'

Early Dynastic III Period: *Za$_3$-mi$_3$ Hymns* 53 (Amgalnum)

Sargonic Period: *Inana and Ebih* 4 (Inana)

Lagaš II Period: *Gudea Cylinder A* viii 27 (Ninĝirsu's heart); *B* vii 24 u$_4$ ⸢ḫuš⸣ 'furious storm' (the *mitum* weapon of Ninĝirsu)

Ur III Period: *Šulgi V* 1 (Enlil), 13 (Šulgi); CBS 11553 (a royal hymn to Šulgi) obv. 13 (Šulgi); *Curse Agade* 149 (Enlil)

Old Babylonian Period: *Šu-ilīšu A* 1 u$_4$ ḫuš du$_7$-ru 'furiously raging storm' (Nergal); 6 u$_4$ gal 'great storm' (Nergal); *Iddin-Dagan D* 3 u$_4$ mir-a 'raging storm' (Ninisina); 10 u$_4$ gal 'great storm' (Ninisina); 11 u$_4$ gu$_3$ dub$_2$-dub$_2$ 'howling storm' (Ninisina); 12 u$_4$ ka ša-an-ša-ša 'overpowering storm' (Ninisina); 13–14 (Ninisina); *LW* 3.6 u$_4$ ḫul-du$_3$ 'malevolent storm' (the countenance of the mythical monster); *Ur-Ninurta F*, segm. A 2 u$_4$ gal-la 'great storm' (Iškur); *Būr-Suen A* 31 u$_4$ sumur(KA) me$_3$-a 'the furious storm in battle' (Ninurta); 37 (Ninurta); *UDAM KI AMUS* (*It Touches like a Storm*) 1–10, 23 (the word/command of the gods); *AGALGAL BUR SUSU* (*Flood Which Drowns the Harvest*) a+88 (Nergal); *LSU* 2 (the devastation caused by An and Enlil); 59 u$_4$ gig-ga 'a troublesome storm' (the devastation caused by Enlil); 70 (devastation); 80β–81 (devastation), 108 u$_4$ gal 'a great storm' (the devastation); *LU* 87–91, 94, 98, 100, 109–11, 172–7, 180–2, 185–7, 189, 196–202, 205, 207, 209 (devastation); *Eršemma 163.1* 4 (Ninurta); *Inana B* 17, 28 u$_4$ du$_7$-du$_7$ 'a charging storm' (how Inana charges forward); 29 u$_4$ gu$_3$ ra-ra 'roaring storm' (how Inana roars); *Inana C* 28 (Inana); *Eršemma*

184 rev. ii 82–3, 85–7 (the devastation caused by Iškur), 94, 99 (Iškur); *Eršemma 185* rev. i 12, 14, 15 (the devastation caused by Iškur); *Nergal B* 2 (Nergal); *Eršemma 45* 1–2, 9 u$_4$-u$_{18}$-lu 'southstorm' (Nergal); *Ninurta C* 6 (Ninurta); *ELA* 544 (Iškur); *Angim* 73–4 (Ninurta); *Lugale* 1, 77 (Ninurta), 688, 691, 694 (Ninurta's weapon)

ulu$_3$; ulu$_3$^{lu}/u$_{18}$-lu; ^{im}ulu$_3$^{lu} 'southwind'

Sargonic Period: *Temple Hymns* 339 (Iškur)

Ur III Period: *Šu-Suen D* 33, 36 ulu$_3$ maḫ 'massive southwind' (Ninurta)

Old Babylonian Period: *Šu-ilīšu A* 6 ^{im}ulu$_3$ (Nergal); *Iddin-Dagan D* 3 ^{im}u-lu$_3$^{lu} (the power of Ninsina), 68 ⸢u⸣lu$_3$^{lu} (the decision of Enlil$^?$), 81 ulu$_3$^{lu} ḫuš-a 'furious southwind' (Aruru); *Išme-Dagan S* 13 (Išme-Dagan); *LW* 4.15; *Ur-Ninurta F*, segm. A 4, B 2 (Iškur); *LU* 191 (devastation); *Inana B* 21 (Inana's power); *Inana C* 22 (devastation caused by Inana); *Eršemma 45* 1–2, 9 (Nergal); *Ninurta C* 59 ^{im}ulu$_3$^{lu} (Ninurta); *Inana and Šu-kale-tuda* 188 (Inana's power and rage); *Lugale* 8 (Ninurta's terror)

1.2.1.3 Flora

Old Babylonian Period: *LW* 3.16 zar 'hay (stacks)' (the destroyed population); 3.17 buru$_{14}$ 'harvest (crop)' (the flooded land of Sumer and Akkad); *Lipit-Eštar 49* gi 'reed' (those who are hostile to Lipit-Eštar and are broken by his weapon); *Eršemma 163.1* 6 zi$_3$ 'flour; meal' (the lands dispersed by Ninurta); *163.1* 6 še 'grain; barley' (the lands destroyed by Ninurta); *163.1* 9 gi 'reed' (the enemy land trampled down by Ninurta); *Eršemma 168* 36 še-mu-ra 'threshed grain/barley' (the children of the rebellious who were carried off by the storm); *Eršemma 185* rev. i 32 še-garadin 'grain sheaves' (the little ones who were carried off by the storm); *Dumuzi's Dream* 69 ^{ĝeš}bulug taškarin 'a boxwood needle' (the fingernails of Dumuzi's sister); *Lugale* 6 še 'grain; barley' (the neck of the insubordinate which was reaped by Ninurta); *Inana and the Numun-Grass* 59 buru$_{14}$ 'harvest' (all the kinds of luxuriant plants the shepherd brought to Inana)

1.2.2 Man-made objects

1.2.2.1 Weaponry or war devices

Ur III Period: CBS 11553 (a royal hymn to Šulgi) obv. 5 gu$_4$-si-AŠ 'battering ram' (Šulgi), 8 ĝeš-bur$_2$ 'trap' (Šulgi), 10 sa-šu$_2$-uš-gal 'net' (Šulgi), 11 ^{ĝeš}mitum 'the mace' (Šulgi), 12 ⸢x x x⸣-IB$_2$-ur$_3$-da-tab-ba '. . . siege-shield' (Šulgi); *Šu-Suen D* 4 gu$_4$-si-AŠ 'battering ram' (Ninurta)

Old Babylonian Period: *LW* 3.13 ĝir$_2$ 'knives' (the haunches of the mythical monster), 3.14 ^{uruda}šum-me 'saw' (the muscles of the mythical monster); 4.9 ti mar-uru$_5$-a 'arrows in a quiver', 4.12 ĝeš-bur$_2$ 'trap' (how Sumer was caught in destruction); *LU* 194 ĝeš-bur$_2$ 'trap' (how

Sumer was overturned); *Inana C* 26 niĝ$_2$-⌜ḫuš⌝ 'pitfall' (Inana); 27 ^{ĝeš}es$_2$-ad 'trap' (Inana); *Inana I* 13 tukul il$_2$-la 'a raised weapon$^?$' (Inana); *Eršemma 184* rev. ii 99 ^{ĝeš}tukul 'weapon' (Iškur)

1.2.2.2 Tools

Old Babylonian Period: *LW* 3.5 $^{ĝešgana}{}_2$ĝušur 'harrow' (the scales of the mythical monster); 4.24 ^{ĝeš}naĝa$_3$ 'mortar; pestle' (how the enemies destroyed Sumer and Akkad); 80β $^{ĝešgana}{}_2$ĝušur 'harrow' (the storm/devastation); 80β ^{ĝeš}al 'hoe' (how the city was struck); *Ninurta D* 3^{uruda} du$_5$ x x '. . . axe' (how Ninurta felled trees); 4^{uruda} du$_5$ gal 'great axe' (how Ninurta struck down walls)

1.2.2.3 Other man-made objects

aga 'crown'

Old Babylonian Period: *Lugale* 9 aga-zi; 'the true crown' (Ninurta);

bad$_3$ 'wall'

Ur III Period: *Šu-suen D* 27–8 bad$_3$ gal 'a great wall' (Ninurta)

gi-sig 'reed fence'

Old Babylonian Period: *Angim* 118 (how Ninurta's battle smashes the mountains)

^{gi}muru$_x$(KID.MAḪ) 'reed mat'

Old Babylonian Period: *UDAM KI AMUS* (*It Touches the Earth like a Storm*) 17 (the word of a god); *AGALGAL BUR SUSU* (*Flood Which Drowns the Harvest*) a+82 (the word of a god)

tug$_2$ 'garment' or gada 'linen'

Old Babylonian Period: *LU* 203 uri$_2^{ki}$-ma tug$_2$-gin$_7$ ba-e-dul gada-gin$_7$ ba-e-bur$_2$ '(the storm) covered Urim like a garment, was spread out over it like a linen cloth'; *Inana and the Numun-Grass* 61 gu$_3$ šu niĝin$_2$-na-ni an-ur$_2$-ra tug$_2$-gin$_7$ im-mi-in-dul gada-gin$_7$ im-mi-in-bur$_2$ 'Her (Inana) resounding cry covered the horizon like a garment, was spread over it like a cloth.'

amu(m) 'raft'

Old Babylonian Period: OB *Atra-hasīs* III iv 8, 9 (the people destroyed by the Flood)

karpatu(m) '(clay)pot'

Old Babylonian Period: OB *Atra-hasīs* III iii 10 (Anzu shattered the noise of the land)

1.2.3 Other images

ga 'milk'

Old Babylonian Period: *LSU* 64 ga-gin$_7$ ur-e ba-an-de$_2$ 'like milk poured to the dog' (how Ningirsu wasted Sumer)

^{d}gibil; ^{d}gibil$_{6}$; izi; ga-an-ze$_{2}$-er; ^{d}*girrum*(gira$_{3}$[NE/BIL.GI]) 'fire; flame'
Old Babylonian Period: *Iddin-Dagan D* 4 ^{d}gibil$_{6}$ (the upraised fierce face of Ninisina that rips the bodies of the enemy); *LW* 3.5 izi (the back of the mythical monster); 3.9 ga-an-ze$_{2}$-er (the tongue of the mythical monster); 4.6 ⌜d⌝gibil (Nergal); *LU* 201 izi (how the storm blazes); OB *Gilgameš* III (YBC 2178) iii 111 ^{d}*girrum*(gira$_{3}$ [NE/BIL.GI] (Huwawa's speech); the *Debate between Tree and Reed* 186 izi (how an arrow is shot from the quiver)

kaš 'beer'
Old Babylonian Period: *Inana B* 82 kaš du$_{10}$-ga 'sweet beer' (the tears shed by En-hedu-ana to Inana)

šika '(pot)sherds'
Old Babylonian Period: *LU* 192, 210 šika ku$_{5}$-da 'broken (pot)sherds' (the destroyed people in Urim)

u$_{3}$-dub$_{2}$ 'coal; ember'
Old Babylonian Period: *LW* 3.9 (the tongue of the mythical monster)

uš$_{7}$ 'spittle'; uš$_{11}$ 'poison'; ze$_{2}$ 'bile'
Old Babylonian Period: *Inana C* 28 uš$_{11}$ 'poison' (Inana's attack); *Lugale* 106 uš$_{11}$-ze$_{2}$-a 'bilious poison' (Ninurta's attack); *Lugale* 107 ze$_{2}$ 'bile' (Ninurta's attack); *Lugale* 229 uš$_{7}$ 'spittle' (Ninurta's attack)

2 Abstract

me 'divine power or ordinances'
Ur III Period: YBC 3654 40 (Ninurta$^{?}$)

mūtum 'death'
OB *Gilgameš* III (YBC 2178) iii 112 (Huwawa's breath)

qablu(*m*) 'battle'
Old Babylonian Period: OB *Atra-hasīs* III iii 12 (how the Flood passed over the peoples);[16] III viii 13 (the Flood)

In addition to the above images that are mostly identifiable as either similes or metaphors by their formal features, there are numerous topoi, stock-strophes, or formulaic expressions (Ferrara 1995: 81–117) in the textual sources gathered in Vol. 2 of Chen (2009) which are not marked formally as similes or metaphors and thus have not been listed above. But these should still be identified as figures of speech. For example, the depiction of destruction in terms of burning is commonplace: *LU* 179 (^{d}gibil), 186 (izi), 187 (izi-ĝi$_{6}$-edin-na 'a fiery glow'), 188 (izi), *Inana B* 13; *Lugale* 86, 689 (izi); *Inana and the Numun-Grass* 14, 22, 26, 28, 29, 51, 52. Sometimes, these depictions are mixed with similes which blur the distinction between literal and figurative expressions: see *LU* 186–8 u$_{4}$-da igi-ba izi mu-un-bar$_{7}$-bar$_{7}$-e uĝ$_{3}$-e še am$_{3}$-ša$_{4}$ | u$_{4}$ mir-mir-da izi-ĝi$_{6}$-edin-na bar ba-da-an-tab | an-bar$_{7}$ bar-šeĝ$_{3}$ il$_{2}$-il$_{2}$-la-gin$_{7}$ izi im-ma-an-bar$_{7}$-bar$_{7}$ 'In front of the storm, a fire

[16] Compare SB *Gilgameš* XI 110–11.

blazes—the people groan. With the raging storm a fiery glow burns. Like the haze that rises at noon, the fire blazes';[17] 201 u$_4$ izi-gin$_7$ bar$_7$-e uĝ$_3$-e su bi$_2$-ib-dar 'the storm blazing like fire ripped the flesh of the people'; *Lugale* 93–4 ku$_6$-bi engur-ra u$_4$ mi-ni-ib-ra ka mu-un-ba-ba-e | edin-na maš$_2$-anše-bi u$_2$-ku-uk mi-ni-ib-du$_{11}$ bur$_5$-re-eš šu mi-ni-ḥu-uz$_3$ 'The storm flooded the fish there in the subterranean waters, their mouths snapped (for air). It burned the animals of the steppe, and roasted them as locusts.'

The fact that mixed images, even with the images based on mutually exclusive phenomena in *realia*, such as storm/flood and fire/burning, are juxtaposed side by side, suggests the author attempted to build a heightened literary effect with regard to destruction. To achieve such effect, images are sometimes compounded, which means one image is used to illustrate another; e.g. *LSU* 2 u$_4$-de$_3$ mar-uru$_5$-gin$_7$ teš$_2$-bi i$_3$-gu$_7$-e 'The storm, like a flood, devours all'; 107–8 a-ma-ru du$_6^!$(ki) al ak-e šu im-ur$_3$-ur$_3$-re | u$_4$ gal-gin$_7$ ki-a ur$_5$ mi-ni-ib-ša$_4$ a-ba-a ba-ra-e$_3$ 'The devastating flood was levelling (everything). Like a great storm it roared over the earth, who could escape it?' Without referring to a specific weather disaster, both u$_4$ 'storm' and mar-uru$_5$/a-ma-ru 'flood' in *LSU* clearly signify the catastrophe ordered by An and Enlil for the destruction of Sumer and Akkad. Other examples of compounded images can be found in CBS 15120 rev. 5′ [ ] nam-gu$_2$ ^{d}iškur a-ma-ru uru$_2$ ⸢ur$_3^?$⸣-ra '. . . the oppression (of) Iškur, the flood which sweeps away (like) floodwaters'; *LU* 98 u$_4$ uru$_2$-gin$_7$ gul-lu-ba ni$_2$-bi ha-ma-la$_2$-la$_2$ 'The terror of the storm, destructive as a flood, hangs (heavily) on me.'

The examples such as *LSU* 2, 107–8 and *LU* 98 also indicate that the flood image often not only occurs in juxtaposition, but also can be used interchangeably, with other meteorological images, especially the images of storm and wind/tempest, on the basis of their close meteorological and literary associations or for stylistic variation. Like a-ma-ru and mar-uru$_5$, other meteorological images can also use the verb zi 'to rise': im-ḫul 'evil wind' (*Inana and Ebih* 137); ab 'sea' (*Gudea Cylinder A* viii 23; B x 19); a 'water' (CBS 11553 obv. 15; *LW* 5.20; *UDAM KI AMUS* (*It Touches the Earth like a Storm*) 20; *AGALGAL BUR SUSU* (*Flood Which Drowns the Harvest*) 46, a+85; *ELA* 565); uru$_{18}$ 'flood' (*Šu-Suen Historical Inscription B* i 43–4); mir 'northwind; storm' (*Šu-ilīšu A* 15); u$_{18}$-lu 'southwind' (*Išme-Dagan S* 13).

Another particularity about the image clusters is that the flood and other meteorological images are often employed in close association with the images of ferocious animals (e.g. lions, wild bulls, snakes), birds of prey (e.g. eagles, falcons), or mythical creatures (e.g. the Anzud Bird). Such association may be based on the shared fearsomeness in the character, movement, or roaring of these creatures and the meteorological phenomena. As will be discussed in

[17] Line 88 follows MS P; compare MS Y$_1$ an-bar$_7$ bar-šeĝ$_3$ il$_2$-il$_2$-la-ba ⸢izi⸣ mu-un-bar$_7$-bar$_7$ 'at noon, when the haze rises, the fire blazes' (Samet 2009: 265–6) where no equative case ending -gin$_7$ is found.

Chapter 4, these associations can also be observed in the OB *Atra-hasīs* III iii 7–10 '[Anzu rent] the heavens with his talons. [He . . .] the land and shattered its noise [like a pot]'; 15–17 '[The Flood] bellowed like a bull, the winds [roar] ed like a screaming eagle.'

The image clusters occur in high density and frequency in divine and royal hymns and laments, which constitute the majority of textual sources gathered in Vol. 2 of Chen 2009. Most of the image clusters are depictions of the power of the divine, mythical, and royal figures involved and of the effects of destruction brought about by their power. In general, while the hymns tend to focus on the depiction of this power, the laments emphasize more the effect of destruction. However, this distinction may not be strictly observed, as seen in *Angim* and *Lugale*.

Mythical

Related to Mythical Figures

As noted earlier, the flood or tempest is often used to signify the invincible power and wrath of deities, other mythical beings, and human rulers in figures of speech. But it can also refer to the actual meteorological catastrophe controlled, unleashed, or invoked by divine beings and human rulers through mythical forces.

Early Dynastic III Period: *Stele of the Vultures* obv. x 4

Sargonic Period: *Inana and Ebih* 4, 136

Old Babylonian Period: *LSU* 107; *Inana B* 78; *Inana C* 19; *Inana F* 9; *Death of Bilgames* N_1 iv 10; STVC 87 B 6″; the Mê-Turan version 72, 152, 162; *Inana and Šu-kale-tuda* 188; *Angim* 141; *Lugale* 82–3, 114, 229; OB *Atra-hasīs* II vii 44, 46; III i 37, iii 11, 15, 20, 23, 53, iv 25, v 42, vi 21, viii 9; the *Sumerian Flood Story* 137, 156, 202, 203

In this sense, the flood or tempest has become a mythical weapon or a destructive agent waging war at the behest of the divine and human protagonists on their opponents. In a few instances, the flood is portrayed as a mythical creature/monster or a personified being: *LW* 3.3; *Lugale* 82–3; OB *Atra-hasīs* II vii 44–6; *Inana and the Numun-Grass* 9, 19. All these sources are from the Old Babylonian period.

Related to Mythical Occasions

The flood/Flood is used in several instances to refer to ominous and trying occasions, in which the divine election of the protagonists or their superhuman strength and resilience are highlighted.

Ur III Period: *Ur-Namma C* 57–9 (the election of Ur-Namma by Enlil); *Šulgi A* 60–70 (the superhuman strength of Šulgi); *Year Name 22 of Ibbi-Suen* (the superhuman strength and resilience of Ibbi-Suen)

Old Babylonian Period: *Išme-Dagan A* 120 (the election of Išme-Dagan); the *Instructions of Ur-Ninurta* 1–18 (the installation of Ur-Ninurta as king by Ninurta); *Death of Bilgames* STVC 87 B 1″–6″; the Mê-Turan version 69–75 (the survival of Ziusudra); *ELA* 571–6 (the survival of the people of Aratta); OB *Atra-hasīs* III viii 10, 18 (the survival of the human race); the *Sumerian Flood Story* 203 (the survival of Ziusudra, the antediluvian king); *Rulers of Lagaš* 1–7 (the survival of the human race)

However, both the W-B 444 version of *SKL* 39–40 and the *Rulers of Lagaš* 1–10 refer to the Flood as an occasion that terminated the institution of kingship in the antediluvian era. So the institution had to be reinstated after the Flood. *Inana and the numun-grass* 1–34 allude to the Flood as the time of origin of the *numun*-grass. As will be discussed further in Chapter 2, the Flood used in this mythical sense tends to carry various aetiological functions, and is often characterized by a chronographical (representing the watershed between the antediluvian and post-diluvian eras) or quasi-chronographical (representing the primeval era) sense.

Different Types of Flood/Tempest

Just as there are different types of flood or tempest in the figurative usage, different types of flood may be discerned in the mythical usage of flood/tempest terminology.

Localized and regular flood/tempest

Most of the examples listed in the mythical usage above seem to be based on this type of flood, though the scale or effect of it may have been exaggerated or dramatized: *Stele of the Vultures* obv. x 4; *Inana and Ebih* 4, 136; *LW* 3.3; *LSU* 107; *Inana B* 78; *Inana C* 19; *Inana F* 9; *Inana and Šu-kale-tuda* 188; *Angim* 141; *Lugale* 82–3, 114, 229.

Cosmic and primeval flood/tempest

The tempest (mar-uru$_5$) in *Šulgi A* 62–8 and the flood (a-ma-ru) in *Year Name 22 of Ibbi-Suen* 3–4 seem to allude to the cosmic and primeval storm that symbolizes the marriage between Earth and Heaven at the beginning of the cosmos as portrayed in the prologues of literary sources such as the *Barton Cylinder* i 1–14 (van Dijk 1964).

The primeval flood catastrophe

The primeval flood catastrophe described or alluded to in the *Death of Bilgames*, the *Atra-hasīs Epic*, the *SKL* (W-B 444 and W-B 62), and the *Rulers of Lagaš* falls in this category. What distinguishes the primeval flood catastrophe from the cosmic and primeval tempest/storm is that, on the mythical time line, the latter took place before the time of creation and, in fact, represents an event of cosmogony and theogony. The former, however, marks the end of the primeval era. In the prologue of *Inana and the Numun-Grass* 2–13, the two mythical events seem to be conflated as one.

Literal

Two obvious examples for this usage, both from the Old Babylonian period, are: CBS 7849 iii 16′ a-ma-ru [. . .] 'the flood . . .'; *Proverb* 13.34 [. . .] ⸢bu⸣-ra-gin$_7$ a uru$_2$ (URU×UD)-ke$_4$ gu$_3$ al-de$_2$-de$_2$-[e] '. . . like a torn out . . . the flood$^{?}$ waters were gushing'. The flood in both of these sources refers to localized meteorological phenomena.

Complex Usage

As already pointed out by Westenholz (1992: 381–7; 1996: 189–94) and Black (1998: 12–13), one needs to attend to different levels of meaning in order to fully appreciate the Mesopotamian poetic language. In many cases, the distinction drawn between the figurative, mythical, and literary usages above to facilitate scholarly analysis cannot be carried too far. In the mental process of the ancient scribes, singers, and audience, the vivid memory of regular floods or related weather phenomena in real-life experience in Mesopotamia, the mythical forces perceived as being responsible for the meteorological phenomena, and the symbolic representations of the power and wrath of deities and human rulers by these fearsome natural phenomena may all be at work simultaneously.

For example, it would be in vain to try to determine when or where the literary, mythical, or figurative meaning stops or begins in passages such as *Inana B* 78 kur a-ma-ru ĝiri$_3$-ni-še$_3$ i$_3$-nu$_2$ 'the (foreign) lands (and) the flood lie at her (Inana's) feet'; *Inana F* 9 mar-uru$_5$ ma-an-ze$_2$-⸢eĝ$_3$⸣ ⸢dal$^{?}$⸣-ḫa-mun ma-<an-ze$_2$-eĝ$_3$> 'He (Enlil) gave me (Inana) the tempest/flood and he gave me the dust cloud'; *Inana and Šu-kale-tuda* 188 ⸢^{im}⸣[u$_{18}$]-⸢lu⸣ mar-uru$_5$ ḫuš igi-še$_3$ mu-un-[še-ĝen]$^{?}$ 'The southwind and a fearsome tempest/flood went before her (Inana).'

In *Asarluhi A* 21–2 ^{d}asar-lu$_2$-ḫi uru$_5$ maḫ nam gal tar-re | šu bar a-ra$_2$ niĝ$_2$-nam nu-zu-zu 'Asarluhi, the mighty flood that determines great fates, when unleashed, about whose course no one knows anything', the expression uru$_5$ maḫ 'the mighty flood' not only functions metaphorically as it serves as an epithet of the deity. The expression also functions mythically and literally as

Asarluhi is identified with the River of Ordeal whose actual submerging of the accused would mythically determine their fates. The curse formula of *CH* 27b 78–80 *li-is-si-ma* | *ma-su*$_2$ *a-na til*$_2$(DU$_6$) | *a-bu-bi-im li-te-er* 'may he (Adad) thunder and turn his land into ruins of (as left by) a flood' (rendering after Driver and Miles 1955: 105) would be deprived of the efficacy of its intended threat if only interpreted figuratively or idiomatically.[18] In cases such as *Year Name 22 of Ibbi-Suen, Išme Dagan A* 118–23, and the *Instructions of Ur-Ninurta* 1–4, it is difficult to determine whether the flood was only used in a figurative and mythical sense for the catastrophic demise of the Ur III dynasty and its turbulent aftermath, or may refer to an actual meteorological catastrophe that exacerbated the already vulnerable socio-political conditions of the time.

Negative and Positive Aspects

Most of the references to the flood focus on its destructive aspect. The flood is also often associated with battle and weaponry, especially in compositions that deal with warrior deities such as Inana and Ninurta. But when it comes to the storm god Iškur, both the negative and positive aspects of the flood or tempest are presented in an intertwining fashion, as seen in *Ur-Ninurta F* segm. A 1–B 10; *Eršemma 184* rev. ii 68–99. On the one hand, Iškur is the provider of storm rain necessary for irrigation and the growth of agriculture. So his beneficent presence may ensure abundance and harvest. On the other hand, he was also worshipped as a warrior god using violent storms for the devastation of rebellious cities and lands. No doubt the dual character of Iškur portrayed in these sources reflects the delicate condition of precipitation in lower Mesopotamia which may lead to either drought or overflooding. The literary depiction also betrays the attempts of the Mesopotamian to manipulate such a hydrological condition through Iškur's cult in the political and economic life of the time, so that Iškur may bring a sufficient amount of rainfall to ensure agricultural production in Sumer, on the one hand, and dispatch destructive floods to devastate enemy lands, on the other. The dual character of Iškur/Adad can also be observed in the Old Babylonian version of the *Atra-hasīs Epic*, in which the withdrawal of rain by Adad led to drought and famine during the second cycle of destruction (II ii 11–35), and then the excessive rain caused by Adad presumably led to the Flood (III ii 48–53).

[18] See Foster (2005: 134) 'ruins, as if left by the deluge'; or CAD A I 78 'like hills of ruins'.

Diachronic Observations

The above analyses show the persistence and preponderance of the figurative and mythical usage of flood terminology among the textual sources from the Early Dynastic III period to the Old Babylonian period. This usage flourished especially during the Ur III and Old Babylonian periods, which can be observed in the development of the form of the flood or tempest image, the diverse subject-matters the image signifies or illustrates, and the association or clustering of the image with a variety of meteorological and other images. The flourishing of the figurative and mythical usage of flood terminology during the Ur III and Old Babylonian periods seems to have to do with the developments of the divine and royal hymns and the compositions dealing with catastrophe (e.g. the city laments) during these periods. As mentioned earlier, it is in these compositions that the flood and other meteorological images are used most frequently and in high density, to illustrate the power and wrath of divine and royal protagonists, or the catastrophic effects of their power and wrath. These literary developments, as will be discussed in Chapter 4, reflect the political and religious climate of the times, during which the royal courts such as those of the Ur III and Isin-Larsa dynasties were patrons of literary and religious flourishing, which often in turn served the legitimation of the political regimes.

Judging from the typology of floods referred to in the textual sources, it seems clear that most of the references are based on normal and regular flooding whose effect is often dramatized and extended. There are literary sources (e.g. the *Barton Cylinder* i 1–14) already from the Early Dynastic III period that use the cosmic and primeval storm (u_4) and lightning (nim) to symbolize the cosmic marriage between Heaven and Earth which led to theogony and cosmogony. But as far as the available extant evidence is concerned, the depiction of, or the allusion to, the cosmic and primeval flood/tempest (a-ma-ru/mar-uru_5) only emerged starting from the Ur III period, as seen in *Šulgi A* 60–70 and *Year Name 22 of Ibbi-Suen*. It is likely that the cosmic turbulent weather in the two texts may allude to the violent but formative time as depicted in the mythological texts or prologues such as the *Barton Cylinder* (see further discussion in Chapter 2).

The primeval flood catastrophe, or the Flood, is attested even later, with the *Instructions of Ur-Ninurta* being the first textual witness. Both the usage of the term *abūbu* for 'the Flood' and its literary context, especially in terms of its association with various images, in the Old Babylonian version of the *Atrahasīs Epic* suggest that the epic in many ways follows the figurative and mythical usage of flood/tempest terminology in earlier literary traditions (primarily Sumerian).

However, there are two major differences between the Babylonian epic and the Sumerian traditions in terms of the usage of flood terminology: (1) While in the Sumerian traditions the flood most often serves as the signifier and occasionally as the signified in similes or metaphors, the Flood in the epic only serves as the signified in the figurative process, except probably for OB *Atra-hasīs* II vii 44–6 where the flood term may signify the mythical monster. This avoidance of using flood terminology as the signifier indicates that the author of the epic made a conscious attempt to part with the prevalent practice in the literary conventions of the time, so as not to present the flood as a simile or metaphor, but as an actual, albeit still mythologized, meteorological catastrophe. By comparison, the persistent influence of the figurative usage of flood terminology can be observed in the Old Babylonian version of the *Cuthean Legend of Naram-Suen* (iv 8′–9′ *kīma abūbu mê ša ibbašû | ina nišī* [(x)] *maḫriāti* 'Like the Flood of water that arose among the first peoples') where the author still used the flood term as the signifier in the simile even when the term had gained the specialized meaning 'the primeval flood catastrophe'. (2) Whereas most of the usages of flood terminology in earlier traditions refer to flooding that either took place in history or in a mythical realm, the term *abūbu* in the Flood epic deals with the primeval flood catastrophe which by its cosmic scale wiped out the entire antediluvian world. So the Flood in the epic distinguishes itself not only by its unparalleled scale, but also by its temporal or chronographical uniqueness. This historiographical uniqueness of the Flood may also be seen in the temporal clause eĝir a-ma-ru ba-ur$_3$-ra-ta 'After the Flood had swept over' (line 40 of the W-B 444 version of *SKL*) where the Flood is alluded to. As will be discussed in Chapter 2, the author of the epic did not invent the concept of the Flood or this usage of flood terminology. Instead, he followed previous Sumerian traditions about the Flood or the antediluvian era which had emerged in the earlier phase of the Old Babylonian period.

SUMMARY

By examining the orthography of flood terminology in Sumerian and Akkadian, it is shown that the use of a-ma-ru and *abūbu* to convey the specialized meaning 'the primeval flood catastrophe' only started in the Old Babylonian period. And the analysis of figurative, mythical, and literal usages of flood terminology further confirms that the usage of *abūbu* and the literary depictions of the primeval flood catastrophe in the Old Babylonian version of the *Atra-hasīs Epic* still retain many features of the usage of flood terminology in earlier Sumerian literary traditions. In Chapter 4, it will be demonstrated how the Flood epic as a whole, not just the final Flood episode, in its depictions of destruction (and restoration) relies considerably on Sumerian literary traditions in terms of literary topoi and motifs, broader structural or conceptual frameworks, and the characterization of the protagonists.

2

The Primeval Flood Catastrophe Motif

Judging on orthographic and semantic grounds, it was discovered in the previous chapter that the Sumerian term a-ma-ru and the Akkadian term *abūbu* did not gain their specialized meaning 'the primeval flood catastrophe' until the Old Babylonian period. The present chapter seeks to demonstrate that as a historiographical concept and a literary motif, the primeval flood catastrophe also only became part of the literary traditions related to the primeval time of origins from the Old Babylonian period onwards, as far as the extant textual evidence is concerned. To trace the emergence of the concept and the motif, one needs to examine the development of the representations of the primeval time as a whole in a variety of Mesopotamian literary traditions.

In the light of previous research on the representations of the primeval time of origins in Mesopotamian literary traditions,[1] the following study is intended to first focus on the development of the understanding of the primeval time in relation to other conceptual or temporal frameworks (cosmological, mythological, legendary, cultic, historical, and chronographical) in early Mesopotamian traditions from the Early Dynastic III period to the Old Babylonian period. Such a conceptual development is intricately tied in with the literary development of how the motifs dealing with the primeval time were represented and arranged in Mesopotamian literary compositions (Streck 2002; Ferrara 2006). Thus attention will be paid to how, from a narratological standpoint, the sequencing of primeval events may be affected by various considerations in Mesopotamian literary traditions. The current study will also look into various social functions of the literary compositions involved that may have affected the conceptualizations and literary representations of time. Against the background of the development of the temporal or conceptual

[1] See Chen (2009: 121–53) for a review of previous scholarship. For recent studies of the primeval time of origins as represented in ancient Near Eastern and other cultural traditions, see Faraone and Lincoln (2012: 3–13) and the related articles they edited in *ARG* 1 (2012): 1–156 and *JANER* 12 (2012): 1–141.

frameworks in early Mesopotamian literary traditions, the second half of the study will investigate the development of the concept and motif of the primeval flood catastrophe during the Old Babylonian period.

Previous research has already shown that many Mesopotamian literary compositions begin their narration by referring to the distant past as a preamble to the stories to be narrated. Often the temporal settings of the distant past involve the primeval time (*Urzeit*), during which the origins of the cosmos, divine and human lives, social and cultural institutions, and natural phenomena were believed to have been established. Though many literary traditions refer all the way back to the cosmological origins (e.g. the union or separation of heaven and earth), others only go back to the time of the creation of humankind or the organization of the world as the first event. Still other traditions return to the legendary times such as those of Etana, Enmerkar, Lugalbanda, and Gilgameš. Still others start with the even less remote past, e.g. from the time of Naram-Suen as seen in *Curse Agade*.

The temporal frameworks of many Mesopotamian literary traditions can be recognized as mythical because of the involvement of mythical beings such as gods, monsters, and divine-like human rulers. The mythical time, with its fluidity and evasiveness, often lacks specific location on a chronological scale. Yet, such a temporal framework is frequently found interacting and coterminous with the cosmological, legendary, and historical time frames. Closely associated with the mythical time is the cultic or ritual time, in which certain temporal patterns or qualities of time may be (re-)enacted through ritual or cultic practices. Finally, one finds the chronographical time frame as represented by the *SKL* probably as early as the Sargonic period, which first simply connected, and ordered the sequence of, various known legendary and historical rulers. But gradually, beginning in the early Old Babylonian period, this chronographical tradition inserted the Flood as the watershed of history and added the antediluvian section. The chronographical perspective of *SKL* has influenced the temporal frameworks of a number of Sumerian and Akkadian literary compositions. But, as will be demonstrated later in this book, the influence does not go in one direction, because the *SKL* seems to have relied on Sumerian literary traditions for its brief allusions to the primeval time, especially with regard to the origin of kingship and the Flood.

The primeval time often only serves as the background (*Hintergrund*) of the narrated story or history. Contrary to earlier research that did not see much connection between references to the primeval time and the rest of the compositions to which they belong, recent research (e.g. Streck 2002; Ferrara 2006) shows that in content, structure, form, and phraseology the mythological prologue and the main section of a composition are often integrally related. One of the chief concerns of the current study is how and what kind of temporal frameworks and relationships (continuum, punctuation, sequence, and progression) were established as the Mesopotamian narrator or poet moved his narration back and forth through various past and contemporary events or settings. Important research questions include: how is the primeval time with its constituent events temporally connected with the narrated story or history for which the primeval time serves as a background? What roles do the constituent events in the primeval time play in establishing this connection? To what extent are the choice of temporal frameworks and the selection of constituent events in the primeval time influenced by the foreground (*Vordergrund*) of narration? How do Mesopotamian literary traditions make the transition among different temporal frameworks, for example, between the primeval time, and the legendary and historical times?

To study temporal representations in Mesopotamian literary traditions one must also take into account literary and sociological factors that may have had significant bearing on the representations. As already observed in previous scholarship,[2] temporal representations in Mesopotamian literary traditions utilize certain formal and literary devices to indicate temporal settings and to structure the progression of time. During the course of the development of these devices, both continuities and changes can be seen. These literary devices or strategies may in some instances 'disrupt' the 'normal' representation of time out of various narratological and ideological considerations. Sometimes an event or subject may be given priority in narrative sequence, thus causing 'anachronia' in the temporal sequence of a story or history (Ferrara 2006: 54), in order to announce the chief concern and purpose of the composition, or to introduce the protagonist (Wilcke 1977).

Oftentimes temporal representations are dictated by the social functions of compositions. As will be demonstrated below, religious and political ideologies frequently manipulated and reconfigured different temporal frameworks and dimensions of reality in attempts to establish legitimacy, authority, precedence, and superiority for cults, cities, and rulers in question through Mesopotamian literary traditions such as royal hymns, city laments, myths, and epics. Socio-economic factors too played an appreciable role in the ordering of the primeval events in Mesopotamian literary traditions. The so-called contest or disputation literature often betrays competition for supremacy by various economic models, e.g. the agricultural and the pastoral (*Grain and Sheep*). Still, there is an aspect of serious reflection in literary sources that sought to confront certain critical intellectual, theological, and social issues at hand through reckoning with the origins of things (e.g. the *Atra-hasīs Epic*). However, not all the motives behind the literary representations involved aim at achieving serious goals or are based on serious reflections. Clearly some of the temporal frameworks constructed were the result of playful speculations

[2] See Castellino 1957; van Dijk 1964; Wilcke 1975, 1977; Alster 1976*a*, 1976*b*; Black 1992; Dietrich 1995; Streck 2002; Ferrara 2006.

and dramatizations for providing entertainment in royal courts or public squares.

EXAMINATION OF SELECTED TEXTUAL SOURCES

Though extensive research on the textual sources related to the primeval time of origins has been carried out, only thirty-one sources from the Early Dynastic III period to the Old Babylonian period are presented below for analysis due to limited space.

Sources without the Primeval Flood Catastrophe Motif

The Barton Cylinder *(CBS 8383 = Barton MBI No. 1) (Alster and Westenholz 1994: 15–46)*

This twenty-column cylinder coming from 'a date toward the end of the Early Dynastic period, or perhaps Early Sargonic times' only has three-quarters of its original text preserved, with many aspects of the preserved section that are difficult to understand (Alster and Westenholz 1994: 15–17). Due to the broken context, the detailed plot of this text remains largely unclear. One can only derive from the preserved sections a sketch of what this mythological composition is about.

The prologue begins with the cosmic time of origins, first by referring back to the sexual union between Heaven (an) and Earth (ki), which is represented by roaring storm and flashing lightning (i 7–14). After a lacuna, the prologue is found moving on to the sexual union between probably Enlil and Ninhursaĝa which resulted in the latter giving birth to seven twins (ii 1–9) and probably the small watercourses mentioned in ii 14–15. Though Enlil is not referred to in the preserved section as the spouse of Ninhursaĝa, such marital relation may be restored on the basis of the Old Babylonian god list SLT 122–4 (van Dijk 1964: 7–8) and *Lugale*, in which the mother goddess Ninmah/Ninhursaĝa is equated with Enlil's wife Ninlil. As in SLT 122–4, the prologue of the *Barton Cylinder* seems to present Enlil and Ninhursaĝa/Ninlil as the second pair after Heaven and Earth. Thus the cosmic time of origins is primarily expressed in terms of sexual unions (between Heaven and Earth, Enlil and Ninhursaĝa/Ninlil) and sexual reproductions (the birth of the seven twins by Ninhursaĝa and the birth of the small watercourses by the Supreme Divine River). The protagonists involved are deified and personified parts of the cosmos or nature: heaven (an), earth (ki), wind (^{d}en-lil$_2$), mountain (^{d}nin-ḫur-saĝ), river (^{d}id$_2$-maḫ). The ensuing events deal probably with the establishment of abundance (iii 2–6). The main body of the composition concerns the crisis of food supply being interrupted for the cult in Nippur (iii 8–vi 4) and the resolution of the crisis. According to Alster and Westenholz (1994: 38–9), Ninurta, who is presumably the son of Enlil and Ninhursaĝa/Ninlil, seems to play a crucial role in bringing about the resolution. Thus 'the composition is an early example of a myth extolling Ninurta's deeds, like Lugale' (Alster and Westenholz 1994: 39).

Temporal settings of the entire text seem to be primeval. The initial stage of the primeval time involves cosmogony and theogony through a series of sexual unions among the primordial gods and goddesses which led to the birth of rivers. As Castellino (1957: 130–1) has observed, cosmogonic depictions in Mesopotamian literary compositions tend to focus almost exclusively on the organization of the earth. The next stage of the primeval time moves on to describe the establishment of abundance presumably as a result of the creation of rivers (ii 2–6). Then the flow of creation was halted due to the interrupted cultic supply in Nippur. This interruption may have caused the birth goddess Ninhursaĝa to depart from her cultic centre Keš (xii 4). Once the crisis was resolved, abundance of animals occurred in mountains (xiv 3–15), and Ninhursaĝa returned to Keš. The sequence of the events narrated highlights the importance of maintaining the cult in Nippur for the fertility of the earth, a role which was carried out by Ninhursaĝa. The pivotal role of the cult in Nippur has already been announced in the opening lines of the prologue where the union of Heaven and Earth is said to have taken place 'on the sacred area of Nippur' (i 9). The union between Enlil, whose main temple was in Nippur, and Ninhursaĝa as the second primordial couple who engendered the rivers, also stresses the indispensable role of the cult of Nippur for the creation.

The literary or formal device used in the prologue to mark the cosmic beginning is the three-tier adverbial expression u_4-re_2-a u_4-re_2-$še_3$ | na-nam | $ĝi_6$-re_2-a $ĝi_6$-re_2-$še_3$ | na-nam | mu-re_2-a mu-re_2-$še_3$ | na-nam 'In those days, it was to those days; in those nights, it was to those nights; in those years, it was to those years' (i 1–6). This adverbial expression and its variants, according to Black (1992: 73–4, 92–5; see also Streck 2002: 231), were the conventional devices used to mark 'the formalised opening' of many Sumerian mythological compositions from the Early Dynastic III period to the Old Babylonian period.[3]

The literary device to mark the transition from the prologue to the main body of the composition, usually u_4-ba 'in those days, at that time', may have

[3] But as also pointed out by Black (1992: 73–4), these adverbial expressions are not always placed before the motifs pertaining to the cosmic origin. Thus they do not always serve as temporal markers of the cosmic beginning as seen in the *Barton Cylinder*.

been lost in the lacuna at the end of column ii. In vi 5–11 temporal devices are used to introduce Ninurta: nam-⸢ta⸣-⸢e$_3$⸣ | nam-t[a]-⸢e$_3$⸣ | u$_4$ ĝi$_6$-⸢ta⸣ ⸢e$_3$⸣-a | ^{d}nin-urta | nam-ta-e$_3$ | u$_4$ ĝi$_6$-ta e$_3$-a | kuš-⸢piriĝ⸣ bar nam-mi-mu$_4$ 'He came out! He came out! As the day rose from the night, Ninurta came out! As the day rose from the night, he clothed his back in a lion's skin.' The temporal clauses in xv 8–15 mušen a-ba-šub-be$_2$ . . . 'after the bird left it . . .' and the temporal markers in xviii 4–5 u$_4$-bi a-DU ZAL-la | [ĝ]i$_6$-bi [a]-DU šu$_2$-am$_6$ 'That day, passing . . .; that night, darkening . . .' seem to be related to the (re-)establishment of cultic practices at Ninhursaĝa's temple in Keš.

The chief function or purpose of this mythological composition was to exalt the Nippurean cult for its precedence and importance. The pivotal role of the cult can be observed in the narrative sequence in which Nippur (i 9) is mentioned before the union of Heaven and Earth (i 12–14), and the flow of creation was put on hold due to lack of provisions for the cult in Nippur (iv 3–vi 6). From this composition one can see that the sequence of events in the primeval time can be interrupted or reconfigured in narration out of consideration for religious ideology. The Nippurean priest(s), who were presumably responsible for composing this myth, had manipulated the motifs of the primeval time in order to highlight the pivotal role of the Nippurean cult not only for the origin of the world but also for the fertility and abundance of nature.

AO 4153 (= NFT 180 = Sollberger Corpus Ukg. 15) (Sjöberg 2002: 229–39)

This three-column Early Dynastic III mythological text deals with the cosmic beginning. Its temporal setting focuses on the first cosmic couple Heaven (an) and Earth (ki), before the emergence of Enki and Nunki (ii 3), Enlil and Ninlil (ii 4–5), and the sun and moon (iii 3–4). The text seems to be based on the genealogical relations among the primordial gods from a particular tradition of the god list; see the Early Dynastic III god list VA 12573 + 12763 from Fara in which Enki and Ninki/Nunki are the first cosmic couple (van Dijk 1964: 7). Similar to the *Barton Cylinder*, AO 4153 depicts the cosmic beginning in terms of sexual union, but with more suggestive poetic imagery (i 2–ii 2).

Due to the lacuna at the beginning of column i, it is impossible to judge whether this text contains a formalized device to mark the cosmic beginning. But according to Sjöberg's reconstruction of i 1–2 [an-e] | [x] muš ⸢ḫa⸣-mu-ni-sig-sig 'Let An-Heaven [. . .] . . .', there is no such device used. The adverbial expression u$_4$-ba 'on that day; at that time' is used in ii 3 to indicate the absence of Enki and Nunki, Enlil and Ninlil at that point in time when Heaven and Earth were joined. Then the text uses the expressions u$_4$-⸢da⸣ im-ma | ul-[la] im-m[a] (iii 1–2) in front of the reference to the non-existence of the sun and moon (iii 3–4). The expressions in iii 1–2 are translated by Sjöberg 2002: 231 as

'"Today" (:) "last (year)," "the remote (time)" (:) "last (year)."'[4] He thinks that 'these lines conceptualize time before creation as standing still' (2002: 238), which may indeed be the case as there was no counting of time without the sun and moon. Another literary device to mark the temporal setting is the use of negation in ii 3–6 and iii 3–4, a technique which is frequently seen in the portrayals of the primeval time 'als Zeit der Unfertigkeit' (Streck 2002: 240–51).

The function of this mythological composition is uncertain. It may serve as prologue to a larger text (Sjöberg 2002: 229; see also van Dijk 1964: 39).

NBC 11108 (Horowitz 1998: 138–9; Sjöberg 2002: 239–44)

This Ur III Sumerian literary fragment from Nippur only preserves part of the prologue to a larger text. The extant section of the prologue containing thirteen lines traces the beginning of the world to a time even prior to the union of Heaven and Earth. The initial cosmic event that defines the temporal setting is the illumination of the heaven or sky by An (line 1a). But the earth was still left in darkness (line 1b). Lines 2–13 all seem to use negative statements to further define the temporal setting: no irrigation, thus no produce (line 2); no Nippurean cult (line 3); no marriage between Heaven (an) and Earth (ki) (lines 4–6); no light (on earth) (lines 7–8); no vegetation on earth (line 9); the divine power of Enlil not perfected (line 10); the gods of heaven and earth not present (line 13). The sequence of these events in negation as listed here is not logically laid out. There is no obviously discernible principle behind the ordering of the events. And the style of narration is repetitive, as seen in the occurrence of the motif of darkness on earth in both lines 1 and 7–8. The references to the Nippurean cult and Enlil's divine power on this list are not surprising, given that the provenance of this mythological fragment is Nippur. Here, as in the prologue of the *Barton Cylinder*, the Nippurean cult is mentioned prior or adjacent to the motif of the union of Heaven and Earth. No adverbial expression of time is employed in this part of the prologue, presumably because there was no light to regulate time, or no alternation of light and darkness to mark day and night.

Ur-Namma royal hymns

Ur-Namma hymns often depict the ruler as being conceived, given birth to, brought up, elected for kingship, and assisted by the deities (e.g. *Ur Namma C* 17–30, 43–9, 57–9, 70; *Ur-Namma F* 48–9; *Ur-Namma I* segm. B 7–12). In *Ur-Namma C* 111–14, Ur-Namma's birth and kingship are both said to have

[4] However, as pointed out by Sjöberg (2002: 238), it is also possible that these expressions may refer to meteorological phenomena or seasons.

emerged from the primeval time: šu du$_{11}$-ga-e ^{d}nanna-a-me-en | šeš ^{d}bil$_{3}$-ga-mes gu-la-me-en | [dumu] ⸢tu⸣-da ^{d}nin-sun$_{2}$-ka-me-en numun nam-en-na-me-en | [an]-ta nam-lugal ma-ra-e$_{11}$ 'I am the creature of Nanna! I am the brother of Bilgames the Great! I am the son given birth to by Ninsumun. I am the seed of lordship. For me, kingship descended from heaven!' The bold claims made in this passage of self-praise by Ur-Namma freely manipulate the temporal sequence in order to present him as the brother of Gilgameš, a legendary ruler from the remote past. Most astonishingly, by alluding to the opening line of *SKL*, this passage seems to present Ur-Namma as the first king in history: Line 114 [an]-ta nam-lugal ma-ra-e$_{11}$ obviously echoes the opening lines of *SKL*; compare *USKL* obv. i 1–2 ⸢nam⸣-lugal ⸢an-ta⸣ e$_{11}$-da-ba | kiš^{ki} lugal-am 'When kingship had come down from heaven, Kiš was king'. In addition, Ur-Namma is often depicted as being responsible for the establishment of civilization or the organization of the world (see especially *Ur-Namma C*), events which according to Sumerian mythological compositions took place during the primeval time. It is no wonder that at his death (*Ur-Namma A*) the whole society is depicted as collapsing.

Šulgi royal hymns

A number of Šulgi hymns manipulate the motifs of the primeval time in order to depict Šulgi as being conceived, given birth to, nurtured, and chosen or destined for kingship in the primeval time by the primordial or chief deities: *Šulgi A* 7–15; *Šulgi C* segm. A. 21–33; *Šulgi D* 40–60; *Šulgi G* 1–62; *Šulgi P* segm. A 11–14; segm. C 1–66. The following analyses are intended to demonstrate how temporal settings are manipulated in *Šulgi A, Šulgi E*, and *Šulgi O*.

Šulgi A 60–87 depicts how Šulgi, like a falcon, ran at a superhuman speed from Ur to Nippur and back to Ur so as to celebrate a cultic festival at two cities in a single day. The journey was made difficult due to the stormy weather. The section most relevant to our current discussion is lines 62–9:

> On that day (u$_{4}$-bi-a), a storm shrieked, and the west wind whirled around. The northwind and the southwind howled at each other. Lightning together with the seven winds vied with each other in the heavens. Thundering storms made the earth quake, and Iškur roared in the broad heavens. The rains of heaven mingled with the waters of the earth (variant: The rains of heaven vied with the waters of the earth). Small and large hailstones drummed on my back.

This passage most likely alludes to the cosmic beginning when the first primordial couple Heaven and Earth had their sexual union which led to cosmogony and theogony, as depicted in many mythological compositions and prologues.[5]

[5] The motif was adapted in *Enūma eliš* I 5 where Apsu and Tiamat mingled their waters together.

That union was often manifested in turbulent storm, lightning, and rain.[6] For this reason, van Dijk (1964: 31) called the day of cosmic marriage 'le jour de violence par excellence', which 'est devenu aussi le prototype des catastrophes qui dans le cours de l'histoire se sont abattues sur le pays de Sumer'.[7]

The Šulgi hymn thus alludes to this turbulent cosmic event as the temporal setting in which Šulgi made his journey between Ur and Nippur. The purpose of choosing this temporal setting was obviously to highlight the courage and tenacity of Šulgi: 'I, the king, however, did not fear, nor was terrified. I rushed forth like a fierce lion. . . . I celebrated the *ešeš* festival in both Nippur and Ur on the same day' (lines 70–1). The manipulation of temporal concepts can thus be observed both in depicting Šulgi as overcoming the violent weather from the cosmic beginning and in his superhuman speed. Line 86 represents one further example of using the temporal concept of the distant past to underscore Šulgi's incomparable kingship: '. . . since the days of yore (⸢u$_4$⸣ ul-le-a-še$_3$) . . . , no king of Sumer like me has existed for the people' (MSS HJ).

Šulgi E 174–99 represents Šulgi as one who carried out the royal duties to the gods which an unidentified king from the primeval time had failed to do:

> On the day (u$_4$) when the destiny of the lands was determined, the king who in his arrogance . . . , in luxuriance Enlil and Ninlil . . . , . . . for the life of Sumer and Akkad, . . . justice for the Land, canals which he did not maintain . . . , a city which he did not enlarge. . . . The Great Mountain . . . at their side . . . great places. He did not . . . the god of the palace. He . . . to Enlil, and did not offer great gifts in the E-kur, and did not . . . the door-sockets of the gods. . . . songs. What he achieved with his praises, what he creatively decorated with his words, the singer . . . in his songs. I, Šulgi, the king . . . , who cares for holy An, . . . food offerings, who constantly attends upon Enlil . . . , Nanna, . . . the office of *en*; Ninurta, the *ensi* appointed by Enlil, has given me a club and a battle-mace from the E-šu-me-ša. Not since the seed of humankind was germinated, has Enlil ever before been able to give the sceptre of kingship to a king who could control the troops single-handedly.

Note that the reign of the unidentified king from the primeval time is characterized by a series of negative statements. By reversing the negative conditions (Michalowski 1991), the achievements of Šulgi are highlighted. He is presented as the ideal king as defined by the functions of kingship from the primeval time of origins.

Šulgi O contains sections that portray how Šulgi, son of the goddess Ninsun, was conversing with his brother and friend Gilgameš (lines 25–141). Šulgi and

[6] See the *Barton Cylinder* i 7–8, 10–11; AO 4153 ii 2; and *Inana and the Numun-Grass* 2–8.

[7] In this sense, the motif of the cosmic marriage between Heaven and Earth may fit into the category 'Urzeit als Zeit des Weltuntergangs' in the study of Streck (2002: 232, 251), who, however, only lists the motif of the primeval flood catastrophe as an example. The intriguing question is whether the motif of the primeval flood catastrophe was based on the violent stormy weather used to depict the cosmic marriage of Heaven and Earth.

Gilgameš are depicted as praising each other's heroic deeds and accomplishments. Lines 38–48 cast the meeting of the two brothers in the primeval time:

> On the day ($u_4^?$-bi$^?$) when the destiny of the Land was determined, when the seed of all living beings was originally brought forth, when the king appeared radiantly to his comrade—on that day (u_4-ba$^?$), Gilgameš, the lord of Kulaba, conversed with Šulgi, the good shepherd of Sumer, at his shining feet: so that their praise would be sung forever (u_4 ul-le_2-aš), so that it would be handed down for distant days (u_4 su_3-ra_2-aš), so that it should not be forgotten in remote years (mu su_3-ra_2-aš), they looked$^?$ at each other favourably in their mighty heroism.

From the lines quoted above, one finds several temporal devices that are employed to signify different time settings: $u_4^?$-bi$^?$ (line 38) and u_4-ba$^?$ (line 41) mark the distant past, while u_4 ul-le_2-aš (line 44), u_4 su_3-ra_2-aš (line 45), and mu su_3-ra_2-aš (line 46) indicate the distant future. To establish the endurance of Šulgi's kingship, the hymn freely manipulated different temporal settings and used mythological style of perception and writing in order to transcend the boundaries of time. Šulgi was portrayed as existing already in the primeval time together with Gilgameš. Thus both Gilgameš from the legendary time and Šulgi from the historical time have been moved back to a time when destinies were fixed, humankind was created, and kingship was instituted.[8] If the meeting of Gilgameš and Šulgi was intended to match the latter with the former in legendary status with regard to heroism, the projection of the two brothers back to the primeval time was an attempt to gain a sense of precedence and permanence for their kingship.

USKL *(Steinkeller 2003: 267–92)*

This Ur III copy of *SKL* starts with a brief allusion to the primeval time during which kingship descending from heaven was first granted to the Kiš dynasty: ⸢nam⸣-lugal ⸢an-ta⸣ e_{11}-da-ba | Kiš^{ki} lugal-am_3 'When kingship descended from heaven, Kiš was king' (obv. i 1–2).[9] The second dynasty is presumably Uruk as reconstructed by Steinkeller 2003: 271 at the end of obv. iii.[10] This chronographical text lists the Ur III dynasty as the last dynasty, mentioning only the first two rulers from that dynasty: Ur-Namma and Šulgi (rev. vi 32–4). Note that unlike the W-B 444 version of *SKL* from the Old Babylonian period, there is no reference to either the Flood or the antediluvian period in the *USKL*.

[8] See also line 60 of the same hymn where Šulgi praised Gilgameš for bringing kingship from Kiš to Uruk. Both passages seem to be based on the same chronographical tradition as seen in the *SKL* that kingship, first granted to Kiš, was transferred to Uruk. Here, as in the *USKL* and BT 14 + P_3, there is no reference or allusion to either the antediluvian dynasties or the Flood.

[9] See also the Old Babylonian copy of *SKL* BT 14 + P_3 i 1–4 (Klein 2008: 80) and the *History of the Tummal* 1–6 for Kiš being the first dynasty.

[10] See also BT 14 + P_3 i 27 (Klein 2008: 81).

Temporal settings of the text change from the primeval to the legendary and the historical. The text traces Mesopotamian political history back to the primeval time when kingship first descended from heaven, i.e. was granted by the gods. This primeval event marks the starting point of the temporal sequence in the text. As a stylistic device signifying the primeval time, the opening line ⸢nam⸣-lugal ⸢an-ta⸣ e$_{11}$-da-ba 'When kingship descended from heaven' is equivalent to the three-tier adverbial expression u$_{4}$-re-a . . . ĝi$_{6}$-re-a . . . mu-re-a . . . 'In those days . . . , in those nights . . . , in those years . . .' in Sumerian mythological compositions.

For this ideological text, it is not just kingship itself that originated from the gods during the primeval time. More importantly, by prefacing the king list with the opening line, the author intended to stress that the pattern of kingship or hegemony in Mesopotamia, i.e. that it could only be exercised by one city at a given time and for a limited period, was already fixed when kingship was first instituted. This conception of kingship is echoed in *LSU* 367–8: 'From time immemorial, since the Land was founded, until the population multiplied, who has ever seen a reign of kingship that would take precedence (for ever)?'; 461–2 'My son, the city that was built for you in joy and prosperity, it was given to you as your reign, the destroyed city, the great wall, the walls with broken battlements: all this is part of the (appointed) reign.' The function of the opening line of *USKL*, therefore, is primarily to legitimize this particular type of political ideology or historiographical vision.

Lugale *(van Dijk 1983)*

This mythological composition, whose earliest textual attestations are from the Old Babylonian period, may have been composed during the Ur III period. The text contains several major events: the defeat of the monster Asag (lines 22–333), the building of the mountains for irrigation and agriculture (lines 334–67), the renaming of Ninhursaĝa (lines 368–410), the fixing of the destinies of the stone warriors (lines 411–647) (Black 1992: 77). Some of the events (e.g. Ninurta's combat with Asag) were drawn from different mythological traditions regarding Ninurta. But other events (e.g. the building of the mountains and invention of agriculture) may have been elaborated by the author on the basis of traditional motifs as seen in the *Barton Cylinder*. The author had arranged the events in such a way so as to make them follow one another in a more or less logical (associative) and temporal sequence.

After the defeat of Asag for his father Enlil, Ninurta renamed it as Stone and called its entrails the underworld (lines 327–9). Then Ninurta went on to organize other aspects of the world, namely, piling up the stones as mountains so as to channel the waters from melted snow downstream for the purpose of irrigation, a deed which brought praise to his father Enlil (lines 334–67). To please his mother Ninmah, Ninurta used the mountains he had piled up with stones to honour her, by calling her Ninhursaĝa (Lady Mountain) and by fixing the destiny of the mountains so that they might be at his mother's service (lines 390–410). Afterwards, to respond to the request of his aunt Aruru (Enlil's sister), Ninurta fixed the destinies of the stone warriors whom he had slain (lines 411–644). Overall, stones, mountains, and family relations or obligations play crucial roles in the plot to tie different events together.

The temporal setting of the composition is mythical and primeval. This can be seen in the combination of the story of Ninurta's combat against Asag in the mythical time and the origins of irrigation and agriculture in the primeval time. The portrayal of the primeval time in lines 334–67 is readily recognizable by style and content. This aetiological story about the origin of irrigation and agriculture through Ninurta's building of the mountains uses the negation-reversal technique to highlight Ninurta's achievement.

A number of adverbial expressions of time are used throughout the composition: u_4-bi-a 'at that time' (line 22) to introduce the conflict between Ninurta and Asag; u_4-ba 'on that day' (line 72) to indicate Ninurta getting ready to fight against Asag; i_3-ne-eš$_2$ u_4-da 'at that time; on that day' (line 180) to indicate the time of the fierce attack of Asag against Ninurta; kur-ra u_4-ta im-ma-ra-[zal] | ^{d}utu silim-ma mu-na-⸢an⸣-[du$_{11}$] 'In the mountain, the day came to an end. The sun bade it farewell' (lines 300–1) to mark the time of Ninurta's victory over Asag; [u_4]-da-ta 'from today on' (line 327) to indicate the time of renaming Asag; u_4-bi-a 'at that time' (line 334) to introduce the conditions of the world before Ninurta began to organize the stones; i_3-ne-eš$_2$ 'at that time' (line 355) to indicate the good results of Ninurta's efforts to organize the stones; i_3-ne-eš$_2$ u_4-da 'at that time, on that day' (line 360) to indicate how throughout the world, kings of the Land rejoiced for the abundance Ninurta brought through his work; u_4-bi-a 'at that time' (line 368) to introduce the episode of Ninurta's attempt to please his mother Ninmah; i_3-ne-eš$_2$ 'at that time' (line 433) to introduce the destiny of the U stone (emery); i_3-ne-eš$_2$ 'now' (line 461) to introduce the destiny of the Saĝkal stone; i_3-ne-eš$_2$ . . . u_4-da 'at that time . . . on that day' (lines 510–11) to introduce the destiny of the Kagina stone (haematite).

The purpose of this composition was obviously to exalt Ninurta, as indicated by the praises of him in the prologue and epilogue of the text. Lines 662–8 also suggest that the text might have had some functions in a ritual context. The author sought to use Ninurta's exploits to provide aetiological explanations for some natural phenomena, the names and destinies of the divine and mythical beings involved, the qualities of the stones, and the origins of irrigation and agriculture. In the meantime, the composition expresses certain geopolitical aspirations, especially through Ninurta's victory over the recalcitrant mountain regions, which are represented by Asag and his cohort, towards the north-east of Mesopotamia.

Enki and the World Order

This mythological composition celebrates Enki as the organizer of different aspects of the world, for the restoration of the Land (lines 451), which might have suffered from the lack of natural and cultural resources which Enki was to introduce. In terms of content, the temporal setting of this composition is supposedly primeval because it deals with the origins of natural and cultural phenomena, the establishment of the destinies of various cities and regions, and the assigning of roles and responsibilities to different gods and goddesses. But in terms of style, there is little indication of the primeval time. So the narrated events took place in mythical time. Such choice of temporal setting may be understandable given that the author seems to be trying to be as comprehensive as possible in attributing different aspects of the world to Enki's creative efforts without paying particular attention to the order of occurrence, or the process of development, of these events.

To be sure, there are some organizing principles behind the presentation of the events: geographic regions or cities (lines 123–249), different deities and their roles or functions (lines 250–450). There are two passages at the beginning of the composition that deal with Enki's regulation or organization of time for humankind: u_4 šid-e iti e_2-ba ku_4-ku_4 mu šu du_7-du_7-da | mu šu du_7 unkin-e eš-bar $šum_2$-mu-da | eš-bar kin u_4-da si sa_2-sa_2-e-da 'Counting the days and putting the months in their houses, so as to complete the years and to submit the completed years to the assembly for a decision, taking decisions to regulate the days' (lines 17–19); [x x] u_4-de_3 sag̃ ba-ab-gi_4 iti e_2-ba ba-an-ku_4 'he closes up the days . . . , and makes the months enter their houses' (line 44). The adverbial expression i_3-ne-$eš_3$ 'now' (line 451) is used towards the end of the composition to mark the completion of Enki's work.

Inana and Enki

This mythological text tells how Inana went from her city Uruk to meet with Enki her lover/father in Eridu in order to bring the divine powers (the so-called *mes*), cultic personnel, and various cultural objects, indeed the entire civilization from Eridu to Uruk, presumably as a compensation for the sexual relations Enki had with her (segm. B 5). She accomplished her goal by first obtaining these things from Enki while the latter was under the influence of beer. By the time Enki became sober, Inana was already on the Boat of Heaven loaded with all the obtained items to sail back to Uruk. Having overcome a series of obstacles Enki had set up through his minister Isimud at different junctures of the journey, Inana eventually reached Uruk with the items.

The temporal setting of the story is set in the mythical past. There is no stylistic or formal indicator that the narrated events took place during the primeval time. In terms of content, it is clear that the events happened after the primeval time of origins, because the divine powers and the arts of civilization had already been created. The central issue in the composition is the ownership of these powers and arts, for which the author of this composition attempted to show that though these powers and arts had originated in Eridu (as Enki was widely acknowledged as the god of wisdom and arts), they were brought to Uruk by Inana. The transfer of the divine powers and arts from Eridu to Uruk should thus be viewed as the mythical event that tied the primeval time of origins (as represented by the primeval city Eridu) with the time in which the author lived in Uruk, for the purpose of supporting the author's claim to Uruk's acquired cultural superiority, if not precedence in origin.

Various narratological techniques are used to assist the progression of the story. One of the techniques is the contest format, in which contestants often vied with each other for supremacy. In this particular case, it is Enki and his minister Isimud against Inana and her minister Ninšubur, with the former trying to stop the latter from carrying the divine powers and arts to Uruk. Repetition or refrain is yet another technique used, which is always coupled with certain variations to indicate progression in the story. This is best seen in the formulaic exchanges between Enki and his minister Isimud, on the one hand, and Inana and Ninšubur, on the other, during the process of the latter's journey from Eridu to Uruk. One crucial variation in these exchanges is the location Inana's boat had reached at each stage of the journey, until she finally arrived in Uruk. Ordinal numbers are also used to indicate how many times Enki spoke to his minister in order to deter Inana from reaching Uruk with the Boat of Heaven: segm. H 35, 69 (restored), 103, 137 (restored), 171, and 213. Adverbial expressions, u_4-bi-a 'on that day' (segm. B 6) and u_4-ba 'on that day' (segm. B 9), occur at the beginning of the story to announce Inana's journey to Eridu and Enki's foreknowledge of Inana's intention. When Inana finally reached Uruk with the Boat of Heaven, the adverbial expression u_4-ba 'at that time; today' is used three times (segm. H 217, 220, 225) to signify the joyful and momentous occasion.

Enki and Ninhursaĝa

This mythological composition narrates a series of exploits of the god Enki, which brought about some of the things that had not existed in the pristine Dilmun and Sumer. The composition starts with Enki having sex with his spouse/daughter Ninsikila/Damgalnuna in Dilmun, the so-called land of innocence, where there is a lack of both good and bad aspects of the common human world, e.g. no river quay, no diseases (Streck 2002: 207). When Ninsikila complained to Enki for giving her this city that had neither fields, meadows, furrow nor river quay, Enki responded by making these things occur in Dilmun. Then in Sumer, after having an extramarital affair with the birth goddess Nintu/Ninhursaĝa, Enki started a series of incestuous relationships with his daughter Ninsar (goddess of plants), granddaughter Ninkura (goddess of looms), and great-granddaughter Uttu (goddess of weaving). With Nintu/Ninhursaĝa's intervention, Enki's semen was taken out of the womb of Uttu and grown into various plants. But Enki would not even leave these plants alone. Having eaten them, he determined their destinies, defining what kind of plants they were. This deed of Enki enraged Nintu/Ninhursaĝa, who went on to curse Enki, who then fell ill with various diseases. Nintu/Ninhursaĝa was brought by Enlil by means of a fox to provide a remedy for Enki. The birth goddess gave birth to a group of deities such as Ninkasi (patron goddess of beer and brewing) to relieve Enki of his diseases. Probably to prevent Enki from having sexual relations with the offspring who were presumably also engendered by him, the birth goddess determined that some of the gods and goddesses should marry each other. Ensag, the last offspring of this group, became the lord of Dilmun. From a literary-historical point of view, it is clear that different episodes which had originally belonged to separate traditions (Katz 2007, 2008), especially the tradition concerning Enki and his spouse Ninsikila/Damgalnuna and the tradition concerning Enki and Nintu/Ninhursaĝa, were combined together as a whole by the author.

The temporal setting of the mythological story is obviously primeval. In terms of style, the story uses many portrayals in negation to illustrate the conditions of Dilmun and Sumer (lines 3–36) prior to the time when Enki began to introduce various natural and cultural phenomena. Such a negation-reversal technique is frequently used in Sumerian mythological compositions dealing with the primeval time of origins. In terms of content, the story narrates the birth of various deities and the origin of different natural and cultural phenomena.

Several temporal devices are used at different junctures of the narrative. At the beginning of Enki's fulfilment of his promise, one finds i_3-ne-$eš_2$ ^{d}utu u_4 ne-a | ^{d}utu an-na gub-be_2-e 'At that moment, on that day, and under the sun, when Utu stood in heaven' (lines 50–1). These lines are partially repeated at the end of the fulfilment as a refrain: i_3-ne-$eš_2$ ^{d}utu u_4 ne-a ur_5 $ḫe_2$-na-nam-ma 'At that moment, on that day, and under the sun, so that happened' (line 62). So the fulfilment section is bracketed with these adverbial expressions. Another group of temporal expressions is used repeatedly also as refrains during the three cycles of Enki's sexual encounters with Nintu, Ninsar, and Ninkura, to indicate the time the goddesses spent in pregnancy: 'But her one month was one day, but her two months were two days, but her three months were three days, but her four months were four days, but her five months were five days, but her six months were six days, but her seven months were seven days, but her eight months were eight days, but her nine months were nine days. In the month of womanhood, like juniper oil, like oil of abundance, Nintu, mother of the country, like juniper oil, give birth to Ninsar' (lines 75–87; see also lines

102–7, 122–6). Here the time of pregnancy is compressed apparently because the pregnant females were divine.[11] Lastly, Enki's lustful actions are sequenced with temporal expressions: lines 97–8, 117–18, and 152.

Various other literary devices are used to structure the narrative and the sequence of the narrated events. The promise–fulfilment framework with repetition in Enki's transformation of Dilmun for Ninsikila (lines 40–62), for example, provides a sense of enclosure in temporal ordering. The ensuing exploits of Enki are initially structured by refrains and repetitive patterns of Enki's sexual encounters and the giving birth by the goddesses (lines 69–126). But from the generation of Uttu, the narrative begins to break away from the preceding monotonous patterns and starts to introduce fresh events that brought frustration to Enki's attempts to prey on the goddess and to impregnate her. However, it is the negation-reversal technique mentioned earlier that provides the broader structure for the composition. The conditions of Dilmun and Sumer as described in the prologue more or less determine the course and nature of the events in the story: for example, the lack of diseases in Sumer like Dilmun is reversed by Enki's diseases.

It is important to point out that the author did make a distinction between the transformation of Dilmun in the first story and that of Sumer in the second. Dilmun's changes were essentially improvements in terms of its natural resources and agricultural productivity, and its conditions as an ideal quay. The changes in Sumer, however, are cultural and related to physical health, though the creation of the plants in the second story also indicates changes in the ecological environment in Sumer. What the author wanted to stress through this contrast is that Dilmun's transformation turned it into a paradise island without its being tainted by the moral and physical/mental degradation seen in Sumer despite its cultural advancement. Dilmun remained morally pure as it was from the beginning and people there were healthier, thus having no need for the cultural sophistication in Sumer such as the advancement in medical treatment.[12] What made the differences between Dilmun and Sumer, according to the author, was that the former's improvements were achieved through marriage, while the latter's changes were out of wedlock. Undoubtedly, for the author, the former is to be preferred, as expressed in the repeated emphasis on and approval of the pure and ideal state of Dilmun symbolized by Enki's monogamous relationship with Ninsikila in lines 5–10:

> He laid her down in Dilmun, and the place where Enki had lain down with his spouse, that place is still virginal, that place is still pristine. He laid her down all

[11] Compression of time is often used to portray the time span in the mythical realm. It could just be a metaphor or simile to convey the divine transcendence of time; compare Psalm 90: 4 'For a thousand years in your sight are like a day that has just gone by' in the Hebrew Bible.

[12] Though Ensag, a deity who was born in Sumer as a remedy for Enki's pain in his sides, became the lord of Dilmun (line 280).

> alone in Dilmun, and the place where Enki had lain down with Ninsikila, that place is virginal, that place is pristine.

Compare this passage with the author's condemnation of the moral degradation in Enki's extramarital affair with Ninhursaĝa in Sumer as expressed in lines 72–4:

> Enki distributed his semen destined for Damgalnuna (Ninsikila). He poured semen into Ninhursaĝa's womb and she conceived the semen in the womb, the semen of Enki.

This mythological composition was intended to tell how Sumer and Dilmun had evolved into the ways they were known at the time during which the author lived, by using two traditional tales of Enki's exploits as aetiological explanations. There is a strong moral overtone in the contrast of the developments of Dilmun and Sumer. Both regions were pure in the beginning, but Dilmun remained so,[13] while Sumer was defiled, as already announced in the prologue (lines 1–4):

> Pure were the cities—and you are the ones to whom they were allotted. Pure was Dilmun land. Pure was Sumer—and you are the ones to whom it was allotted. Pure is Dilmun land. Pure is Dilmun land. Virginal is Dilmun land. Virginal is Dilmun land. Pristine is Dilmun land.

Thus at least one of the main purposes of the composition was to teach a moral lesson to the general public in Sumer of the advantages of nurturing one's marital relations and the complications of following one's wanton desires.

Enki and Ninmah

This mythological composition, possibly dating back to the Ur III period, combines different traditional stories about Enki (Sauren 1993: 198–208). At least two separate traditions embedded in the text may be discerned: the creation of humankind by Enki and the birth goddesses for the relief of the gods from their toil (lines 9–51); and the contest between Enki and Ninmah over their ability to care for abnormal human creatures they created (lines 52–141). In both stories Enki is exalted for his unparalleled wisdom and ingenuity. These two stories are combined together because they both deal with the creation of human beings and the fixing of their destinies. However, the first story is devoted to describing the creation of humankind in general as a solution to a crisis in the divine world and the common human destiny in service to the gods. The second story, on the other hand, focuses on

[13] Because of the reputation of Dilmun as a land immune from various forms of degradation (e.g. ageing, sickness, and death), later traditions such as the *Sumerian Flood Story* 258–60 portray the Flood hero Ziusudra settling in Dilmun, after having been granted eternal life.

the creation of particular kinds of human beings as a result of the whimsical competition between Enki and Ninmah, and on the destinies of these creatures in service to the human king and queen. The reference to royalty in the second story indicates that it may have been used for court entertainment.

The temporal setting is obviously primeval. In terms of style and form, the composition starts with a prologue (*Enki and Ninmah* 1–8) that contains the three-tier adverbial expression and temporal clauses indicating the primeval time of origins:

> In those days, in the days when the heaven [left] the earth; in those nights, in the nights when the heaven [left] the earth; in those years, in the years when the fates [were determined]; when the Anuna gods were born; when the goddesses were taken in marriage; when the goddesses were distributed in heaven and earth; when the goddesses . . . became pregnant and gave birth; when the gods were obliged? . . . their food . . . for their meals.[14]

The prologue thus harks back to the event of the separation of heaven and earth as the cosmic beginning which had created space in between for the subsequent events to take place. The events of determining the fates and the childbearing of the goddesses in the prologue anticipate the introduction of Namma as 'the primeval mother who gave birth to the senior gods' (line 17), her giving birth to the first human being (line 36), her determining of his fate (line 37) and the fixing of the destinies of abnormal creatures made by Enki and Ninmah in the latter half of the composition. The main clauses of the prologue (lines 9–11: 'the senior gods oversaw the work, while the minor gods were bearing the toil. The gods were digging the canals and piling up the silt in Harali. The gods, dredging the clay, began complaining about this life') announce the crisis to be resolved in lines 12–51.

Other than the three-tier adverbial expression in the opening lines of the prologue, the first half of the composition also uses u_4-ba 'at that time' (line 12) to mark the transition from the prologue to the main body of the composition, and to introduce Enki as the chief protagonist of the story. However, there is no stylistic or formal device to mark the transition from the first story to the second (line 52). Within the second half of the composition, the following expressions are used to structure the sequence of the first round of the contest between Enki and Ninmah: gi_4-bi 'second' (line 62), peš-bi 'third' (line 66), peš-gi 'fourth' (line 69), peš-peš-gi 'fifth' (line 72), peš-bal-gi 'sixth' (line 75).[15] Each time, Ninham created an abnormal human creature (six in total). But

[14] Reconstruction of the first two lines is based on the bilingual version from Nineveh K 1711 + 2168 + 4896 + 4932 as presented by Sauren (1993: 200); compare ETCSL t.1.1.2 and Streck (2002: 197).

[15] Though these expressions are interpreted as ordinal numbers by ETCSL t.1.1.2, they are not normal ordinal numbers (see Thomsen 2001: 83). Note that Edzard 2003: 66 lists peš-bal-gi_4 and peš-peš-gi_4 as cardinal numbers.

each time, Enki managed to fix a favourable destiny to care for the creature by assigning an honourable function for the creature to take up in the royal court. But when it was Enki's turn to create a creature, Ninmah did not know 'how to handle and feed the newborn child' (Sauren 1993: 198 n. 4). Thus Enki won the contest with the score six to zero. The use of the adverbial expression u_4-da 'today' (line 134) in Enki's speech emphasizes the final verdict of Enki's victory over Ninmah.

According to Sauren (1993: 198 n. 4), the contest in the second half of the composition may be 'an apologetic satiric story defending Eridu' and Enki as a male deity triumphing over the birth goddess Ninmah from Nippur for knowing better how to care for the newborn.

Enki's Journey to Nippur

This mythological composition aims to praise Enki's newly constructed temple E-engura in Eridu. The outline of the composition is as follows: the prologue (lines 1–3); description of Enki's construction of his temple (lines 4–17); praise of the temple and Enki by Isimud the minister (lines 18–70); Enki's boat journey from Eridu to Nippur to provide a banquet for the senior gods (lines 71–116); Enlil's praise and blessing for Enki's temple (lines 117–29).

The temporal setting of the story is primeval, as indicated by the temporal proximity and sequence between the events mentioned in the prologue (lines 1–3) and the construction of the temple introduced in lines 4–6:

> In those days, when the fates were determined; in the years when An brought about abundance, and people broke through the earth like green plants, the lord of *abzu*, king Enki, Enki, the lord who determines the fates, built up his temple entirely from silver and lapis lazuli.

The selection of the primeval events in the prologue is not random. The determining of the fates (line 1) is echoed by Enki being the lord who determines the fates (line 5), and possibly by Enlil's pronouncement of blessing upon Enki's temple (lines 117–29). Abundance (ḫe_2-ĝal_2; line 2) is mentioned again when Enki prepares the banquet for the gods in Nippur (line 88). The creation of humankind (line 3) presumably anticipates the cultic personnel serving in Enki's temple (line 48) and their slaughtering of animals for the banquet in Nippur (line 93). Note that there is no adverbial expression u_4-ba used to mark the transition from the prologue to the main body of the composition.

The purpose of the story about Enki's journey to provide the banquet for the senior gods is obviously to gain their approval and blessing for his newly constructed temple. The author of this composition acknowledged the authority of Nippur as the religious centre in Sumer.

Enlil and Sud

This composition provides a folk story concerning the marriage of Enlil and Sud (Ninlil's name before marriage). The whole process of how this marriage came about is depicted with very few mythological elements but largely in an anthropological way, reflecting much of the cultural customs from the time of the author. The story tells how Enlil, after having initially offended Sud in her city Ereš with his casual and rude proposition, resorted to following proper protocol by sending his minister Nuska to approach Sud's mother Nisaba in Ereš with a formal marriage proposal and gifts in order to obtain her consent first for his plan to take Sud as wife. Apparently ready to consent to this plan, Nisaba instructed that Enlil should bring the marriage gifts and presents as promised. She further added that Enlil's sister should come to accompany Sud from her home in Ereš to Nippur. Upon receiving Nisaba's instructions from Nuska, Enlil set about preparing the marriage gifts and then dispatched them to Ereš. Once the gifts had reached Ereš with the wedding party, Nisaba gave her blessing to Sud as she sent her daughter off to Enlil. Enlil's sister Aruru accompanied Sud to the Ekur, Enlil's house in Nippur, where the marriage was consummated. The text concludes with Enlil blessing and renaming Aruru as Nintu, and then Sud as Ninlil.

The temporal setting of the story is supposedly primeval because it deals with the origin of the marriage between Enlil and Ninlil. Stylistically, the negations used in describing the initial stage of the story also point to the primeval time of origins: 'At that time (⸢u$_4$⸣-ba) Enlil had not yet been given a wife in the E-kur; Ninlil's name was not yet famous in the Ki-ur' (Version A, segm. A 9–10). But the anthropological style of characterizing the protagonists and the almost entirely human social environment of the story suggest a setting rather contemporaneous to the time of the author and his audience. This choice of temporal setting seems to be a narratological technique to engage the audience, not by taking them back to the primeval time or taking them out of their normal life experience into the mythical realm, but by bringing the mythical characters from the primeval time into contemporary society and mundane human and cultural experience. Engaging the audience in such a direct way is usually done in Sumerian literary compositions dealing with the primeval times of origins through brief statements in the prologue, as already seen in *Enki and Ninhursaĝa* 1–2 (see also *Enlil and Ninlil* 1–12 discussed later in this chapter). Casting the entire story about mythical beings so thoroughly in a contemporary setting as done in the current composition is indeed rare, not even matched by the Sumerian tales regarding Dumuzi (e.g. *Dumuzi's Dream*).

In addition to the adverbial expression u$_4$-ba used, the adverbial expression u$_4$-da-ta 'From now on' (Version A, segm. A 156, 170; compare Version B 15, 26) is used in Enlil's speech at the close of the composition to indicate the time of renaming Aruru and Sud. The author apparently attempted to use the marriage of Enlil and Sud as an aetiological occasion for the identification of Aruru with Nintu, Sud with Ninlil. The aetiological motive is clearly expressed in the better preserved passage in Version B 26–7a 'From now on, Sud, Enlil is its king and Ninlil is its queen. The goddess without name has a famous name now.' This concluding remark indicates the appearance of what was lacking as stated in the negative statements in Version A, segm. A 9–10.

Besides the above aetiological function, the composition may have been used as a lesson to teach young men aspiring to marriage to follow proper procedures and protocols. As already seen above, the story is packed with detailed descriptions of making a proposal, obtaining parental consent, preparing marriage gifts, arranging the wedding party, parental blessings, rewards for the bridesmaid, and tender treatment of one's bride. Most probably it is due to this sociological and practical function that the composition contains very few mythological elements.

Enlil and Ninlil

Similar in style to the second story in *Enki and Ninhursaĝa*, this mythological composition tells a farcical and lurid story about the lascivious exploits of Enlil as a young man at the expense of an innocent and naïve young woman Ninlil. Thus it represents a different aetiological account of the marriage of Enlil and Ninlil from what is found in *Enlil and Sud*. In spite of the parental warning from her mother Nun-bar-še-gunu of Enlil's lustful intent, Ninlil still fell prey to Enlil's plan and conceived Suen-Ašimbabbar in her womb. After being sent into exile by the divine assembly for raping Ninlil, Enlil under disguise nonetheless managed to impregnate Ninlil three more times with Nergal-Mešlamta-ea, Ninazu, and Enbilulu. As a result, Ninlil was simultaneously carrying four children of Enlil. The composition ends with praise to Enlil and Ninlil.

The temporal setting is supposedly primeval, because the content of the mythological story deals with the union between Enlil and Ninlil and the resultant conceptions of four gods. There are elements of cosmology and cosmogony involved in the sequence of the conceptions: Suen-Ašimbabbar (the moon god) is said to be on the top level in Ninlil's womb, while Nergal-Mešlamta-ea (the god of the Netherworld), Ninazu (the god of the Netherworld, and 'the king who stretches measuring lines over the field'), and Enbilulu (the god of rivers and canals) were on the bottom level.

However, the prologue of this composition (*Enlil and Ninlil* 1–12) is not written in a style indicative of the primeval time of origins.

> There was a city, there was a city—the one we live in. Nippur was the city, the one we live in. Dur-ĝišnimbar was the city, the one we live in. Id-sala is its holy river, Kar-ĝeština is its quay. Kar-asar is its quay where boats make fast. Pu-lal is its

> fresh-water well. Id-nunbir-tum is its branching canal, and if one measures from there, its cultivated land is 50 *sar* each way. Enlil was one of its young men, and Ninlil was one of its young women. Nun-bar-še-gunu was one of its wise old women.

The style and content of the prologue are clearly intended to engage the contemporary audience who lived in Nippur. Both the topographical information and the characterization of the protagonists facilitate easy identification of the environment and personalities in the story by the allegedly youthful audience, whom the author may have intended to entertain.

The adverbial expression u_4-ba 'At that time' is used in line 13 to indicate the transition from the prologue to the main body of the composition. The same expression is used three times in the sense of 'if; in the event of' in the narrative when Enlil was trying to hide from Ninlil (line 69) and when he, in disguise, was trying to have intercourse with her (line 82, 108).

The Debate between Grain and Sheep *(Alster and Vanstiphout 1987: 1–43)*

Though Sumerian disputations (such as the current composition) and narrative compositions (e.g. *Enki and Ninmah*; *ELA*; *Enmerkar and En-suhgir-ana*) may both deal with a contest between two protagonists, the former group of texts is said to be distinct from the latter group in 'a *rhetorical* form' (Vanstiphout 1997: 581 n. 2). While the contest over superiority or precedence in the narrative compositions generally involves actions of protagonists, the contest in the disputations is almost always conducted through debates or disputes.[16] Nonetheless, Sumerian disputations and Sumerian narrative compositions still share certain literary features in common, one of which is that both groups of literature tend to begin their stories with mythological prologues that trace back to the primeval time of origins.

The text under investigation tells how Grain and Sheep, originally not present in the world, had been created first for the divine realm before they were granted by Enki and Enlil to human beings for their sustenance. Complementing each other, they initially served the world well. But at a banquet, under the influence of wine and beer, they began to argue over superiority. Using one's own advantages against the other's disadvantages, their quarrel became increasingly heated until Grain felt hurt at the end of the second round and gave her final speech. At this juncture, Enki began to intervene by saying to Enlil that Grain and Sheep should work together again, yet with the final verdict that Grain had precedence over Ewe.

[16] Except in the *Debate between Bird and Fish* where Fish attacked Bird's nest.

The temporal setting in the first 64 lines is clearly primeval. In terms of content, the prologue harks back to the time when An spawned the Anunna gods upon the Hill of Heaven and Earth, which is narrated as the first primeval event (lines 1–2). The second event is the creation of Grain and Sheep at the same location where the gods had been born. The third event is the gods enjoying the bounty brought about by Grain and Sheep. The fourth event is the granting of Grain and Sheep by Enki and Enlil to human beings as sustenance. The next event is the working together of Grain and Sheep to bring abundance and satisfaction to the world. The following banquet scene (lines 65–70) in which Grain and Sheep apparently intended to celebrate and enjoy the fruit of their labour but lapsed into a dispute is the transition point in narration from the primeval time to, in Alster and Vanstiphout's words, 'what may have been a specific though perhaps repeated point in time' (1987: 3), that is, the perennial conflict between the two economic models, pastoral and agricultural, as represented by Grain and Sheep in ancient Mesopotamia. The banquet and disputation as told from line 65 onwards can still be considered as having taken place in the primeval time. But the event of disputation carries a paradigmatic character that sets the relational pattern between what Grain and Sheep represent in normal life experience at all times.

In terms of form and style, the prologue (lines 1–25) uses a long series of negative statements in describing the economic and life conditions of presumably both gods and human beings prior to the existence of Grain and Sheep. But once they were created by the gods, the conditions were reversed. The negation-reversal technique used in this composition highlights the vital importance of Grain and Sheep for the divine and human worlds alike. Without them, no sustenance and civilization would be possible, which explains why the creation of Grain and Sheep is narrated as the second event after the birth of the Anunna gods. Though human beings had already existed before the arrival of Grain and Sheep (lines 20–5), their creation was not narrated as an event.

The adverbial expression u_4-ba 'at that time; then' is used in the composition to mark the crucial points of the story: the creation of Grain and Sheep at the Hill of Heaven and Earth (line 26); Enki's discussion with Enlil about sending Grain and Sheep from the Hill down to human beings (line 37); the last speech of the dispute which was given by Grain (line 168); and Enki's intervention with Enlil to give the final verdict (line 179). In addition to the stylistic device, thematic (e.g. food or banquet, clothing) and rhetorical patterns are also used to connect the prologue and the dispute (Alster and Vanstiphout 1987: 7–10).

Generally regarded by scholars as serving for entertainment, this composition contains an aetiological motive. Not only does the composition seek to account for the vital importance of, and the complementary, yet conflicting, relation between, the two economic models which Grain and Sheep represent; it also, in the final analysis, attempts to exalt what Grain symbolizes on rhetorical and economic grounds (Alster and Vanstiphout 1987: 12). The composition was obviously made with a bias favouring the perspective of the farmer.

How Grain Came to Sumer

This mythological composition provides an account different from what is seen in the above disputation about how grain or barley came to Sumer. The narrative starts by describing the dire condition of humankind before the existence of grain, barley, or flax (lines 1–2; cf. the *Debate between Grain and Sheep* 20–4). Then An brought these out from the interior of heaven. But Enlil chose to restrict their growth to the Cedar Mountain north of Sumer. In the *Debate between Grain and Sheep* one also finds this motif of restricting Grain and Sheep to the Hill of Heaven and Earth when they were first created (lines 26–34). The current text diverges from the disputation in that while the latter portrays Enki and Enlil as sending Grain and Sheep down from the Hill of Heaven and Earth to the human world, the former says that it was two brothers Ninazu and Ninmada who attempted to bring grain or barley down from the mountain to Sumer, with the help of the sun god Utu. But how the two brothers achieved this venture is no longer preserved in the extant text.

The temporal setting is obviously primeval because it deals with the origin of grain or barley in Sumer. The author plunged directly into the main subject without mentioning any other primeval events; compare the *Debate between Grain and Sheep* 1–2 where the birth of the Anunna gods is first introduced. Similar to the disputation, the creation and existence of human beings is presupposed, but not narrated as a primeval event. In terms of style, again negation is used in the prologue: u_4 re-a ^{d}ezina$_2$ še gu nu-[zu] 'In those days, they did not know grain, barley or flax' (line 2). This negative form of describing the human condition is echoed in the dialogue between the two brothers in the main body of the story: in Ninazu's proposal 'Let us make barley known in Sumer, which knows no barley' (line 20), and Ninmada's reply 'How can we make barley known in Sumer, which knows no barley?' (line 27). Ninmada's question naturally leads to the introduction of Utu who may help them achieve the goal (lines 28–31). The fulfilment of their goal, which is not preserved in the extant text, presumably reverses the negative condition described above.

Two temporal expressions are used in the extant text: u_4 re-a 'in those days' (line 2) to introduce the negative condition of human beings before the existence of grain, barley, or flax, and the imminent creation of these products by An; u_4-ba 'at that time; then' (line 13) to introduce Ninazu, who made the suggestion to his brother about fetching the barley down from the mountain.

The current story and the *Debate between Grain and Sheep* attest to the innovations among ancient authors in composing different aetiological accounts for explaining the origin of grain or barley in Sumer. At the same time, these two compositions follow the same mythological motifs that grain or barley was created by the gods and that it was first inaccessible to Sumer or the human world. The two compositions also share the same style in presentation, for example the negation-reversal technique.

Song of the Hoe

This composition seeks to exalt the tool in manifold ways. Thematically, it explores the omnipresence and indispensable roles of the hoe in various events or settings: the primeval time of origins (lines 1–34), the construction of temples or cultic places (lines 35–73), the exploits of the legendary hero Gilgameš (lines 74–82), nature (lines 83–93), and the realm of human activities—especially in agriculture and architecture (lines 94–106). But many claims of the omnipresence and importance of the hoe in this text are based not on the actual reference to the hoe (^{ĝeš}al), but rather, as already pointed in previous scholarship (see ETCSL t.5.5.4), on the presence of the syllable, or the sound, of al (occasionally ar) in Sumerian words. In many respects, this composition is made up with an ingenious collection and arrangement of Sumerian nouns, verbal forms, and adjectives that contain al/ar. Some of the far-fetched associations between the hoe (^{ĝeš}al) and other Sumerian words with the al/ar syllable or sound may have been based on folk etymology. But most of these associations may have just been the result of the author's own fanciful and forced speculations or wordplays out of his eagerness to see the name of the hoe encoded in almost everything.

The temporal setting of this composition changes from the primeval time of origins during which the hoe was involved in the separation of heaven and earth, the creation of humankind, and the assignment of the roles of important people to serve the gods by Enlil (lines 1–34), to the time (possibly also primeval) of the construction of various temples (lines 35–73), and finally to the legendary era of Gilgameš (lines 74–82). From then on, the text turns to focus on nature (lines 83–93) and the mundane human work setting (lines 94–106). The creation of the hoe is not narrated as a primeval event. So it is unclear whether the creation of the hoe is presupposed. Or the hoe was thought of as self-existing, similar to some of the cosmic principles such as heaven and earth in mythological traditions.

In any case, the emphasis is placed on the leading roles and destiny of the hoe, which started as important events in the primeval time of origins (e.g. lines 2, 16) and continued to unfold in ensuing events (e.g. line 107). The portrayal of the hoe as being involved in the separation of heaven and earth and the creation of humankind is striking in terms of the ordering and conceptualization of time in this composition. By using the hoe to separate heaven and earth, Enlil made daylight break through (line 8). Thus the hoe was instrumental for the starting of time, if the creation or organization of time is thought to have begun with the appearance of (sun)light on the earth (Ferrara 2006: 57, 62). The placing of the existence of the hoe as a cultural object before the creation of humankind in time is equally conspicuous. Both cases of temporal ordering reflect an architectural and agricultural perspective. The separation of heaven and earth is perceived as an architectural undertaking, and the creation of humankind as an agricultural task of loosening the ground and letting the seeds break through the soil.

In terms of form and style, this composition does not use the common devices (e.g. negations or the expression u_4-ba) as seen in other Sumerian mythological compositions dealing with the primeval time of origins to structure or sequence the narrated events. Nonetheless, there are a couple of temporal expressions used in the text. Besides the allusion to the starting of time in line 8 mentioned above, one also finds in line 36 u_4-de_3 al-du_3-e $\hat{g}i_6$ al-mu_2-mu_2 'By day it (the hoe) was building, by night it (the hoe) caused (the temple of Enlil) to grow.' As mentioned above, the chief technique to bind the constituent parts together in the text is the ubiquitous syllable al/ar.

Marriage of Martu

This composition tells a folkloristic story of how Martu, a 'Heros Eponymos' of the Martu nomads, was married to Adĝar-kidu, the daughter of the local deity of the princely land Inab (Klein 1997). The temporal setting of the story is halfway through the development of the primeval time of origins, as described in the prologue (lines 1–6).

> When the city of Inab already existed, but the city Kiritab did not yet exist, when the holy crown already existed, but the holy tiara did not yet exist, when the holy herb already existed, but the holy cedar did not yet exist, when holy salt already existed, but holy alkali did not yet exist, when intercourse and kissing already existed, when giving birth in the fields already existed.

The choice of the motifs mentioned in the prologue is to a certain extent deliberate: the city Inab played a crucial role throughout the story, symbolizing advanced cultural development. Cedar trees are referred to again in the last two lines of the prologue, 'I was the grandfather of the holy cedar, I was the ancestor of the *meš* tree, I was the mother and father of the white cedar, I was the relative of the *hašur* cedar' (lines 7–8), for the identification of the narrator as someone from a time of high antiquity (Streck 2002: 209), who was responsible for transmitting the story. Lastly, intercourse and kissing and giving birth must have existed before Martu's marriage could take place.

Stylistically, the prologue represents an example of what Streck (2002: 192–209) calls 'Bühnen-Prologe', whose focus is 'Die Szenerie und die Akteure', as opposed to 'Zeitreisen-Prologe', which aim at 'Fixierung in ferner Vergangenheit'. Streck (2002: 202) is right when he states that the 'Bühnen-Prologe' such as found in the Marriage of Martu 'schildern zusätzlich die Urzeit, dismal aber nicht im Stadium der Weltentstehung, sondern in einem vorgerückten, jedoch noch unfertigen Stadium der Welt'. The incomplete state of things does not only refer to the fact that civilization had already begun, but that it was yet to be more fully cultivated or unfolded (e.g. line 3 'when the holy herb already existed, but the holy cedar did not yet exist'). It also points to a time when the existing level of civilization had not been as widely spread as it was later on (e.g. line 1 'when the city Inab already existed, but the city of Kiritab did not yet exist'). This definition of incomplete development in terms of cultural disparities fits the plot of the story well: Inab is described as the most culturally developed city (lines 9–10). But the nomadic tribe, to which Martu belonged, that lived on the outskirts of the city, was still lagging behind in cultural development. They still maintained the primitive ways of living: hanging up nets, hunting, and dividing rations (lines 16–40), presumably without the technology for domesticating animals. According to the demands of Adĝar-kidu's father, in order for Martu to marry Adĝar-kidu, Martu had to acquire the skills to domesticate animals so as to provide a more stable source of living, and also to become integrated into the more settled way of life (lines 91–111). The urbanites from Inab were prejudiced against Martu and his people, as indicated by the words spoken to Adĝar-kidu by her girlfriend against Martu (lines 127–39). The vast cultural gap between Adĝar-kidu and Martu seems to be intentionally highlighted in these prejudices: while the former was the daughter of the god of the most developed city Inab, the latter had no established religion.

In the main body of the composition, the following temporal expressions are used to structure the temporal sequence of the story: u_4-ba 'at that time' (line 9) to indicate the transition from the prologue to the beginning of the story; u_4-ne u_4 te-na um-ma-te-a-ra 'That day, as the day drew to an end' (lines 19, 34) to mark the time of Martu and his people distributing rations among themselves, an event that prompted Martu's desire to get married; u_4-ba 'at that time' (line 53) to introduce the episode when Martu went to Inab for the festival where he encountered Adĝar-kidu; u_4 ba-ḫi-a 'the days have multiplied' (line 126) to indicate the fact that though much time had elapsed after Martu presumably had already met the demands of Adĝar-kidu's father, no decision regarding the marriage had yet been made. The chief reasons for this delay, as given in the words of Adĝar-kidu's girlfriend which are referred to above, are the urbanite prejudices against Martu and his people. But despite the prejudices, Adĝar-kidu decided to marry Martu.

The purpose of this composition seems to offer an aetiological story for the integration of the nomadic people, the Amorites, into the settled life of Mesopotamia,[17] in spite of all the cultural disparities and prejudices (Falkenstein 1951: 17).

[17] For the background of the Amorites, see Sallaberger (2007: 444–9) with previous literature.

Curse Agade

The temporal setting of this composition is chronographical, (literary-)historical, and mythical. According to the chronographical scheme of *SKL*, kingship passed from Kiš to Uruk and then to Agade (Kiš→Uruk→Agade in the *USKL*, and the 3rd Kiš dynasty→the 3rd Uruk dynasty→Agade in the W-B 444 version of *SKL*). And among these three cities, only Agade never regained kingship. Apparently following the chronographical tradition of *SKL*, *Curse Agade* offers an aetiological story to account for the terminal demise of the Akkad dynasty. The transfer of kingship from one city to another is the normal pattern or principle in the political ideology of *SKL*. It is this pattern that structures the dynastic events in the *SKL*. And such pattern or principle is depicted as having been determined and sanctioned by the gods in the primeval time when kingship was first granted to humanity. Just as kingship was passed on from Kiš to Uruk and to Agade, it too would be passed on from Agade to another city. But the ruler of Agade Naram-Suen was represented as trying to stop this pattern of kingship. He made attempts for seven years through extispicy to obtain divine approval for building the temple of Inana in order to secure Agade's power. After these efforts had failed, Naram-Suen launched a sacrilegious attack on the temple of Enlil, who was believed to be chiefly responsible for establishing the fate or pattern of kingship, in order to force the hand of Enlil. Because of this act of hubris, Agade was cursed by the gods that it would be permanently destroyed. The moral lesson of the story is that one should accept the transient power of kingship as ordained by the gods. By fighting against this fate, one would only make things worse and eliminate any chance of recovery due to the turn of fate. Had Naram-Suen not attacked the Ekur, Agade could have regained its glory like other cities in the *SKL*.

Sumerian compositions dealing with catastrophe such as *Curse Agade* developed distinct literary motifs. But some of these motifs are evidently based on those concerning the primeval time of origins. In terms of content, the powers that were withdrawn from Agade (e.g. lines 60–76; compare the powers mentioned in the Sumerian composition *Inana and Enki*), and the cosmic structure (lines 120–1) and different aspects of civilization that were destroyed in Agade, Nippur, and Sumer, are the very things that are said to have been established during the primeval time of origins. In terms of style, there is no more use of the types of prologue, either *Zeitreisen-Prolog* or *Bühnen-Prolog* (Streck 2002), seen among the mythological compositions dealing with the primeval time of origins. However, the portrayals of the conditions of destruction, such as seen in *Curse Agade* 171–5 quoted below, are the same as the negative depictions in the prologues of the mythological compositions dealing with the primeval time.

> (For the first time) since cities were built and founded, the great agricultural tracts produced no grain, the inundated tracts produced no fish, the irrigated

orchards produced neither syrup nor wine, the gathered clouds did not rain, the *mašgurum* did not grow.

Just as the mythological compositions dealing with the primeval time of origins use the negative–positive reversal to emphasize the dynamics of creation, the compositions dealing with catastrophe such as *Curse Agade* use the positive–negative reversal to underscore the dynamics of destruction. In the final analysis, the negative descriptions in the compositions dealing with catastrophe represent the inversion of the creation and organization of the world which took place in the primeval time of origins (see Tinney 1996: 44–5). In *Curse Agade*, for example, the destroyed Nippur, Agade, and Sumer as a whole are a world returning to the pre-organized, pre-civilized, and, to some extent, even pre-created world. Note that this inversion is not restricted to those depictions styled in the form of negation. Many portrayals of destruction in the affirmative seem to be intended as reversals of the portrayals of the creation and organization of the world in mythological compositions dealing with the primeval time of origins.

The following temporal devices are used in the text: u_4-ba 'At that time' (line 7) to introduce Inana and her constructive works in Agade; u_4-ba 'At that time' (line 25) to introduce another series of Inana's constructive works in Agade; u_4 nu–5-am_3 u_4 nu–10-am_3 'It was not five days, it was not ten days' (line 66) to indicate the time when Ninurta withdrew the royal symbols from Agade; ^{d}na-ra-am-^{d}suen mu 7-am_3 mu-un-ge-en | lugal mu 7-am_3 šu saĝ-$ĝa_2$ du_{11}-ga a-ba igi im-mi-in-du_8-a 'Naram-Suen was immobile for seven years! Who has ever seen a king act so anomalously for seven years!' (lines 92–3) to indicate the length of time during which Naram-Suen humbled himself in order to appeal to Enlil to change the unfavourable decision regarding the fate of Agade; u_4-ba 'At that time' (line 176) to indicate the time of economic hardship as a result of the foreign invasions caused by Enlil in Sumer; u_4-ba 'At that time' (line 193) to indicate the time when Enlil renovated his temple which had been damaged and pillaged by Naram-Suen; um-ma u_4-ta ba-ra-ab-tak_4-a | ab-ba u_4-ta ba-ra-ab-tak_4-a | gala-maḫ mu-ta ba-ra-ab-tak_4-a | u_4 7 $ĝi_6$ 7-$še_3$ 'The old women who survived those days, the old men who survived those days, the chief lamentation singer who survived those years, for seven days and seven nights' (lines 196–9) to indicate the length of time when the survivors lamented for Nippur; u_4-ba 'At that time' (line 210) to indicate the time when the gods started to curse Agade in order to comfort Enlil; 2-kam-ma-$še_3$ 'for the second time' (lines 222, 266, 275) to indicate that the gods repeatedly curse Agade. Note that, unlike many mythological compositions dealing with the primeval time of origins which have been examined previously, the usage of the adverbial expression u_4-ba 'at that time' in this composition is no longer restricted to marking important events or temporal transitions in the story. Its usage in line 25 has become merely a structuring device on the literary level rather than a temporal device for sequencing the narrated events.

The functions of the text seem to be didactic, in order to inculcate, probably to incumbent or prospective rulers, the political ideology of *SKL* and reverence towards the Nippurean cult.

LSU

The temporal setting of this Sumerian composition dealing with catastrophe is both (literary-)historical and mythical. Historically, it portrays the destruction of the Ur III dynasty when Ibbi-Suen was the ruler. In both content and style, many motifs of destruction found in this composition are inversions of those found in Sumerian mythological compositions dealing with the primeval time of origins as well as in divine and royal hymns. As stated in the opening of the text, the destruction depicted in *LSU* was to overturn what was previously ordained, presumably during the primeval time of origins (lines 1, 27). The portrayals of the destruction of temples and cultic services, the removal of human kingship, the invasion of foreigners, and the collapse of the whole socio-political structure in Sumer also are obvious inversions of the motifs or topoi in divine and royal hymnic compositions.

However, promises of and appeals for restoration as seen towards the end of the composition (lines 464–518) are represented as a further inversion, a return to the created order and developed society in the primeval time of origins, or 'a re-creation' (Tinney 1996: 45). The author pleaded on behalf of Ur and Sumer that the gods would never change the order again (*LSU* 494–513). The restoration of course is represented as a return not only to the norms of the created order as found in the mythological compositions dealing with the primeval time, but also to the norms (e.g. the destruction of foreign enemies or their submission to Sumer; lines 483–92) aspired to in royal hymns.

To a large extent, this lament was composed to endorse the political ideology and the chronographical principle as propagated through the *SKL* with regard to the transience of kingship at each of its recipient cities. The political ideology and the chronographical principle are even elevated to the divine level: thus it was not Ibbi-Suen but Nanna/Suen who is represented as having to reckon with the transience of his divine kingship in Ur (lines 360–70, 460–2). Furthermore, according to *LSU* 364–9 (see also 461–2), the political ideology and the chronographical principle of *SKL* are represented as having been established in the primeval time:

> The judgment of the assembly cannot be turned back, the word of An and Enlil knows no overturning, Ur was indeed given kingship (but) it was not given an eternal reign. From time immemorial, since the Land was found, until the population multiplied, who has ever seen a reign of kingship that would take precedence (for ever)? The reign of its kingship had been long indeed but had to exhaust itself.

Thus the transience of kingship, even for the divine in each of their cities, had already been predetermined at the primeval time of origins by An and Enlil. In correlation with what is taught in *Curse Agade, LSU* inculcates the idea that only by accepting this fate might there be hope for possible future restoration of Ur's glory.

The following temporal expressions are used in the composition: u_4-ba 'on that day' (line 75) to mark the time when Enlil sent down the Gutians from the mountains; u_4 mud-e 'on the bloody day' (line 80α) to indicate the time of slaughter as a result of the invasion of the Gutians; u_4-ba 'on that day' (line 81) to indicate the time of cosmic catastrophe; u_4-ba 'on that day' (line 99) to indicate the destruction of kingship in Ur; u_4-ba 'On that day' (line 163) to mark probably the time of the implementation of Enlil's command to attack Sumer and Ur; u_4-ba u_4 'then the day' (line 171) to introduce the destruction of Lagaš; u_4-bi-a nin-e u_4-da-a-ni sa_2 nam-ga-mu-ni-ib-du_{11} | ^{d}ba-u_2 lu_2-u_{18}-lu-gin_7 u_4-da-a-ni sa_2 nam-ga-mu-ni-ib-du_{11} 'And then the Queen also reached the end of her time, Ba'u, as if she were human, also reached the end of her time' (lines 173–4) to indicate that even the divine rulers were not immune from transience; u_4-bi-a 'On that day' (line 214) to indicate the time when the people of Sumer were forced to live in darkness because of the destruction brought by the storm; $\hat{g}i_6$-a x x-ke_4 ḫa-ba-gub-bu-da-na u_4-de_3 ba-ra-an-tuku 'By night [. . .] . . . by day . . .' (line 236) with an unclear function due to the broken context; 2-kam-ma-$še_3$ 'For the second time' (line 261) to indicate the second time when Enlil sent down the Elamites from the mountains for Sumer's destruction; u_4 3-e $\hat{g}i_6$ 3-e la-ba-da-ti$^{?}$ x x [. . .] iri ^{ĝeš}al-e ba-ab-r[a-aḫ] 'Three days and three nights did not pass [. . .] the city was raked (as by) a hoe' (line 264); u_4 ul kalam ki gar-ra-ta za_3 $u\hat{g}_3$ lu-a-$še_3$ 'From time immemorial, since the Land was founded, until the population multiplied' (line 367) to indicate the pattern of transient kingship as having been established for eternity since the primeval time of origins.

The lament in its support of the transient character of kingship with regard to the Ur III period is said to have been manipulated by the early rulers of the Isin dynasty for establishing themselves as rightful successors of the Ur III dynasty (Michalowski 1983: 242–3; 1989: 6–7). The depictions of destruction and restoration in this text likewise may have been used as political rhetoric by the same Isin rulers for legitimation of their regimes, especially Išme-Dagan, who was explicitly portrayed in *LW* and *NL* as the divinely chosen hero to bring about restoration. However, Išme-Dagan is not mentioned in *LSU* (see further discussion in Chapter 4).

Year Name 22 of Ibbi-Suen *(Civil 1987: 27–8; de Maaijer and Jagersma 1997–8: 282; Frayne 1997: 365)*

This historical text states 'Year Ibbi-Suen, the King of Ur, made firm Ur and URU×UD stricken by a flood/tempest which was ordered by the gods that blurred the boundaries of heaven and earth.'[18] It is unclear whether the word a-ma-ru refers to an actual meteorological catastrophe, or is used metaphorically to depict the dire condition the country was facing (Gomi 1984: 211–42; Jacobsen 1953: 36–45). It is possible that both interpretations might be applicable. Despite the uncertainty surrounding the interpretation of the flood term, what remains clear is that the year name was intended to praise the superhuman strength or ability of Ibbi-Suen through a destruction-restoration scenario, a form of rhetoric which has been frequently manipulated in royal hymns and inscriptions.

The temporal setting is historical, cosmic, and mythical. Though taking place during the reign of Ibbi-Suen in Sumer, the catastrophe is represented, in its scale and effect, as blurring or confusing the boundaries of heaven and earth: za$_3$ an-ki im-suḫ$_3$-suḫ$_3$-a 'it ("the flood") blurred/confused the boundaries of heaven and earth'. As already noted earlier, the separation of heaven and earth is frequently considered in Mesopotamian mythological traditions as the first cosmic event through which space and time were made available for the subsequent events to unfold.[19] The depiction of scale and effect of the flood in the year name is apparently an inversion of this event symbolizing the cosmic beginning. According to the year name, the catastrophe is depicted as being sent by the gods. The year name stresses that against all odds—the cosmic catastrophe and the divine opposition—Ibbi-Suen was able to restore the flattened Ur and URU×UD. The combination of historical, cosmic, and mythical settings is to highlight the unprecedented achievement of the ruler.

Sources with the Primeval Flood Catastrophe Motif

The Instructions of Ur-Ninurta *(Alster 2005: 221–40)*

This composition, inscribed on an originally six-column *Sammeltafel* together with at least two other Sumerian compositions, absorbs materials from diverse literary traditions: mythological prologues dealing with the primeval time of origins (lines 1–4), royal hymns (lines 5–18), and didactic literature (lines 19–71) (Alster 2005: 223–4). Such a collection or selection 'reflects the

[18] *Year Name 22 of Ibbi-Suen*: mu ^{d}i-bi$_2$-^{d}suen lugal uri$_2^{ki}$-ma-ke$_4$ a-ma-ru niĝ$_2$-du$_{11}$-ga diĝir-re-ne-ke$_4$ za$_3$ an-ki im-suḫ$_3$-suḫ$_3$-a uri$_2^{ki}$ uru$_2$(URU×UD)^{ki} tab-ba bi$_2$-in-ge-en.

[19] e.g. *Bilgames, Enkidu, and the Netherworld*, version A 8 an ki-ta ba-da-bad-ra$_2$-a-ba 'when heaven was separated from the earth'; also *Lugalbanda in the Mountain Cave*, segm. A 1 [u$_4$ ul an ki-ta bad-ra$_2$-a-ba] 'In the days of yore when heaven was separated from earth' (reconstructed from OB catalogues; ETCSL c.1.8.2.1); *Enki and Ninmah* 1–2 u$_4$-re-a-ta u$_4$ an ki-bi-ta ba-an[-e$_3$-a-ba] | ĝi$_6$ re-a-ta ĝi$_6$ an ki-bi-ta ⸢ba⸣-[e$_3$-a-ba] 'In those days, in the days when the heaven [left] the earth; in those nights, in the nights when the heaven [left] the earth'. On this motif, see Streck (2002: 235); Ferrara (2006: 47–63) for discussion.

ambitions of the royal court of King Ur-Ninurta' (Alster 2005: 224) in order to legitimize and praise Ur-Ninurta, on the one hand, and to inculcate diligence in those who served him, on the other. Ur-Ninurta is represented in the relevant sections (lines 12–36) as being chosen by Ninurta, pious and wise, thus deserving to be rewarded with a long life or reign.

The temporal setting of lines 1–18 (Plate 6) is primeval, though Ur-Ninurta was a ruler from the middle of the Isin dynasty.

1 After the days of yore had come to an end,
2 after nights had become far remote from those distant nights,
3 after years had become remote from remote years,
4 after the Flood had swept over,
5 the one given wisdom by Enki,
6 the one . . . by Nisaba,
7 the one who takes counsel with . . . Inana,
8 —in order to organize the plans of Sumer;
9 —in order to abolish wickedness, to implement righteousness,
10 —in order to let the people return to their dwelling places,
11 —in order to consolidate the foundation of Ur-Ninurta's shepherd[ship],
12 on that day, (Ninurta), the lord of Ešumeša, (installed the one) born in Nippur (= Ur-Ninurta)
13 [the one chosen in his] heart [by] Suen,
14 the 'home-born slave' of [(. . .$^?$)] Ninurta,
15 —in order (for him, i.e. Ninurta) to install (him, i.e. Ur-Ninurta) for long days,
16 in Nippur, his beloved city,
17 he installed him for long days to last,
18 —in order not to [terminate$^?$ his sovereignty$^?$] of the Land.[20]

Stylistically, the three-tier adverbial expression or its variant, which often appears in the opening lines of the prologue, is the standard temporal device to introduce the primeval time of origins in Sumerian mythological compositions (see Black 1992: 71–101; Streck 2002: 231 for discussion):

Bilgames, Enkidu, and the Netherworld Version A 1–10
In those days, in those distant days, in those nights, in those remote nights, in those years, in those distant years; in days of yore, when all that is fitting had been brought into manifest existence, in days of yore, when all that is fitting had been

[20] u$_4$-ul-li-a-ta u$_4$-ub-ba til-la-[a-ta] | gig-re be$_2$-ri ĝi$_6$ ba-su$_3$-[da-a-ta] | mu-su$_3$-da mu ba-ši-[su$_3$-da-a-ta] | eĝir a-ma-ru ba-ĝar-ra-[a-ta] | ĝeštu$_2$ šum$_2$-ma ^{d}en-ki-[ga-ta] | KA.KA ^{d}nisaba-[(x)-t]a | ša-ak-šu ^{d}⸢x⸣ ⸢x⸣-inana-ta | ĝeš-ḫur kalam-ma-ke$_4$ si-sa$_2$-e-si | niĝ$_2$-erim$_2$ ḫa-la-mi-it-te niĝ$_2$-gi-na gin-te | uĝ$_3$-e dur$_2$-bi ki-bi gi$_4$-gi$_4$-te | [nam]-sipa ur-^{d}nin-urta suḫuš-bi gi-ne-te | ⸢u$_4$⸣-⸢ba⸣ [(x)]-[x]-la lugal e$_2$-šu-me-ša$_4$ ⸢u$_3$⸣-tu-da nibru^{ki} | ša$_3$ x [x EN$^?$].ZU-⸢na⸣-ka | emedu$_2$ (ama-a-⸢tu⸣) [(x)]-^{d}nin-urta-ka | u$_4$-su$_3$-še$_3$ ba-⸢an⸣-[(x)-s]i$_3$-⸢ga⸣-te | nibru^{ki} iri ki-[a]ĝ$_2$-ĝa$_2$-ta | u$_4$-su$_3$-še$_3$ da-ru-[še$_3$ . . .]-ĝar | ⸢x⸣ kalam-ma-ke$_4$ ⸢u$_4$⸣ nu-⸢da⸣-⸢x⸣-[(x)]-te (thus MS A; Alster 2005: 227–8).

for the first time properly cared for, when bread had been tasted for the first time in the shrines of the Land, when the ovens of the Land had been made to work, when heaven had been separated from earth, when earth had been delimited from the heaven, when the fame of humankind had been established.

Enki and Ninmah 1–8
In those days, the days when heaven [left] earth; in those nights, the nights when heaven left earth; in those years, in the years when the fates were [determined]; when the Anuna gods were born; when the goddesses were taken in marriage; when the goddesses were distributed in heaven and earth; when the goddesses . . . became pregnant and gave birth; when the gods were obliged[?] . . . their food . . . for their meals.

Enki's Journey to Nippur 1–3
In those days, when the fates were determined; in the year when An brought about abundance, the people broke through the earth like green plants.

ELA 6–11
In those days of yore, when the destinies were determined, the great princes allowed Unug Kulaba's E-ana to lift its head high. Plenty, and carp floods, and the rain which brings forth dappled barley were then increased in Unug Kulaba.

How Grain Came to Sumer 2–3
In those times, they (humankind) did not know grain, barley or flax. An brought these down from the interior of heaven.

Lugalbanda in the Mountain Cave A 1–5
[In days of yore when heaven was made remote from earth], [. . .] of yore [when] the crown was bound, [in . . .] of yore when at ancient harvests . . . barley was eaten[?] . . . , when boundaries were laid out and borders were fixed, when boundary-stones were placed and inscribed with names. . . .

According to the above textual witnesses, the adverbial expression or its variant is closely associated with, or generally used to introduce, the separation of heaven and earth, and the fixing of destinies as two of the important events upon which the ensuing events depended. But out of narratological considerations, this expression may also introduce events or subjects more immediately relevant to the central theme of the composition: for example, the bestowing of grain or barley by An (*How Grain Came to Sumer* 2–3); niĝ$_2$-du$_7$-e 'that which is fitting' and ninda '(cultic) bread' (*Bilgames, Enkidu, and the Netherworld* Version A 4–6).

In the prologue of the *Instructions of Ur-Ninurta*, the expression eĝir a-ma-ru ba-ĝar-ra-[a-ta] 'after the Flood had swept over' (line 4) has become part of the stylistic and temporal devices for signalling the primeval time—though still second to the three-tier adverbial expression. The Flood has also become the starting point of the temporal sequence of the narrated events (Chen 2012). The selection of the event of the Flood is apparently deliberate for the destruction-restoration rhetoric: In order to reorganize the plans of Sumer (line 8), to reinstall justice (line 9), to help the people with their resettlement (line 10), and to restore religion (lines 19–36) and agriculture (lines 37–71), kingship must first be re-established (lines 11–18). Thus Ur-Ninurta was presented as the royal hero chosen by Ninurta to restore order and society after the catastrophe.

The destruction-restoration rhetoric had been used earlier, as already seen in *Year Name 22 of Ibbi-Suen*. The same rhetoric had also been used by Išme-Dagan as seen in *LW* and *NL*. *Išme-Dagan A* 118–23 contain phraseology and ideology similar to that in the *Instructions of Ur-Ninurta*.[21] However, while the word a-ma-ru 'flood' is used in a metaphorical sense to refer to the catastrophic demise of the Ur III dynasty and its turbulent aftermath in both the royal hymn of Išme-Dagan and the *Instructions of Ur-Ninurta*,[22] the word a-ma-ru began to refer to a primeval catastrophe in the latter text due to the fact that the flood terminology is now couched in the literary context of the primeval time of origins, as indicated by the prologue. From a chronographical point of view, Ur-Ninurta is presented in this text as the first postdiluvian king. The chronographical traditions related to the Flood may have not yet existed at the time of Ur-Ninurta. Rather, it was the literary innovation of combining the destruction-restoration rhetoric in the Ur III and Isin royal ideology and the mythological prologue dealing with the primeval time of origins as seen in the *Instructions of Ur-Ninurta* that may have given rise to the concept and motif of the primeval flood catastrophe, which in turn influenced the chronographical traditions (see Glassner 2004: 109).

Besides the adverbial expression of time in the opening three lines, ⌜u$_4$⌝-⌜ba⌝ 'On that day' (line 12) is used to mark the time when Ninurta installed Ur-Ninurta as king. The temporal expressions u$_4$-su$_3$-še$_3$ 'for long days' (lines 15, 17) are used to convey the long life or reign which Ninurta determined for the king.

Old Babylonian version of the Instructions of Šurrupak *(Alster 2005: 56–100)*

This didactic text contains the wisdom teaching of a father to his son. The first twelve lines of the text run as follows:

1 In those days, in those far remote days;
2 in those nights, in those far-away nights;

[21] *Išme-Dagan A* 118–23 (TCL 15 9 obv. iii 25′–30′ // PBS X 2 9 rev. i 21–6 ^{d}iš-me-^{d}da-gan dumu ^{d}da-gan-na-me-en | ^{d}en-lil$_2$ lugal kur-kur-ra-ke$_4$ | [eĝir a]-⌜ma⌝-ru ur$_3$-ra-ta | [u$_4$ du$_{10}$-du$_{10}$-ga]-ni-še$_3$ maš$_2$-e ḫe$_2$-bi$_2$-in-pa$_3$-de$_3$ | [e$_2$-kur-še$_3$] igi ḫul$_2$ ḫe$_2$-em-ši-in-⌜bar⌝ | [ki-en]-gi-re gu$_3$ zi-de$_3$-eš ⌜ḫu⌝-[mu-un-de$_2$] 'I am Išme-Dagan, son of Dagan, whom Enlil, the lord of all the lands, after the flood had swept over, chose by extispicy on his most favourable day. He looked at the Ekur happily indeed, spoke approvingly to Sumer' (Langdon 1917: 149; Römer 1965: 46; Flückiger-Hawker 1999: 66–7).

[22] See van Dijk 1964: 32; Römer 1965: 70 n. 348; Jacobsen 1981: 527.

3 in those years, in those far remote years;
4 in those days, the intelligent one, the one of elaborate words, the wise one, who lived in the land;
5 the man from Šuruppak, the intelligent one, the one of elaborate words, the wise one, who lived in the land;
6 the man from Šuruppak, gave instructions to his son;
7 the man from Šuruppak, the son of Ubār-Tutu;
8 gave instructions to his son Ziusudra:
9 'My son, let me give instructions; let my instructions be taken!
10 Ziusudra, let me speak a word to you; let attention be paid to them!
11 Don't neglect my instructions!
12 Don't transgress the words I speak!'[23]

By comparison, the Early Dynastic III versions from Abū Ṣalābīkh and Adab (see Alster 2005: 176–7, 196) contain neither the three-tier adverbial expression in the opening lines, nor u$_4$-ba 'In those days' (line 4) to mark the transition from the prologue to the main body of the text, nor the name Ziusudra. These elements were evidently added together with the mythological prologue and the allusion to the Flood during the Old Babylonian period when the text underwent updating. As seen above, the *Instructions of Ur-Ninurta* likewise joins the mythological prologue to a didactic composition, but with a hymnic section dealing with the installation of Ur-Ninurta in between. The purpose of updating the *Instructions of Šuruppak* was probably to make this didactic text conform to the prevalent literary style and the chronographical scheme of the time, and to lend to its wisdom teaching a higher status of antiquity and authority.

As a result of the literary and conceptual updating, the normal life setting of the Early Dynastic III versions of this didactic text has acquired a primeval framework, as indicated by the three-tier adverbial expression in lines 1–3. The Old Babylonian version basically follows the same temporal presentation as found in the prologue of the *Instructions of Ur-Ninurta* (lines 1–4). Though there is no explicit reference to the Flood, as one can find in line 4 of the *Instructions of Ur-Ninurta*, the presence of Ziusudra, the Sumerian name of the Flood hero, indicates that the Flood as a primeval event is conceived as the starting point of the temporal sequence in this text. The family from which this wisdom teaching allegedly originated has been turned into the last antediluvian dynasty. Likewise, the instructions passed on from the father to the

[23] u$_4$ re-a u$_4$ su$_3$-ra$_2$ re-a | ĝi$_6$ re-a ĝi$_6$ bad-ra$_2$ re-a | mu re-a mu su$_3$-ra$_2$ re-a | u$_4$-ba ĝeštu$_2$-tuku inim-galam inim-zu-a kalam-ma ti-la-a | šuruppak^{ki} ĝeštu$_2$-tuku inim-galam inim-zu-a kalam-ma ti-la-a | šuruppak^{ki}-e dumu-ni-ra na na-mu-un-ri-ri | šuruppak^{ki} dumu ubar-tu-tu-ke$_4$ | zi-u$_4$-su$_3$-ra$_2$ dumu-ni-ra na na-mu-un-ri-ri | dumu-ĝu$_{10}$ na ga-ri na-ri-ĝu$_{10}$ ḫe$_2$-dab$_5$ | zi-u$_4$-su$_3$-ra$_2$ inim ga-ra-ab-d[u$_{11}$] ĝizzal ḫe$_2$-em-ši-ak | na-ri-ga-ĝu$_{10}$ šu nam-bi$_2$-bar-re | inim du$_{11}$-ga-ĝu$_{10}$ na-ab-ta-bal-e-de$_3$ (Alster 2005: 226–40).

son have also become part of the wisdom from high antiquity, i.e. antediluvian wisdom, the pursuit of which became a major theme in Sumerian and Babylonian Gilgameš traditions (e.g. the *Death of Bilgames* and the Standard Babylonian version of the *Gilgameš Epic*).

W-B 62 version of SKL *(Langdon 1923b: 251–9)*

This chronographical source contains the antediluvian section, listing only the names of the rulers in each of the five antediluvian cities and the number of years they reigned. The descriptive formulae are restricted to the summary of the number of ruler(s) and years of his/their reign in each city and the final summary of the entire antediluvian era in the closing line. Only the rulers in the last antediluvian dynasty in the city Šuruppak are provided with the familial relationship, which evidently derived from the *Instructions of Šuruppak*. But the genealogical style of this familial relationship and the chronographical style of this king list as a whole are based on those in the *SKL* proper (see the *USKL*).

The temporal setting is antediluvian from a chronographical perspective. The Flood stands as the last, climactic event that brought the antediluvian era to an end. It seems that once the flood catastrophe had been considered as a primeval event in Sumerian literary traditions around the time of Ur-Ninurta, the temporal perspective on this event in some traditions gradually shifted from what took place *after* the Flood (e.g. the *Instructions of Ur-Ninurta* 4 eĝir a-ma-ru ba-ĝar-ra-[a-ta] 'after the Flood had swept over') to what had happened *prior to* it (e.g. line 18: lugal [*pa*]-*nu* a-ma-ru 'kings [be]fore the Flood' in W-B 62). Attempts at reconstruction of, or speculation on, what had happened before the Flood were made in earnest especially when the Flood motif was adopted in the chronographical and literary sources. As the Flood became the watershed in the chronographical time line in the *SKL*, efforts began to be made to extend and apply the chronographical framework of the *SKL* proper (i.e. the original list such as the *USKL* without any reference to the Flood) to the time prior to the Flood, until the whole antediluvian section was constructed.

W-B 444 version of SKL *(Jacobsen 1939)*

While the antediluvian section may exist independently as seen in the case of W-B 62, it is joined with the king list proper in chronographical sources such as W-B 444.[24] Compared with W-B 62, the antediluvian section in W-B 444 is more developed in style and form. Not only have more stylistic formulae in

[24] Compare the *Dynastic Chronicle* (Glassner 2004: 126–34).

line with the king list proper been inserted, the opening line of the king list proper has also been added to the beginning of the antediluvian section [nam]-lugal an-ta e$_{11}$-de$_{3}$-a-ba 'When kingship came down from heaven' (line 1). Furthermore, the allusion to the Flood as the watershed in the chronology has also been inserted between the antediluvian section and the king list proper: a-ma-ru ba-ur$_{3}$-«ra-ta» | eĝir a-ma-ru ba-ur$_{3}$-ra-ta 'Then the Flood swept over. After the Flood had swept over' (lines 39–40). In such a chronographical framework, the primeval time of origins, specifically with regard to the establishment of kingship, had to take place twice. The first time was in the beginning of the world, with the second time immediately following the Flood which had allegedly swept away the entire antediluvian establishment. Line 39 a-ma-ru ba-ur$_{3}$-«ra-ta» 'Then the Flood swept over' serves as the concluding remark for the antediluvian section; while line 40 eĝir a-ma-ru ba-ur$_{3}$-ra-ta 'After the Flood had swept over' functions as the new introductory formula for the king list proper, which is now the postdiluvian section (see the *Rulers of Lagaš* 1).[25] The traditional introductory formula of *SKL* nam-lugal an-ta e$_{11}$-de$_{3}$-a-ba 'After kingship had descended from heaven' is now relegated to the second place (line 41 in W-B 444).

As already pointed out earlier, the opening line of *USKL* ⸢nam⸣-lugal ⸢an-ta⸣ e$_{11}$-da-ba 'When kingship descended from heaven' serves primarily to legitimize the particular type of political ideology and historical vision of this chronographical tradition. The antediluvian section in W-B 444 performs a similar function. As the pattern of kingship or hegemony originally embedded in the *SKL* proper (now the postdiluvian section) is established in the antediluvian section, the political ideology and historical vision of *SKL* gains renewed credibility because the antediluvian era is considered as a time of high antiquity and prestige.

The Rulers of Lagaš *(Sollberger 1967: 279–91)*

This text, composed in a scribal school (line 200), contains an elaborate mythological prologue (lines 1–67) to be followed by a chronographical section listing only the rulers of Lagaš (lines 99–199).[26] The way the prologue was presented is instructive:

1 After the Flood had swept over,
2 and the destruction of the land had been brought about;
3 when humankind was made to endure,

[25] Compare Hallo (1963*b*: 57) who considered line 40 of W-B 444 as 'transitional' from the antediluvian section to the king list proper.

[26] Lines 68–98 are missing between the end of obv. ii and the beginning of rev. iii on the tablet, see Sollberger (1967: 288–9).

4 and the seed of humankind was preserved,
5 and the black-headed people rose on their own accord;
6 After An and Enlil
7 had called the name of humankind
8 and established rulership;
9 but when kingship, the crown of the cities,
10 had not yet come out from heaven.[27]

Evidently, as a stylistic and temporal device, the expression eĝir a-ma-ru ba-ur₃-ra-ta 'After the Flood had swept over' has replaced the three-tier adverbial clause u₄ re-a-ta ... ĝi₆ re-a-ta ... mu re-a-ta ... 'In those days ..., in those nights ..., in those years ...' (or its variants) to stand at the beginning of the prologue and to introduce the starting point of the temporal sequence.[28] Conceptually, it is the Flood, rather than the separation of heaven and earth or the fixing of destinies, that is selected as the first primeval event from which the temporal sequence of the text starts.

The following lines deal with the resumption of the primeval time in order to restore different aspects of civilization. Note that humankind was preserved during the Flood (lines 3–5), so that it did not have to be created again, though lines 6–7 seem to suggest a second creation of humankind (Sollberger 1967: 282).

Stylistically, the primeval character of the temporal setting is also signalled by the ample use of negations in the descriptions of the living conditions of human beings and their society (lines 6–13, 17–37). The use of negations is even extended into the chronographical section (lines 107–8). Negations are used, as usual, as a dynamic technique, so as to highlight the epoch-making and creative achievements of the chief deity Ninĝirsu and the rulers of Lagaš who reversed the negative conditions.

Judging from the temporal sequence of the mythological prologue of this text, it becomes clear that the Flood as a primeval event has been promoted both stylistically and conceptually to the first position in narration, so much so that even the primeval era of origins is now relegated to a position in the text after the Flood in the narrative sequence (see Van Seters 1989: 53), though all these shuf-flings are done ingeniously in terms of the temporal sequence, given that the primeval time of origins had to start anew after the Flood.

The chronographical section seems to follow the *SKL* stylistically. Sollberger (1967: 279–80; see also Glassner 2004: 146) argues that the Lagaš text was

[27] [eĝir a-m]a-ru ba-ur₃-ra-ta | [u₃] ˹gel˺- le-eĝ₃ kur-ra-ke₄ ba-an-ĝar-ra-ta | ˹nam-lu₂˺-ulu₃ da-re-eš i-ak-a-ba | numun nam-lu₂-˹ulu₃˺ im-mi-in-tak₄-a-ba | uĝ₃ saĝ ge₆-ga ni₂-bi-a im-mi-in-il₂-la-a-ba | u₄ an-ne₂ ᵈen-lil₂-le | nam-lu₂-ulu₃ mu-bi sa₄-a-ta | u₃ nam-ensi₂ in-˹ĝar-ra˺-ta | nam-˹lugal˺ aga ˹iri-am₃˺ | an-t[a nu]-ub-ta-an-e₃-[a-ba] (Sollberger 1967: 280–91).
[28] Compare the prologue of the *Instructions of Ur-Ninurta* where eĝir a-ma-ru ba-ĝar-ra-[a-ta] 'after the Flood had swept over' is still second to the three-tier adverbial expression.

composed in reaction to the W-B 444 version of *SKL* which omits Lagaš and its rulers entirely. While the *SKL* chronicles the movement of kingship from one city to another, the Lagaš text is fully devoted to documenting the accomplishments of the chief deity of Lagaš, Ninĝirsu, and the rules in Lagaš from the primeval time to the time of Gudea. Ideologically, the Lagaš text attempted to show that contrary to the transient exercise of kingship in other cities as recorded in *SKL*, kingship or rulership in Lagaš is 'permanent and uninterrupted—even though it was invested in different families it remained always in Lagaš' (Sollberger 1967: 279). And the exercise of kingship or rulership in Lagaš was not manifested in military feats as shown in the *SKL* for the dynasties it records, but primarily in cultural achievements related to the development of agriculture, irrigation, religion, and writing. Similar to the *SKL*, however, the Lagaš text traces its political and cultural history back to the primeval time of origins, but after the Flood. The text stresses that kingship or rulership in Lagaš had not been interrupted since then. The choice of the Flood as the starting point is also deliberate, so as to highlight, again, the epoch-making and creative achievements of Ninĝirsu and the rulers of Lagaš. This is the same destruction-restoration rhetoric as used in the *Instructions of Ur-Ninurta*.

In addition to [eĝir a-m]a-ru ba-ur_3-ra-ta 'after the Flood had swept over' (line 1), other temporal devices used in the text include: u_4-ba 'In those days' (line 14) to indicate the time of the primeval era when human beings still enjoyed longevity; u_4-ba 'In those days' (line 17) to indicate the time when Lagaš was suffering from drought and famine due to lack of irrigation systems; ⸢u_4⸣-bi-a 'In those days; then' (line 57) to mark the time when Ninĝirsu caused barley to grow; u_4-ba 'In those days' (line 107) to mark the time when there was no writing; u_4-ba 'In those days' (line 109) with an unclear function due to the broken context.

The Death of Bilgames, *the Mê-Turan version (Cavigneaux and Al-Rawi 2000; Veldhuis 2001: 141–7)*

This Sumerian composition offers an aetiological story on how Gilgameš became a governor and a judicial authority in the Netherworld. In the meantime, it also tries to tackle the theological question as to why Gilgameš could not escape death in spite of being a son of the goddess Ninsun and having an unparalleled career. Judging from the relevant passage quoted below, the text attests to the convergence of several strands of tradition: mythological compositions dealing with the primeval time of origins, antediluvian traditions, the Flood epic, and the Gilgameš tradition.

The temporal setting of the story is legendary and mythical, as the story in the main part tells how the legendary hero on his sickbed dreamed of the Anunna gods determining his final fate. In his dream, the gods reviewed Gilgameš's heroic deeds and achievements in his career. His two important achievements, as far as the gods were concerned, were his establishment of temples and his restoration of the lost cultic rites with the antediluvian *mes* which he retrieved through his journey to visit the Flood hero Ziusudra (lines 56–60; 147–51). On account of these achievements, Enlil advised them not to let Gilgameš be taken away by death. In response, Enki reminded the divine assembly of the decision made immediately after the Flood:

159 In those days, in those distant days,
160 in those nights, in those distant nights,
161 in those years, in those distant years,
162 after the assembly had made the Flood sweep over,
163 it was the seed of humankind that we were to destroy.
164 Among us I was the only one for life$^?$, and he remained alive$^?$.
165 Ziusudra kept the name of humankind alive$^?$.
166 Since that day I swore by the life of heaven and earth,
167 since that day I swore that humankind shall not live forever. . . .
168 Now, this is what is to be shown to Bilgames,
169 He cannot be spared because of his mother.[29] (// lines 69–79)

The reminiscence of the decision made after the Flood is to affirm that Ziusudra was the only person whom the divine assembly had allowed to continue to enjoy eternal life on account of his contribution to save the human race and thus the divine society as well. But no one from the generations born after the Flood could have the same privilege, because, according to this Sumerian tradition (see also the *Atra-hasīs Epic*), death had been instituted after the Flood. Therefore Gilgameš could not escape the fate of mortality regardless of his half-divine birth. This episode of Gilgameš's dream contains two separate allusions to the Flood: one stresses the contribution of Gilgameš in restoring the cultic rites through the antediluvian knowledge which he brought back from the Flood hero; the other emphasizes the immutable decision of Enki that after the Flood human beings were not to have eternal life again. The function of the second allusion overrides that of the first.

The style of recalling the primeval time in the first four lines of Enki's reply to Enlil in the passage quoted above is very similar to the opening lines of the *Instructions of Ur-Ninurta* (lines 1–4). Both texts have the three-tier adverbial expression before the temporal clause related to the Flood. Together with lines 1–10 of the *Instructions of Šuruppak*, all these three texts make allusions to the

[29] u$_4$-re-ta u$_4$-⸢su$_3$⸣-[da-re-ta] | ĝi$_6$-re-ta ĝi$_6$-⸢su$_3$⸣-[da-re-ta] | mu-re-ta mu- su$_3$-[da-re-ta] | pu-uḫ-rum a-ma-ru ba-NIR-ra-[ta] | numun nam-lu$_2$-ulu$_3$-ur$_2$ ḫa-la-me-de$_3$ x [. . .] | murub$_4$-me-a zi saĝ-dili-me-en ⸢nam-ti⸣-[am$_3$] | zi-us$_2$-<ra> dili mu nam-lu$_2$-ulu$_3$ nam-ti-am$_3$ | u$_4$-bi-ta zi an-na zi ki-a mu-un-pa$_3$-da-nam | u$_4$-bi-ta nam-lu$_2$-ulu$_3$-ur$_2$ nu-mu-ti-am$_3$ mu-ni-pa$_3$ | e-ne-še$_3$ ^{d}GIŠ.BIL$_2$-ga-mes igi-bi ba-ni-ib-tu | šu nam-ama-a-ni nu-mu-un-da-TE.TE-ed-nam (the Mê-Turan version; Cavigneaux and Al-Rawi 2000: 31; Veldhuis 2001: 141–7).

Flood after the three-tier adverbial expression. In all three cases (see also the *Rulers of Lagaš*), the Flood is treated as the first event in the temporal framework. The reason for this choice in the current text is that the Flood was the decisive event that changed human destiny regarding immortality/mortality.

In addition to the three-tier adverbial expression (lines 159–61) and the following temporal clause (line 162), other stylistic devices used to mark the temporal sequence in the above-quoted passage include: u_4-bi-ta 'since that day' (lines 166, 167) to stress the time when the decision was made for human beings not to have eternal life; e-en-$še_3$ 'now' (line 168) to make the transition from the time of the Flood to the time of judging the case of Gilgameš.

ELA *(Kramer 1952a: 40–3; Vanstiphout 2003: 88–9; Mittermayer 2009: 148–9)*

This is one of the Sumerian narrative compositions that celebrate the heroic deeds of the legendary rulers of Unug (Enmerkar, Lugalbanda, and Gilgameš) in rivalry with the mountainous region Aratta and the Kiš dynasty (Vanstiphout 2003: 1). The contest in this text starts with Enmerkar demanding from Aratta submission to Unug and supply of precious raw materials for the embellishment of temples in Sumer. Refusing to submit, the lord of Aratta challenged Enmerkar with a riddle, which led to the subsequent three cycles of contest, through which Enmerkar emerged as the winner. The contest demonstrates not only Enmerkar's 'superior intelligence and cleverness' but also the technological superiority of Sumer in wheat and textile production, in manufacturing, and in the invention of the cuneiform writing system (Vanstiphout 2003: 54) for resolving the seemingly impossible tasks at hand.

The temporal setting of the story mixes the primeval with the legendary. According to the *USKL* or the W-B 444 version of *SKL*, the first Unug dynasty comes after the primeval time. But in order to highlight Unug/Sumer's precedence or Enmerkar's superiority, the story is cast in the primeval time of origins in several of its main themes or motifs, as can be seen by both content and style. The overarching theme of the text is the invention of trade or commerce, the lack of which led to the events of the story. In the prologue section (lines 6–21), one finds the description of this condition of lack of trade in a series of negative statements:

> In those days, when the destinies were fixed, the Great Princes granted Unug-Kulab's Eana head-lifting pride. Opulence, carp floods and rains that bring forth dappled wheat abounded in Unug-Kulab. The land Dilmun did not yet exist, when the Eana of Unug-Kulab was already well-founded, and the Gipar of Holy Inana and Kulab, the Brickwork, glinted like silver in the lode. [. . .] was not yet

> *imported*; there was no trading; [. . .] was not *exported*; there was no commerce. [Gold], silver, copper, tin, blocks of lapis lazuli, [and the mountain ores,] were not yet brought down from the highlands. [. . .] there was no bathing for the festival; [. . .] were no sitting [. . .].

This passage depicts the time when Unug was blessed with abundance of wheat production, while the mountain region had precious metals. But there was no trade relation to facilitate the exchange of these materials which each region needed from the other: Unug needed the precious metals and stones for the embellishment of temples in Sumer, while Aratta needed wheat to cope with famine. But at the end of the story, trade agreements were established between the two regions with the help of the gods. The reference to the existence of Unug prior to Dilmun as made in lines 12–13 is meaningful in the context of the establishment of trade. Dilmun, as already pointed out by Vanstiphout (2003: 12), is 'a symbol for foreign trade', presumably due to its ideal quay (see *Enki and Ninmah*). Thus this reference not only indicates that Unug existed prior to Dilmun, but also that the establishment of trade between Unug and Aratta, allegedly as a result of the pioneering efforts of Enmerkar and Unug, albeit initially in an attempt to impose hegemony over Aratta, pre-dated that of Dilmun, regardless of Dilmun's legendary status of antiquity.

Line 58 'When I then bring back the powers from Eridu' ($eridu^{ki}$-ta me de_6-a-mu-ne; compare line 89) expresses Enmerkar's intention to transfer the divine powers, especially in terms of lordship (nam-en-na; line 59), from Eridu to Unug. Eridu is acknowledged here as the first city that received the divine endowment of these powers. As may be recalled, in *Inana and Enki*, it was Inana who transferred the powers from Eridu to Unug (see the repeated use of the same Sumerian verb de_6 'to carry' in *Inana and Enki*, segm. I 1–106). In the present text, this feat was attributed to Enmerkar. But this event is supposed to have taken place after the establishment of trade between Unug and Aratta in the light of the temporal sequence of the story.

Lines 135–55 contain the so-called spell of Nudimmud, which, according to Vanstiphout (2003: 65, 93–4), conveys the prospect of the Sumerian language becoming the *lingua franca*, in the form of prophecy based on Enmerkar's ambition to unify the broader Mesopotamian region under the cultural influence of Sumer. The style of negation found in lines 136–9 'On that day, there will be no snake, no scorpion, there will be no hyena, nor lion, there will be neither (wild) dog nor wolf, and thus there will be neither fear nor trembling, for man will then have no enemy' is often used in Sumerian mythological compositions for depicting the primeval time of origins. Though the Sumerian language becoming the *lingua franca* is referred to as a future event in the narrated time, from the perspective of the author this was already a past event that took place in the primeval time of origins. Underlying this temporal conception is an aetiological motive to explain the supremacy of the Sumerian language during the time of the author. The invention of the cuneiform writing on clay tablets by Enmerkar in order for the messenger to deliver the solution to the last riddle (lines 503–6), an event which also presumably took place in the primeval time of origin, is yet another aetiological story, explaining the prevalent use of cuneiform as an international means of writing for administrative, business, and communication purposes during the time of the author (Vanstiphout 2003: 54). Other technological inventions, such as wheat and textiles production and manufacturing of goods that are attributed to Enmerkar with the help of Nisaba and Enki, likewise represent an aetiological motive to account for these technologies as originating from Unug in the primeval time.

It is still a matter of debate as to whether the flood term (a-ma-ru) mentioned in lines 564–76, where the lord of Aratta praised Inana for saving Aratta from bowing to the hegemony of Unug, refers to the Flood.

564 Inana, Lady of all the lands,
565 like a rising torrent, encircles for them (the people of Aratta)!
566 The people are those who were chosen from (other) peoples.
567 They are people whom Dumuzi made stand out from (other) peoples,
568 they are ones who firmly established the holy words of Inana!
569 Let Urigiĝala, the house-born slave of Dumuzi. . . .
570 . . . [. . .]
571 They were those who had stood in . . . the flood/Flood.
572 After the flood/Flood had swept over,
573 Inana, Lady of all the lands,
574 out of her great love for Dumuzi,
575 sprinkled the water of life upon them,
576 and make the Land (Sumer) subject to them![30]

Mittermayer (2009: 86–9, 308–9) argues that this passage contains a reference to the antediluvian era. According to her, the narrator of the story tried to draw a parallel between what the ancient people of Aratta had experienced at the time of the Flood and what the people of Aratta in the story were experiencing. She further suggests that the passage is related to the antediluvian king list tradition in which Dumuzi is listed as a ruler from the city Badtibira.

However, there is no hint in the context of the above passage that the Sumerian term a-ma-ru alludes to the Flood as depicted in the *Atra-hasīs Epic* or referred to in the chronographical traditions such as W-B 444. For the

[30] ^{d}inana nin kur-kur-ra-ke$_4$ | a maḫ e$_3$-a-gin$_7$ mu-un-na-NIĜIN | lu$_2$-bi-ne lu$_2$ lu$_2$-ta suḫ-a | lu$_2$ ^{d}dumu-zi-de$_3$ lu$_2$-ta e$_3$-a-me-eš | inim ku$_3$ ^{d}inana ki-bi-še$_3$ ĝar-ĝar-me-eš | ur igi-ĝal$_2$-la ⸢emedu⸣ ^{d}dumu-zi-da ḫe$_2$-ši-im-⸢x(-x)⸣ | ⸢x x x x x x x x⸣ [(x) x] | ⸢x a⸣-ma-ru-ka gub-ba-me-eš | [eĝ]ir a-ma-ru ba-⸢ur$_3$⸣-ra-ta | ^{d}inana nin kur-kur-ra-ke$_4$ ¦ nam-gal ki aĝ$_2$ ⸢^{d}⸣dumu-zi-da-ke$_4$ | a nam-ti-la-ka m[u]-un-ne-su$_3$-su$_3$ | gu$_2$ kalam-ma-ka [ĝ]eš mu-un-ne-en-ĝal$_2$ (Mittermayer 2009: 148–9).

current author, most likely the term is used metaphorically, referring to the catastrophic drought and famine in conjunction with the imposition of hegemony by Unug which the people of Aratta had just experienced in the story.[31] The people of Aratta were delivered from their plight thanks to a timely storm which relieved the drought and brought about the harvest (lines 542–55). This recent experience seems to be mythologized in the above-quoted passage through a brief mythological tale involving Inana and her lover Dumuzi (see also *Inana and the Numun-Grass*). This tale presumably existed earlier than, and independently of, the antediluvian king list tradition (Chen 2012).

The following temporal expressions are found in the text: u$_4$ re-a nam ba-[tar-ra-ba] 'In those days, when the destinies were fixed' (line 6) to mark the primeval setting of the story; u$_4$-ba 'in those days' (line 33) to mark the transition from the prologue to the main body of the text and to introduce the protagonist Enmerkar; [x] NE u$_4$ šu$_2$-uš-ta um-[ta]-ab-il$_2$-ke$_4$-eš | [x] NE u$_4$ te-en-e um-ma-[te]-e-ta 'Having carried [*their burdens*$^?$] all day, [. . .] when the day has drawn to an end' (lines 97–8) as part of Inana's speech to Enmerkar to indicate that the people of Aratta would support Enmerkar's demand for Aratta's submission; u$_4$-ba 'on that day' (lines 136, 141, 147) in the spell of Nudimmud to indicate the future day when the Sumerian language would become the *lingua franca*; ĝi$_6$-u$_3$-na-ka 'at night' . . . an-bar$_7$-gan$_2$-ka 'at daybreak' (lines 158–9; 161–2) as part of Enmerkar's instructions to the messenger to travel to Aratta without delay; u$_4$ im-zal ⸢^{d}utu⸣ im-ta-e$_3$-a-ra | ^{d}utu kalam-⸢ma-ka saĝ x-x-il$_2$⸣ 'When day broke, to the rising Sun, the Sun of the Land raised his head' (lines 308–9) to mark the time when Enmerkar joined the Tigris and Euphrates as part of the solution to the first riddle; u$_4$-bi-a 'at that time' (line 317) to mark the time when Nisaba assisted Enmerkar to solve the first riddle; ⸢eĝir⸣-ba 'after' (line 363) with an unclear function due to the broken context; u$_4$ im-zal 'when day broke' (line 391) and i$_3$-ne-še$_3$ 'now' (line 392) to mark the time when the lord of Aratta was to pose the second challenge; u$_4$-ba 'at that time' (line 497) to mark the time when Enmerkar was to invent cuneiform writing to convey his message; u$_4$-bi-ta inim im-ma gub-bu nu-ub-ta-ĝal$_2$-la | i$_3$-ne-še$_3$ ^{d}utu u$_4$ ne-a ur$_5$ ḫe$_2$-en-na-nam-ma-am$_3$ 'Before that day, there had been no putting words on clay; but now, when the sun rose on that day—so it was' (lines 504–5); u$_4$-ba 'At that moment' (line 542) to mark the time when the storm god Iškur intervened to relieve Aratta of drought and famine; eĝir a-ma-ru ba-ur$_3$-ra-ta 'After the flood/Flood had swept over' (line 572); u$_4$-bi-ta 'Since that day; after that day' (line 586) to mark the time when Inana helped Unug and Aratta establish trade with each other.

[31] See a maḫ e$_3$-a-gin$_7$ 'like a rising torrent' in line 565 which is another example of figurative and mythical use of a meteorological phenomenon in the immediate context.

As pointed out by Vanstiphout (2003: 1), though 'the actual form of the texts and the tablets themselves date almost exclusively from the Isin-Larsa period (2017–1763 B.C.E.)', this and other compositions related to the legendary rulers of Unug originated in the Ur III period. 'The ideological reasoning involved runs somewhat like this', says Vanstiphout (2003: 8): 'in the remote times of the glorious rulers of Unug the foundations were laid for Sumer's preeminence among nations—and this preeminence persists in the present Ur III state' (see also Michalowski 2010: 7–25). The reference to the Flood was supposedly included during the Isin-Larsa period when the text took on its current form.

Inana and the Numun-Grass *(Kramer 1980: 87–97)*

This mythological composition is an aetiological myth explaining the origin of the loathsome grass and how it was controlled by Inana with the help of Dumuzi. The first half of the composition traces the mythological origin of the grass back to the primeval time, which is made clear in the prologue section.

1 The *abba* instructed, the *abba* [instructed]:
2 When the rain rained, when the walls were demolished,
3 when it rained scorching potsherds,
4 when one confronted another defiantly.
5 when there was copulation—he also copulated,
6 when there was kissing—he also kissed,
7 when the rain said: 'I will rain,'
8 when the wall said: 'I will rain.'[32]
9 when the Flood said: 'I will sweep everything away.'
10 Heaven impregnated (lit. spoke), Earth gave birth,
11 She gave birth also to the *numun*-grass.
12 Earth gave birth, Heaven impregnated (lit. spoke),
13 She gave birth also to the *numun*-grass.
14 His luxuriant reeds carried fire.
15 They who defied it, who defied it,
16 The *umma* who had survived the days,
17 the *abba* who had survived the days,
18 the chief *gala* priest who had survived the years,
19 whoever had survived the Flood—

[32] See 'When it had then said, "I will demolish walls"' by Kramer (1980: 93), who thought that the subject im-e 'the rain' is omitted by the scribe 'probably for poetic effect'. Kramer's rendering involves emending not only e$_2$-gar$_8$-e 'the wall' for im-e, but also ga-šeĝ$_3$ 'I will rain' for ga-gul 'I will destroy' in line 8; compare e$_2$-gar$_8$ ba-gul-la-ba 'when the walls were demolished' in line 2. In any case, line 8 seems to be corrupt.

20 the *numun*-grass crushed them with labour,
21 crushed them with labour, and made them crouch in the dust-heap.[33]

In Sumerian mythological prologues, stormy weather is used metaphorically to depict the cosmic union or reproduction (cosmogony), as seen in mythological compositions from the Early Dynastic III period such as the *Barton Cylinder* i 7–14 and AO 4153 (NFT 180 = Sollberger Corpus Ukg. 15) ii 2. As pointed out by van Dijk (1964: 21), this primeval event was conceived as both 'le prototype de toute violence destructive' and 'naissance de la vie'. While the Early Dynastic III sources only use the storm, lightning, and thundering images to portray the cosmic union, *Inana and the Numun-Grass* adds the flood image. The author of this composition did not seem to distinguish between the primeval storm which was used traditionally for the depiction of the cosmic union of Heaven and Earth, on the one hand, and the primeval flood as a possibly new motif for introducing the primeval time of origins, on the other. Together they are represented as one mythical event that starts off the temporal and narrative sequence. The mixing of these two literary motifs in this composition suggests that when the flood catastrophe was first regarded as a primeval event it was associated with the cosmic beginning (cosmogony) rather than the closing and climactic event in the primeval time of origins (as seen in the *Atra-hasīs Epic* or the W-B 444 version of *SKL*).

In terms of the stylistic and temporal devices used for introducing the primeval time of origins, note that line 9 of *Inana and the Numun-Grass*, u$_4$ a-ma-ru ĝe$_{26}$-e ga-ur$_3$-ur$_3$ im-mi-in-du$_{11}$-ga-ba 'when the Flood said: "I will sweep everything away"', may allude to the temporal clause eĝir a-ma-ru ba-ur$_3$-ra-ta 'After the Flood had swept over'. The temporal clause in line 9, couched in the mythological prologue of the primeval time of origins, makes it explicit that the term a-ma-ru here refers to the primeval flood. The passage um-ma u$_4$-da ba-ra-ab-tak$_4$-a | ab-ba u$_4$-da ba-ra-ab-tak$_4$-a | gala-maḫ mu-da ba-ra-ab-tak$_4$-a 'The *umma* who had survived the days, the *abba* who had survived the days, the chief *gala* priest who had survived the years' in lines 16–18 is presumably an allusion to the three-tier adverbial expression u$_4$-re-a ... ĝi$_6$-re-a ... mu-re-a ... 'In those days ..., in those nights ..., in those years ...'. Unlike what we have seen in the *Instructions of Ur-Ninurta*,

[33] ab-ba na mu-un-di ab-ba na mu-un-[di] | im ba-šeĝ$_3$-ĝa$_2$-ba e$_2$-ĝar$_8$ ba-gul-la-[ba] | šika bar$_7$-bar$_7$-ra ba-šeĝ$_3$-ĝa$_2$-ba | lu$_2$-ra lu$_2$ gi$_4$-ba gaba ba-ri-a-ba | mu ba-du$_{11}$-ga-ba in-ga-an-du$_{11}$ | še ba-su-ub-ba in-ga-an-su-ub | u$_4$ im-e ĝe$_{26}$-e ga-šeĝ$_3$ im-mi-in-du$_{11}$-ga-ba | u$_4$ e$_2$-gar$_8$-e ĝe$_{26}$-e ga-šeĝ$_3$ im-mi-in-du$_{11}$-ga-ba | u$_4$ a-ma-ru ĝe$_{26}$-e ga-ur$_3$-ur$_3$ im-mi-in-du$_{11}$-ga-ba | an in-du$_{11}$ ki in-tu-ud | $^{u}{}_2$numun$_2$ in-ga-an-tu-ud | ki in-tu-ud an in-du$_{11}$ | $^{u}{}_2$numun$_2$ in-ga-an-tu-ud | gi lum-lum-ma-ni izi ba-an-la$_2$ | ri-a-ri-a-bi gaba ba-ri-a-bi | um-ma u$_4$-da ba-ra-ab-tak$_4$-a | ab-ba u$_4$-da ba-ra-ab-tak$_4$-a | gala-maḫ mu-da ba-ra-ab-tak$_4$-a | mu-lu a-ma-ru-ta ba-ra-ab-tak$_4$-a | $^{u}{}_2$numun$_2$ kiĝ$_4$-gi$_4$-a ba-an-gaz | kiĝ$_2$-gi$_4$-a ba-an-gaz saḫar-ḪUB$_2$-be$_2$ ba-tuš (Kramer 1980: 88–94).

the current Sumerian composition places the temporal clause related to the Flood prior to the allusion to the three-tier adverbial expression. What the above observations show is that while the Flood motif is conflated with the primeval storm motif symbolizing the violent but creative cosmic beginning, the temporal clause related to the Flood is gaining the upper hand over the three-tier expression.

The second half of the composition (lines 35–66) starts with temporal clauses that hark back to the opening lines quoted above: 'When the rain rained, when the walls were demolished, when it rained scorching potsherds; they who defied Dumuzi; the rain rained, the walls were demolished, the cowpen was demolished, the sheepfold was ripped out' (lines 35–9). These passages are followed by the natural explanation of the origin of the *numun*-grass as growing in the marsh areas by the banks of the Tigris and Euphrates after the heavy rain (lines 39–44).

The tracing of the mythical and natural origins of the *numun*-grass is for the purpose of keeping it under control, a common literary phenomenon as seen in Mesopotamian magical texts such as *An Incantation against Toothache* (CT 17 50) and *An Incantation against the Mote* (BAM 510 iv 41–5) (Foster 2005: 969, 995). The current text offers several views on how the control of the loathsome grass was done through magical and ritual means: by Inana setting a raven on the top of the grass bundle with the help of Dumuzi (lines 32–4); by Inana hurling a vicious storm on the head of the grass (line 62); and by Inana pronouncing the fate of the grass (lines 63–6). According to Kramer (1980: 91 n. 7), the association of Inana with the *numun*-grass in this text is presumably based on the long-known tradition that the grass 'was utilized for Inana's bed in the Sacred Marriage Rite . . . and that there may have been some connection between our myth and the ritual act'. If this was indeed the case, the *numun*-grass, which had little practical value, was finally subdued and utilized in the Inana cult. It is likely that the text was meant to be recited regularly in ritual settings in order to enact the mythical and magical power for controlling the grass.

Old Babylonian version of the Atra-hasīs Epic *(Lambert and Millard 1969)*

As convincingly demonstrated by Moran (1987: 245–55), the entire story is largely presented in the form of crisis and resolution. The first crisis is already announced in the opening lines I 1–6 (Plates 7 and 8):

1 When gods were (like) men,
2 they bore the work and carried the soil-bucket,
3 the drudgery of the gods was indeed great.
4 The forced labour was heavy, the misery was much.

5 The great Anunnaki, the seven,
6 were burdening the Igigi-gods with forced labour.[34]

The crisis eventually evolved into a rebellion against Enlil. To resolve the crisis, Enki proposed that the ringleader of the rebellion be slaughtered so that his flesh and blood could be mixed with the clay for the creation of human beings who might take the role of the labouring gods. Though this solution initially worked well, human beings in their boisterous growth eventually disturbed Enlil, thus triggering a new series of crises and resolutions. Though on the surface the crises manifested themselves as conflicts or confrontations between Enlil and humankind, essentially they were driven by the contests between Enlil (the god who had absolute power) and Enki (the god who embodied wisdom). To eliminate human disturbance, Enlil sent plague, drought, and famine to diminish their growth. But Enki sympathized with his human creatures and instructed his servant Atra-hasīs to ward off and survive the three rounds of devastation Enlil sent. Finally, in his fury and frustration, Enlil decided to launch the Flood to wipe out humankind entirely once for all. But Enki in his foresight saved Atra-hasīs and his family in the midst of the catastrophe so that the human race could start anew and carry on the tasks of the gods. Had Enki not done that, the same crisis that beset the divine world and Enlil in the beginning would undoubtedly recur. To prevent human beings from running into the same conflict with Enlil, various measures—including death, infant mortality, and the institutions of women devoted to religious services so that they would not marry and bear children—were set up to curb human population growth. The *Atra-hasīs Epic* represents a profound intellectual and theological work seeking to provide aetiological explanations for the human and social conditions in relation to the divine world.

The temporal setting of this composition is primarily antediluvian. The earliest event the story refers to is the allocation of cosmic territories by Anu, Enlil, and Enki (I 11–18). But the narration of this event is preceded by the announcement of the crisis regarding the heavy labour imposed on the Igigi gods by the Anunnaki (I 1–6). Though the imposition of heavy labour on the Igigi is temporally later than the event of the allocation of cosmic territories, it is this event that led to the subsequent series of crises and resolutions. As will be demonstrated in detail in Chapter 4, the author ingeniously used the motif of noise (*rigmu* or *ḫubūru*) to tie all the major events together and to provide a cause-and-effect structure in the temporal sequence of the story. The last narrated event of the story is the fixing of human destinies in order to control human population growth after the Flood (III vii 1–9).

[34] *inūma ilū awīlum* | *ublū dulla izbilū šupšikka* | *šupšik ilī rabīma* | *dullum kabit mād šapšāqum* | *rabûtum Anunnakkū sibittam* | *dullam ušazbalū* ^{d}*I⌈gigi⌉* (Lambert and Millard 1969: 42–3).

The temporal devices used in the text are as follows: the temporal clause *inūma ilū awīlum* | *ublū dulla izbilū šupšikka* 'When gods were (like) man, they bore the work and carried the soil-bucket' (I 1–2) to announce the first cause of the crises; [*šanātim im*]*nû ša šupšikki* | [. . .] x 40 *šanātim atram* | [x x *du*]*llam izbilū mūši u urri* 'They [cou]nted years of forced labour, excessive [. . .] for forty years [. . .] they bore the work night and day' (I 36–8) to indicate the length of time during which the Igigi gods had to bear the forced labour; *mišil maṣṣarti mūšum ibašši* 'It was night, halfway through the watch' (I 70, 72) to mark the time when the rebel gods surrounded Enlil's temple Ekur; [*u_4-mi-šam-m*]*a ir*-[*ṣe*-x (. . .)] x-*na-a-ṭu* '[Every day]. [. . .] . . .' (I 178) as part of Enki's speech to Enlil to indicate that every day there was an outcry or lament from the Igigi gods who were suffering from the heavy labour; *ina arhi sebūti u šapatti* 'On the first, seventh, and fifteenth day of the month' (I 206, 221) as part of Enki's instructions to the Anunna gods to indicate the time when Enki would make a purifying bath to prepare for the creation of human beings out of the flesh and blood of the slaughtered god; *aḫ-ri-a-t*[*i-iš u_4-mi up-pa iš-mu*]-⸢*u_2*⸣ 'In future [days] they [heard the drum]' (I 227) to signal the time of the existence of human beings probably through their heartbeat; *pānami* ^{d}*mami nišasīki* | *inanna bēl*[*et*] *kala ilī* | *lū š*[*um*]*ki* 'Formerly [we used to call] you "Mami", now let your n[am]e be "Mistress-of-All-the Gods" (Bēlet-kala-ilī)' (I 246–8) to mark the time of the name change of Mami due to her contribution to the creation of human beings; [*simānu*] *šīmati issû ešra arḫa* | *ešru arḫu illikamma* '[At the] destined [time$^{?}$], they summoned the tenth month. The tenth month arrived' (I 280–1) to indicate the length of pregnancy; 9 *ū*[*mi l*]*innadi libittum* 'Let the brick be in place for nine days' (I 294) and 9 *ūmī* [*lišš*]*akin ḫidûtum* 'Let there be rejoicing for nine days' (I 303) to indicate the length of time for the birth ritual; [*ul illikma* 600].600 mu-ḫi-a '[Twel]ve hundred years [had not gone by]' (I 352) to indicate the time that had elapsed between the creation of human beings and the beginning of conflict between human beings and Enlil; *ul illikma* 600.600 mu-ḫi-a 'Twelve hundred years had not yet gone by' (I 416; II i 1) to mark the interval between the end of the first cycle and the beginning of the second cycle of conflict between human beings and Enlil; *ina šērēti ibbara lišaznin* | *lištarriq ina mūšimma* | *lišaznin nalša* 'May he rain down mist in the morning, may he stealthily rain down dew in the night' (II ii 16–18; see the refrain II ii 30–2) as part of Enki's instructions to human beings to bribe the storm god Adad for relieving the drought; [*ū*]*mišamma ibtanakki* | [*m*]*uššaki izabbil* | [*in*]*a šērēti* 'Every day he would weep, bringing dream offerings in the morning' (II iii 4–6) and *anāku ina mūš*[*i* . . .] 'In the night I [. . .]' (II iii 24) to indicate that Atra-hasīs sought Enki's help by day and night; *ištīta šattam ikulā labīra* | *šanīta šattam u_2-na-ad/ṭ-d/ṭi-a nakkamtam* | *šaluštum šattum illik*[*amma*] | *ina bubūtim zīmūšina* [*ittakrū*] 'The first year they ate old grain, the second year they exhausted$^{?}$ their stores. When the third year came, their features [had changed] through hunger' (II iv

9–12) to depict the worsening famine as the years went by; *bā' abūbi* 7 *mūšīšu iqbīšu* 'He told him of the coming of the seven-day Flood' (III i 37) as part of Enki's speech to Atra-hasīs about the duration of the catastrophe; 7 *ūmī* 7 *mūš[iātim]* 'For seven days and seven nights' (III iv 24) to mark the actual duration of the catastrophe.

As seen previously in this chapter, Sumerian traditions from the Early Dynastic III period and the Ur III period had already explored the subject of the primeval time of origins on literary, intellectual, and ideological levels. Explorations as such are often presented in the form of crisis and resolution. The motif of the creation of human beings to relieve the gods of their toil, for example, can already be found in *Enki and Ninhursaĝa*, *Lugale*, and the *Song of the Hoe*. Natural and economic crises such as drought and famine and how the crises were resolved are common motifs (e.g. the *Barton Cylinder*, *Lugale*, *How Grain Came to Sumer*, the city laments). There are also ample cases of depictions of catastrophe, even in the image of storm and flood, as an inversion of creation (e.g. *Curse Agade*, *LSU*, *Year Name 22 of Ibbi-Suen*). Conflicts and contests among gods or mythical beings are also themes frequently found in Sumerian mythological compositions (e.g. *Lugale*, *Enki and Ninmah*, *Enki and Inana*). And the primeval era being the time when destinies were fixed is the most pivotal notion undergirding many of the literary, intellectual, and ideological explorations. Thus, literarily and conceptually, the *Atra-hasīs Epic* relied on previous Sumerian traditions to a substantial degree (see Lambert and Millard 1969: 15–27; Clifford 1994: 74–82).

But the reliance on traditions does not diminish the creativity of this monumental Babylonian literary production, which can be primarily seen in how the primeval events were arranged: the cause-and-effect sequence and the progression in crescendo are the two salient organizational features. Events are not only well connected so that one naturally led to another, with the innovative use of the motif of noise; they are also presented as moving in the direction of the final devastation: the Flood. Compared with the Sumerian compositions dealing with catastrophe such as *Curse Agade* and the city laments, the Babylonian Flood epic possesses a narrative sequence and a temporal scheme that are more structured.

In comparison with the adverbial expressions of time used in the Sumerian mythological compositions dealing with the primeval time of origins, the temporal markers used in the *Atra-hasīs Epic* are also more specific in terms of providing the exact length of days, months, and years for the narrated events.[35] Such specificity can already be seen in Sumerian chronographical

[35] Such temporal specificity can also be seen in the Old Babylonian version of the *Cuthean Legend of Naram-Suen*. The specific dating of the Flood underwent further development in the biblical account of the Flood in the *Book of Genesis* and *Berossos* which added calendrical calculations of the event (See Guillaume 2003: 55–82; Jacobus 2003: 83–114).

traditions such as the *SKL*. But as noted by Lambert and Millard (1969: 20–1), the antediluvian tradition represented by the *Atra-hasīs Epic* diverges substantially from the *SKL* (e.g. W-B 444 and W-B 62) that contains antediluvian history, especially with regard to the number of rulers (if Atra-hasīs is to be considered as an antediluvian ruler in the epic) and the length of the antediluvian period. The Sumerian chronographical sources and the Babylonian epic also differ conceptually: while the former views the Flood as bringing a total discontinuity to what had existed in the antediluvian era, the latter suggests that there is some continuity, especially given the survival of the Flood hero. Also different from W-B 444, the *Atra-hasīs Epic* views the antediluvian era as a time when human destinies were not permanently established. Instead, the era was a process through which human destinies were finally fixed. In W-B 444, patterns of human individual and social life, such as the limited human lifespan and the limited length of hegemony of each city, were already determined from the beginning of the world. But in the *Atra-hasīs Epic*, some of these patterns, such as human mortality, were fixed only after the Flood. Nonetheless, even W-B 444 acknowledges that the Flood had altered the human condition for the generations coming after it. Thus life expectancy has dropped substantially in the postdiluvian era. Lastly, in terms of functions, while the antediluvian era in W-B 444 was used to legitimize the political ideology and historical perspective of *SKL*, the antediluvian era in the *Atra-hasīs Epic* was meant to offer aetiological explanations for human and social conditions in general.

The Sumerian Flood Story *(Civil 1969: 140–5)*

Because of the lacuna of 36 lines in the first column of the tablet CBS 10673 + CBS 10867 (Plates 9 and 10), it is difficult to make sense of the meaning of the speech presumably made by Enki in i 37–46:

> . . . sets up . . . 'I will . . . the perishing of my humankind; for Nintu, I will stop the annihilation of my creatures, and I will return the people from their dwelling grounds. Let them build many cities so that I can refresh myself in their shade. Let them lay the bricks of many cities in pure places, let them establish places of divination in pure places, and when the fire-quenching . . . is arranged, the divine rites and lofty *mes* are perfected and the earth is irrigated, I will establish well-being there.'

The lacuna and i 37–46 may constitute the prologue of the text, in which the events to take place in the main body of the composition are anticipated or announced through the speech of Enki. But the events referred to in the speech are in a reverse order of the events to be narrated in the rest of the text.

Starting from i 47, the text recounts the creation of human beings by An, Enlil, Enki, and Ninhursaĝa (i 47–8), and the creation of animals (lines 49–50).

After another lacuna, the text only preserves the end of another speech, probably by Enki again as above: 'I will oversee their labour. Let . . . the builder of the Land dig a solid foundation' (ii 86–7), which seems to deal with the preparation for the founding of cities. The following lines have to do with the descent of kingship from heaven (ii 88–9), the perfection of divine rites and lofty *mes* (ii 90; as the fulfilment of i 45); the establishment of the five antediluvian cities (ii 91–8; as the fulfilment of i 41); and the establishment of the irrigation system (ii 99–100; as the fulfilment of i 46). After another lacuna, the text is already in the episode of the Flood, which starts from the lamenting of Nintu for her creatures who were consigned to destruction through the Flood by the gods (iii 140; iv 157; anticipated in i 38–9) and ends with the settlement of Ziusudra in Dilmun for saving the human race from total annihilation (vi 260; anticipated in i 38–40). From there on, the text is broken again.

The temporal setting of the text is mostly antediluvian. The preserved sections of the text first deal with the creation (of human beings and animals) and organization of the world (kingship, cities, and irrigation). But the episode of the Flood takes up most of the space of narration, occupying four columns out of this six-column tablet (cols. iii–vi). Temporal devices used in the text include: the temporal clauses an ^{d}en-lil$_2$ ^{d}en-ki ^{d}nin-ḫur-saĝ-ĝa$_2$-ke$_4$ | saĝ-ge$_6$-ga mu-un-dim$_2$-eš-a-ba 'When An, Enlil, Enki and Ninhursaĝa had fashioned the black-headed people' (i 47–8); [u$_4$ x] x nam-lugal-la an-ta e$_{11}$-de$_3$-a-ba | ⌜men⌝-maḫ ^{ĝeš}g[u-z]a-nam-lugal-la an-ta e$_{11}$-a-ba '[When . . .] of kingship descended from heaven, when the lofty crown and the throne of kingship descended from heaven' (ii 88–9); u$_4$-bi-a 'Then; on that day' (iii 140) to mark the time when Nintu lamented for her people being devastated; u$_4$-ba 'At that time' (iii 145) to introduce the king Ziusudra and mark the time when he sought Enki's help; u$_4$ šu$_2$-uš-e 'Every day' (iii 148; compare [*ū*]*mišamma* 'every day' in OB *Atra-hasīs* II iii 4) to indicate that Ziusudra daily sought communication with Enki, who was presumably under oath not to divulge the divine plan to annihilate humankind by the Flood; ⌜e-ne⌝-še$_3$ 'now' (iv 161) with an unclear function due to the broken context; u$_4$ 7-am$_3$ ĝi$_6$ 7-am$_3$ | a-ma-ru kalam-ma ba-ur$_3$-ra-ta | ^{ĝeš}ma$_2$ gur$_4$-gur$_4$ a-gal-la im-ḫul tuk$_4$-tuk$_4$-a-ta 'After the Flood had swept the Land, and the waves and windstorms had rocked the huge boat for seven days and seven nights' (v 203–5; cf. 7 *ūmī* 7 *mūš*[*iātim*] 'For seven days and seven nights' in OB *Atra-hasīs* III iv 24) to mark the period of the storm and Flood; u$_4$-ba 'At that time' (vi 258) to mark the time when the gods settled Ziusudra in Dilmun.

This composition has evidently absorbed material from different strands of tradition. Both in content and style, it has followed older Sumerian mythological prologues or compositions in its descriptions of the primeval time of origins in i 47–ii 100. In ii 88–97 where the descent of kingship and the founding of the five antediluvian cities are referred to, the text most likely follows the antediluvian section of a chronographical source such as W-B 444. Both the phraseology used with regard to the descent of kingship and the names and order of the antediluvian cities in this passage correspond with lines 1–32 of W-B 444. But instead of listing human rulers from these cities as seen in W-B 444, the present text portrays these cities as being given to different gods.[36] The only human ruler in the entire antediluvian era was the Flood hero Ziusudra. In this regard, the *Sumerian Flood Story* corresponds to the *Atra-hasīs Epic*. But contrary to the Babylonian Flood epic in which the Flood hero is not explicitly represented as a ruler, the present text repeatedly stresses the royal identity of Ziusudra (iii 145; v 209, 211; vi 254, 258). In terms of the plot, phraseology, and temporal markers, the episode of the Flood story in the current text also seems to tally with the *Atra-hasīs Epic*. One major difference between the Sumerian story and the Babylonian epic is the name of the Flood hero. For the name Ziusudra, the current text seems to depend on the Sumerian antediluvian traditions such as the W-B 62 version of *SKL* or the *Instructions of Šuruppak*. Another major difference between the current Sumerian text and the Babylonian Flood epic is that while the Sumerian text represents Ziusudra as being granted eternal life by the gods, the Babylonian epic does not seem to contain this motif due to the fact that human mortality was only instituted after the Flood in this text, which makes granting eternal life to Atra-hasīs from the antediluvian era unnecessary. Phraseologically, iv 158–9, 160 of the current text (as part of Enki's speech to Ziusudra with regard to the finality of the divine decision to destroy the Land by the Flood) apparently follow *LSU* 364–5, 369 (as part of Enlil's speech to his son Nanna/Suen with regard to the finality of the divine decision to destroy Ur) respectively.

Judging on the basis of its selection and adaptation of the traditional materials, the current Sumerian text's representations of the antediluvian era and the Flood story seem to be a reaction to the political ideology promulgated in W-B 444. Such rewriting was achieved by manipulating antediluvian history. Contrary to W-B 444, the current Sumerian text uses a different version of antediluvian history to demonstrate that kingship, once having descended from heaven, rather than being transient as portrayed in W-B 444 in its shift among the five antediluvian cities, is stable, as represented by the idealized royal figure Ziusudra who reigned for the entire antediluvian era. Furthermore, kingship, rather than being annihilated by the Flood according to W-B 444, not only survived the catastrophe but also even gained a permanent and transcendent status, as reflected in Ziusudra who was granted eternal life. The repeated emphasis on Ziusudra as king, and the only king in the antediluvian era, in the current text is no coincidence. Ziusudra seems to have been deliberately omitted by W-B 444 as the last antediluvian ruler precisely because his

[36] See the city laments in which the divine, rather than human, rulers of the cities were emphasized.

presence undermines the ideological stance of *SKL*. W-B 444 and the *Sumerian Flood Story* attest to the opposing ideological usages of the antediluvian era and the Flood. While the former sought to use the antediluvian era and the Flood to prove the transience of kingship, the latter attempted to use them to underscore the permanent nature of kingship, regardless of the divine opposition (see also *Year Name 22 of Ibbi-Suen*).

SYNCHRONIC OBSERVATIONS

The textual sources examined above indicate that the primeval time of origins was represented in various genres in ancient Mesopotamian traditions: mythological compositions, hymns, disputations, didactic compositions, chronographies, city laments, and year names. In terms of the distribution within each individual composition, representations of the primeval time can occur in the prologue section or sporadically in different sections of a composition. In many cases, the primeval time is the subject of the entire composition. The primeval time can also serve as either the background or foreground of the main events narrated in a composition. The length of descriptions of, or references to, the primeval time can be either brief or elaborate.

The primeval setting is easily recognizable by the content or style of narration. In terms of content, events dealing with origins such as cosmogony, theogony, the creation of humankind and animals, the organization of the world (e.g. the creation of mountains, rivers, and canals), the rise of various aspects of civilization, and the emergence of various natural and social phenomena are all indicative of such a setting. In terms of style, the three-tier Sumerian adverbial clause u_4-re-a . . . $\hat{g}i_6$-re-a . . . mu-re-a . . . 'In those days . . . , in those nights . . . , in those years . . .' and its variants are frequently used to introduce the primeval time in mythological sources. Often this clause precedes the first primeval event in the temporal sequence of the text. In the chronographical sources, the *USKL* and the W-B 444 version of *SKL* use the temporal clause nam-lugal an-ta e_{11}-da-ba 'When kingship descended from heaven' to mark the primeval time. In the prologue sections of the *Instructions of Ur-Ninurta* and the *Rulers of Lagaš*, the temporal clauses related to the Flood eĝir a-ma-ru ba-ĝar-ra-a-ta and eĝir a-ma-ru ba-ur_3-ra-ta 'After the Flood had swept over' and variants are used for introducing the primeval time. But in the *Instructions of Ur-Ninurta* the clause stands in conjunction with the three-tier adverbial expression, while in the *Rulers of Lagaš* the clause alone is used. Furthermore, negative statements or propositions are frequently employed to depict the conditions of the primeval time that were to be inverted in the main body of the text. In addition, the adverbial expression u_4-ba or u_4-bi-a 'On that day; at that time' is used for various temporal and structural functions: to mark the transition from the prologue to the main body of the composition, to mark the vital junctures or events in the temporal sequence of the story, and to introduce protagonists.

The selection and order of primeval events vary in the textual sources. Some texts refer to the union or separation of heaven and earth as the first event. Others refer to the fixing of the destinies. In the *USKL* and W-B 444, the descent of kingship from heaven is presented as the first event. Still others allude to the Flood as the beginning point of the temporal sequence (e.g. the *Rulers of Lagaš*). And the choice and sequence of the rest of the primeval events also vary in the textual sources. Though certain general structuring principles such as the crisis-resolution or contest format can be observed in many sources, rules for temporal ordering or factors that affect the temporal sequence may differ substantially among the sources. Not infrequently, the selection and ordering of primeval events in the mythological prologue are influenced by the subjects, events, or protagonists in the main body of a composition.

The relationship of the primeval time with other temporal frameworks can be fluid. Legendary or historical royal figures (e.g. Enmerkar, Gilgameš, Ur-Nammu, Šulgi, Ur-Ninurta) are often represented as existing in the primeval time. Conversely, events that were supposed to have taken place in the primeval time, such as the marriage between Enlil and Sud/Ninlil, can be cast in the temporal and social settings contemporaneous with the author. In the city laments and some of the Isin royal hymns (see also *Year Name 22 of Ibbi-Suen*), the cosmic, natural, and social structures established in the primeval time of origins are often represented as being destroyed in historical times by catastrophes and subsequently being restored. Similar conceptions of the destruction of the primeval order to be followed by restoration can be seen in representations in W-B 444 and the *Rulers of Lagaš*. According to these texts, the events that destroyed the primeval order took place in the remote and mythical past, rather than in the recent course of history as in the city laments. But in both groups of texts, the primeval time of origins had to start anew due to the catastrophes that interrupted the normal course of history and destroyed the previous world structure.

In terms of functions and purposes, the primeval time being a time when the destinies were fixed was frequently used to lend support to competing claims to precedence or superiority by different cities, cultic centres, deities, human rulers, economic models, and political ideologies or philosophies. For example, W-B 444, the *Sumerian Flood Story*, and the *Rulers of Lagaš* all utilized and manipulated the representations of antediluvian history or the Flood in attempts to legitimize their dialectically different views on kingship or rulership. It is also common for many aetiological stories that were intended to explain certain natural, cultural, and social phenomena to cast their temporal setting in the primeval era. One needs to be aware, however, that there can be different aetiological stories to account for the origins of things. For example, both *Enlil and Sud*, and *Enlil and Ninlil* offer aetiological stories for how Enlil and Ninlil became a couple. But the plots as well as purposes of the stories are dramatically different. While the former composition seeks to condemn inappropriate propositions and promote proper procedures and protocols for making marriage proposals, the latter composition takes delight in telling the lascivious exploits of Enlil at the expense of Ninlil for lurid entertainment. The *Debate between Grain and Sheep* and *How Grain Came to Sumer* also provide different accounts about the origin of grain in Sumer.

DIACHRONIC OBSERVATIONS

Development of Representations of the Primeval Time of Origins

The textual sources from the Early Dynastic III period to the Old Babylonian period which have been examined above attest to the continuity of literary representations regarding the primeval time in Sumerian and Babylonian traditions. In terms of content, it is taken for granted that the primeval time is a time in which the cosmos, the world, and human society originated. There is also an enduring convention in the textual sources to trace the earliest event in narration back to the cosmic beginning symbolized by events such as the union or separation of heaven and earth. In terms of style, as already discussed above, the textual sources utilized similar stylistic techniques or temporal devices, such as the negative–positive reversal, the adverbial expressions of time, the crisis-resolution scheme, and the contest scenario, for depicting, staging, sequencing, or structuring the primeval events. The chronographical framework and the political philosophy of *SKL* had exerted a persistent influence in various literary traditions, e.g. *Curse Agade*, *LSU*, the *Sumerian Flood Story*, and the *Rulers of Lagaš*.

Innovations were achieved in various ways. Conceptually, innovations can be frequently seen in the manipulations of temporal concepts or frameworks. On the one hand, legendary, historical, and contemporary events and characters may be projected back to the primeval time (e.g. *Ur-Namma C*, *Šulgi E*, *ELA*). On the other hand, primeval events or characters may be brought forward into historical and contemporary settings (e.g. *Enlil and Sud*, *Šulgi A*, *Year Name 22 of Ibbi-Suen*, *Curse Agade*, *LSU*). Innovations may also come in the form of ideological responses or reactions to previous traditions, for example *Inana and Enki* (in reaction to the traditions concerning Eridu being the cultural centre), the *Sumerian Flood Story* and the *Rulers of Lagaš* (which seem to have been composed in reaction to the *SKL*).

Literarily, innovative representations often emerged as a result of unique ways of combining and arranging various motifs or stories from previously separate traditions, for example *Lugale*, *Enki and Ninhursaĝa*, *Enki and Ninmah*, the *Instructions of Ur-Ninurta*, the *Instructions of Šuruppak*, the W-B 444 version of *SKL*, the *Rulers of Lagaš*, the *Death of Bilgames*, *ELA*, *Inana and the Numun-Grass*, the *Atra-hasīs Epic*, and the *Sumerian Flood Story*. As a result of synthesizing previous traditions, stories concerning the primeval history became more elaborate, as seen in *Lugale* and the *Atra-hasīs Epic*. Such synthesizing endeavours were carried out not only with regard to motifs and stories, but also in terms of genre, form, and style. Cross-fertilization among mythological narratives, laments, hymns, chronographies, disputations, and didactic texts flourished especially in the Old Babylonian period. The *Instructions of Ur-Ninurta*, for example, has combined the mythological prologue, the royal hymn, and didactic literature. The *Rulers of Lagaš* and the *Sumerian Flood Story* have incorporated the style of the mythological prologue and the chronographical style and framework of *SKL*. *Inana and the Numun-Grass*, the *Atra-hasīs Epic*, and the *Sumerian Flood Story* have absorbed the style of the laments.

Development of the Primeval Flood Catastrophe Motif

To trace this development, it is important to start with the observation that the primeval flood catastrophe emerged as a major innovation for the representation of the primeval time of origins both in terms of content and style during the Old Babylonian period. Prior to this innovation, it was conventional for mythological compositions to use the three-tier adverbial expression u_4-re-a . . . $ĝi_6$-re-a . . . mu-re-a . . . 'In those days . . . , in those nights . . . , in those years . . .' and its variants to indicate the primeval time, more precisely, often the beginning or the most defining event of the primeval time. The first primeval event the mythological compositions typically chose is either the union or separation of heaven and earth, or the fixing of destinies. In the chronographical sources such as the *SKL*, the conventional stylistic formula to mark the beginning point of temporal sequence is nam-lugal an-ta e_{11}-da-ba 'After kingship had descended from heaven' (see the *USKL* and BT 14) with the establishment of kingship as the first and only primeval event.

Judging from the textual evidence, the *Instructions of Ur-Ninurta* is the first textual source that uses the temporal clause eĝir a-ma-ru ba-ĝar-ra-[a-ta] 'After the Flood had swept over' (line 4) as part of the stylistic devices to introduce the primeval time. But in this textual source, the temporal clause related to the Flood is still second to the three-tier adverbial expression (lines 1–3). In terms of content, the Flood has already become the first primeval event in the temporal sequence of narration. The *Instructions of Ur-Ninurta* thus stands out as a crucial step in the development of the temporal conception and stylistic presentation of the primeval time. A similar style of presentation and temporal conception of the primeval time can be found in the prologue of the *Instructions of Šuruppak* and the relevant sections in the *Death of Bilgames*. In the W-B 444 version of *SKL*, stylistically, the temporal clause eĝir a-ma-ru ba-ur$_3$-ra-ta 'After the Flood had swept over' (line 40), preceding the conventional stylistic marker nam-lugal an-ta e$_{11}$-de$_3$-a-ba 'when kingship descended from heaven' (line 41), introduces the second beginning of the world. In terms of the temporal conception, the Flood was treated as the first event prior to the re-establishment of kingship. In the *Rulers of Lagaš*, the temporal clause [eĝir a-m]a-ru ba-ur$_3$-ra-ta 'After the Flood had swept over' (line 1) alone is used to introduce the primeval time of origins. And the Flood again is considered as the first event in the temporal sequence. In the prologue of *Inana and the Numun-Grass*, the Flood conflates with the union of heaven and earth as the first event in the temporal sequence of the text. The above textual sources attest to the increasing popularity of the temporal clause regarding the Flood as a stylistic device and the Flood as an event signalling the (re)beginning of time. In fact, the popularity of the Flood as a stylistic and temporal marker of the primeval time had reached such a height that the older stylistic and temporal devices were either relegated to second place (W-B 444), replaced (the *Rulers of Lagaš*), or assimilated (*Inana and the Numun-Grass*), by it.

The reconstruction of the development of the Flood motif should be approached from the conceptual and literary perspectives. As noted earlier and as will be discussed further in Chapter 4, *Year Name 22 of Ibbi-Suen* and the city laments depict the destruction of the Ur III dynasty as caused by a meteorological catastrophe in the form of an inversion of the creation order. According to these textual sources, the restoration brought about by the royal heroes (Ibbi-Suen or Išme-Dagan) is nothing short of a re-creation or re-enactment of the primeval time of origins. Such destruction-restoration rhetoric is encapsulated in *Išme-Dagan A* 118–23: 'I am Išme-Dagan, son of Dagan, whom Enlil, the lord of all the lands, after the flood had swept over, chose by extispicy on his most favourable day. He lo[oked] at the Ekur happily, and sp[oke] approvingly to Sumer.' The flood in the temporal clause 'after the flood had swept over' (eĝir a-ma-ru ur$_3$-ra-ta) of this passage clearly refers to a recent catastrophe during Išme-Dagan's days. But when the similar temporal clause appears in the mythological prologue of the *Instructions of Ur-Ninurta* eĝir a-ma-ru ba-ĝar-ra-[a-ta] 'After the Flood had swept over' (line 4), the literary context clearly signals that the word a-ma-ru is used here as referring to a primeval event. It seems that the destruction-restoration rhetoric which had been used earlier to refer to a recent historical catastrophe was projected back into the primeval time of origins as the prototype of world-ending catastrophe (see van Dijk 1983: 33; Dalley 2005: 275–85) in the *Instructions of Ur-Ninurta*.

Arguably, it is the above literary and ideological responses to the catastrophic demise of the Ur III period that gave rise to the motif of the primeval flood catastrophe and the basic plot of the Flood story that involves a royal hero who restored the devastated world and was consequently granted a long or eternal life. The motif and the plot developed in several directions during the Old Babylonian period. As will be demonstrated in detail in Chapter 3, the two-generation or three-generation genealogies of the Flood hero were formed on the basis of the familial relations in the *Instructions of Šurrupak*. Following the chronographical framework and style of *SKL*, antediluvian history was also constructed with the Flood hero's family being the last antediluvian dynasty located in Šuruppak (the W-B 62 version of *SKL*). Then the antediluvian section was joined with the *SKL* proper. Thus in the W-B 444 version of *SKL*, the temporal sequence starts with the primeval era signalled by line 1 ([nam]-lugal an-ta e_{11}-de_3-a-ba 'After kingship had descended from heaven') and proceeds to the antediluvian history containing five dynasties (lines 2–38). The Flood brought the antediluvian era to an end (line 39 a-ma-ru ba-ur_3-«ra-ta» 'Then the Flood swept over') and inaugurated the beginning of a new era (eĝir a-ma-ru ba-ur_3-ra-ta | nam-lugal an-ta-ed_3-de_3-a-ba 'After the Flood had swept over, when kingship came down from heaven'). Thereafter, the normal history resumes (lines 42 ff.).

Literarily, the emergence of the Flood motif had led to diverse dramatic representations during the Old Babylonian period: those from Isin which exalted Enlil, Ninurta, and the Isin rulers (e.g. the *Instructions of Ur-Ninurta*); those from Unug[?] which exalted Inana, her spouse Dumuzi, and their protégés (e.g. *Inana and the Numun-Grass*); and the tradition from Eridu which exalted Enki and his protégé the Flood hero.[37] It is the Flood myth from Eridu that became most popular in Mesopotamian literary traditions. The original story was probably composed in the early Old Babylonian period, and was subsequently elaborated, most notably in the *Atra-hasīs Epic*. Rather than serving as the mythological *background* (as seen in the *Instructions of Ur-Ninurta*, the *Instructions of Šuruppak*, the W-B 444 version of *SKL*, the *Rulers of Lagaš*, the *Death of Bilgames*, and *Inana and the Numun-Grass*), the Flood has become the *foreground* of the story. The ingenious contribution of the Babylonian epic lies in its combining different previous traditions, including mythological motifs regarding the primeval time of origins (e.g. the first story in *Enki and Ninmah*), themes related to contests between gods (e.g. the second story in *Enki and Ninmah*), elements from didactic and critical literature, motifs regarding catastrophe from the city laments (see Chapter 4), and the Flood story. The epic arranges the traditional materials into a well-sequenced and sweeping narrative that culminates in the Flood story.[38] Thus the Flood has

[37] That the primeval flood story originated from Eridu may explain why Eridu was listed as the first antediluvian city in the chronographical traditions as seen in the W-B 62 and W-B 444 versions of *SKL*.

[38] This composition history of the *Atra-hasīs Epic* has already been hinted at by Lambert and Millard (1969: 23), Clifford (1994: 74–82), and Horowitz (1998: 143 n. 48).

not only become part of the foreground of the Babylonian epic, it is also represented as the climactic event in the epic (see also the *Sumerian Flood Story*).

Other representations of the Flood motif in the Old Babylonian period also involved syncretism. The *Sumerian Flood Story* apparently assembled materials from the chronographical sources such as the W-B 444 version of *SKL* and the mythological narrative compositions such as the city laments and the earlier Flood story. Likewise, the *Rulers of Lagaš* and the *Dynastic Chronicle* joined the mythological narrative composition and the chronographical sources, but giving more emphasis to the chronographical sections than what is seen in the *Sumerian Flood Story*. In the *Death of Bilgames* and the *Ballade of Early Rulers*, the antediluvian tradition and the Flood story began to converge with Gilgameš traditions (see Chapter 3).

SUMMARY

The above study has examined the emergence of the Flood motif within the broader development of representations of the primeval time of origins in Mesopotamian traditions (primarily Sumerian) from the Early Dynastic III period to the Old Babylonian period. It is observed that in terms of temporal conceptions and stylistic features, the Flood motif and the temporal clause regarding the Flood were innovations that took place starting from the time of Ur-Ninurta (*c.*1923–1896 BC), as a result of the literary and ideological responses to the catastrophic demise of the Ur III period. The following chapters will examine in detail the development of the antediluvian traditions (Chapter 3) and the formation of the Babylonian Flood epic (Chapter 4).

3

Antediluvian Traditions

This chapter investigates the complex development of diverse Mesopotamian traditions regarding the Flood hero, the last antediluvian rulers, and the antediluvian era as a whole. It also identifies the major sources involved in the development of the traditions, and unravels the conceptual and literary processes through which the traditions emerged and evolved.

THE FLOOD HERO AND THE LAST ANTEDILUVIAN RULERS

It is well known that the name of the Flood hero varies among the Mesopotamian sources. In the oldest version of the Flood epic he is called Atra-hasīs (^{m}*atram-ḫasīs*, meaning 'one (who is) exceeding in wisdom'. In an Old Babylonian manuscript of the *Gilgameš Epic* (OB VA + BM), his name is *ūta-na'ištim rūqu* 'Ūta-na'ištim the Distant' (George 2003: 153). In the Standard Babylonian version of the *Gilgameš Epic*, it is either ^{m}UD-*napišti*(zi) *rūqu*, ^{m}UD-*napišti*(zi), or ^{m}UD-*napišti*(zi)^{tim}. But in two instances, he is called Atra-hasīs (SB *Gilgameš* XI 49, 197), which betrays the influence of the *Atra-hasīs Epic* on the Standard Babylonian *Gilgameš Epic* (Tigay 1982: 216–17). The Sumerian name of the Flood hero Ziusudra (zi-u$_4$-su$_3$-ra$_2$ 'life of prolonged, or distant, days') occurs in the Old Babylonian version of the *Instructions of Šuruppak*; the W-B 62 version of *SKL*; the *Sumerian Flood Story*; the *Death of Bilgames*; the *Ballade of Early Rulers*; the *Dynastic Chronicle*; an omen text reconstructed from the Middle Assyrian, Neo-Assyrian, and Neo-Babylonian fragments (George 2003: 113); and Berossos' *Babyloniaca* (Xisuthros).

Also, despite some basic agreement, there is considerable divergence concerning the number of rulers for the last antediluvian dynasty in Mesopotamian traditions. The fluidity of the traditions as a whole has long been observed.[1] In

[1] See Finkelstein 1963: 45–51; Lambert and Millard 1969: 15–21; Galter 2005: 269–96.

the extant copies of the chronographical sources, W-B 62 lists three generations: Ubār-Tutu, SU.KUR.LAM, and Ziusudra. SU.KUR.LAM is read by most scholars as Šuruppak (Jacobsen 1939: 76 n. 32; George 2003: 154),[2] though Langdon (1923*b*: 258–9) reads as Arad. The former view is obviously correct, as the name of the city Šuruppak is written the same way in the W-B 62 version of *SKL*, lines 15, 17. Among these three generations, only the last two are represented in W-B 62 as rulers in the last antediluvian city Šuruppak. The W-B 444 and MS 2855 version of *SKL* present only one ruler Ubār-Tutu from the city Šuruppak. The relevant lines in the UCBC 9-1819 version of *SKL* are fragmentary. According to the reconstruction of Finkelstein (1963: 43), this king list contains Ubār-Tutu and possibly Ziusudra from Šuruppak. Both the *Dynastic Chronicle* (attested in Neo-Assyrian copies whose original composition may go back to the Old Babylonian period) and *Babyloniaca* (*c*.300 BC) present Ubār-Tutu and Ziusudra (Otiartes and Xisuthros respectively in *Babyloniaca*) as the last antediluvian rulers, with only one difference: while in the former source the two rulers were from Šuruppak, in the latter they were from Larak.

Among the mythological or epic sources, the royal identity of Atra-hasīs is not openly stated but may be implied in his commanding and intermediate role in the Flood epic. Other than Enlil's shrine Ekur in Nippur, the epic mentions no specific antediluvian city (Lambert and Millard 1969: 19). Whether Atra-hasīs was presented as the only ruler in the antediluvian era in the Babylonian Flood epic (Lambert and Millard 1969: 20–1) remains unclear. But Ziusudra was definitely regarded as the only antediluvian ruler in the *Sumerian Flood Story*. Presumably he is associated with the last antediluvian city Šuruppak mentioned in the story, though this association is nowhere spelled out in the current state of the text. The Standard Babylonian version of the *Gilgameš Epic*, closer to the chronographical traditions than to the Old Babylonian versions of the *Atra-hasīs Epic* in this respect, has Ubār-Tutu and UD-napišti (IX 6, X 208, XI 23) from Šuruppak (XI 11, 23), exactly the same genealogical and geographic presentations as in the *Dynastic Chronicle* except for the Akkadian designation ^{m}UD-*napišti* for the Sumerian name Ziusudra.

Among the didactic sources, the Old Babylonian version of the *Instructions of Šuruppak* presents three generations: Ubār-Tutu, the man from Šuruppak, and Ziusudra.[3] Modern scholars have not reached consensus as to whether Šuruppak^{ki} should be reckoned as a personal name (Jacobsen 1939: 76 n. 32; Krebernik 1998: 241, 319; George 2003: 154–5)[4] or an epithet based on the

[2] The toponym Šuruppak is normally written SU.KUR.RU^{ki} (Krebernik 1998: 239).

[3] OB *Instructions of Šuruppak* 7–8, 74–5, 77–8, 144–5, 147–8: šuruppak^{ki} dumu ubar-tu-tu-ke$_4$ | zi-u$_4$-su$_3$-ra$_2$ dumu-ni-ra na na-mu-un-ri-ri '—the man from Šuruppak, the son of Ubār-Tutu—gave instructions to his son Ziusudra' (Alster 2005: 57, 71–2, 81–2).

[4] The view of Šuruppak as a personal name was first propagated by Jacobsen (1939: 76 n. 32; see also George 2003: 154–5), together with Zimmern and Landsberger, in an attempt to explain

toponym Šuruppak, i.e. 'the man from Šuruppak' or 'the Šuruppakean' (Alster 2005: 32, 104–5). As will be shown in the following discussion, the disagreement over the interpretation of Šuruppak^{ki} in the *Instructions of Šuruppak* goes all the way back at least to the time of the Old Babylonian period.

How should the above divergence and commonality among the traditions surrounding the Flood hero and the last antediluvian rulers be explained? Why are there different names for the Flood hero? Even among the Babylonian sources alone there are two different names or epithets, Atra-hasīs and Ūta-na'ištim/UD-napišti the Distant. How can one explain the presentation of one (W-B 444 and MS 2855), two (the *Dynastic Chronicle* and *Babyloniaca*), or three (W-B 62 and the Old Babylonian version of the *Instructions of Šuruppak*) rulers in the last antediluvian dynasty? What could have been the reason behind the omission of Ziusudra in W-B 444? Why is Atra-hasīs not explicitly identified as a ruler in the Flood epic? And when Ziusudra is identified as a ruler in the *Sumerian Flood Story*, why is he presented as the only ruler during the entire antediluvian era? What is the historical relationship between the mythological traditions, the chronographical traditions, and the didactic traditions concerning the development of the representations of the Flood hero and the last antediluvian rulers?

To answer the above questions concerning the growth of the antediluvian traditions and how these traditions were related to one another during the course of their development and transmission, it is necessary to start by examining the interpretive history of the Early Dynastic III versions of the *Instructions of Šuruppak*. This didactic source proves vital for the development of the antediluvian traditions. Many of the above divergent traditions, the current author would argue, are the results of ancient attempts to make sense of the ambiguities in the opening lines of the Early Dynastic III versions of the *Instructions of Šuruppak* and to update the genealogical information in these lines with contemporary traditions.

the extra generation that stands in between Ubār-Tutu and Ziusudra in W-B 62. This attempt was basically motivated by the belief that the two-generation list comprising Ubār-Tutu and Ziusudra in the *Dynastic Chronicle* and *Babyloniaca* was canonical, while the three-generation list comprising Ubār-Tutu, SU.KUR.LAM/Šuruppak, and Ziusudra in W-B 62 was an aberration resulting from the later scribal misunderstanding of the toponym Šuruppak, serving as the epithet of Ziusudra in line 16 of W-B 62 zi-u_4-su_3-ra_2 dumu SU.KUR.LAM 'Ziusudra, the one from Šuruppak', for the epithet of Ziusudra's father 'Ziusudra, the son of Šuruppak'. The above view has been challenged on the basis of the expression Šuruppak^{ki} UR_2.AŠ dumu-ni-ra na na-ri-ri in one of the Early Dynastic III versions of the *Instructions of Šuruppak* (i.e. the Adab version; compare Šuruppak^{ki} UR_2.AŠ in the Abū Ṣalābīkh version) by Lambert and Millard (1969: 19) and Alster (2005: 104–5), who argue that this Early Dynastic expression suggests that the generation of the father called 'Šuruppak' or 'the man from Šuruppak' originated from an Early Dynastic III tradition. But this latter interpretation is far from being conclusive, as the Early Dynastic III sources, particularly the Adab version, obviously contain ambiguities, with which the ancient traditions also seem to have struggled and come up with divergent interpretations (see the following discussions).

Didactic Sources

Early Dynastic III Versions of the Instructions of Šuruppak

The *Instructions of Šuruppak* comprises a set of instructions a father gives to his son, a traditional type of didactic composition (Alster 2005: 22). The text is attested in many versions from different historical periods and different Mesopotamian sites (Alster 2005: 47–53). The earliest versions we have available are from the Early Dynastic III period: the Abū Ṣalābīkh version, ED_1 (Plate 11), and the Adab version, ED_2 (Plate 12). In the following section we shall examine the opening lines of both versions that are relevant to our current discussion.

AbS-T 1–5 (Alster 2005: 176)
ĝeštu$_2$ inim-zu | [ka]lam [t]i-la | [šuruppak U]R$_2$.[A]Š | [ĝeš]tu$_2$ inim-zu | kalam ti-la | šuruppak dumu na [n]a-mu-ri | dumu-ĝu$_{10}$ na ga-ri | GIŠ.PI.[TUG$_2$] ḫe$_2$-m[a]-ak

The intelligent one, the wise one, who lived in the land, the man from Šuruppak, UR$_2$.AŠ; the intelligent one, the wise one, who lived in the land, the man from Šuruppak, gave instructions to his son: 'My son, let me give [you] instructions. Let attention be paid to them!' (compare AbS-T 16′, 26′, 46′, 146′–7′, 171′)

Adab segm. 1.1–9 (Alster 2005: 196)
[ĝeštu$_2$-tuku inim-galam inim-zu-a]m$_6$ | [kalam-m]a [ti]-la-am$_6$ | [šurupp]ak^{ki} [U]R$_2$.AŠ | [ĝeš]tu$_2$-[tu]ku inim-[galam inim]-zu-am$_6$ | [kalam-m]a [ti-la-am$_6$] | [šuruppak^{ki}] UR$_2$.AŠ | dumu-ni-ra na na-ri-ri | [dumu-ĝu$_{10}$ na ga-ri] | GIŠ.PI.[TUG$_2$] ḫe$_2$-m[a]-ak

The intelligent one, the one of artistic words, the wise one, who lived in the land; the man from Šuruppak, UR$_2$.AŠ; the intelligent one, the one of artistic words, the wise one, who lived in the land, the man from Šuruppak, UR$_2$.AŠ, gave instructions to his son: '[My son, let me give you instructions.] Let attention be paid to them!' (compare Adab segm. 2.7)

The opening lines of the two Early Dynastic III versions basically agree with each other in structure and wording. There are, however, two obvious differences. The first is found in the intellectual attributes described in line 1. Parallel to ĝeštu$_2$ 'the intelligent one' in ED_1 (AbS-T 1–2), ED_2 (Adab segm. 1.1) has a more elaborate description, ĝeštu$_2$-tuku inim-galam 'the intelligent one, the one of artistic words'. Though fragmentary on the tablet, this phrase can be reasonably restored from the corresponding line in Adab segm. 1.4 [ĝeš]tu$_2$-[tu]ku inim-[galam] as well as from that in the Old Babylonian version, which is closer to ED_2 overall than to ED_1 (Alster 2005: 176, 195). Another difference between the two versions is that ED_2 has UR$_2$.AŠ after Šuruppak^{ki} in Adab segm. 1.6, while this epithet is absent in ED_1 (AbS-T 3)—though it appears to be present in the closing line of ED_1 (AbS-T 171′): šuruppak U[R$_2$].A[Š]$^?$

dumu na ri-ri-ga '(These are instructions which) the man from Šuruppak, UR_2.AŠ, gave as instructions to his son.' It is difficult to judge which one of these two versions is more original in the light of these differences. The motivations for adding the above elements to ensure more clarity and for eliminating the elements to avoid redundancy are equally possible.

Leaving the uncertainty of the relative date of the traditions represented by the two Early Dynastic versions aside, we are confronted by the issue as to whom the above intellectual characteristics as described in the opening lines of this didactic text (AbS-T 1–2; Adab 1.1–5) are attributed. The syntax of the opening lines of the AbS-T version is sufficiently clear that these characteristics should belong to the father giving the instructions, who is introduced first before the initial reference to the son receiving the instructions in AbS-T 3–4. There might be some ambiguity in the Adab version, depending on how one interprets the Sumerian phrase šuruppak^{ki} UR_2.AŠ. The ancient interpretive traditions of this text, however, unanimously regard the one giving the instruction, identified as the man of Šuruppak, as one being described by these intellectual attributes.[5] From the perspective of the didactic scenario of the *Instructions of Šuruppak*, it is clear that the one giving the instructions should be accorded these attributes, rather than the one receiving the instructions.

The pivotal issue in the Early Dynastic versions of the *Instructions of Šuruppak* for the development of the names of the last antediluvian rulers, however, is the interpretation of the Sumerian phrase šuruppak UR_2.AŠ in ED_1 (AbS-T 2) and šuruppak^{ki} UR_2.AŠ in ED_2 (Adab segm. 1.3, 6). With regard to the meaning of UR_2.AŠ, both Alster (2005: 104) and Steinkeller (quoted in Davila 1995: 202 n. 21) think that it is related to ušbar$_x$. However, while Alster equates UR_2.AŠ with the Akkadian expression *emu rabû* 'father-in-law', Steinkeller, not excluding that explanation in kinship terms, prefers to regard UR_2.AŠ as 'the phonetic (or archaic) spelling for the later uš-bar "weaver"'. Whatever the precise meaning UR_2.AŠ once had, modern scholarship offers three options for the interpretation of the Sumerian phrase šuruppak UR_2.AŠ or šuruppak^{ki} UR_2.AŠ:

1 'Šuruppak, i.e. UR_2.AŠ' (Alster 1974: 25; Krebernik 1998: 319 n. 779) In this view, šuruppak or šuruppak^{ki} is understood as the personal name of the father giving the instructions. UR_2.AŠ is taken as the epithet (or personal name$^?$) of Father Šuruppak, on the basis of the position of this designation in ED_2 (Adab segm. 1.3, 6).

[5] Compare Old Babylonian version of the *Instructions of Šuruppak*, line 5: šuruppak^{ki} ĝeštu$_2$-tuku inim-galam inim-zu-a kalam-ma ti-la-a 'the man from Šuruppak, the intelligent one, the one of elaborate words, the wise one, who lived in the country' (see also MSS Ur_1, P, Sch_1; Alster 2005: 56).

2 'Šuruppak, to UR_2.AŠ' (Civil and Biggs 1966: 2)
UR_2.AŠ is regarded as the name of the son receiving the instructions.

3 'the man of Šuruppak, to UR_2.AŠ' (Alster 2005: 104–5, 176, 196)
Here šuruppak^{ki} or šuruppak is viewed as the epithet of the father based on the toponym Šuruppak. Alster argues that the ki-determinative at least in the Adab version does not seem to support the reading of Šuruppak as a personal name.[6]

The three modern scholarly views regarding the interpretation of the Sumerian phrase šuruppak UR_2.AŠ in ED_1 (AbS-T 2) and šuruppak^{ki} UR_2.AŠ in ED_2 (Adab segm. 1.3, 6) as summarized above basically agree that šuruppak^{ki} or šuruppak refers to the father; and UR_2.AŠ is the designation of either the father or the son. However, according to the ancient traditions to be examined below, there are other interpretive options for the expression šuruppak UR_2.AŠ or šuruppak^{ki} UR_2.AŠ in the Early Dynastic III versions of the *Instructions of Šuruppak*.

To a large extent, the diverse ancient and modern interpretations of the Sumerian expression šuruppak UR_2.AŠ in ED_1 (AbS-T 2) and šuruppak^{ki} UR_2.AŠ in ED_2 (Adab segm. 1.3, 6) are caused by the ambiguities in the syntax of the opening lines of the Adab version. In the AbS-T version, UR_2.AŠ signifies the epithet of Šuruppak and stands in apposition to that personal name/epithet built on toponym: the man from Šuruppak, UR_2.AŠ. The syntax seems to suggest that this is the only option (see AbS-T 2–3). In the Adab version, however, three options seem possible:

1 UR_2.AŠ can be viewed as the epithet of the man from Šuruppak: the man from Šuruppak, UR_2.AŠ.

2 UR_2.AŠ represents the personal name/epithet of the father giving the instructions, while šuruppak^{ki} is treated as a toponym: in Šuruppak^{ki}, UR_2.AŠ. According to this and the case above, there are only two generations referred to in the text: UR_2.AŠ the father, and the son receiving the instructions. Compare the *Dynastic Chronicle* and *Babyloniaca*; also partially in W-B 62 and W-B 444.

3 UR_2.AŠ may also be taken as the epithet of the father of the man from Šuruppak: the man from Šuruppak, (son of) UR_2.AŠ. In this case, three generations are involved. See line 7 of the Old Babylonian version of *Instructions of Šuruppak*, which adds dumu 'son of': šuruppak^{ki} dumu

[6] According to Alster (2005: 104), $^{lu}{}_2$*šuruppakû* in SB *Gilgmaš* XI 23: $^{lu}{}_2$*šuruppakû mār*(dumu) ^{m}*ubara-*^{d}*tutu* and the Akkadian translations of šuruppak^{ki} in the *Instructions of Šuruppak*, ^{m}*šurippakû* (Akk_1) or *šurippakû* (Akk_2), should likewise be translated 'the man from Šuruppak' or 'the Šuruppakean', instead of a personal name (compare the opposing view in George 2003: 154–5).

ubar-tu-tu-ke$_4$, assuming that Ubār-tutu parallels UR$_2$.AŠ. The epithet is dropped in line 5 of the Old Babylonian version of the *Instructions of Šuruppak* presumably for the sake of clarity. The author of the Old Babylonian version seems to have access to a source similar to the AbS-T version, in which Šuruppak must be treated as the personal name/epithet of the father giving the instructions.

The first and third options can be confusing, as UR$_2$.AŠ in the latter case still qualifies Šuruppak or signifies the epithet of the man from Šuruppak, with the supposed abbreviation of the genealogical notation dumu 'son of' in front of UR$_2$.AŠ.

In neither version should UR$_2$.AŠ be treated as the epithet of the son (or the grandson) receiving the instructions from the man from Šuruppak, as interpreted by Civil and Biggs (1966: 2) and Alster (2005: 176, 196). The syntax in both versions rules out the possibility that the epithet of the son receiving the instructions can be referred to as early in the text as AbS-T 2 or Adab segm. 1.3–5, by UR$_2$.AŠ. Biggs 1966: 78 has already noted that in the Early Dynastic III version, i.e. the AbS-T version, the son receiving the instructions is not named. Though Alster (2005: 32) argues that the epithet UR$_2$.AŠ is the Early Dynastic parallel to Ziusudra, the name of the son receiving the instructions in the Old Babylonian version, one must agree with Lambert and Millard (1969: 19) and Krebernik (1998: 319 n. 779) who have pointed out that UR$_2$.AŠ can be in no way identified with Ziusudra.

Old Babylonian Version of the Instructions of Šuruppak

The Old Babylonian version (Plate 13) is reconstructed by Alster on the basis of the extant Old Babylonian copies of the text. By comparing the opening lines of this version with those of the Early Dynastic versions, one will see some of the procedures and techniques by which the author(s) of the Old Babylonian version interpreted and adapted the Early Dynastic versions.

OB *Instructions of Šuruppak* 1–12 (Alster 2005: 56–7)

u$_4$ re-a u$_4$ su$_3$-ra$_2$ re-a | ĝi$_6$ re-a ĝi$_6$ bad-ra$_2$ re-a | mu re-a mu su$_3$-ra$_2$ re-a | u$_4$-ba ĝeštu$_2$-tuku inim-galam inim-zu-a kalam-ma ti-la-a | šuruppak^{ki} ĝeštu$_2$-tuku inim-galam inim-zu-a kalam-ma ti-la-a | šuruppak^{ki}-e dumu-ni-ra na na-mu-un-ri-ri | šuruppak^{ki} dumu ubar-tu-tu-ke$_4$ | zi-u$_4$-su$_3$-ra$_2$ dumu-ni-ra na na-mu-un-ri-ri | dumu-ĝu$_{10}$ na ga-ri na-ri-ĝu$_{10}$ ḫe$_2$-dab$_5$ | zi-u$_4$-su$_3$-ra$_2$ inim ga-ra-ab-d[u$_{11}$] ĝizzal ḫe$_2$-em-ši-ak | na-ri-ga-ĝu$_{10}$ šu nam-bi$_2$-bar-re | inim du$_{11}$-ga-ĝu$_{10}$ na-ab-ta-bal-e-de$_3$

In those days, in those remote days; in those nights, in those faraway nights; in those years, in those remote years; in those days, the intelligent one, the one of elaborate words, the wise one, who lived in the land; the man from Šuruppak, the intelligent one, the one of elaborate words, the wise one, who lived in the land; the man from Šuruppak, gave instructions to his son; the man from Šuruppak, the son of Ubār-Tutu; gave instructions to his son Ziusudra: 'My son, let me give instructions; let my instructions be taken! Ziusudra, let me speak a word to you; let attention be paid to them! Don't neglect my instructions! Don't transgress the words I speak!'

The adding of the introduction in lines 1–3, the motif of mythical origin, which had already occurred in the prologues of literary texts in the Early Dynastic period (Biggs 1974: 57), is obviously significant (Galter 2005: 281). This introductory formula has been discussed in detail in Chapter 2. For now our discussion will focus on the section in the Old Babylonian version that parallels the Early Dynastic versions, as indicated in the following comparative chart:

AbS-T 1–5	**Adab Segm. 1.1–9**	**OB Version 4–12**
1	1.1–2	4
		u$_4$-ba
ĝeštu$_2$	[ĝeštu$_2$-tuku	ĝeštu$_2$-tuku
inim-zu |	inim-galam inim-zu-a]m$_6$ |	inim-galam inim-zu-a
[ka]lam [t]i-la	[kalam-m]a [ti]-la-am$_6$	kalam-ma ti-la-a
2	1.3–5	5
[šurupp]ak U]R$_2$.AŠ |	[šurupp]ak^{ki} [U]R$_2$.AŠ |	šuruppak^{ki}
[ĝeš]tu$_2$	[ĝeš]tu$_2$-[tu]ku	ĝeštu$_2$-tuku
inim-zu |	inim-[galam inim]-zu-am$_6$ |	inim-galam inim-zu-a
kalam ti-la	[kalam-m]a [ti-la-am$_6$]	kalam-ma ti-la-a
3		6
šuruppak		šuruppak^{ki}-e
dumu		dumu-ni-ra
na [n]a-mu-ri		na na-mu-un-ri-ri
	1.6–7	7–8
	[šuruppak^{ki}] UR$_2$.AŠ |	šuruppak^{ki} dumu ubar-tu-tu-ke$_4$ |
	dumu-ni-ra	zi-u$_4$-su$_3$-ra$_2$ dumu-ni-ra
	na na-ri-ri	na na-mu-un-ri-ri
4	1.8	9
dumu-ĝu$_{10}$	[dumu-ĝu$_{10}$	dumu-ĝu$_{10}$
na ga-ri	na ga-ri]	na ga-ri
		na-ri-ĝu$_{10}$
		ḫe$_2$-dab$_5$
5	1.9	10
		zi-u$_4$-su$_3$-ra$_2$
		inim ga-ra-ab-d[u$_{11}$]
GIŠ.PI.[TUG$_2$]	GIŠ.PI.[TUG$_2$]	ĝizzal
ḫe$_2$-m[a]-ak	ḫe$_2$-m[a]-ak	ḫe$_2$-em-ši-ak

11
na-ri-ga-ĝu$_{10}$
šu nam-bi$_2$-bar-re

12
inim du$_{11}$-ga-ĝu$_{10}$
na-ab-ta-bal-e-de$_3$

Lines 4–8 quoted above show that the Old Babylonian version closely follows the Adab version (or a tradition similar to the Adab version) from the Early Dynastic III period. The descriptions in lines 4–5, for example, are nearly verbatim quotations from Adab segm. 1.1–5, except for the dropping out of the mimation after the enclitic copula -a and UR$_2$.AŠ after šuruppak^{ki}.

Furthermore, lines 7–8 of the Old Babylonian version are essentially built on the basis of Adab segm. 1.6–7. The Old Babylonian version presumably interpreted, or misunderstood, UR$_2$.AŠ in the Adab version, neither as the epithet of the father giving the instructions nor as the son receiving them (as interpreted by modern scholars), but as the epithet of the grandfather (Steinkeller quoted in Davila 1995: 202 n. 21),[7] dubbed by the Old Babylonian version as 'Ubār-Tutu', a name which is of Akkadian origin, meaning 'foreigner of (protected by) the god Tutu' (Alster 2005: 106). Such an interpretation of UR$_2$.AŠ by the Old Babylonian version may have been prompted by the fact that the patriarchal lineage of the man from Šuruppak was expected in this position according to certain genealogical conventions. This interpretation may also have been facilitated by the partial resemblance between the sign ušbar$_3$ = UR$_2$×U$_2$-AŠ (Alster 2005: 104) and the sign ubar, though the rationale behind the insertion of Tutu (tu-tu), the name of a city deity of Borsippa (Foster 2005: 129 n. 4), remains inexplicable (Steinkeller quoted in Davila 1995: 202 n. 21). Thus by interpreting, or possibly misunderstanding, the archaic UR$_2$.AŠ as the name of the father of the man of Šuruppak with the added qualification dumu 'son of' and by inserting the name of the son receiving the instructions, the Old Babylonian version presented three generations in this didactic text: Ubār-Tutu, the man from Šuruppak, and Ziusudra.[8]

[7] Nevertheless, the expression dumu ubar-tu-tu-ke$_4$ 'the son of Ubār-Tutu', which comes immediately after šuruppak^{ki}, as a whole functions as an epithet of the father giving the instructions. Thus the Old Babylonian version's interpretation and qualification of UR$_2$.AŠ in the Early Dynastic version tend to support the first modern interpretation of UR$_2$.AŠ summarized earlier.

[8] Compare the observations of Galter (2005: 281), who writes 'Šuruppak wird als Sohn Ubaratutus und Vater Ziudsuras in die Familie des letzten Königs vor der Flut eingeführt.' However, Galter does not explain in detail the transmission process.

There is evidence that the author of the Old Babylonian version was handling two parallel traditions. Line 6 šuruppak^{ki}-e dumu-ni-ra na na-mu-un-ri-ri 'the man from Šuruppak[9] gave instructions to his son' clearly follows a tradition similar to the Abū Ṣalābīkh version, AbS-T 3 šuruppak dumu na [n]a-mu-ri, which differs from Adab segm. 1.6 in lacking UR_2.AŠ after the name Šuruppak. Lines 6–8 of the Old Babylonian version indicate that this version has conflated two divergent traditions by juxtaposing them side by side: line 6 ≈ AbS-T 3; lines 7–8 ≈ Adab segm. 1.6–7.

The Old Babylonian version's omission of the epithet of the man of Šuruppak in line 5, in disagreement with AbS-T 2 and Adab segm. 1.3, 6 which both contain UR_2.AŠ after the name of Šuruppak, should be considered as an attempt to avoid the ambiguities as seen primarily in the Adab version. Šuruppak^{ki} in lines 5 and 7 of the Old Babylonian version can now be unequivocally interpreted as the man from Šuruppak, the father who gives instructions to his son. And it is he who should be accorded the intellectual attributes in the opening lines of the didactic text. So overall, on the basis of the passages we have discussed, it appears that the Old Babylonian version sought to clarify the ambiguities in the opening lines of the Early Dynastic versions concerning the generations involved in the didactic setting, by adding to or subtracting from the earlier versions.

Given the fact that the same names in the three-generation family mentioned in the Old Babylonian version of the *Instructions of Šuruppak* also occur in some of the chronographical traditions as the names of the last antediluvian rulers, an important historical question arises as to which one of the two branches of traditions developed first. Wilcke (1978: 202) suggests that the development in the Old Babylonian version of the *Instructions of Šuruppak* was due to the influence from the antediluvian king list tradition.[10]

At least in part, the name of Ubār-Tutu can be considered as deriving internally from the *Instructions of Šuruppak*, as the result of an attempt to make sense of UR_2.AŠ (ušbar$_x$) in the Early Dynastic versions, regardless of whether such attempt was first made by the Old Babylonian version or an earlier tradition. But the genealogical form added by the Old Babylonian version through the insertion of dumu in front of Ubār-Tutu (for UR_2.AŠ) seems more at home in the chronographical tradition, as the formula PN_1 dumu PN_2 'PN_1, the son of PN_2' is frequently used in the dynastic succession in the king list traditions as early as the Ur III

[9] The added ergative morpheme -e after šuruppak^{ki} suggests the attempt by the Old Babylonian version to stress that this toponym refers to the subject of the sentence.

[10] 'die Herrscher-Familie *Ubār-Tutu*—Šuruppag—Ziusudra ursprünglich nichts mit dem seinem Kind und Schwiegerkind ratenden Šuruppag zu tun hat und diese Namen erst später wegen der Namens-gleichheit mit dem „König" Šuruppag eindrangen'.

period.[11] Furthermore, the name Ziusudra, added by the Old Babylonian version of the *Instructions of Šuruppak*, must have come from external sources as well, because there is nothing in the Early Dynastic versions that could have given rise to this name (Lambert and Millard 1969: 19; Krebernik 1998: 319 n. 779). Though the name Ziusudra occurs in the mythological traditions (see the *Sumerian Flood Story*, the *Death of Bilgames*), the didactic traditions (see the *Ballade of Early Rulers*), the omen tradition mentioned earlier (see George 2003: 113) as well as the chronographical traditions (e.g. W-B 62, the *Dynastic Chronicle, Babyloniaca*), only in the chronographical traditions is Ziusudra presented in familial relationship, either with Ubār-Tutu as his father (the *Dynastic Chronicle, Babyloniaca*), or with Ubār-Tutu as his grandfather and the man from Šuruppak as his father (W-B 62). Thus it is quite certain that Ziusudra in the Old Babylonian version of the *Instructions of Šuruppak* was borrowed from the chronographical traditions, especially a tradition which is similar to the W-B 62 version of *SKL*. Wilcke's view that the development of the three-generation family in the Old Babylonian version of the *Instructions of Šuruppak* was the result of an attempt to adapt the Early Dynastic III versions of this didactic composition according to the existing chronographical tradition, therefore, seems to be warranted.

The chronographical sources must have gone through some essential adaptations in order to fit into the context of the *Instructions of Šuruppak*, which has little to do with the royal court, but is more at home in an agricultural and common social setting (Lambert and Millard 1969: 19; Alster 2005: 26, 33). The precepts given were for commoners to learn practical skills and virtues in order to lead a successful and secure life, rather than for the preparation of a ruler. Alster (2005: 33) rightly points out that 'it would be ludicrous or even quite insulting that such advice as "don't steal anything" (l. 28) were to be understood as seriously addressed to a future king'. Thus even with the genealogical relationship expanded and the name of Ziusudra added in the Old Babylonian version on the basis of the chronographical or antediluvian king list tradition, the didactic text still contains no explicit reference to the royal identity of any of the generations listed (contra Finkelstein 1963: 48–9).

Our investigation so far shows that prior to the development of the three-generation presentation (Ubār-Tutu, the man from Šuruppak, and Ziusudra) in the Old Babylonian version of the *Instructions of Šuruppak*, the tradition that contains the last antediluvian rulers already existed in the chronographical sources. The following study will turn to focus on those sources to see how they developed.

[11] See *USKL* ii 9 aka dumu en-me-barag-ge-si 'Aka, son of En-me-barage-si'; iii 14–15 mes-nun-ne$_2$ | dumu na-an-ne$_2$ 'Mes-nunne, son of Nanne'; iv 24 sar-ga-li$_2$-sar-ri$_2$ dumu na-ra-am-^{d}suen-ke$_4$ 'Sar-gali-sarrī, son of Narām-Suen' (Steinkeller 2003: 270–2).

Chronographical Sources

Among the seven published chronographical sources (MS 2855, W-B 444, W-B 62, UCBC 9-1819, Ni 3195, the *Dynastic Chronicle*, and *Babyloniaca*)[12] which contain the antediluvian section in their current condition, the last antediluvian dynasty is preserved in only five of them:

MS 2855 (early OB$^?$) line 19: ubur-tu$_3$-tu$_3$ mu 36,000 i$_3$-ak ‘Ubur-Tutu reigned 36,000 years.’ (Friberg 2007: 238)

W-B 444 (mid-OB) lines 32–5: šuruppak(SU.KUR.RU^{ki}) ⸢ub⸣ur(⸢DAG⸣.KISIM$_5$×⸢GA⸣)$^?$-tu$_3$-tu$_3$ | lugal-am$_3$ mu 18,600 i$_3$-ak | 1 lugal | mu-bi 18,600 ib$_2$-ak ‘(In) Šuruppak, Ubur-Tutu was king; he reigned 18,600 years. One king reigned 18,600 years.’ (Jacobsen 1939: 74–7)

W-B 62 (possibly OB$^?$[13]) lines 15–17: ^{m}šuruppak(SU.KUR.LAM) dumu ubur$_x$(DAG$_2$.KISIM$_5$×DIŠ$^?$)-tu-tu mu 28,800 | ^{m}zi-u$_4$-su$_3$-ra$_2$ dumu šuruppak(SU.KUR.LAM)-ke$_2$ mu 36,000 | 2 lugal šuruppak(SU.KUR.LAM^{ki}) ‘The man from Šuruppak, son of Ubūr-Tutu, (reigned) 28,800 years. Ziusudra, son of the man from Šuruppak, (reigned) 36,000 years. Two kings from Šuruppak.’ (Langdon 1923*b*: 258–9)

The *Dynastic Chronicle* (earliest extant copies from around the time of Assurbanipal 668–627 BC) lines 11–13: šuruppak^{ki} ubār-^{d}[tu-tu lu]gal-e m[u ... in-ak] | zi-u$_4$-su$_3$-ra dumu u[bār-^{d}tu-tu mu ... in-ak] | 2-am$_3$ lugal-e-ne bal[a šuruppak^{ki} mu ...] ‘In Šuruppak, Ubār-[Tutu], the king, [reigned ...] years. Ziusudra, son of [Ubār-Tutu, reigned ... years]. Two kings, the dynasty [of Šuruppak, reigned ... years].’ (Lambert 1973: 273, 275)

[12] IM 63095, a fragment of a recension of *SKL* from Tell Harmal which was discovered by Goetze and cited in Finkelstein (1963: 39 n. 1, 45 n. 21, 47 n. 26), is said to have preserved an antediluvian section. But the text has not yet been published and is thus unavailable. The tablet is dated to the early Old Babylonian period (see Vincente 1995: 238). There is still an Uruk list of rulers and sages, known from a manuscript dating to the Hellenistic period, *c.*165 BC (van Dijk 1962: 44–52; see also Galter 2005: 291; Beaulieu 2007: 6), that contains an antediluvian section. But this list omits the dynasty of Šuruppak. Instead, it has Enmeduranki, the king of Sippar, the next to last antediluvian dynasty in Šuruppak according to W-B 444, W-B 62, UCBC 9-1819, as the last antediluvian king. Galter (2005: 291) suggests that the dynasty of Šuruppak was intentionally left out by the author in order to arrive at the number seven. But it is quite possible that this list reflects a genuine antediluvian chronographical tradition (originating from Sippar$^?$) that concludes with the dynasty of Sippar, as hinted at by a bilingual inscription of king Nebuchadnezzar I (1126–1104 BC), entitled ‘*The Seed of Kingship*’ (see Lambert 1967: 126–38; 1974: 427–40; Frame 1995: 23–8; Foster 2005: 376–80); *Erra and Ishum* IV 50, and *Babyloniaca*.

[13] Jacobsen (1939: 58 n. 106) followed Zimmern and dated the tablet to ‘the end of the 3d millennium B.C.’, while recent scholars are uncertain of its date (Edzard 1980–3: 78; Vincente 1995: 238).

> *Babyloniaca* (around 300 BC) Book 2, F3: 'Then came the rule of Amempsinos (Ensipazianna), the Chaldean from Larankhos (Larak). He was king for eighteen *saroi*. Then came the rule of Otiartes (Ubār-Tutu), a Chaldean from Larankhos. He reigned eight *saroi*. Then after the death of Otiartes, his son Xisuthros (Ziusudra) reigned eighteen *saroi*. During his reign the Great Flood occurred.' (Verbrugghe and Wickersham 1996: 48)

According to Finkelstein (1963: 43), the damaged section concerning the last antediluvian dynasty in UCBC 9-1819 (no later than Samsu-iluna, 1749–1712 BC) may be reconstructed as follows: lines 14–17 [šuruppak(-še$_3$) ubur-] tu-tu | [mu . . . in-ak] | [zi-u$_4$-su$_3$-ra$_2$ dumu] | ubur-[tu-tu mu] 18,000 + . . . in-ak '[to (or "in") Šuruppak, Ubūr]-Tutu [reigned . . . years]. [Ziusudra, son of] Ubūr-[Tutu], reigned 18,000 + . . . years' (see also Galter 2005: 279). At least it is quite plausible that the toponym Šuruppak and the personal name Ubūr-Tutu were originally included in the text.

To trace the historical relationships among the data regarding the last antediluvian dynasty in the chronographical sources, it is important to compare them with each other as well as with the relevant passages from the Early Dynastic III and Old Babylonian versions of the *Instructions of Šuruppak* and the Standard Babylonian version of the *Gilgameš Epic*. According to the following comparisons, all these ancient sources tend to follow three genealogical schemes:

1 One-generation scheme: Ubār-Tutu

W-B 444 (*SKL*) 32–5	**MS 2855 (*SKL*) 19**
In Šuruppak,	
Ubār-Tutu was king;	Ubār-Tutu
he reigned 18,600 years.	reigned 36,000 years.
One king reigned 18,600 years.	

2 Two-generation scheme: Ubār-Tutu and Ziusudra

UCBC 9-1819 (*SKL*) 14–17	***The Dynastic Chronicle* 11–13**	***Babyloniaca* Book 2, F3**	**SB *Gilgameš* IX 6; X 208; XI 23**
[(In) Šuruppak	In Šuruppak	A Chaldean from Larankhos,	
Ubār-]Tutu	Ubār-[Tutu], the king,	Otiartes	
[reigned . . .	[reigned . . .]	reigned	

years.	years.	eight *saroi*.	
		After the death of Otiartes,	
Ziusudra,	Ziusudra,	Xisuthros,	UD-napišti/the man from Šuruppak,
son of] Ubār-[Tutu] reigned 18,000 + . . . years.	son of [Ubār-Tutu, reigned . . . years].	his son reigned eighteen *saroi*.	son of Ubār-Tutu
	Two kings, the dynasty [of Šuruppak, reigned . . . years].		

3 Three-generation scheme: Ubār-Tutu, the man from Šuruppak, and Ziusudra

W-B 62 (*SKL*) 15–17	**OB *Instructions of Šuruppak* 7–8**
The man from Šuruppak, son of Ubār-Tutu, (reigned) 28,800 years.	The man from Šuruppak, son of Ubār-Tutu,
	gave instructions to
Ziusudra, son of the man from Šuruppak, (reigned) 36,000 years. Two kings from Šuruppak.	Ziusudra, his son.

The name Ubār-Tutu is featured in all of the sources that have preserved the last antediluvian dynasty, no matter which generation this name represents, either the solo generation in W-B 444 and MS 2855, the first of the two generations in the *Dynastic Chronicle* (possibly UCBC 9-1819 as well; with Berossos listing Otiartes/Ubār-Tutu under the Larak dynasty), or the first of the three generations in W-B 62. If our view propounded earlier, that Ubār-Tutu is an interpretation (or misunderstanding) of UR$_2$.AŠ in the Early Dynastic III versions of the *Instructions of Šuruppak*, stands correct, then the fact that Ubār-Tutu is a common feature in the chronographical sources implies that the development of the last antediluvian dynasty in the chronographical sources must have depended on the *Instructions of Šuruppak*. If this is indeed the case, W-B 444 and the *Dynastic Chronicle* seem to have interpreted the Sumerian phrase Šuruppak^{ki} UR$_2$.AŠ (the Adab version) or Šuruppak UR$_2$.AŠ (the Abū Ṣalābīkh version) differently from the Old Babylonian version of the *Instructions of Šuruppak*. Instead of treating Šuruppak^{ki} or Šuruppak as the epithet of the father providing the counsels, W-B 444 and the *Dynastic Chronicle* regarded the toponym as being in a locative construction (though without the corresponding locative morpheme -a), i.e. '(In) Šuruppak', an interpretation which may have been prompted by the need for the name of the last antediluvian city in the chronographical traditions.[14] In so doing, Ubār-Tutu became the first generation. Ziusudra then, in the *Dynastic Chronicle*, became the son of Ubār-Tutu, with the added qualification dumu u[bār-^{d}tu-tu] 'son of U[bār-Tutu]' (line 12).

Berossos' account apparently follows the above tradition, as it too presents Ubār-Tutu (Otiartes) and Ziusudra (Xisuthros) in a father–son relationship. Yet, as mentioned earlier, Berossos deviated from the *Dynastic Chronicle* and the rest of the chronographical sources in that he presented Ubār-Tutu and Ziusudra as coming from the city Larak, instead of Šuruppak.

In presenting three generations in the last antediluvian dynasty: Ubār-Tutu, the man from Šuruppak, and Ziusudra, W-B 62 certainly follows the same interpretation of Šuruppak^{ki} UR$_2$.AŠ (the Adab version) or Šuruppak UR$_2$.AŠ (the Abū Ṣalābīkh version) in the Early Dynastic versions of the *Instructions of Šuruppak* as seen in the Old Babylonian version of the *Instructions of Šuruppak*. In addition to qualifying UR$_2$.AŠ (Ubār-Tutu) with dumu, as seen in the Old Babylonian version of the *Instructions of Šuruppak*, W-B 62 also defines Ziusudra as dumu šuruppak(SU.KUR.LAM)-ke$_2$ 'son of the man from Šuruppak'. The summary formula of the last antediluvian dynasty 2 lugal SU.KUR.LAM^{ki} 'two kings in Šuruppak' (line 17) further suggests that the author of this chronographical source seems to have been aware of the two-generation scheme as represented in the *Dynastic Chronicle*. Thus only two generations are acknowledged as rulers though the text lists all three generations. But unlike the *Dynastic Chronicle* which has Ubār-Tutu and Ziusudra as the last antediluvian rulers, W-B 62 presents the man from Šuruppak and Ziusudra.[15] Thus W-B 62 had conflated the two-generation tradition and the three-generation tradition when constructing the last antediluvian dynasty.[16]

Another case of the conflation of the divergent traditions may be observed in the genealogical relationship of ^{m}UD-*napišti*(zi) and Ubār-Tutu in SB *Gilgameš* IX 6 ^{m}UD-*napišti*(zi) *mār*(dumu) ^{m}*ubara*-^{d}*tutu* 'UD-napišti, son of Ubār-Tutu'; X 208 ^{m}UD-*napišti*(zi) *mār*(dumu) ^{m}[*u*]-*bar*-*t*[*utu* (. . .)] 'UD-napišti, son of [U]bār-T[utu]'; XI 23 $^{lu}{}_{2}$*šuruppakû mār*(dumu) ^{m}*ubara*-^{d}*tutu* 'O

[14] Compare eridu(NUN)^{ki} a$_2$-lu-lim lugal '(In) Eridu, Alulim (was) king)' (line 3); bad$_3$-tibira^{ki} en-me-en-lu$_2$-an-na '(In) Bad-tibira, Enmenluanna' (line 11); la-ra-ak^{ki} en-sipa-zi-an-na '(In) Larak, Ensipazianna' (line 20); zimbir(UD.KIB.NUN.NA^{ki}) en-me-en-dur$_2$-an-na '(In) Sippar, Enmenduranna' (line 26) in W-B 444. Note in all these cases, as well as šuruppak(SU.KUR.RU^{ki}) ⸢ub⸣ur(⸢DAG⸣.KISIM$_5$×⸢GA⸣)$^{?}$-tu$_3$-tu$_3$ '(In) Šuruppak, Ubūr-Tutu' (line 32), the locative morpheme is missing after the toponyms.

[15] Note that Finkelstein (1963: 45) and Friberg (2007: 240) in their comparative charts of antediluvian kings list Ubār-Tutu as the first ruler in the last antediluvian dynasty in W-B 62; compare the correct listing in Finkelstein (1963: 46) and Galter (2005: 279).

[16] An alternative explanation for the three-generation but two-ruler presentation for the last antediluvian dynasty in W-B 62 might be that the author of this chronographical source attempted to keep the total number of the antediluvian rulers at ten, thus counting one less generation from Šuruppak as a ruler.

man of Šuruppak, son of Ubār-Tutu' (George 2003: 666–7, 690–1, 704–5). On the one hand, the genealogical relationship follows the presentation of the two-generation dynasty comprising Ubār-Tutu the father and ^{m}UD-*napišti*(zi)/Ziusudra the son, as seen in the *Dynastic Chronicle*. $^{[i]ri}$*šuruppak* is definitely taken as the name of the last antediluvian city (XI 11–14), in which the last antediluvian rulers dwelled, an interpretation of Šuruppak^{ki} in the Early Dynastic III versions of the *Instructions of Šuruppak* which can also be found in W-B 62 and W-B 444. On the other hand, XI 23 $^{lu}{}_{2}$*šuruppakû mār*(dumu) ^{m}*ubara-*^{d}*tutu* 'O man of Šuruppak, son of Ubār-Tutu' reflects the interpretation of Šuruppak^{ki} UR$_2$.AŠ or Šuruppak UR$_2$.AŠ in the Early Dynastic III versions of the *Instructions of Šuruppak* by W-B 62 and the Old Babylonian version of the *Instructions of Šuruppak*. The mixing of the divergent traditions led to a fascinating result: the man from Šuruppak is no longer the father of ^{m}UD-*napišti*(zi)/Ziusudra, but ^{m}UD-*napišti*(zi)/Ziusudra himself! This shows that while the author (or editor) of the Standard Babylonian version of the *Gilgameš Epic* adopted the rendering of Šuruppak^{ki}/Šuruppak UR$_2$.AŠ as represented in the traditions such as W-B 62 and the Old Babylonian version of the *Instructions of Šuruppak*, he nonetheless adhered to the two-generation genealogical scheme as seen in the *Dynastic Chronicle*. Thus the identity of 'the man from Šuruppak' had to be redefined. There is no other choice for identifying this figure in the two-generation framework for the last antediluvian dynasty but ^{m}UD-*napišti*(zi)/Ziusudra.

The presentation of Ubār-Tutu in MS 2855 and W-B 444 as the only ruler from Šuruppak in the last antediluvian dynasty (omitting Ziusudra) is most peculiar among the chronographical sources. Jacobsen (1939: 76 n. 34) thought that the omission of Ziusudra in W-B 444 may have resulted from the composite nature of the antediluvian section of W-B 444: with Ubār-Tutu belonging to an independent antediluvian king list tradition (e.g. W-B 62) and Ziusudra being the hero in the Flood epic. During the process of joining these two originally separate traditions, the author of W-B 444 failed to incorporate Ziusudra in the antediluvian king list. Jacobsen's explanation is predicated on his assumption that the antediluvian tradition and the Sumerian expression a-ma-ru . . . ba-ur$_3$-ra-ta in lines 39–40 of W-B 444 originated in the mythological or epic source (1939: 64 n. 118). According to Jacobsen, the temporal construction eĝir . . . -ta in W-B 444 line 40 was added by the author of W-B 444. But as already suggested earlier in this book, the phrase eĝir a-ma-ru ba-ur$_3$-ra-ta in line 40 of W-B 444 as a whole was a stylistic formula first used in *Išme-Dagan A* and the *Instructions of Ur-Ninurta*, compositions which were independent of the Flood epic.

Rebuffing Jacobsen's explanation, Finkelstein (1963: 47–8) believed that the omission of Ziusudra in W-B 444 was 'deliberate'; yet he did not appear to state why it was so, except for pointing out that such omission is not related to the number of the antediluvian rulers included in the chronographical traditions.

But Finkelstein's ensuing discussion on the divergent traditions regarding the royal identity of Ziusudra in Mesopotamian sources (1963: 48–9) implies that the omission of Ziusudra in W-B 444 might have been influenced by those traditions (e.g. the *Ballade of Early Rulers*, and the omen text referred to by George 2003: 113) that do not openly acknowledge the royal status of Ziusudra (see Galter 2005: 280). But given that all other chronographical sources, except for MS 2855, have preserved the last antediluvian dynasty and include Ziusudra (W-B 62, the *Dynastic Chronicle*, and *Babyloniaca*; see also the epic source SB *Gilgameš* IX 6; X 208; XI 23), the omission of Ziusudra in WB 444 is enigmatic.

One might possibly interpret the absence of Ziusudra in W-B 444 in the light of the literary history of the *Instructions of Šuruppak*. If one assumes an evolutionary stage at which the name Ubār-Tutu had already occurred in place of UR_2.AŠ in the Early Dynastic III versions of the *Instructions of Šuruppak* (e.g. Adab segm. 1.6–7 [šuruppak^{ki}] UR_2.AŠ | dumu-ni-ra na na-ri-ri) without the qualification of dumu, and the name Ziusudra was not yet added, is it possible that the author of W-B 444 might have interpreted Ubār-Tutu as the only ruler from Šuruppak in the last antediluvian dynasty? Since the son receiving the instructions was not named, he might have been simply ignored. However, since W-B 444 had combined the antediluvian section and the king list proper with the introductory, concluding, and transitional remarks, and had adapted the antediluvian section according to the king list proper (Jacobsen 1939: 55–68, especially n. 118), by adding the formulae for dynastic total and the change of dynasty, and the formulae introducing single rulers and the first rulers of a dynasty (Jacobsen 1939: 29–51), it seems that this chronographical source developed later than those traditions lacking these features, such as the traditions reflected in W-B 62, UCBC 9-1819, and Ni 3195. If some of these traditions (W-B 62, and possibly UCBC 9-1819) had already included Ziusudra, it would be difficult to think that the author of W-B 444 was still unaware of or overlooked Ziusudra as the last antediluvian ruler (Finkelstein 1963: 48). Nor is it conceivable from the perspective of the factual data that W-B 444 could reach a stage in the development of the antediluvian chronographical tradition that included all other names of the antediluvian cities and rulers (as seen in the *Dynastic Chronicle*) except for Ziusudra, because this name was still unknown to or accidentally omitted by the author of W-B 444 (Lambert and Millard 1969: 20). Thus Finkelstein (1963: 47) may indeed be right in viewing the omission of Ziusudra in W-B 444 as deliberate. But what could have been the reason for such a deliberate omission?

The rationale for the omission of Ziusudra in W-B 444 might have been rooted in the particular political ideology promulgated by *SKL*: that kingship or hegemony could only manifest itself in one city at a time in ancient Mesopotamia and its periphery. The idea of the relentless shift or rotation of political supremacy among different cities for the legitimization of the incumbent rulers in place of the preceding dynasty might have prevented the inclusion of a ruler, presumably already known by then as the Flood hero who had gained eternal life, in the king list as the last antediluvian ruler. Eternal life for the last antediluvian ruler might imply his eternal reign,[17] which obviously would not be congruent with the *SKL*'s underlying political philosophy that emphasizes the discontinuity of kingship.

The omission of Ziusudra in W-B 444 may furthermore be understood in the light of the function of the antediluvian section in this chronographical source, which had been used by the Isin rulers as a 'historical charter' (Michalowski 1983: 241–3) for their assumption of power.[18] The antediluvian section was added to the king list proper (Jacobsen 1939: 57–68) in such a way as to project *SKL*'s ideology back in the remote past, in the time of mythical origin (see Chapter 3). The opening line of the king list proper, nam-lugal an-ta e$_{11}$-de$_3$-a-ba 'after kingship had descended from heaven' (line 41 of W-B 444; compare nam-lugal an-ta e$_{11}$-da-ba in *USKL* obv. i 1 and BT 14 + P$_3$ i 1), is duplicated and placed at the beginning of the antediluvian section (Hallo 1963*b*: 56). The formula for the change of dynasty was added: GN$_1^{ki}$ ba-šub nam-lugal-bi GN$_2^{ki}$-še ba-de$_6$ (W-B 444 i 8–10; compare another *SKL* version IM 63095 as commented on in Finkelstein 1963: 42, 45 n. 21) or GN$_1^{ki}$ ba-šub-be$_2$-en nam-lugal-bi GN$_2^{ki}$-še ba-de$_6$ (W-B 444 i 18–19, 24–5, 30–1)[19] 'GN$_1$ fell$^{?}$; its kingship was taken to GN$_2$', which correlates with the parallel formulae in the king list proper, such as GN$_1^{ki}$ ^{geš}tukul ba-an-sig$_3$ nam-lugal-bi GN$_2^{ki}$-še$_3$ ba-de$_6$ 'GN$_1$ was smitten with weapons; its kingship was carried to GN$_2$' (see

[17] Eternal/prolonged life and eternal/prolonged reign are two interrelated blessings which were often sought after in royal hymns for the royal patrons.

[18] The study of Dahl (2007: 9–11) seems to imply that the *SKL* might have been used not only to bolster the claims of the Isin rulers as the rightful successors of the preceding Ur III dynasty with the ideology of a relentless shift of hegemony, but also to legitimize the Isin rulers against the competing claims to the throne among their royal kinsmen with the almost strict presentation of patrilineal succession—though in some cases, fratrilineal succession may have been the reality. For example, Amar-Suen, Šū-Suen, and Ibbi-Suen may all have been Šulgi's sons. But in the W-B 444 version of *SKL* only Amar-Suen is presented as Šulgi's son, while Šū-Suen is presented as Amar-Suen's son and Ibbi-Suen as Šū-Suen's son (Dahl 2007: 4, 19).

[19] The first- or second-person singular pronominal ending in ba-šub-be$_2$-en is difficult to explain. Jacobsen's rendering 'I drop (the topic) City A' (1939: 71–5) implies the intrusion of the scribe's own voice in the text. Finkelstein (1963: 41–2), however, argued that the verb šub should not be rendered as 'to drop' but 'to fall, throw down, overthrow, etc.' and translated the finite verb chain as 'I will bring to an end (the ascendancy of) City A, etc.', assuming the speaker is a deity from a mythological or epic source, on the basis of which the above formula for the change of dynasty in W-B 444 was formed. It might be important to point out that the verb šub is used in *NL* 14, 28, 36, 42, 58, 99, 280, 281, often in the sense of 'to fall' or 'to neglect'. In *NL* 99, the verb is applied to the city Nippur, uru$_2$-bi uru$_2$ šub-ba im-ma-ni-in-ku$_4$-ra-am$_3$ 'That city he (Enlil) turned into a neglected city.' Glassner (2004: 119, 121) renders ba-šub-be$_2$-en as 'I abandoned (City A)' in W-B 444 i 17, 23, 29.

Jacobsen 1939: 29–38). Then the temporal clause that alludes to the flood catastrophe was adopted from the royal hymnic compositions such as *Išme-Dagan A* and the *Instructions of Ur-Ninurta* and placed right in front of the king list proper: a-ma-ru ba-ur$_3$-«ra-ta» | eĝir a-ma-ru ba-ur$_3$-ra-ta | nam-lugal an-ta e$_{11}$-de$_3$-a-ba | kiš^{ki} nam-lugal-la 'The Flood swept over. After the Flood had swept over, when kingship descended from heaven, kingship was in Kiš' (W-B 444 i 39–42). This chronographical arrangement signifies that the primeval flood catastrophe had destroyed kingship, which called for its re-establishment by the gods. Thus the Flood as well as the antediluvian era in W-B 444 served as a mythical foundation for the paradigm of political re-establishment or the destruction-restoration rhetoric propagated by the *SKL* and Isin-Larsa royal hymns. In such an ideological framework the author of W-B 444 may have found it difficult to include Ziusudra who was acknowledged as both the last antediluvian ruler and the Flood hero from antediluvian traditions independent of the king list proper.

Other chronographical sources presumably had no problems with Ziusudra because they did not seem to use the antediluvian tradition ideologically, which can partly be seen from the lack of conscious efforts to join the antediluvian tradition and the king list proper together and to adapt the antediluvian tradition according to the formulae and the ideology of the king list proper among some sources. For example, W-B 62 is an independent antediluvian tradition detached from the king list proper which only comprises a simple list without some of the formulae characteristic of W-B 444. Though containing a formula of change of dynasty (GN$_1^{ki}$ bala-bi ba-kur$_2$ nam-lugal-bi GN$_2^{ki}$-še$_3$ ba-nigin 'the dynasty of GN$_1$ changed; its kingship passed to GN$_2$'), the *Dynastic Chronicle* has no introductory formula comparable to that of W-B 444 i 1. The antediluvian tradition was joined with the king list proper in this chronographical source apparently due to antiquarian interests, as indicated by the allusions to the Flood epic. The same explanations may be applied to the inclusion of Ziusudra in Berossos' account, a text of an even later date which obviously was also motivated by antiquarian interests in its incorporation of the chronographical tradition as well as the Flood epic. It is impossible to judge UCBC 9-1819 and Ni 3195 because the section of the last antediluvian dynasty has been damaged. At least from the extant portions of these two antediluvian sources we see no introductory formula as found in line 1 of W-B 444.

W-B 444's deliberate omission of Ziusudra as the last antediluvian ruler due to its emphasis on the dynastic discontinuity brought by the Flood and on the legitimization of political re-establishment may find resonance in the *Rulers of Lagaš*, another ideologically laden chronography but from the late Old Babylonian period which alluded to the survival of humankind after the Flood but omitted the Flood hero in its introductory section. Its intertextual connection with W-B 444 i 40–1 seems certain on account of the chronological sequence and the phraseology used in the prologue:[20]

> After the Flood had swept over and brought about the destruction of the countries; when humankind was made to endure, and the seed of humankind was preserved and the black-headed people all rose; when An and Enlil called the name of humankind and established rulership, but kingship and the crown of the city had not yet come out from heaven.[21]

Despite some of the differences between the *Rulers of Lagaš* and W-B 444, both chronographical sources stress the discontinuity of the antediluvian establishment. Though the human race had survived, the sustaining civilization was gone and must be re-established in order for the human race to flourish. In particular, kingship (nam-lugal) or rulership (nam-ensi$_2$), an essential aspect of civilization, had to be reinstated by the gods. The purpose of emphasizing the discontinuity of the antediluvian or ante-catastrophic establishment for both W-B 444 and the *Rulers of Lagaš* is to accentuate the achievement of the postdiluvian and post-catastrophic establishment. This is also the case for *LW, NL, Išme-Dagan A*, and the *Instructions of Ur-Ninurta*, with the latter two texts sharing basically the same phraseology with W-B 444 and the *Rulers of Lagaš* when introducing the post-catastrophic era.[22]

While *LW, NL, Išme-Dagan A*, the *Instructions of Ur-Ninurta*, and W-B 444 used this destruction-restoration ideology to legitimize the power of the Isin rulers, the *Rulers of Lagaš* appropriated the same ideology for the glorification of the Lagaš dynasty. The extensive portrayals of the dire situation of humankind immediately after the Flood (lines 1–49) in the Lagaš text serve as a preparation for the dramatic reversal in the ensuing enumeration of the cultural achievements of the Lagaš rulers: the ongoing digging of the irrigation system, writing and the rise of the scribal and administrative classes (lines 107, 183, 185, 192, 196), the development of cults through temple-building (lines 154–5, 171), and the construction of cities, including the

[20] Other evidence of intertextual relationship between W-B 444 and the *Rulers of Lagaš* can be seen from the use of similar stylistic formulae (e.g. mu X i$_3$-ak, 'he reigned X years') and a fantastic number of years for the reign of the early rulers in both texts. According to Sollberger (1967: 279), the *Rulers of Lagaš* was composed in reaction to the king list 'whose author had ignored the rulers of Lagaš'.

[21] *Rulers of Lagaš* 1–10: [eĝir a]-ma-ru ba-ur$_3$-ra-ta | [u$_3$] ⸢gel⸣-le-eĝ$_3$ kur-ra-ke$_4$ ba-an-ĝar-ra-ta | ⸢nam-lu$_2$⸣-ulu$_3$ da-re-eš i-ak-a-ba | numun nam-lu$_2$-⸢ulu$_3$⸣ im-mi-in-tak$_4$-a-ba | uĝ$_3$ saĝ ge$_6$-ga ni$_2$-bi-a im-mi-in-il$_2$-la-a-ba | u$_4$ an-ne$_2$ ^{d}en-lil$_2$-le | nam-lu$_2$-ulu$_3$ mu-bi sa$_4$-a-ta | u$_3$ nam-ensi$_2$ in ⸢ĝar-ra⸣-ta | nam-⸢lugal⸣ aga ⸢iri-am$_3$⸣ | an-t[a nu]-ub-ta-an-e$_3$-[a-ba]. Phraseologically, the lines quoted here from the *Rulers of Lagaš* also show close intertextual connections with the *Sumerian Flood Story* 88–9, 157, 259 (Sollberger 1967: 279).

[22] *Išme-Dagan A* 120 eĝir a-ma-ru ur$_3$-ra-ta; the *Instructions of Ur-Ninurta* 4 eĝir a-ma-ru ba-ĝar-ra-[a-ta]; W-B 444 i 40 eĝir a-ma-ru ba-ur$_3$-ra-ta; the *Rulers of Lagaš* 1 [eĝir a]-ma-ru ba-ur$_3$-ra-ta 'after the flood/Flood had swept over'.

building of the palace and city walls (lines 155, 186, 187). These cultural achievements are but a continuation of the restoration that began with the re-establishment of agriculture initiated earlier presumably by Ninurta (Sollberger 1967: 284) in lines 50–65. The juxtaposition of negative depictions and their reversals is very similar to what we have already seen in *NL*, in which the catastrophe ushers in the restoration by Enlil and his chosen human agent Išme-Dagan.

The emphasis on postdiluvian re-establishment under direct divine assistance in the *Rulers of Lagaš* implies that the inclusion of Ziusudra either as the last antediluvian ruler or as the Flood hero is not only unnecessary, but also counterproductive. Thus Ziusudra (as well as the whole antediluvian history) is omitted even when the text clearly alludes to the Flood story, most likely a version similar to the *Sumerian Flood Story*. By contrast, the *Dynastic Chronicle*, which also alluded to the Flood story, but did so at greater length and evidently relied on the *Atra-hasīs Epic*, includes Ziusudra as the last antediluvian king in its antediluvian king list and presumably as the Flood hero as well in its fragmentary section of the Flood epic.

The traditions such as W-B 444 and the *Rulers of Lagaš* that emphasize postdiluvian re-establishment through direct divine intervention form a sharp contrast with the traditions that stress the indispensable role of the Flood hero for the recovery of civilization in the postdiluvian era. The latter traditions are often represented by the compositions, generally didactic in nature, that are related to the legendary ruler Gilgameš: for example, the *Death of Bilgames* and the Standard Babylonian *Gilgameš Epic*. According to these traditions, the recovery of antediluvian civilization was only possible because of the survival of the Flood hero who had not only preserved the knowledge from the antediluvian era but had also transmitted that knowledge in some way or another to the people of the postdiluvian period. In the Gilgameš traditions, it was Gilgameš who brought back from the Flood hero the once-lost antediluvian knowledge which was most essential for the maintenance of human society and the Land of Sumer.

If one compares lines 1 and 41 of W-B 444[23] with the *Death of Bilgames*, the Mê-Turan version 56–61,[24] the conceptual difference between these two sources becomes clear. While the chronographical source portrays civilization as having to be reinstituted after the Flood, presumably through direct divine

[23] nam-lugal an-ta e$_{11}$-de$_3$-a-ba 'When kingship descended from heaven'.

[24] e$_2$ diĝir-re-e-ne ki ĝar-ĝar-ra-a-ba | zi-u$_4$-su$_3$-ta$^{!}$-aš ki-bi-a saĝ im-ma-ni-t[i] | me ki-en-gi-ra-ke$_4$ ki u$_4$ ⸢ba-ḫa⸣-la-me-eš ⸢x⸣ [(x x)]/u$_4$ ul-⸢-li⸣-še$_3$ | ⸢a$_2$ aĝ$_2$⸣-ĝa$_2$ bi-lu-da$_{10}$ kalam-ma-aš ⸢im-ta-a-ni⸣ | šu-⸢luḫ ka-luḫ x (x) si mu-un-si-sa$_2$⸣-e | a-⸢ta$^{?}$ x⸣ [. . .] ⸢x⸣ 'Having founded many temples of the gods, you reached Ziusudra in his dwelling place. Having brought down to the land the divine powers of Sumer, which at that time were forgotten forever, the orders, and the rituals, he$^{?}$ carried out correctly the rites of hand washing and mouth washing' (thus MS M$_1$; compare the Mê-Turan version 147–52; N$_1$ iv D 5–9; SB *Gilgameš* I 42–4).

intervention (e.g. the *Rulers of Lagaš* 6–10), because it had been completely destroyed by the Flood, the Gilgameš tradition represents civilization as being preserved during the Flood through the Flood hero Ziusudra/^{m}UD-napišti and passed on to Gilgameš.

There is, however, considerable fluidity in how antediluvian civilization or knowledge was preserved and transmitted. In general, the Old Babylonian sources tend to be reticent about how exactly the Flood hero preserved antediluvian civilization. Both the Old Babylonian version of the *Atra-hasīs Epic* and the *Sumerian Flood Story* only recount the preservation of humankind and other living creatures by the Flood hero during the Flood. But the late sources offered explicit information with regard to the intermediary role of the Flood hero in preserving antediluvian knowledge. SB *Gilgameš* XI 86, for example, went on to add that the Flood hero also carried on board ⸢*mārī*(dumu)^{meš}⸣ *ummâni kalīšunu* 'artisans of all kinds'. After the Flood, these artisans supposedly helped revive human civilization.

In the *Seed of Kingship* (Lambert 1967: 128–31; 1974: 434–40), a bilingual text (Sumerian and Akkadian) that exalts Nebuchadnezzar I (1125–1104 BC), one finds a different account about how antediluvian knowledge was transmitted.[25] Though being celebrated for reviving antediluvian civilization like Gilgameš (the *Seed of Kingship* 4, 7), the Babylonian king did not rely on the Flood hero (as known in the Flood epic) or the last antediluvian king called Ziusudra from Šuruppak (as known in the chronographical sources) for information. Instead, he had presumably inherited antediluvian knowledge through Enmeduranki, king of Sippar in the antediluvian era, from whom Nebuchadnezzar I was said to have descended biologically (the *Seed of Kingship* 8–9; for the historical context, see Foster 2005: 376–7).

The antediluvian tradition reflected in the *Seed of Kingship* corresponds well with *Erra and Ishum* IV 50, which describes Sippar as the only antediluvian city spared from the destruction of the Flood, and the Uruk list of antediluvian rulers and sages known from a manuscript dating to the Hellenistic period (van Dijk 1962: 44–52; Galter 2005: 291), which presents Enmeduranki as the last antediluvian king. The same tradition that regards Sippar as the last antediluvian city or dynasty has also been preserved in the highly synthetic account of Berossos who, in addition to including the tradition of Ubār-Tutu/Otiartes and Ziusudra/Xisuthros (normally identified as coming from Šuruppak but here from Larak), recorded that, prior to

[25] That civilization was brought from Eridu (the first antediluvian city) to Uruk (a postdiluvian city) by Inana (*Inana and Enki*) or Enmerkar (*ELA* 58, 89) may represent different traditions, from the city Uruk of course, regarding the transmission of antediluvian knowledge. Likewise, the notion that the seven antediluvian sages laid the foundation for the wall of Uruk (SB *Gilgameš* I 21; XI 326) may be understood accordingly. All of these seem to be attempts to promote the prestige of Uruk by connecting the city with the hoary past, see also SB *Gilgameš* I 15.

the arrival of the Flood, Xisuthros was instructed by Kronos[26] 'to bury together all the tablets, the first, the middle, and the last, and hide them in Sippar, the city of the sun' so that after the Flood people could retrieve them and rebuild Babylonia (F4a). The tablets presumably contained the knowledge and arts humans had learned from the eight antediluvian sages coming up from the Erythraean Sea.[27] Thus antediluvian knowledge in Berossos' account was to a certain extent independent of the Flood hero, the king as well as the gods. It was the sages and the means of writing that played the decisive role (Galter 2005: 294), which reflects the rising independence of the scholarly tradition in late Mesopotamian culture, as observed by Beaulieu (2007: 15–19).

Though it is the late sources that tend to provide more information on the issues of the preservation and transmission of antediluvian civilization, the intermediary role of the Flood hero in these cultural tasks can already be deduced from how the protagonist Ziusudra or antediluvian kingship was portrayed in the *Sumerian Flood Story* (as well as the *Death of Bilgames* mentioned earlier). In this late Old Babylonian composition (Poebel 1914*a*: 66–9; Civil 1969: 138–9), Ziusudra the Flood hero is not only acknowledged as an antediluvian ruler, but also the only ruler in the antediluvian era. If we compare the *Sumerian Flood Story* (CBS 10673 + CBS 10867) with W-B 444, the intertextual relationship between the two texts as well as their dialectically opposing views with regard to antediluvian kingship become immediately apparent:[28]

***SKL* (W-B 444)**	***The Sumerian Flood Story* (CBS 10673 + CBS 10867)**
(1) [nam]lugal an-ta e$_{11}$-de$_3$-a-ba When kingship descended from heaven	(88) [u$_4$ x] x nam-lugal-la an-ta e$_{11}$-de$_3$-a-ba [When . . .] of kingship descended from heaven,
	(89) men maḫ ^{ĝeš}gu-za nam-lugal-la an-ta e$_{11}$-a-ba when the exalted crown and throne of kingship descended from heaven,
(2) eridu^{ki} nam-lugal-la kingship was in Eridu.	

[26] The father of Zeus, parallel to Enki being the father of Marduk; see Verbrugghe and Wickersham (1996: 49 n. 17).

[27] Although the Erythraean Sea (τῆς Ἐρυθράς Θαλάσσης) literally means 'the Red Sea' to the Greeks, it included the Indian Ocean and the Persian Gulf (see Verbrugghe and Wickersham 1996: 48).

[28] The following comparative chart is partially based on that of Jacobsen (1939: 65 n. 119), who, however, did not point out the opposing conceptions of antediluvian kingship in these two texts.

(3–38) (list of 5 antediluvian cities and 8 antediluvian kings)	(92–7) (list of antediluvian cities assigned to their patron deities)[29]
* inclusion of antediluvian kings and their succession * omission of Ziusudra as the last antediluvian king and the Flood hero	* omission of antediluvian kings and their succession * inclusion of Ziusudra as the only antediluvian king and the Flood hero
(39) a-ma-ru ba-ur$_3$-«ra-ta» Then the Flood swept over.	(202) a-ma-ru ugu kab-du$_{11}$-ga ba-an-da-ab-ur$_3$-e The Flood swept over the capitals. (203) u$_4$ 7-am$_3$ ĝi$_6$ 7-am$_3$ After, for 7 days and 7 nights,
(40) eĝir a-ma-ru ba-ur$_3$-ra-ta After the Flood had swept over	(204) a-ma-ru kalam-ma ba-ur$_3$-ra-ta the Flood had swept over the land, (205) ^{ĝeš}ma$_2$ gur$_4$-gur$_4$ a gal-la im-ḫul tuku$_4$-tuku$_4$-a-ta and waves and windstorms had rocked the huge boat.
(41) nam-lugal an-ta e$_{11}$-de$_3$-a-ba and when kingship had descended from heaven,	(206–the end) (the survival and apotheosis of the Flood hero Ziusudra being repeatedly called king)
(42) kiš^{ki} nam-lugal-la kingship was in Kiš.	

Though adopting a similar conceptual framework and phraseology to the chronographical sources such as W-B 444, the *Sumerian Flood Story* unequivocally shows that kingship, personified and idealized by the Flood hero Ziusudra, not only persisted regardless of the divine intention to destroy it by the Flood (line 160), but also achieved a transcendent status with the apotheosis of Ziusudra after it had contributed to the preservation of humankind and other living creatures at the time of destruction (line 259).[30] Thus there is no need for the reinstitution of kingship after the Flood.

The *Sumerian Flood Story*'s omission of the antediluvian kings and its representation of the Flood hero Ziusudra as the only king in the antediluvian era may not only have been conditioned by the author's particular understanding of kingship in response to *SKL*'s political ideology, but may also have

[29] In terms of the names and order of the antediluvian cities, the *Sumerian Flood Story* seems to have borrowed from W-B 444 or a similar king list tradition (Jacobsen 1981: 526). But the form in which the cities were presented and the idea that these cities were assigned to their patron deities are at variance with W-B 444. And these features do not seem to have originated in the *Sumerian Flood Story*; instead, they may have been adapted from earlier Sumerian traditions such as *LSU*.

[30] The exaltation of kingship in the *Sumerian Flood Story* has also been noted by Vladimir V. Emelianov as referred to in Annus (2002: 129, 131–2).

been influenced by the Flood epic (the *Atra-hasīs Epic*), which our text seems to have abbreviated and adapted.[31] As observed by Lambert and Millard (1969: 20–1), the antediluvian tradition in the *Atra-hasīs Epic* is independent of the king list tradition (see also Jacobsen 1939: 76 n. 34), for it is unlikely that it had included the antediluvian rulers in the lost lines in Tablet I 307–51. So the Flood hero Atra-hasīs seems to be the only king in the antediluvian era in this tradition, though the extant text gives no explicit indications of Atra-hasīs' royal identity. The *Sumerian Flood Story* was the first attested mythological source that openly identified the Flood hero as king, as some king list traditions represented by W-B 62 from the Old Babylonian period had done in their antediluvian sections.

The above examination so far shows that the genealogy of the last antediluvian dynasty most likely had originated in the chronographical traditions. Based on the available sources, it is concluded that the two-generation scheme comprising Ubār-Tutu and his son known as Ziusudra might have occurred at a date earlier than the three-generation scheme consisting of Ubār-Tutu, the man from Šuruppak, and Ziusudra. The one-generation scheme in W-B 444 (and MS 2855) may be a result of deliberate omission of Ziusudra for ideological reasons. As far as the name or epithet of each generation is concerned, both the name Ubār-Tutu and the epithet 'the man from Šuruppak' developed on the basis of the Sumerian expression Šuruppak^{ki} UR_2.AŠ or Šuruppak UR_2.AŠ in the opening lines of the Early Dynastic III versions of the *Instructions of Šuruppak*. UR_2.AŠ in the *Instructions of Šuruppak* later evolved into Ubār-Tutu. The three-generation scheme with 'the man from Šuruppak' defined as dumu Ubār-Tutu 'son of Ubār-Tutu' emerged later in the context of the Old Babylonian version of the *Instructions of Šuruppak* in the process of updating the Early Dynastic III version on the basis of the two-generation genealogy in

[31] That the Flood narrative in the last four columns of the *Sumerian Flood Story* (CBS 10673 + CBS 10867) has a close relationship with the Flood epic represented by the OB *Atra-hasīs Epic* has long been known. Poebel (1914*a*) tended to see their relationship as CBS 10673 + CBS 10867's dependence on the *Atra-hasīs Epic*. Civil (1969: 139, 171 nn. 153, 202) also argues for the Sumerian composition's reliance on an Akkadian model; see also Hallo (1990: 199). Lambert and Millard (1969: 14), however, contend that 'the relative dates' of these compositions cannot be determined, though they seem to have been composed around the same time, i.e. the latter half of the Old Babylonian period. The basic plot is almost the same, except that the Sumerian story represents a telescoped version of what is found in the *Atra-hasīs Epic*, probably in order to keep the whole story contained in one tablet. Poebel's assessment (1914*a*: 65) of the Sumerian text's adaptation of the earlier Flood narrative tradition is quite illuminating: 'Our text does not relate the various incidents of the story in the quiet and steady progression usually found in historical narrative, but often merely alludes to some striking incident and without wasting any time on details jumps abruptly to some other incident. A good illustration for this is found in the third column, where line 17′ merely tells us that Enki held counsel in his heart without betraying what the subject of his deliberation was. Our poem evidently belongs to that class of historical poetry which was not intended to impart new historical facts with which the person who listened to the poem or song was quite familiar.'

the chronographical traditions. However, where the name Ziusudra and its Akkadian counterparts ^{m}UD-*napišti*(zi) *rūqu*, ^{m}UD-*napišti*(zi), or ^{m}UD-*napištim*(zi)*tim* in the Standard Babylonian *Gilgameš Epic* originated from still remains a puzzle, which will be tackled later in this chapter.

Mythological Sources

It has been shown above that the *Instructions of Šuruppak* played an important role in the development of antediluvian traditions in the chronographical sources during the Old Babylonian period. The examination below will demonstrate how the same didactic composition had influenced the development of antediluvian traditions in the mythological or epic sources.

The *Instructions of Šuruppak* presents a traditional didactic scenario in which the father gave practical instructions to his son on how to succeed in life and work. In the Flood story, the communication between Enki and the Flood hero is likewise presented in a didactic fashion. The opening formulae in Enki's instructions to the Flood hero prior to the Flood, for instance, are reminiscent of those in the father's instructions to the son in the didactic source:

ED III version of the *Instructions of Šuruppak* (AbS-T) 4–5 (Alster 2005: 177)
dumu-ĝu$_{10}$ na ga-ri | GIŠ.PI.[TUG$_2$] ḫe$_2$-m[a]-ak
My son, let me give [you] instructions, let attention be paid to them! (// Adab segm. 1.8–9)

OB version of the *Instructions of Šuruppak* 9–10 (Alster 2005: 57)
dumu-ĝu$_{10}$ na ga-ri na-ri-ĝu$_{10}$ ḫe$_2$-dab$_5$ | zi-u$_4$-su$_3$-ra$_2$ inim ga-ra-ab-d[u$_{11}$] ĝizzal ḫe$_2$-em-ši-ak
My son, let me give instructions; let my instructions be taken! Ziusudra, let me speak a word to you; let attention be paid to them!

OB *Atra-hasīs* III i 18–21
šipra ša aqabbûku | *šuṣṣir atta* | *igāru šitammianni* | *kikkišu šuṣṣirī kala siqrī*$^{!}$*ya*
Observe the message that I will speak to you: Wall, listen to me! Reed wall, obey all my words!

The *Sumerian Flood Story* (CBS 10673 + CBS 10867) 154–5
iz-zi-da inim ga-ra-ab-du$_{11}$ inim-[ĝu$_{10}$ ḫe$_2$-dab$_5$] | na ri-ga-ĝu$_{10}$ ĝizz[al ḫe$_2$-em-ši-ak]
Side-wall, let me speak a word to you; [let my] word be [taken]; [let atten]tion [be paid] to my instructions.

SB *Gilgameš* XI 21–3
kikkiš kikkiš igār igār | *kikkišu šimēma igāru ḫissas* | ^{lu_2}*šuruppakû mār*(dumu) ^{m}*ubara-*^{d}*tutu*
Reed fence, reed fence! Brick wall, brick wall! Listen, O reed fence! Pay heed, O brick wall! O man of Šuruppak, son of Ubār-Tutu.

The above textual sources will be analysed in detail through the following comparative chart:

ED Version of the *Instructions of Šurrupak* **4–5**	**OB Version of** the *Instructions of Šurrupak* **9–10**	**OB *Atra-hasīs*** **III i 18–21**	**CBS 10673 + CBS 10867** **153b–5**	**SB *Gilgameš*** **XI 21–3**
dumu-ĝu$_{10}$	dumu-ĝu$_{10}$			*kikkiš kikkiš*
				igār igār
				kikkišu
na ga-ri	na ga-ri			
	na-ri-ĝu$_{10}$	*šipra ša aqabbûku*		
	ḫe$_{2}$-dab$_{5}$	*šuṣṣir atta*		*šimēma*
		igāru	iz-zi-da	*igāru*
		šitammianni		*ḫissas*
	zi-u$_{4}$-su$_{3}$-ra$_{2}$			$^{lu}{}_{2}$*šuruppakû*
				mār ^{m}*ubara-*^{d}*tutu*
	inim		inim	
	ga-ra-ab-d[u$_{11}$]		ga-ra-ab-du$_{11}$	
		kikkišu		
		šuṣṣirī kala siqrīya	inim-[ĝu$_{10}$	
			ḫe$_{2}$-dab$_{5}$]	
			na ri-ga-ĝu$_{10}$	
GIŠ.PI.[TUG$_{2}$]	ĝizzal		ĝizz[al	
ḫe$_{2}$-m[a]-ak	ḫe$_{2}$-em-ši-ak		ḫe$_{2}$-em-ši-ak]	

According to the above comparison, both the Old Babylonian version of the *Atra-hasīs Epic* as well as the *Sumerian Flood Story* seem to follow the repetitive style of the Old Babylonian version of the *Instructions of Šuruppak* 9b–10a: na-ri-ĝu$_{10}$ ḫe$_{2}$-dab$_{5}$ | zi-u$_{4}$-su$_{3}$-ra$_{2}$ inim ga-ra-ab-d[u$_{11}$] 'let my instructions be taken! Ziusudra, let me speak a word to you' // iz-zi-da inim ga-ra-ab-du$_{11}$ inim-[ĝu$_{10}$ ḫe$_{2}$-dab$_{5}$] 'Side-wall, let me speak a word to you; [let my] word be [taken]' (the *Sumerian Flood Story* 154) // *šuṣṣir atta* | *igāru šitammianni* 'You observe! Wall, listen to me!' (OB *Atra-hasīs* III i 19–20). The mythological sources all agree that the instructions were communicated through a fence or a wall because Enki was bound by an oath not to assist humankind. This motif was first developed in the *Atra-hasīs Epic*, then was followed by the *Sumerian Flood Story* and finally elaborated in the Standard Babylonian *Gilgameš Epic*. However, the *Gilgameš Epic* differs from the *Atra-hasīs Epic* and the *Sumerian Flood Story* in that it unexpectedly gives away the identity of the human recipient of Enki's instruction by inserting $^{lu}{}_{2}$*Šuruppakû mār*(dumu) ^{m}*ubara-*^{d}*tutu* 'O man of Šuruppak, son of Ubār-Tutu' in the Flood story, which indicates that the author of the Standard Babylonian version was familiar with the *Instructions of Šuruppak*, probably the Akkadian translation of it (George 2003: 879; also 154).

As mentioned earlier, the SB version's addressing the Flood hero as ^{lu_2}*šuruppakû* 'the man of Šuruppak' is unparalleled.

In addition, as the instructions in the didactic sources were given by the father to the son mostly in negative terms,[32] so were the repeated instructions which Enki gave to Atra-hasīs styled in the negative.[33] These negative instructions in the *Atra-hasīs Epic* were followed by Enki's further advice for the people to bribe the gods who were directly responsible for the drought, famine, and plague—pragmatic instructions which were aimed at warding off Enlil's attacks by manipulating cultic worship. While the father gave instructions to his son four times in the *Instructions of Šuruppak*,[34] Enki also instructed Atra-hasīs four times on how to cope with Enlil's attacks in the *Atra-hasīs Epic*.

The critical wisdom or the vanity theme expressed through the Nothing-is-of-Value passage in the lines 252–3 of the *Instructions of Šuruppak*[35] may resonate with Enki's instructions to Atra-hasīs before the coming of the Flood in OB *Atra-hasīs* III i 22–3.[36] The parallel passages to OB *Atra-hasīs* III i 22–3 in SB *Gilgameš* XI 24–6 demonstrate an even closer connection between the Flood story and the *Instructions of Šuruppak* by identifying the Flood hero as ^{lu_2}*šuruppakû mār*(dumu) ^{m}*ubara-*^{d}*tutu* 'the man from Šuruppak, son of Ubār-Tutu'.

The advice given by Enki to Atra-hasīs in the plague cycle for the people not to reverence their personal or city deities but to sacrifice to the gods directly responsible for the catastrophe reflects not only the defiant attitude expressed in the Sumerian compositions of catastrophe such as *Ur-Namma A*, but also the critical tone exhibited in the letters the Babylonians wrote to their personal gods as well as in the didactic compositions during the Old Babylonian period (Lambert 1960: 12).[37]

The above evidence of influence of the *Instructions of Šuruppak* and the didactic traditions on the Flood epic leads us to consider why Enki and

[32] For instance, e$_2$ na-[bur$_3$] x [x x] | [x]-gaz na-ak x sir$_2^?$ [na]-⸢bar⸣$^?$ | ninta$_x$(SAL+NITAḪ) mi-si ⸢na⸣-x (= ḪI×DIŠ+GIŠ$^?$) [m]e-zu [x] x 'Don't break into a house . . . ; don't commit murder; [don't] mutilate yourself [with an] axe$^?$! don't [make] a young man best man; [don't humiliate] yourself!' (AbS-T 19′–20′; Alster 2005: 178).

[33] *e t[a]-ap-la-ḫa* ⸢*i*⸣*-li-ku-un* | *e tu-[sa]-al-li-a [i]š-ta-ar-ku-un* 'Do not reverence your gods; do not pray to your goddesses' (OB *Atra-hasīs* I vii 378–9; cf. I viii 393–4, 405–6; II ii 9–10, 21–2).

[34] Best preserved in AbS-T 3, 26′, 46′, 146′–7′.

[35] niĝ$_2$-nam nu-kal zi ku$_7$-ku$_7$-da | niĝ$_2$ nam-kal-kal-en niĝ$_2$-e me-kal-kal 'Nothing at all is of value, but life should be sweet tasting. Don't appreciate things (too much); (because then) things will evaluate you (i.e. you will become dependent on their evaluation)' (Alster 2005: 96–7).

[36] *ubbut bīta bini eleppa* | *makkūra zērma* | *napišta bulliṭ* 'Destroy your house, build a boat, spurn property and save life.'

[37] Though the blasphemous instructions in the Flood epic find no counterparts in the *Instructions of Šuruppak*, they can be seen in another well-known didactic text composed later in the first millennium BC: *Dialogue of Pessimism* 58–61: *ē arad anāku* ^{udu}*niqâ ana ilīyāma ul eppuš* | *lā teppuš bēlī lā teppuš* | *ila tulammadsūma kī kalbi arkīka ittanallak* | *šumma parṣi šumma ila lā tašāl šumma mimma šanâmma irriška* '"No, slave, I will by no means sacrifice to my god." "Do not sacrifice, my lord, do not sacrifice. You can teach a god to run after you like a dog, whether he asks of you rites, or 'Do not consult a god,' or anything else"' (Lambert 1960: 146–9).

Atra-hasīs were made the protagonists in the Babylonian Flood epic. As noted earlier, the Early Dynastic III versions of the *Instructions of Šuruppak* characterize the father giving the instructions as ĝeštu$_2$ inim-zu 'the intelligent one, the wise one' in AbS-T 1–2 and ĝeštu$_2$-tuku inim-galam inim-zu-am$_6$ 'the intelligent one, the one of artistic words, the wise one' in Adab segm. 1.1, 4 (though there are ambiguities in the Adab version). The Old Babylonian version also makes it clear that it was the father giving the instructions who was the one so described. The name Atra-hasīs (^{m}*atram-ḫasīs*) in the Flood epic means 'one (who is) exceeding in wisdom',[38] which corresponds to the descriptions of the father giving the instructions in the *Instructions of Šuruppak*.[39] Note specially that the Akkadian word *ḫasīsu* (n. 'ear; wisdom') or *ḫassu* (adj. 'clever, wise') is lexically equivalent to the Sumerian terms ĝeštu$_2$ and ĝeštu$_2$-tuku (n. 'ear; wisdom'; adj. 'wise').[40] The equivalence is already indicated by the use of ĝeštu$_2$ for *ḫasīs* by the scribe of the Neo-Assyrian recension of the Flood epic: [*bēl t*]*ašīmti* ^{m}*atra-ḫasīs*(geštu$_2$) *amēlu* 'the sagacious one, the man Atra-hasīs' (K 3399 + 3934 [S] rev. iv 17, v 27). By describing the one who received the instructions as wise, the Flood epic seems to offer an interpretation of the Early Dynastic III versions which is different from that of the Old Babylonian version of the *Instructions of Šuruppak*. However, if one takes into account the fact that Enki, the one giving the instructions in the Flood epic and whose role parallels that of the advice-giving father in the *Instructions of Šuruppak*, is the god of wisdom *par excellence* in Mesopotamian culture, it then seems that the representation of the didactic scenario in the Flood epic may not totally contradict that of the *Instructions of Šuruppak*. The author of the epic portrays both Enki, the one who gave the instructions, and his perceptive human servant the Flood hero as wise.

The description of Ziusudra in the *Sumerian Flood Story* 147 inim si$_3$-si$_3$-ge 'the articulate one' may be considered as parallel to the Adab segm. 1.1, 4 and Old Babylonian version of the *Instructions of Šuruppak* 4–5 inim-galam 'the articulate one'. As in the *Atra-hasīs Epic*, the description here is also about the one receiving the instructions.

Given the above analyses, it seems warranted to conclude that the name Atra-hasīs was based on the descriptions of the advice-giving father in the *Instructions of Šuruppak*. Both the *Atra-hasīs Epic* and the *Sumerian Flood*

[38] The construction (*w*)*atram-ḫasīs* is unusual in that it contains 'an adjective with the ending -*a*(*m*), instead of a substantive in the endingless construct state, preceding a substantive in the genitive' (Reiner 1984: 177; see also von Soden 1960: 163–71), in this case, with no inflectional ending; compare *ellam qāti* 'pure of hand', *aklam išātim* 'consumed by fire', *rabītam libbi* 'great of heart', *rapaš uzni* 'broad of understanding/ear', *palkât uzni* 'wide of understanding/ear', which were also studied by Reiner (1984: 177–82). This construction may be a kind of accusative of respect (see Huehnergard 2005: 173). The same construction also occurs in Arabic. The current author is indebted to Professor John Huehnergard for pointing to Reiner's study.

[39] Compare the rendering of the expression ĝeštu$_2$ inim-zu in AbS-T 1, 2 according to Biggs (1966: 78): 'The [most] intelligent, the [most] knowledgeable in word'.

[40] See Alster (2005: 189) who equates ĝeštu$_2$ with ĝeštu$_2$-tuku.

Story show that their authors were familiar with this didactic source. The non-royal setting of the didactic composition helps explain why Atra-hasīs was not explicitly depicted as a ruler in the Babylonian epic.

TRADITIONS ABOUT ZIUSUDRA AND ŪTA-NA'IŠTIM/ ᴹUD-NAPIŠTI THE DISTANT

If the Babylonian name of the Flood hero Atra-hasīs was based on the Old Babylonian version of the *Instructions of Šuruppak*, where did the Sumerian name Ziusudra come from? This name, as mentioned earlier, originated in the Sumerian chronographical traditions where it represents the last antediluvian king. This is also the name of the Flood hero in the *Sumerian Flood Story* and the *Death of Bilgames*. Later, as the Babylonian and Sumerian traditions related to the Flood were adapted in the Babylonian Gilgameš traditions, the Flood hero began to take on a new name, ^{m}UD-*napišti*(zi), together with its variants. The following section is devoted to investigating the development of the name Ziusudra in the chronographical traditions and the historical relationship between this name and its alleged Akkadian counterpart ^{m}UD-*napišti*(zi) and its variants.

Problems with the Identification of the Two Literary Figures

Ancient traditions had already begun to associate Ziusudra with Ūta-na'ištim/ UD-napišti, as seen in the Middle Assyrian and Babylonian copy of the *Instructions of Šuruppak*[41] and the Neo-Assyrian copy of a group vocabulary.[42] Likewise among modern scholars it has been generally accepted that ^{m}UD-*napišti*(zi) *rūqu*, the name of the hero in the Standard Babylonian version of the *Gilgameš Epic*, is the Akkadian interpretation or even direct translation of zi-u$_4$-su$_3$-ra$_2$: UD parallels with u$_4$ 'day, or days', *napištu* with zi 'life', and *rūqu* with su$_3$-ra 'distant, far away'.[43] Given the long-standing association of the Sumerian and Akkadian names, almost all scholars take the view that both the Sumerian and Akkadian names represent the same legendary figure, that is, the Flood hero, and that the identification of these two figures with each other started even as early as in the Old Babylonian version of the *Gilgameš Epic* (OB VA + BM).

Philological Distinctions

Though himself subscribing to the above view, George (2003: 152–3) has recently challenged the equation of the Sumerian and Akkadian names,

41 ^{m}UD-*napu*[*šte*] (Alster 2005: 57, 71).
42 zi-sud$_3$-da = UD-*na-puš$_2$-te* (George 2003: 96, 152).
43 See Clay 1922: 23; Ravn 1955: 49; Tigay 1982: 229–30; Durand 1988: 423; Alster 2005: 32.

specifically the normalization of ^{m}UD-*zitim* as *ūm-napištim* 'day of life', that is, treating UD and *napištim* in the bond form to correspond with the genitive construction zi-u_4-su_3-ra_2 'life of prolonged (or distant) days'. His objection to such normalization is basically twofold: (1) Such reading ignores the name of the hero in the Old Babylonian version of the *Gilgameš Epic* (OB VA + BM): *u_2-ta-na-iš-tim*, which is supported by the Manichaean Middle Persian translation of the Flood hero, At(a)nabīš (*'tnbyš*). The genitive case of *na'ištim, napišti* or *napištim* in the Akkadian construction is problematic. George proposes to treat it as an abnormal form of the accusative, as in other Old Akkadian names, and thus normalizes *u_2-ta-na-iš-tim* as *ūta-na'ištim* 'I/he found life'[44] and ^{m}UD-*zi^{tim}* as *ūta-napištī* 'I found my life'. And (2) 'a translation of zi u_4 sù.ra into Akkadian would not invert regens and rectum'.

In support of George's position above, one can point out further philological problems in treating *ūta-na'ištim*/^{m}UD-*napišti*(zi) *rūqu* as the Akkadian equivalent of zi-u_4-su_3-ra_2. These problems primarily have to do with the different shades of meaning the Akkadian word *rūqu* (adj. 'distant, remote', based on the verb *rêqu*), as part of the Akkadian epithet, and the Sumerian word su_3 '(to be) distant; (to be) remote, long-lasting', as part of the Sumerian epithet, take in the literary contexts where they are often found. Though both words can have temporal as well as spatial dimensions in meaning, the Akkadian word *rūqu* as part of the epithet *ūta-na'ištim rūqu* or ^{m}UD-*napišti*(zi) *rūqu* most certainly refers to the spatial remoteness in the Babylonian *Gilgameš Epic*. In the epic Gilgameš from Uruk undertook a perilous and humanly impossible journey to a distant place in the far east where he met this legendary figure called *ūta-na'ištim rūqu* or ^{m}UD-*napišti*(zi) *rūqu* who was said to have obtained eternal life. The motivation behind such a heroic undertaking is the fear of death on the part of Gilgameš after his beloved friend and comrade Enkidu died young. The notion of Gilgameš having gone through a long and difficult journey in order to reach the legendary hero is already sufficiently clear in the extant Old Babylonian version of the *Gilgameš Epic* (OB VA + BM). The Standard Babylonian version offers a more elaborate and dramatized story of this journey in Tablets IX, X, and XI. The frequently used phrase *rūqatu urḫu, urḫu rūqatu*, or *arḫu rūqatu* 'a distant road' (I 9; IX 54; X 9, 43, 50, 64, 66, 116, 123, 141, 143, 241, 243)[45] to refer to the long journey Gilgameš undertook to reach the legendary

[44] Already translated as such by Heidel and Speiser as noted in George (2003: 152); also by Komoróczy (1975: 61) followed by Abusch (1993: 11).

[45] It is generally understood that this expression finds parallel in *ur-ḫa-am re-qe_2-e-tam* in OB VA + BM iv 11, with *re-qe_2-e-tam* being treated as the feminine singular of the adjective *rēqum* 'far, distant', which corresponds with *rūqatu* from the adjective *rūqu* in the Standard Babylonian version. But due to the problems of 'the intruding vowel' *-e-* and the '*plene* writing of that vowel', George (2003: 284) suggests regarding *re-qe_2-e-tam* as the feminine verbal adjective of *raqûm*/*reqûm* 'to hide' and thus normalizing it as *reqētam* 'hidden'.

hero may indicate a conscious effort to resonate with the adjective *rūqu* in the hero's epithet.[46] Taken to refer to the spatial remoteness, *rūqu* apparently qualifies *ūta-na'ištim* or ^{m}UD-*napišti*(zi) as a whole—thus the translation 'Ūta-na'ištim the Distant' or 'UD-napištim the Distant'—rather than *ūta*/UD or *na'ištim*/*napišti* separately. For this reason, the epithet can function without the adjective, at least according to the Standard Babylonian version in which the legendary hero is often simply called ^{m}UD-*napišti*(zi) or ^{m}UD-*napištim*(zi)^{tim}.

By contrast, the Sumerian word su$_3$ is always used for its temporal dimension whenever it is juxtaposed with the words of temporal duration such as u$_4$ 'day(s)', mu 'year(s)', bal 'term, reign', and zi/ti-la/nam-ti 'life' in Sumerian literature. Such usage frequently occurs in royal hymns from the Ur III and Isin-Larsa periods that sought divine favour to bless incumbent rulers with a prolonged life and reign, often in return for their exemplary services to the gods and the Land of Sumer. In the context of royal hymns, the expressions such as zi u$_4$ su$_3$ (or nam-ti u$_4$ su$_3$) 'to prolong life', bal u$_4$ su$_3$ 'to prolong reign', and nam-lugal u$_4$ su$_3$ 'to prolong kingship' are closely related in meaning and function. Similar expressions uttered on behalf of royal personages are also found in the restoration section towards the end of the city laments: *LSU* 507; *LW* (segm. H) 33; *NL* 314. The topoi of extended days or reigns, furthermore, can be applied to deities (e.g. *LU* 112–13), and cities (e.g. *LSU* 515; *LE* [the Nippur version] segm. C 44; *NL* 236–7). The Sumerian word su$_3$ in all of these temporal applications, related to the kingship or hegemony of human and divine rulers or city-states, points to the remote future. But the word su$_3$ can also be used to refer to the remote past, especially in passages that allude to the mythical past.[47] Also different from the Akkadian word *rūqu* in the epithet Ūta-na'ištim the Distant (*ūta-na'ištim rūqim*) in the Old Babylonian version of the *Gilgameš Epic* (VA + BM) or UD-napišti the Distant (^{m}UD-*napišti rūqi*) in the Standard Babylonian version of the *Gilgameš Epic* the Sumerian word su$_3$ is an integral part of the epithet of the Flood hero zi-u$_4$-su$_3$-ra 'life of prolonged or distant days' that qualifies u$_4$. Therefore the word cannot be detached from the rest of the epithet.

[46] Though the expression *ana ālik urḫi rūqati pānūšu mašlū* 'his face was like one who had travelled a distant road' is apparently idiomatic, for it is not only applied to Gilgameš (SB *Gilgameš* X 9, 43, 50, 116, 123) but also to the hunter (SB *Gilgameš* I 121).

[47] Compare the Old Babylonian version of the *Instructions of Šuruppak* 1–3: u$_4$ re-a u$_4$ su$_3$-ra$_2$ re-a | ĝi$_6$ re-a ĝi$_6$ bad-ra$_2$ re-a | mu re-a mu su$_3$-ra$_2$ re-a 'In those days, in those remote days; in those nights, in those faraway nights; in those years, in those remote years'; see also the *Instructions of Ur-Ninurta* 1–3; the *Death of Bilgames*, the Mê-Turan version, segm. F 27–9.

Conceptual and Literary Differences

The above philological distinctions suggest that the Sumerian name Ziusudra and the Akkadian name Ūta-na'ištim the Distant at one time belonged to two separate traditions. They represent two distinct literary figures who were only associated with each other secondarily. Further evidence supporting this hypothesis can be derived from conceptual and literary differences in the representations of Ziusudra in the Sumerian traditions related to the Flood and Gilgameš, on the one hand, and Ūta-na'ištim the Distant in the Babylonian *Gilgameš Epic*, on the other hand, from the Old Babylonian period onwards.

According to the Babylonian *Gilgameš Epic*, the legendary figure whom Gilgameš strove to meet in a remote region was best known for having found (eternal) life, as indicated by his name Ūta-na'ištim 'I/he found life' in OB VA + BM. Undoubtedly, this characterization of the legendary figure is closely tied in with Gilgameš's desperate quest for eternal life and his failure to achieve that objective; see OB VA + BM i 8′,[48] ii 10′?,[49] iii 2 (compare SB *Gilgameš* I 41, IV 245?, IX 76, XI 7, 25, 208, 213). And it is exactly this failed attempt of Gilgameš to obtain eternal life that led to the occasion for presenting the central message of the epic: that one must learn to accept death as the ultimate human destiny. The name of the legendary hero Ūta-na'ištim the Distant in OB VA + BM fits well in the epic: Gilgameš's failure to find life (OB VA + BM i 8′ // iii 2 *balāṭam ša tasaḫḫuru lā tutta* 'You cannot find the life that you seek') contrasts starkly with the success of the legendary hero Ūta-na'ištim 'I/he found life'.[50] The wordplay involved in the contrast of Gilgameš and Ūta-na'ištim has already been observed by Komoróczy 1975: 61 (see also Abusch 1993: 11). In SB *Gilgameš* XI 2–7, this contrast is acutely expressed in Gilgameš's puzzlement as he spoke to ^{m}UD-*napišti*(zi) *rūqu* in the hope that the latter would disclose the secret (see also IX 76–7):

2 *anaṭṭalakkumma* ^{m}UD-*napišti*(zi)
3 *minâtūka ul šanâ kī yâtīma atta*
4 *u atta ul šanâta kī yâtīma atta*

[48] Though Gilgameš's desire to meet Ūta-na'ištim the Distant is only latent in OB VA + BM until Gilgameš went to Sursunabu, the boatman of Ūta-na'ištim the Distant—probably a literary strategy to build up suspense—the purpose of his journey to search for eternal life is clearly expressed from the beginning, i.e. when he first met Šamaš. The Standard Babylonian version, by contrast, breaks this suspense and introduces UD-napišti from the outset to be followed by repeated announcements about the legendary hero with all the figures who aided Gilgameš on his way to the hero (Šamaš, IX 6; the Scorpion-man, IX 75; Šiduri/the ale-wife, X 73, 87; Ur-šanabi, X 150), a repetitive style typical of the late version.

[49] See Abusch (1993: 10), who suggests that *balāṭum* 'life' in this line *ištu warkīšu ul ūta balāṭam* 'after he (Enkidu) was gone I did not find life' does not mean 'eternal life' but 'a meaningful life or perhaps the state of being/feeling alive'.

[50] Note that *tutta* and *ūta* both derive from *watû* 'to find'. Also *na'ištum* and *balāṭum* are equivalent in meaning.

5 ⸢*gummurka*⸣ *libbī ana epēš tuqunti*
6 [x] x *aḫ̮ī* ⸢*nad*⸣*ât elu ṣērīka*
7 [*att*]*a* ⸢*kīkī*⸣ *tazzizma ina puḫur*(ukkin) *ilī*(dingir)^{meš} *balāṭa tešû*

2 As I look at you, UD-napišti
3 your form is not different, you are just like me,
4 you are not different at all, you are just like me.
5 I was fully intent on doing battle with you,
6 [but] in your presence my hand is stayed.
7 How was it you attended the gods' assembly, and found life?[51]

Such contrast suggests that the legendary hero had at one time sought eternal life like Gilgameš.[52] In short, the characterization of the literary figure Ūta-na'ištim the Distant in the Old Babylonian epic (likewise UD-napištim in the Standard Babylonian version) is to a large extent conditioned or shaped by the characterization of the protagonist Gilgameš, the leitmotif of seeking eternal life, and the wisdom lesson of learning to accept human fate in the Babylonian epic. The meeting between Ūta-na'ištim the Distant and Gilgameš was based on the former's possession of what the latter desperately wanted for himself but in the end still failed to obtain.

In the Sumerian and Babylonian versions of the Flood story from the Old Babylonian period, however, the motif of seeking eternal life seems lacking. According to the *Sumerian Flood Story* (lines 256–7), life (eternal) was simply granted to Ziusudra—presumably as a reward for his contribution to the preservation of humankind and the religious rites—without his deliberate effort to search for it.

With the relevant section of OB *Atra-hasīs* III vi 47–8 being damaged, it has long been assumed that the Babylonian Flood epic originally contained the episode of the Flood hero being granted eternal life, as in the *Sumerian Flood Story*. But George (2003: 507–8) has recently argued on the basis of the Mê-Turan version of the *Death of Bilgames* segm. F 27–9 that both this Sumerian passage and the *Atra-hasīs Epic* represent the belief that death was instituted after the Flood. According to George, OB VA + BM (iii 1–5) and the Standard Babylonian version of the *Gilgameš Epic* reflect another tradition that regards

[51] Compare the *Death of Bilgames* (the Mê-Turan version) 66–7, 156–7 where Enlil presented Gilgameš's case to the gods to see whether the ruler might be able to have eternal life: if Ziusudra, being a human being, was allowed to live forever, will Gilgameš be spared from death because of his divine birth by his goddess mother? The oath Enki swore after the Flood dictated that no human being was to be allowed to live forever again. But the question is whether this decision would be applied to someone like Gilgameš. Enlil's words seem to suggest that by birth Gilgameš was more qualified than Ziusudra for eternal life.

[52] A similarity which is pointed out by the Gilgameš traditions such as the *Ballade of Early Rulers* 11; the omen apodoses reconstructed from a Middle Assyrian fragment (A 6′–7′) and a Neo-Babylonian fragment (c 2′–3′) (as quoted by George 2003: 113–14); and SB *Gilgameš* XI 25.

death as being established at the creation. The *Sumerian Flood Story* is obviously to be identified with the latter tradition. That the *Atra-hasīs Epic* would represent death as such is consistent with a central theme of the epic. The unrestrained human growth in numbers and presumably in lifespan which had eventually led to the Flood had to be checked if further outbreaks of the catastrophe were to be avoided. Thus human mortality and other measures of population control were introduced at the end of the epic. If death was only introduced after the Flood, Atra-hasīs and supposedly a few others who survived the catastrophe with him might not be subject to this fate because they were born prior to the Flood (George 2003: 508). The implication of this argument is that it was not necessary for Atra-hasīs to be granted eternal life.[53] Also as noted earlier, the emphasis of the closing section of the Babylonian epic is on the survival of the human race in general rather than on the immortality of the Flood hero.

The motif of seeking eternal life in the Flood story incorporated in SB *Gilgameš* XI 24–6 must be a later addition. If one compares this passage with its counterpart in OB *Atra-hasīs* III i 22–3 it is obvious that the phrase *še'i napšāti* 'seek life' in SB *Gilgameš* XI 25 was inserted as a result of the adaptation of the Flood story and the recharacterization of the Flood hero in the Babylonian *Gilgameš Epic* (see also SB *Gilgameš* IX 76; XI 7).

OB *Atra-hasīs* III i 22–3	**SB *Gilgameš* XI 24–6**
ubbut bīta bini eleppa	*uqqur bīta bini* ^{ĝeš}*eleppa*
	muššir mešrâmma še'i napšāti
makkūra zērma	[*m*]*akkūru zērma*
napišta bulliṭ	*napišti bulliṭ*
Destroy the house,[54] build a boat!	Destroy the house, build a boat!
	Abandon riches and seek life!
Spurn property and save life.	Spurn property and save life.

Likewise, among the extant Sumerian compositions related to Gilgameš from the Old Babylonian period, the motif of seeking eternal life by

[53] That the motif of Enlil granting eternal life to the Flood hero is found in the Middle Babylonian recension of the *Atra-hasīs Epic* from Ras Shamra Ugaritica v. 167 = RS 22.421 rev. 1–4 (Lambert and Millard 1969: 132–3) and the Neo-Babylonian/Achaemenid recension of the *Atra-hasīs Epic* MMA 86.11.378A, Plates 59, 60, rev. v 15–23 (Lambert 2005: 198–200), is a result of influence from the Standard Babylonian version of the *Gilgameš Epic;* See Chen 2009 (Vol. 2): 370–4.

[54] The rendering 'Destroy the house' for *ubbut bīta* in OB *Atra-hasīs* III i 22a follows Lambert and Millard (1969: 88–9), who regard *ubbut* as D imperative singular of *abātu* 'to destroy'. Foster (2005: 247; based on Hoffner 1976: 241–5) considers *ubbut* as D imperative singular of *abātu* 'to run away; to flee from', and translates the phrase 'Flee [the] house'. The former rendering is supported by SB *Gilgameš* XI 24a *uqqur bīta*.

Gilgameš, especially through a legendary figure who had sought and found eternal life himself, is also lacking originally (Tigay 1982: 33). The motif was only added secondarily due to the influence of the Babylonian *Gilgameš Epic*. Though the fear of death, not so much prompted by Enkidu's death (*Bilgames, Enkidu, and the Netherworld*) as by human mortality in general (*Bilgames and Huwawa A*), and the mortality of Gilgameš in particular (the *Death of Bilgames*), had already become a dominant issue in these compositions, it was dealt with differently from what we see in the Babylonian *Gilgameš Epic*.

For example, seeking eternal life was apparently not a solution in *Bilgames and Huwawa A*. Gilgameš portrayed in this text evidently accepted death as an unchangeable reality (see also the *Ballade of Early Rulers*), even for a renowned ruler like him who was born of the goddess Ninsun. This attitude can be seen in words to Utu the sun god from whom he sought help to overcome Huwawa in order to fell the cedar trees in the mountains:

> *Bilgames and Huwawa A* 21–33 (compare 4–7; *Bilgames and Huwawa B* 5–21)
> Utu, I have something to say to you—a word in your ear! I greet you—please pay attention! In my city people are dying, and hearts are full of distress. People are lost—that fills me with dismay. I craned my neck over the city wall: corpses in the water make the river almost overflow. That is what I see. That will happen to me too—that is the way things go. No one is tall enough to reach heaven; no one can reach wide enough to stretch over the mountains. Since a man cannot pass beyond the final end of life, I want to set off into the mountains, to establish my renown there. Where renown can be established there, I will establish my renown; and where no renown can be established there, I shall establish the renown of the gods.

Two things in the above passage stand in sharp contrast with the Babylonian epic. (1) Unlike the epic, the Gilgameš portrayed here did not need to be lectured on the inescapable reality of death. (2) In the light of his candid acknowledgement of that reality, one can see why the fear of death did not drive him to seek eternal life. Instead, he resorted to a heroic attempt to establish a lasting legacy or name, which can be viewed as a more realistic form of extending one's life than seeking eternal life (Jacobsen 1980: 19–21; Tigay 1982: 6–7).

The sections parallel to the Sumerian passage quoted above in the Babylonian *Gilgameš Epic*, OB *Gilgameš* III (the Yale tablet) iv 140–3, 160; v 188 and SB *Gilgameš* II 234–6, have adapted Gilgameš's proposal to venture into the Cedar Mountain. As a result of the adaptation, Gilgameš's proposal, which originally was directed to Enkidu (*Bilgames and Huwawa A* 4–7) and then Utu (*Bilgames and Huwawa A* 21–33), has now been collapsed into one directed to Enkidu (OB III 140–62). The motif of Gilgameš's fear of death in the Sumerian text was suppressed so as to postpone the presentation of the motif until after the death of Enkidu (see also George

2003: 193).[55] Gilgameš was recharacterized as being unafraid of death[56]—which reflects his youthfulness,[57] at least not until after the death of Enkidu.[58] The truncated passage from the Sumerian composition *Bilgames and Huwawa A* 21–33 in OB III iv 140–3, 160; v 188 with the added 'Nothing is of Value' motif in OB III 142–3 make the journey to the Cedar Mountain no longer motivated so much by the fear of death as by the venturesome spirit or 'youthful bravado' (George 2003: 193). Since immortality is unattainable,[59] and life is so short and filled with mundane activities, one should venture to do something that has eternal value—even if it means risking one's life. Most significantly, Gilgameš's own acknowledgement of unattainable immortality and death as an unchangeable reality in the Sumerian composition was transformed into a wisdom lesson that had to be taught to him by Šamaš and the ale-wife in OB VA + BM and by UD-napišti in Tablets X and XI of the Standard Babylonian version of the *Gilgameš Epic*. The delayed motifs of Gilgameš's fear of death and of his acknowledgement of human fate in the Babylonian epic are conditioned by the attempts of the author(s) to arrange the traditional tales about Gilgameš into an integrated epic with a new narrative structure (see also Tigay 1982: 3–10) so that Gilgameš's journey to search for eternal life can become a driving theme in the latter half of the epic.

As already noted earlier, the fear of death did not lead Gilgameš to seek eternal life but eternal fame in *Bilgames and Huwawa A*. However, George (2003: 97–8) has recently revived a view first proposed, but later abandoned, by Kramer (1944*b*: 13 n. 48, 18 n. 82; 1947: 4 n. 2), that the Sumerian expression lu$_2$ ti-la in the incipit of *Bilgames and Huwawa A*[60] should be interpreted as 'the Living One' referring to the long-lived legendary hero Ziusudra or

[55] Note the similarities between the dialogues of Gilgameš with Utu in *Bilgames and Huwawa A* 17–33, the dialogues of Gilgameš with Šamaš and the ale-wife in OB VA + BM, and the conversations of Gilgameš with Šamaš, the scorpion-man, Šiduri, Ur-šanabi, and ^{m}UD-*napišti*(zi) in Tablets IX and X of the Standard Babylonian version of the *Gilgameš Epic*.

[56] See OB *Gilgameš* III iv 144, 147, 156–7; SB *Gilgameš* II 232, IV 233, 245.

[57] See OB *Gilgameš* III v 191–2; SB *Gilgameš* II 289–90.

[58] See SB *Gilgameš* IX 5, X 61, 62, 138, 139.

[59] OB *Gilgameš* III iv 140–1 *mannu ibrī elû šam*[*ā'ī*] | *ilūma itti* ^{d}*šamšim*(utu) *dāriš u*[*šbū*] 'Who is there, my friend, that can climb to the sky? Only the gods have [dwelled] forever in sunlight', which is approximately parallel to *Bilgames and Huwawa A* 28–30 lu$_2$ suku$_x$-ra$_2$ an-še$_3$ nu-mu-un-da-la$_2$ | lu$_2$ daĝal-la kur-ra la-ba-an-šu$_2$-šu$_2$ | murgu ĝuruš-e ti-la saĝ ti-le-bi-še$_3$ la-ba-ra-an-e$_3$-a 'No one is tall enough to reach heaven; no one can reach wide enough to stretch over the mountains. Since a man cannot pass beyond the final end of life', are omitted in Tablet II of the Standard Babylonian version of the *Gilgameš Epic*. The reason for this omission clearly has to do with the attempt of the late version's author to avoid the potential contradiction between this passage concerning Gilgameš's acknowledgement of unattainable immortality and his later pursuit of eternal life upon the death of Enkidu.

[60] en-e kur lu$_2$ ti-la-še$_3$ ĝeštu$_2$-ga-ni na-an-gub | en ^{d}bil$_4$-ga-mes-e kur lu$_2$ ti-la-še$_3$ ĝeštu$_2$-ga-ni na-an-gub 'Now the lord once decided to set off for the mountain where the man lives; Lord Gilgameš decided to set off for the mountain where the man lives.'

Ūta-na'ištim/UD-napišti the Distant. George (2003: 16, 97, 111–12) thinks that the same expression found in *Šulgi O* 91[61] and *Bilgames, Enkidu, and the Netherworld*, the Mê-Turan version, segm. B 70–1,[62] should be interpreted likewise.[63] If George's interpretation is correct, then the motif of seeking eternal life, particularly through a long-lived figure or the Flood hero, could have originally existed in the Sumerian traditions concerning Gilgameš. George (2003: 97–8) even goes as far as to assert that:

> . . . the incipit means that the tale we know as Bilgames and Huwawa must once have included a narrative of Gilgameš's journey [to] Ziusudra. The mismatch between opening lines and plot in the poem as handed down in Old Babylonian schools can most easily be explained as having arisen as a result of the abridgement of a much longer text by expunging the episode concerning Ziusudra.

For scholars such as Matouš (1960: 86), Lambert (1961: 183), and Steiner (1996: 187–90), however, lu$_2$ ti-la in the incipit of *Bilgames and Huwawa A* refers to Huwawa. Though George (2003: 97) argues that 'nothing we learn of him [Huwawa] corroborates or explains why he might bear such an epithet', the mythical monster is referred to as lu$_2$ in lines 94–5.[64] Further support for interpreting lu$_2$ ti-la as referring to Huwawa may be found in those passages that describe the monster as living in the mountains.[65] The story of *Bilgames and Huwawa A* is about Gilgameš's attempt to establish lasting fame by defeating Huwawa who was born (line 156) and living in the formidable mountains where cedars grew (lines 21–33).[66] The text contains no motif of seeking eternal life through a long-lived legendary figure. That motif is not only irrelevant to the plot but also contradicts the tenet of the passages (*Bilgames and Huwawa A* 4–7, 21–33) which indicate Gilgameš's motive for his quest for eternal fame, i.e. his acknowledgement of the inescapability of

[61] a-ba za-gin$_7$ kaskal kur-[ra-ke$_4$ si im-sa$_2$] ḫar-ra-an x [x DU] 'Who else like you (Gilgameš) has gone directly on the road to the mountains and has travelled the way to . . . ?'

[62] lugal-[e (. . .)] nam-ti-la i$_3$-kin-[kin] | en-e kur ⸢lu$_2$ ti⸣-la-še$_3$ $^{\text{ĝeš-tug}}_2$ĝeštu-ga-[ni] ⸢na⸣-an-gub 'The king began to search for life. Now the lord once decided to set off for the mountain where the being/man lives.'

[63] See Cavigneaux (2000: 5–6 n. 33), who holds the same interpretation that lu$_2$ ti-la in *Bilgames and Huwawa A* refers to Ziusudra or Ūta-na'išti/UD-napišti the Distant.

[64] en-na lu$_2$-bi lu$_2$-u$_{18}$-lu ḫe$_2$-a im-ma-zu-a-a-aš diĝir ḫe$_2$-a im-ma-zu-a-aš | ĝiri$_3$ kur-še$_3$ gub-ba-ĝu$_{10}$ iri^{ki}-še$_3$ ba-ra-gub-be$_2$-en 'until I discover whether that being (i.e. Huwawa) was a human or a god, I shall not direct back to the city my steps which I have directed to the mountains.'

[65] See *Bilgames and Huwawa A* 138, 142, 148C, 148N, 148Y, 148II, 148SS (kur-ra tuš-a-zu ba-ra-zu kur-ra tuš-a-zu ḫe$_2$-zu-am$_3$ 'No one really knows where in the mountains you live; they would like to know where in the mountains you live.' Note that a different Sumerian verb is used in these instances: tuš 'to sit (down); to dwell' instead of ti 'to live; to sit (down); to dwell'.

[66] Compare Ninurta's killing of Asag, who also lived in the mountains according to *Lugale*. For parallels between Ninurta mythology and the Gilgameš traditions, see van Dijk 1983: 21, 42; Annus 2002: 168–71.

death and unattainable immortality. Even George (2003: 17) concedes that 'this figure [Ziusudra] plays no role in the story of Gilgameš's expeditions to the Cedar Forest as it survives'[67].

In *Šulgi O* 91, lu_2 ti-la should also be interpreted as referring to Huwawa (Klein 1976: 289). The occurrence of this expression and the motif of seeking eternal life in the closing lines of the Mê-Turan version of *Bilgames, Enkidu, and the Netherworld* segm. B 69–71 should be considered as indicative of the attempt of a redactor who was well acquainted with the Babylonian epic to join this Sumerian composition with the incipit of *Bilgames and Huwawa A*. This redactional phenomenon has already been pointed out by George (2003: 16–17):

> Any attempt to consider the story of Gilgameš's expedition to the Cedar Forest as a sequel of the story in which Enkidu was taken prisoner in perpetuity in the Netherworld defies logic, for it is very much the living Enkidu that accompanies Gilgameš to Huwawa's lair. It seems to me that the two texts have been joined by someone familiar with the Babylonian epic, in which the grief and horror that Enkidu's death provokes in Gilgameš impel the hero on a search for eternal life. . . . The three-line bridge therefore is not evidence for a cycle of Sumerian poems. Instead it reveals that the epic story told by the Babylonian poems was already so well embedded in the literary mind in the early eighteenth century BC that people began to adapt the Sumerian poems to fit the expectations aroused by that poem.[68]

[67] Though theoretically it is conceivable that the incipit might have been added secondarily (compare *Bilgames and Huwawa B*, which contains no such incipit) in order to correspond with the Babylonian *Gilgameš Epic* where Gilgameš's defeat of Huwawa and his pursuit of the long-lived legendary figure were arranged in succession (George 2003: 16–17, 97). But again, given the conceptual incompatibility between *Bilgames and Huwawa A* 21–33 and the motif of seeking immortality, it is unlikely lu_2 ti-la even as a later insertion refers to Ziusudra/Ūta-na'ištim.

[68] As mentioned earlier, the motifs of Gilgameš's fear of death and his seeking eternal life are delayed until after the death of Enkidu in both the Old and Standard Babylonian versions of the *Gilgameš Epic*. Regardless of the fragmentary state of the OB III ii and SB *Gilgameš* II 162–93 sections which precede the episode of Gilgameš's proposal to venture into the Cedar Mountain, there seem to be indications that the Babylonian epic may have drawn inspiration from *Gilgameš, Enkidu, and the Netherworld* to formulate the occasion that prompted Gilgameš to journey into the Cedar Mountain. The sadness of Enkidu described in these sections may have to do with his having overheard Ninsun's words to Gilgameš with regard to 'Enkidu's strange birth and lack of family' (George 2003: 456 on SB *Gilgameš* II 175–7). With his strength deteriorating (OB III ii 85–7; SB *Gilgameš* II 187) as a result of his humanization by the harlot in an earlier episode, the reminder of his lack of family must have made Enkidu fearful of the prospect of his afterlife, as graphically depicted in *Bilgames, Enkidu, and the Netherworld*, according to which those who lack family to provide them with proper funeral rites and afterlife care dwell wretchedly in the Netherworld. To distract Enkidu from his sadness, Gilgameš proposed that they go on an expedition to the Cedar Mountain (George 2003: 192, 456). Concerns for Enkidu's afterlife persist in the epic, especially in the adoption of Enkidu by Ninsun (SB *Gilgameš* III 121–8), which makes Enkidu and Gilgameš brothers (but their close companionship is already foretold through Gilgameš's dreams prior to their meeting; see SB *Gilgameš* I 246–98), so that the latter could

The original Sumerian composition, without the motif of seeking eternal life, has a different attitude towards mortality. Death was feared of course. Its final, firm grip on humans was never doubted. Enkidu's plight implies that the realm of death should be approached with reverence. His temporary$^{?}$ release from the Netherworld was for the purpose of informing Gilgameš and all those who were still alive of the different conditions or fates of the deceased, so that those who were still living could learn to lead more fulfilled lives, particularly through familial relations, and to take better care of the cult of deceased family members (see one of the versions from Ur, UET 6 60).

So far it has already been shown that the motif of seeking eternal life, especially through a long-lived legendary figure, was originally absent in two of the relevant Sumerian tales concerning Gilgameš: *Bilgames and Huwawa A*; and *Bilgames, Enkidu, and the Netherworld*. Fear of death either prompts the protagonist to seek eternal fame or serves as a reminder for the audience to make the most of their (family) lives and to care for the cult of the deceased. In the *Death of Bilgames*, the motif of seeking eternal life, though not overtly stated but only hinted at,[69] may have underpinned the plot of this Sumerian tale. The Sumerian tale was presumably composed in order to provide aetiological explanations as to why Gilgameš,[70] though being the son of the goddess Ninsun and having had a celebrated career, still could not escape death, but became governor and a judicial authority in the Netherworld as he had been known since the Ur III period (see *Ur-Nammu A*). However, this underpinning motif of seeking or aspiring to eternal life in the *Death of Bilgames* is quite different from what is found in the Babylonian epic. Whereas in the epic Gilgameš underwent a long journey in pursuit of eternal life, in the

provide a proper burial for the former (SB *Gilgameš* V 256–7; VII 139–47; VIII). The Standard Babylonian version has evidently utilized the notion of the significance of family for the welfare of the deceased in the afterlife from *Bilgames, Enkidu, and the Netherworld* for the depiction of the relationship between Bilgames and Enkidu throughout the epic. The Sumerian story is also attached to the end of the Standard Babylonian version of the epic as an appendix. This arrangement is logically correct because the Sumerian story deals with what Enkidu experienced in the Netherworld, which cannot be placed in front of the episode of the journey to the Cedar Mountain in Tablet II, as the redactor who joined *Bilgames, Enkidu, and the Netherworld* and *Bilgames and Huwawa A* attempted to do by adding the three-line concluding remarks to the former Sumerian text.

[69] *Death of Bilgames* (N_2) v 12–14 [kur gal] ^{d}en-lil$_2$-le a-a diĝir-re-e-ne-ke$_4$ | [en ^{d}]GIŠ.BIL$_2$-games ma-mu$_2$-da /[. . .] x$^{?}$ DU$^{?}$ bala-da-bi | [^{d}GIŠ.BI]L$_2$-ga-mes nam-zu nam-lugal-še$_3$ mu-tum$_2$ [(x)] ti da-ri$_2$-še$_3$ nu-mu-un-tum$_2$ 'Oh Gilgameš! Enlil, the Great Mountain, the father of gods, has made kingship your destiny, but not eternal life—Lord Gilgameš, this is how to interpret . . . the dream.' Note that the Mê-Turan version of the *Death of Bilgames* lacks these lines, which may imply that they were later additions.

[70] The text may have originally been composed in the Ur III period (Cavigneaux and Al-Rawi 2000: 7, 10) and later adapted in the middle of the Old Babylonian period, which can be discerned on the basis of the allusions to the Flood epic and the Flood hero Ziusudra in the extant copies dated to the Old Babylonian period.

Death of Bilgames there was no such journey mentioned in the review of Gilgameš's career. The idea of eternal life was brought up only at the very end of Gilgameš's life in this Sumerian tale when he went to face the gods for the final judgment of his destiny. Furthermore, unlike what is depicted in the epic, that Gilgameš was taught the lesson of the inescapable fate of mortality by Utu and the ale-wife in OB VA + BM or by ^{m}UD-napišti in Tablets X and XI of the Standard Babylonian version of the *Gilgameš Epic*, in the Sumerian tale the lesson was announced to Gilgameš as a verdict by a deity in the divine assembly.[71]

Though both the Flood hero Ziusudra and the Flood epic are alluded to in the *Death of Bilgames*, they are not connected with Gilgameš's pursuit of immortality through a long-lived legendary figure as seen in the Babylonian epic. In the Sumerian composition, Gilgameš reached Ziusudra in order to obtain antediluvian knowledge for the restoration of civilization destroyed by the Flood.[72] The reference to Gilgameš's journey to Ziusudra serves to highlight that regardless of Gilgameš's great contribution as a cultural hero, he still could not escape death. The allusions to the Flood epic[73] play a similar role in the tale: despite Gilgameš's divine birth through his goddess mother Ninsun, he was still to be counted as human, thus subject to the human destiny established by the gods after the Flood that, apart from Ziusudra, no one would be allowed to live forever again.[74] It is important to note that Gilgameš's journey to Ziusudra for the restoration of antediluvian civilization and his learning of the ineluctable human fate through the recounting of the Flood story represent two separate events in Gilgameš's life: one is listed as part of his heroic career, and the other comes only at the very end of his life.

On the basis of the above philological and literary analyses, it can be concluded that the legendary hero Ūta-na'ištim the Distant in OB VA + BM is not to be identified with the Flood hero Ziusudra. The Old Babylonian version of the *Gilgameš Epic* in its extant form contains little evidence supporting this identification, except that Ūta-na'ištim like Ziusudra from the *Sumerian Flood Story* had achieved extraordinary longevity or immortality.[75]

[71] *Death of Bilgames* (N_1 and N_2) v 12–27; (N_1) vi 12–15; (the Mê-Turan version) 184–92.

[72] *Death of Bilgames* (N_1) iv 5–11; (the Mê-Turan version) 56–64, 147–54.

[73] Extant only in the Mê-Turan version, segm. F 23–37, 116–30.

[74] This composition could well have been a critique on the Ur III and Isin rulers who aspired to eternal life as befitting the divine birth or status they ascribed to themselves as well as the cultural re-establishment they claimed to have achieved in their royal hymns.

[75] Ziusudra and Ūta-na'ištim the Distant are not the only ones known in Mesopotamian tradition for having evaded death or having achieved spectacular longevity. Etana and other early rulers listed in the *SKL* must also have been inspiring examples. For instance, in a letter sent by a Babylonian astrologer to Esarhaddon or Ashurbanipal, the former wished for the Assyrian ruler a fantastic long reign like that of Alulim, the first antediluvian ruler in the W-B 62 and W-B 444 versions of *SKL* (Parpola 1993: 120; Galter 2005: 282 n. 68).

Though it is uncertain as to whether these two literary figures originally sprang from a common tradition,[76] at least one can be certain that they once developed separately and were associated with different conceptual frameworks and plots. The above conclusion is also corroborated by the fact that the legend surrounding the hero in the Babylonian *Gilgameš Epic* is in many respects alien to the Flood tradition. For example, the ale-wife or Šiduri (the Standard Babylonian version), and Sursunabu (OB VA + BM) or Ur-šanabi (in the Standard Babylonian version), the boatman of Ūta-na'ištim/UD-napištim, through whose help Gilgameš finally reached the legendary hero, are not part of the Flood epic.[77] Furthermore, it has long been established that the Flood story had originally existed independently of the Gilgameš traditions (Tigay 1982: 19, 214–50; Geoge 2003: 18–25). The story was first alluded to in the *Death of Bilgames* in the Old Babylonian period and later on was borrowed extensively in the Standard Babylonian version of the *Gilgameš Epic* probably around the Middle Babylonian period. It was also the *Death of Bilgames* among all extant Gilgameš traditions that first referred to Ziusudra but did not associate him with Gilgameš's search for eternal life. Thus it seems that the Old Babylonian version of the *Gilgameš Epic* had no connection with either the Flood hero or the Flood story.

Origins of the Two Strands of Tradition

As mentioned above, much of the characterization of Ūta-na'ištim the Distant in OB VA + BM was developed internally in the literary context of the Babylonian *Gilgameš Epic*. But outside the Gilgameš traditions, the same legendary figure is also said to have once been approached by Sargon (2334–2279 BC), the first ruler of the Dynasty of Akkad, in an Old Babylonian

[76] Theoretically it is possible that the legendary figure Ūta-na'ištim the Distant was developed on the basis of the Flood hero Ziusudra, who, according to the *Sumerian Flood Story* 260 (kur-bal kur dilmun-na ki ^{d}utu e_3-$še_3$ mu-un-ti-eš 'They settled him in an overseas country, in the land Dilmun, where the sun rises'), was relocated by the gods after the Flood. This motif is also reflected in the *Gilgameš Epic* where Ūta-na'ištim/UD-napištim the Distant is described as being situated roughly in the same geographic location, in the east across the sea, see especially OB VA + BM iv 11 *urḫam reqētam waṣā'u šamši*(utu)^{ši} 'hidden road where the sun rises' (George 2003: 495 n. 180; see also 496–7; and Horowitz 1998: 36). Equally conceivable is the possibility of such a depiction of Ziusudra in the *Sumerian Flood Story* being influenced by the Ūta-na'ištim tradition (Alster 2005: 32 n. 8). Given that possessing longevity/immortality and living in humanly inaccessible locations are typical characterizations of legendary or mythical figures (e.g. Etana, Huwawa) in ancient mythology, one may also conjecture that both traditions had a common source. From there on they went their separate ways as dictated by the literary context of each tradition before they finally converged and exchanged motifs with each other repeatedly in the course of transmission.

[77] Berossos' account that Xisuthros had a pilot (George 2003: 151) most likely attests to a late development, possibly due to the influnce of the Standard Babylonian version of the *Gilgameš Epic*.

legend, in which the name is written a bit differently: *u_2-ta-ra-pa-aš$_2$-tim* (Westenholz 1997: 58, 69; George 2003: 152). In the text of a Late Babylonian tablet BM 92687 that contains the so-called 'Mappa Mundi' or 'The Babylonian Map of the World', [^{m}]$^{⌈d⌉}$UD-zi^{tim} is listed with Sargon of Akkad as well as Nūr-Dāgan of Burušhanda 'who are associated with far-away places' (Horowitz 1998: 36; George 2003: 152). The legendary figure Ūta-na'ištim was thus portrayed as having been approached by royalty in order to achieve fame, as indicated by the above text regarding Sargon, probably because it would take superhuman strength to undergo the journey to reach him.[78] Barely discernible in the Gilgameš traditions,[79] this quest for fame seems to have become subordinate to the two other more important motives for Gilgameš's meeting with the legendary hero: obtaining eternal life and retrieving knowledge for restoring antediluvian civilization. The latter motive was definitely developed in association with the Ziusudra tradition.

It is quite likely that the Sumerian epithet Ziusudra developed in the context of royal hymnic compositions from the Ur III period onwards as a topos of the royal figures being rewarded with a prolonged life or reign due to their alleged contributions to the (re-)establishment of cultic and public services. This may explain why the literary figure Ziusudra was closely associated with royalty and the motif of restoration of civilization. Though reflecting the perennial aspiration to eternal life on the part of ancient rulers, the topos developed in the royal hymnic compositions does not seem to be associated with the motif of seeking eternal life as found in the Babylonian *Gilgameš Epic*. The name zi-u_4-su_3-ra 'life of prolonged or distant days' resembles so many of the stock expressions of that royal aspiration, zi u_4 su_3 (or nam-ti u_4 su_3) 'to prolong life' and bala u_4 su_3 'to prolong reign', attested especially in royal hymns from the Ur III period to the Isin-Larsa period (see Appendix III in Chen 2009: 418), that one wonders whether zi-u_4-su_3-ra had ever been used as an epithet of royalty.

Convergence of Traditions

The convergence of the Ziusudra tradition and the Gilgameš tradition may have to do with the royal status of Gilgameš, a renowned ruler from 'the heroic age of Sumer' (George 2003: 6). Because of such status, Gilgameš, like some of the other rulers from the Ur III and Isin-Larsa periods onwards, was expected to revive civilization (especially the cultic rites) as instituted by the

[78] Legendary or historical royal figures made journeys to the Cedar Mountain for a similar reason (George 2003: 93–4).

[79] See SB *Gilgameš* I 42 *kāšid dannussu ana* ^{m}UD-*napišti*(zi) *rūqi* 'reaching UD-napišti the Distant by his strength'.

gods. With the emergence of the Flood motif and antediluvian traditions during the early Old Babylonian period, the lost civilization to be revived was generally believed to be antediluvian. Since almost no legendary figure is more reputed than the Flood hero for possessing antediluvian knowledge (Enmeduranki, the antediluvian ruler of Sippar, is another example; see the *Seed of Kingship*), the inclusion of Ziusudra in the *Death of Bilgames* and the ensuing adaptation of Ūta-na'ištim/^{m}UD-napišti after the Flood hero in the Babylonian *Gilgameš Epic* are not surprising.

The Sumerian Compositions about Gilgameš

The identification of the legendary figure Ūta-na'ištim the Distant in the Old Babylonian version of the *Gilgameš Epic* with the Flood hero seems to start with the adaptation of the Sumerian tales about Gilgameš in the light of the Babylonian *Gilgameš Epic* during the eighteenth century BC. The insertion of the three closing lines in the Mê-Turan version of *Bilgames, Enkidu, and the Netherworld*, segm. B 69–71 mentioned above, can be adduced as an example.[80] As George (2003: 16–17) points out, the insertion was intended to join this Sumerian tale with the incipit of *Bilgames and Huwawa A* 1–2.[81] The attempt to impose the motif of seeking eternal life and the sequence of events (something related to Enkidu triggered Gilgameš's desire to venture into the Cedar Mountain; OB III ii–iii; SB *Gilgameš* II 172–301) from the Babylonian epic on the reading of the Sumerian tales, rather awkwardly, is obvious. The Sumerian expression lu$_2$ ti-la originally referred to Huwawa in the incipit of *Bilgames and Huwawa A*. But once connected with the motif of seeking eternal life, this designation began to point to the legendary hero Ūta-na'ištim the Distant whom Gilgameš sought to meet in the Babylonian epic. If this is the case, the order of mentioning Gilgameš's journey to Ūta-na'ištim the Distant before Gilgameš's journey to defeat Huwawa seems to be at odds with the normal sequence in the Babylonian epic. In the epic Gilgameš first travelled to the Cedar Mountain before he went to find the long-lived hero (see the *Death of Bilgames* in which Gilgameš's killing of Huwawa also precedes his trip to Ziusudra).

[80] ⌜ša$_3$⌝ ba-sag$_3$ ⌜mu-ra⌝-a-⌜ni⌝ ba-uš$_2$ | lugal-[e (. . .)] nam-ti-la i$_3$-⌜kin⌝-[kin] | en-e kur ⌜lu$_2$ ti⌝-la-še$_3$ $^{\text{⌜ĝeš-tug}}$$_2$ĝeštu-ga⌝-[ni] ⌜na⌝-an-gub 'His heart was smitten, his insides were ravaged. The king began to search for life. Now the lord once decided to set off for the mountain where the being/man lives.'

[81] *Bilgames and Huwawa A* 1–2: en-e kur lu$_2$ ti-la-še$_3$ ĝeštu$_2$-ga-ni na-an-gub | en ^{d}GIŠ.BIL$_2$-ga-mes-e kur lu$_2$ ti-la-še$_3$ ĝeštu$_2$-ga-ni na-an-gub 'Now the lord once decided to set off for the mountain where the being/man lives; lord Gilgameš decided to set off for the mountain where the being/man lives.'

Plate 1. Obverse of a six-column clay tablet inscribed with SB *Gilgameš* XI 165–XII 1 (MS C: K 2252+, cols. iv–vi) from the Library of Ashurbanipal. Part of the inscription (SB *Gilgameš* XI 165–206) pertains to the Flood hero, identified as UD-napišti the Distant, recounting the Flood story to Gilgameš. (Photograph courtesy of the British Museum. © The Trustees of the British Museum.)

Image courtesy of the Ashmolean Museum

Plate 2. The Weld-Blundell Prism inscribed with the *SKL* (W-B 444 = AN1923.444, Ashmolean Museum, University of Oxford). The list contains the antediluvian and postdiluvian sections and references to the Flood. (Photographs reproduced from the Cuneiform Digital Library Initiative website: http://cdli.ucla.edu/cdlisearch/search/index.php?SearchMode=Text&txtID_Txt=P384786. © Ashmolean Museum, University of Oxford.)

Plate 3. Upper edge and obverse of a clay tablet inscribed with an Ur III version of the *SKL* (*USKL* obv. i 1–iii 15). The list contains neither the antediluvian section nor any reference to the Flood. (Photographs reproduced from Steinkeller 2003: 287. © Piotr Steinkeller.)

Plate 4. Brockmon Collection duplicate of the *SKL* (BT 14): obverse (top), reverse (middle), lower edge of the reverse (bottom left), and the right side of the reverse (bottom right). The list contains neither the antediluvian section nor any reference to the Flood. (Photographs courtesy of the Hecht Museum, University of Haifa. © Faculty of Humanities, University of Haifa.)

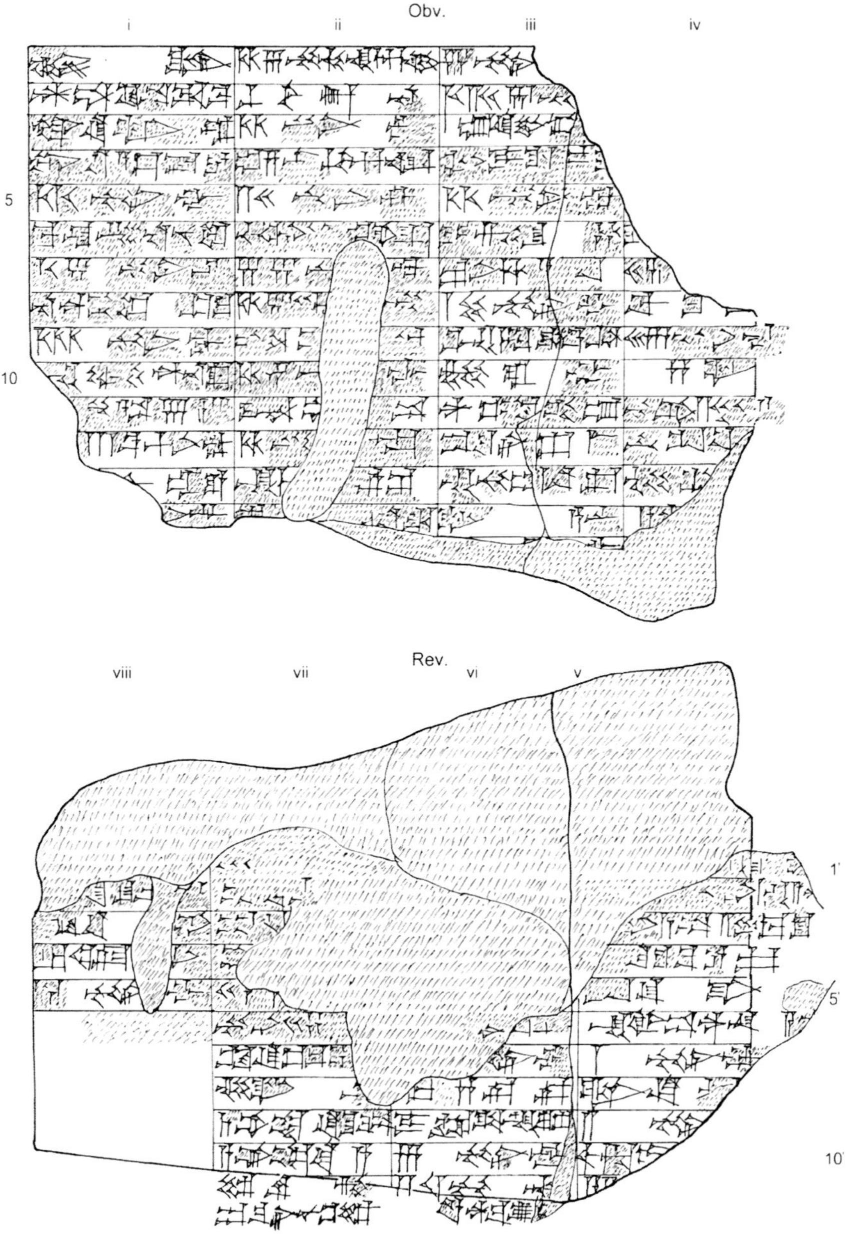

Plate 5. Brockmon Collection duplicate of the *SKL* (BT 14). (Drawings reproduced from Klein 2008: 89. © [2008] American Schools of Oriental Research. All rights reserved. Republished here by permission of the American Schools of Oriental Research.)

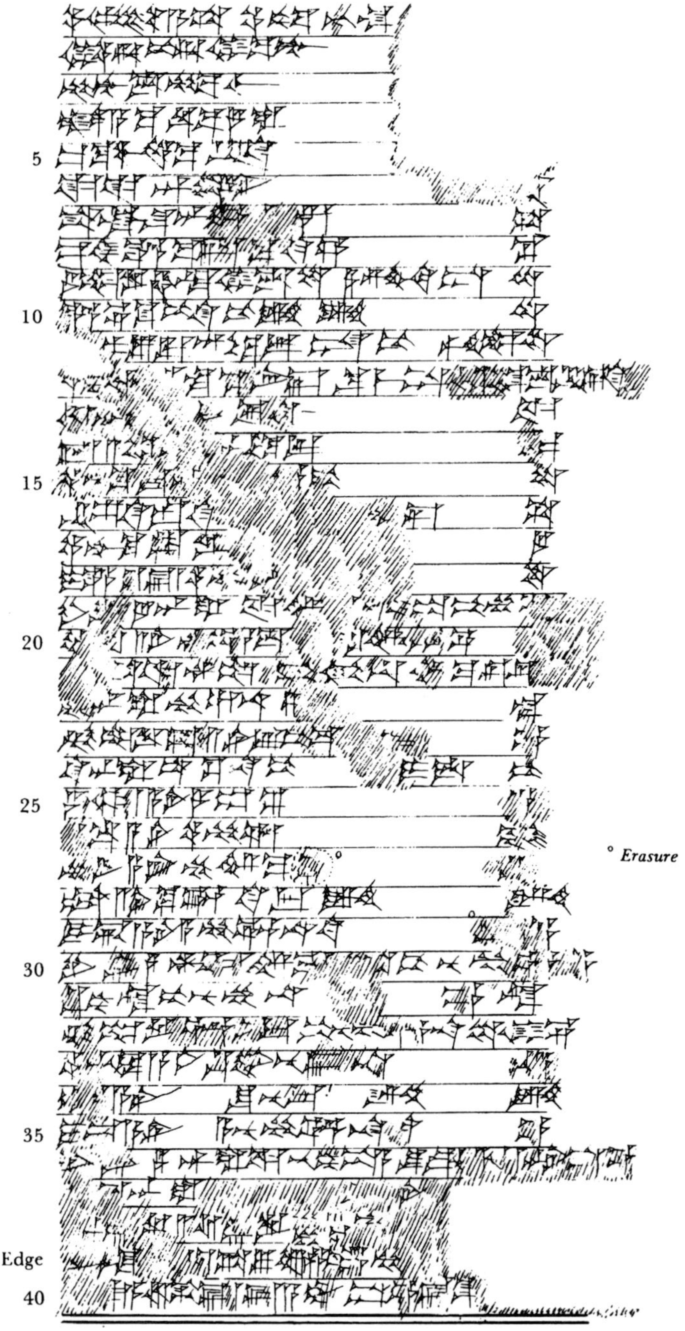

Plate 6. Obverse of a clay tablet inscribed with the *Instructions of Ur-Ninurta* 1–40 (MS A: IM 55403 = TIM 9, 1). Line 4 eĝir a-ma-ru ba-ĝar-ra-[a-ta] 'after the Flood had swept over' represents the earliest textual witness to the use of the Sumerian term a-ma-ru for conveying the specialized meaning 'the Flood'. (Drawing reproduced from van Dijk 1976: plate 1. © J.J.A. van Dijk.)

Plate 7. Obverse of several joined clay fragments inscribed with OB *Atra-hasīs* I 1–227 (MS A: BM 78941 + 78943, obv. i 1–iv 58). This section of the epic covers the events from the division of the cosmos among the senior gods to the creation of human beings in order to relieve the junior gods from labour. (Photograph courtesy of the British Museum. © The Trustees of the British Museum.)

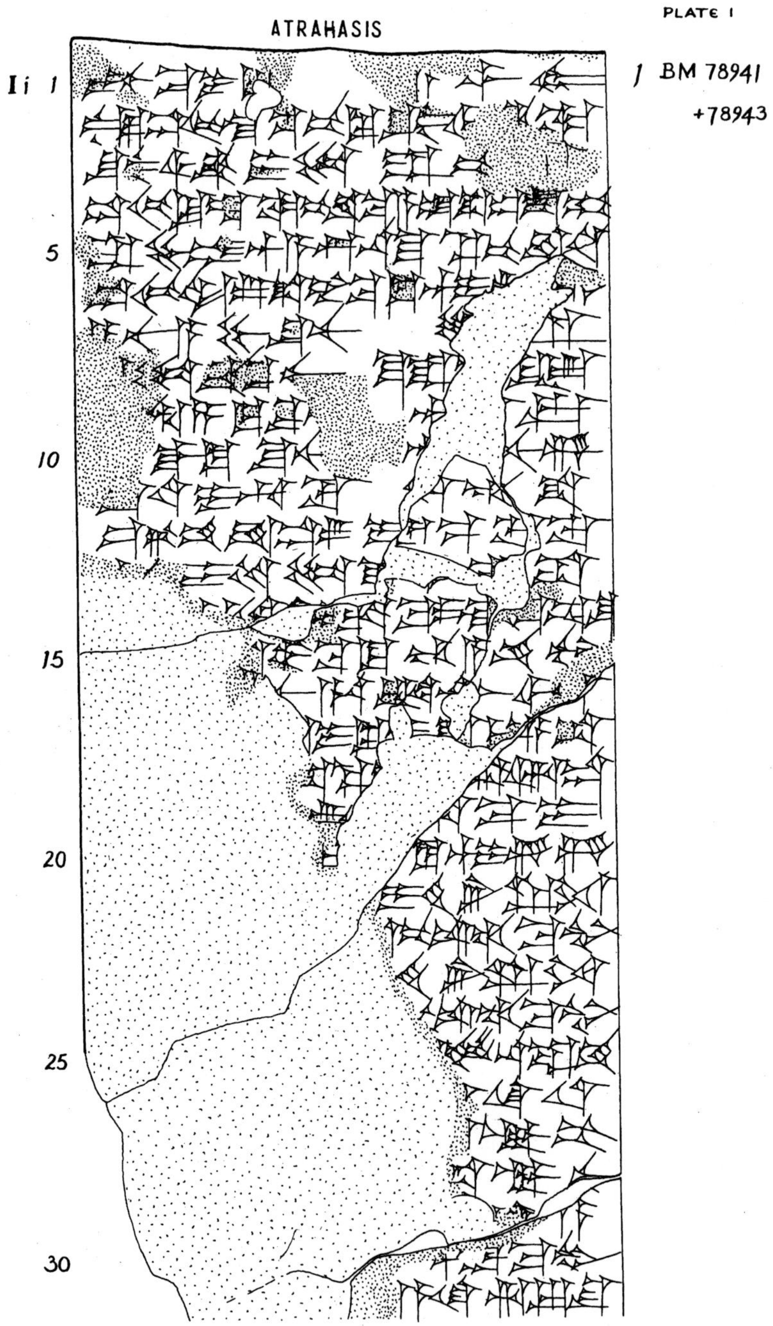

Plate 8. Part of the joined clay fragments inscribed with the opening lines of the Old Babylonian version of the *Atra-hasīs Epic* (MS A: BM 78941 + 78943, obv. i 1–31). These lines announce and depict a crisis in the divine world that led to the rest of the story. (Drawing by A. Millard in Lambert and Millard 1965: plate 1. Courtesy of the British Museum. © The Trustees of the British Museum.)

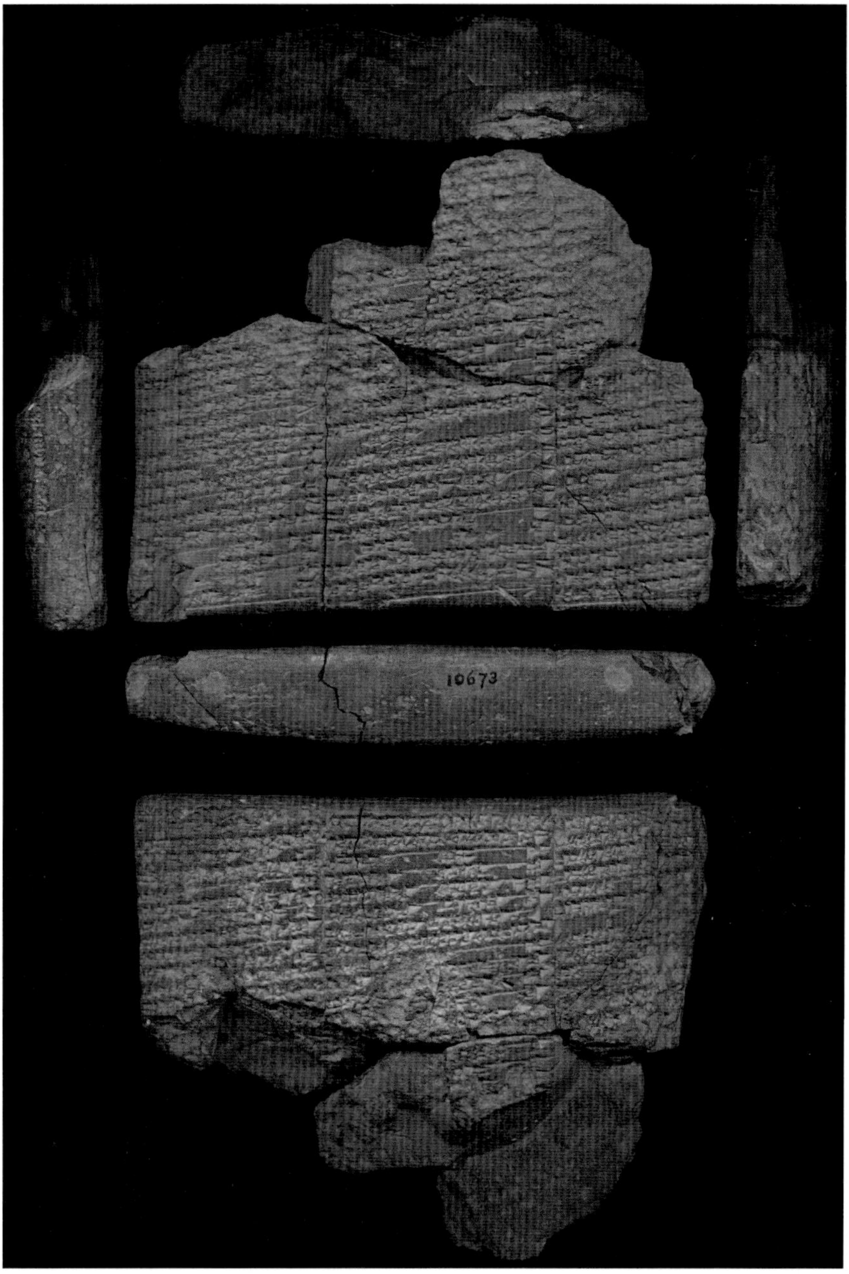

Plate 9. Clay tablet inscribed with the *Sumerian Flood Story* (CBS 10673 + CBS 10867). (Photographs reproduced from the Cuneiform Digital Library Initiative website: http://cdli.ucla.edu/cdlisearch/search/index.php?SearchMode=Text&txtID_Txt=P265876. © The University of Pennsylvania Museum of Archaeology and Anthropology.)

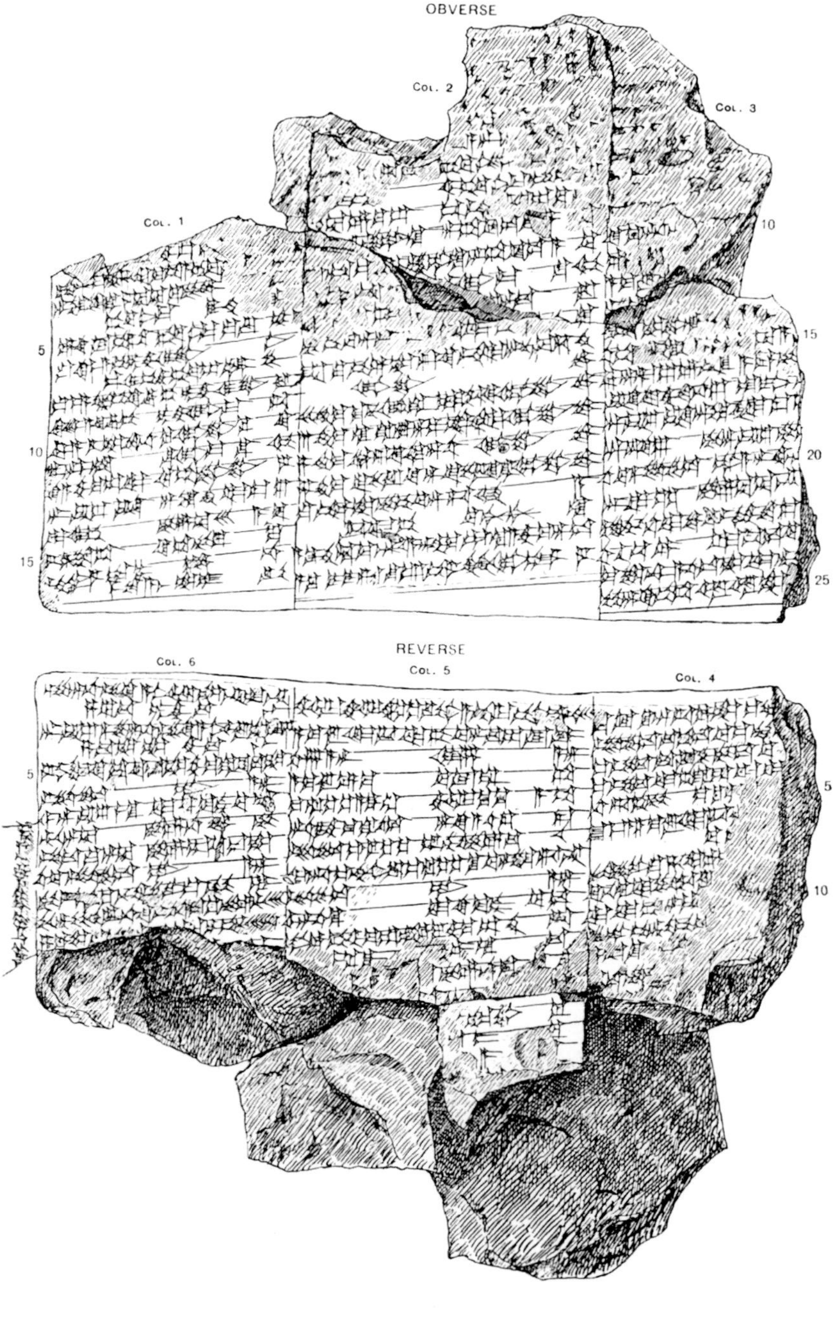

Plate 10. Clay tablet inscribed with the *Sumerian Flood Story* (CBS 10673 + CBS 10867). (Drawings reproduced from Poebel 1914*b*: plate I. © The University of Pennsylvania Museum of Archaeology and Anthropology.)

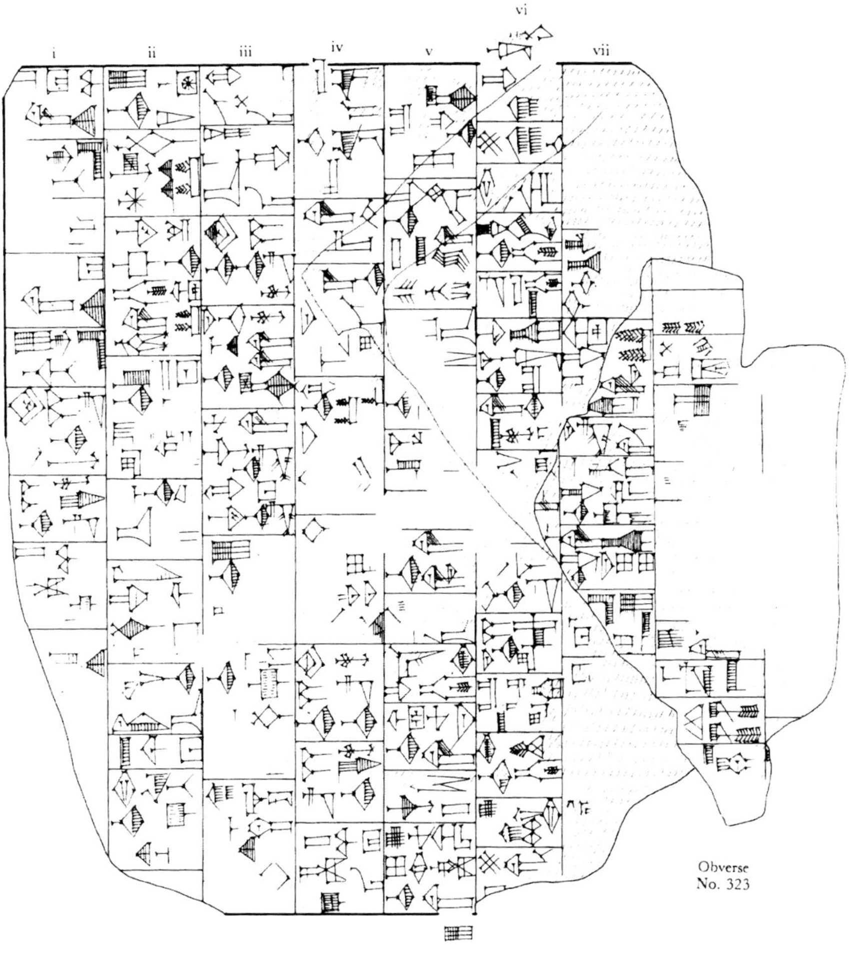

No. 256

Plate 11. Obverse of two joined clay fragments inscribed with the Early Dynastic III version of the *Instructions of Šuruppak* from Abū Ṣalābīkh, AbS-T 1–73′ (ED_1: AbS-T 393 + 323 = OIP 99 256 + 323, obv. i 1–viii 11′). (Drawing by R. Biggs reproduced from Civil 1984: 282 [Figure 1]. © The University of Chicago Press.)

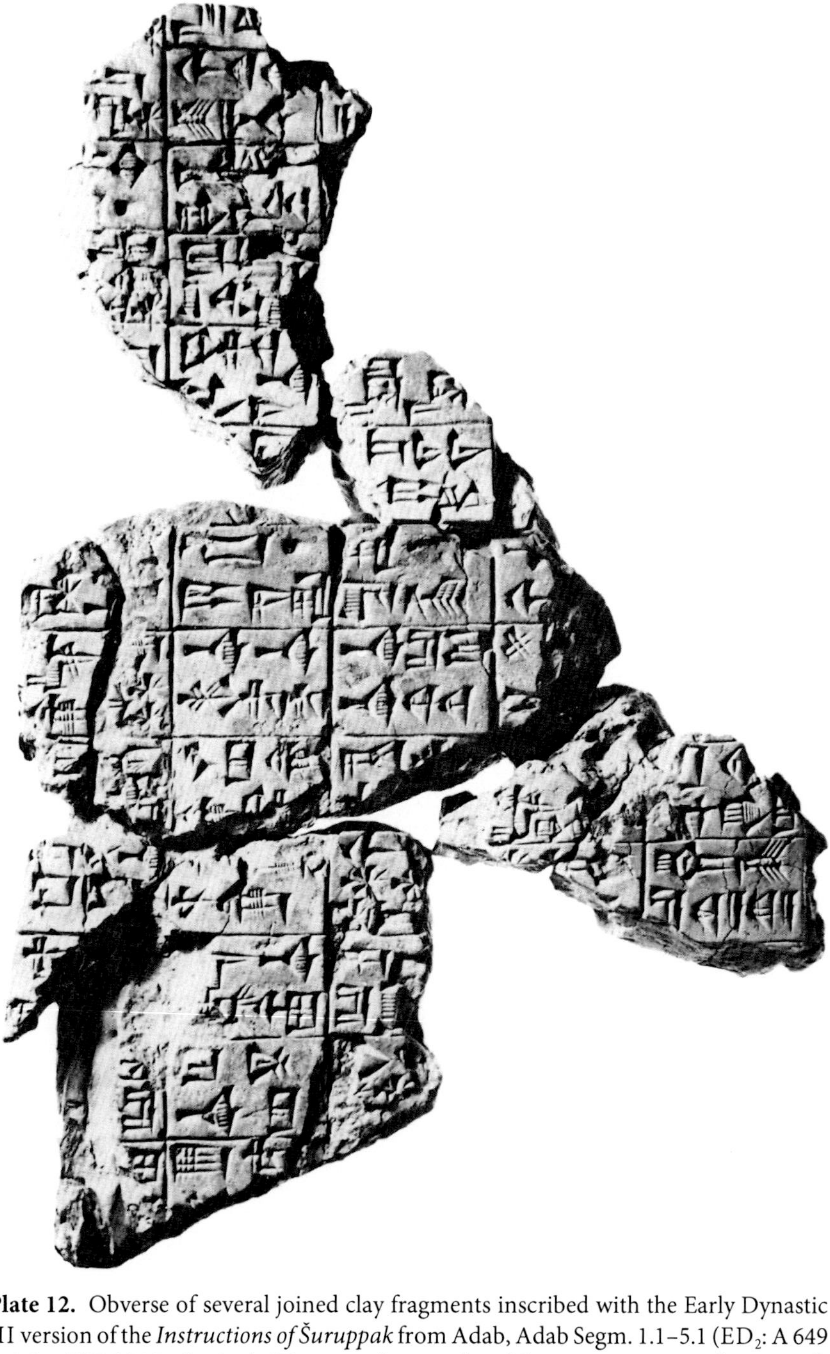

Plate 12. Obverse of several joined clay fragments inscribed with the Early Dynastic III version of the *Instructions of Šuruppak* from Adab, Adab Segm. 1.1–5.1 (ED_2: A 649 + 645 = OIP 99 58, obv. i–v). (Photograph reproduced from Biggs 1974: 58 [Figure 30]. © The Oriental Institute Museum, University of Chicago.)

Plate 13. Obverse of a clay tablet inscribed with the Old Babylonian version of the *Instructions of Šuruppak* 1–25 (MS Sch_1: the Schøyen Collection MS 2788). Note that in lines 1–3 the mythological prologue dealing with the primeval time of origins was added, and that in lines 8 and 10 the name Ziusudra was inserted, in comparison with the Early Dynastic III versions of the *Instructions of Šuruppak*. (Photograph courtesy of the Schøyen Collection. © The Schøyen Collection, Oslo and London.)

Plate 14. Obverse of a clay tablet inscribed with the antediluvian king list from the Schøyen Collection, MS 2855 (obv. 1–12). '(Photograph courtesy of the Schøyen Collection. © The Schøyen Collection, Oslo and London.)'

Plate 15. Clay tablet inscribed with *LSU* 65–88 (obverse), 100–15 (reverse), which show metaphorical depictions of the flood and storm (MS A: AN1926.396, Ashmolean Museum, University of Oxford); e.g. 'On that day, Enlil sent down Gutium from the mountains. Their advance was as the flood of Enlil that cannot be withstood' (*LSU* 75–6); 'The devastating flood was levelling (everything), like a great storm it roared over the earth, who could escape it?' (*LSU* 107–8); 'The storms gather to strike like a flood/tempest' (*LSU* 113). (Photographs reproduced from Michalowski 1989: plate 1. © Ashmolean Museum, University of Oxford.)

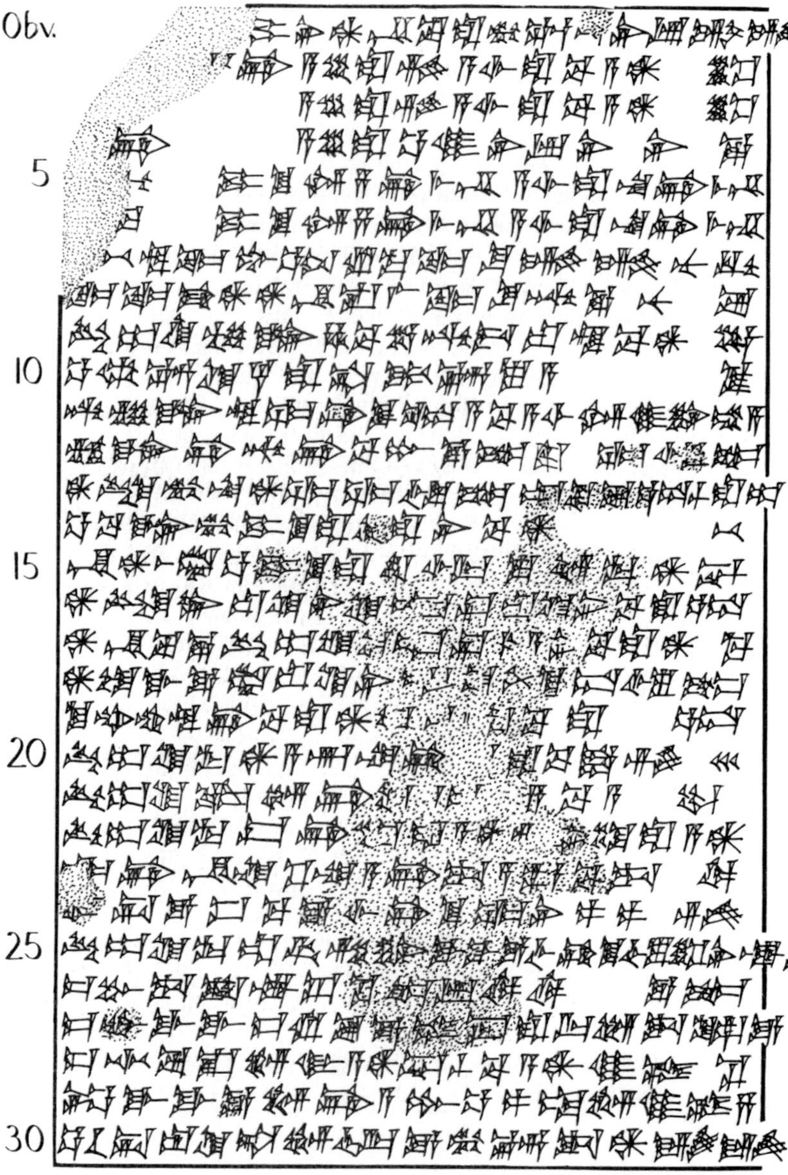

Plate 16. Obverse of a clay tablet inscribed with *LSU* 360–386a (UET 6/2 132, obv. 1–30). Part of the inscription, *LSU* 364–70 (UET 6/2 132, obv. 7–13) 'The verdict, the word of the divine assembly cannot be reversed. The pronouncement by An and Enlil knows no overturning . . .', was quoted in lines 158–61 of the *Sumerian Flood Story* (see CBS 10673, col. iv 9–12 in Plates 9 and 10). (Drawing by C. J. Gadd. Reproduced from Gadd and Kramer 1966: plate CXLVII. © The Trustees of the British Museum.)

The Ballade of Early Rulers

The earliest textual evidence of Ūta-na'ištim the Distant being identified with Ziusudra is to be found in the *Ballade of Early Rulers*, a Sumerian text of the vanity or 'Nothing is of Value' (niĝ$_2$-nam nu-kal) theme. The text is dated to the Hammurabi dynasty (*c.*1792–1750 BC) by Alster (2005: 295 n. 38):

The *Ballade of Early Rulers* 9–14 (Alster 2005: 301–2)[82]

9 [me-a ^{m}a-lu-lu lu]gal-e mu 3,600 × 10-am$_3$ in-ak
10 [me-a e-ta-na lu]gal-e lu$_2$ an-še$_3$ bi$_2$-in-e$_3$-de$_3$
11 [me-a ^{m}bil$_3$-ga-meš z]i-u$_4$-su$_3$-ra$_2$-gin$_7$ nam-ti i$_3$-kin-kin
12 [me-a ^{m}ḫu-wa-wa (. . .) ki] ba-an-za-za dab$_5^{?}$-ba$^{?}$-ta
13 [me-a ^{m}en-ki-du$_3$ nam-kal-ga-ni kal]am$^{?}$-ma$^{?}$ nu$^{?}$-dar-ra-ke$_4$
14 [me-a lu]gal-e-ne dub-saĝ u$_4$-ul-li$_2$-a-ke$_4$-ne

9 Where is Alulu, the king who reigned 36,000 years?
10 Where is Etana the king, the man who ascended to heaven?
11 Where is Gilgameš, who, like Ziusudra, sought (eternal) life?
12 Where is Huwawa, who was caught in submission?
13 Where is Enkidu, whose strength was not defeated$^{?}$ in the land?
14 Where are those kings, the vanguards of former days?

The convergence of the Ziusudra tradition and the Ūta-napištim tradition came about presumably due to their common characteristics: both heroes were represented as possessing immortality (or longevity) and living apart from human society. But as mentioned earlier, the name Ziusudra was not yet associated with the motif of seeking eternal life in the *Death of Bilgames*. But here it definitely is, because of which the name can be identified as the Sumerian counterpart of Ūta-na'ištim the Distant. Just as the legendary hero Ūta-na'ištim ('I/he found life') the Distant was characterized in the light of the depiction of Gilgameš in the Babylonian epic, so was the Flood hero Ziusudra here understood in terms of seeking eternal life. Indeed, Ziusudra in this text has become the predecessor of Gilgameš in pursuit of immortality, a notion which is not even obvious in the characterization of Ūta-na'ištim in the Old Babylonian version of the *Gilgameš Epic*.

By listing Ziusudra/Ūta-na'ištim in front of Huwawa, the *Ballade of Early Rulers* seems to follow the odd sequence of Gilgameš's journeys as created by the closing lines in the Mê-Turan version of *Bilgames, Enkidu, and the Netherworld* (segm. B 69–71). The Sumerian phrase nam-ti i$_3$-kin-kin 'he sought (eternal) life' in the *Ballade of Early Rulers* 11 closely parallels the phrase nam-ti-la i$_3$-kin-[kin] in the Mê-Turan version of *Bilgames, Enkidu, and the*

[82] The quotation here follows MS B. The broken sections are 'tentatively reconstructed' by Alster (2005: 300) on the basis of the Syro-Mesopotamian sources that date to a time around 1300 BC.

Netherworld, segm. B 70. The same expression nam-ti i$_3$-kin-kin occurs again in the *Ballade of Early Rulers* 21 'For him who gives [the good things of] the gods, the food provider, life is found!' (Alster 2005: 305).[83] This line presumably refers to Ziusudra, on the basis of the episode of feeding the gods after the Flood in the *Sumerian Flood Story*.[84] Lastly, the *Ballade of Early Rulers* overall seems to resonate with the pessimistic passages from lines 4, 23–30 of *Bilgames and Huwawa A*, the Sumerian tale to which *Bilgames, Enkidu, and the Netherworld* was supposed to be attached by the inserted closing lines of the Mê-Turan version. It is therefore reasonable to assume that the composition of the *Ballade of Early Rulers* had relied on the Mê-Turan version of *Bilgames, Enkidu, and the Netherworld* as well as *Bilgames and Huwawa A*. If this is the case, the author of this pessimistic text also had interpreted the Sumerian expression lu$_2$ ti-la found in the above two Sumerian tales as referring to Ziusudra/Ūta-na'ištim. The name Ziusudra here does not seem to have been drawn from a mythological source (e.g. the *Death of Bilgames*), but instead from a chronographical source, such as the W-B 444 version of *SKL*. Note that Ziusudra (the last antediluvian ruler) is mentioned in conjunction with Alulu (the first antediluvian ruler) and two postdiluvian rulers: Etana (the thirteenth ruler of the first Kiš dynasty) and Gilgameš (the sixth ruler of the first Uruk dynasty). The earliest evidence of identification of Ūta-na'ištim with Ziusudra in the *Ballade of Early Rulers* already attests to a rather complex web of intertextual relationship between the Sumerian tales about Gilgameš, the Babylonian *Gilgameš Epic*, and the chronographical source.

The Omen Apodoses about Gilgameš

In the omen apodoses (George 2003: 113–14) reconstructed from the Middle Assyrian fragment A (VAT 9488) and the Neo-Babylonian fragment

[83] MS A: [niĝ$_2$-sa$_6^?$-ga] diĝir-re-e-ne bi$_2$-in-šum$_2$-ma-am$_3$ | [. . .]-⌜gu$_7^?$⌝-ra nam-ti i$_3$-kin-kin; MS B: [niĝ$_2$-sa$_6^?$-ga diĝir]-re-e-ne bi$_2$-in-šum$_2$-ma-am$_3$ | [. . .] x(could be gu$_7$) nam-ti i$_3$-kin-kin; MS D: [niĝ$_2$-sa$_6^?$-ga diĝir-r]e-e-ne bi$_2$-in-šum$_2$-ma-am$_3$ | ⌜u$_2$⌝-⌜gu$_7$-gu$_7$⌝ nam-ti i$_3$-kin-kin. According to ePSD, the Sumerian verb kin is attested 108 times, all from the Old Babylonian period. The only three times this verb is used in juxtaposition with nam-ti are found in *Bilgames, Enkidu, and the Netherworld* (the Mê-Turan version) segm. B 70; and the *Ballade of Early Rulers* 11, 21.

[84] As mentioned earlier, the motif of eternal life being a reward for the person who restored or provided offerings to the gods originated from the Ur III and Isin-Larsa royal hymnic compositions. The Isin-Larsa rulers were frequently referred to in their royal hymns as providers (written u$_2$-a) to the gods, as seen in *NL* 162. Tinney (1996: 158) points out that the epithet is 'rare in texts attributed to earlier kings'. The expression u$_2$-gu$_7$-gu$_7$ 'food provider' in the *Ballade of Early Rulers* 21, as restored and read by Alster (2005: 305, 311) from MS D (CBS 1208, pl. 31, rev. ii 3′), is noted by Alster as forming 'another parallel to a composition inscribed on the same *Sammeltafel*, Hymn to Marduk with Blessing for a King, Composition 1:21 in Alster 1990, 12 (previously Alster and Jeyes, 1986, 3 ii 3): diŋir ú-gu$_7$-ám a-silim ⌜nam(?)⌝-ti-la u$_4$-sù-du ŋiš-šub-ba-zu ŋá-ŋá "May it be your lot to be a god consuming the food and healthy water of long life!"' (Alster 2005: 311).

c (Rm 907), one can see that the name Ziusudra, which formerly had only been represented as the Sumerian equivalent to Ūta-na'ištim the Distant in the Sumerian sources of the Gilgameš tradition in the Old Babylonian period, now was even adopted in the Akkadian sources where the name Ūta-na'ištim/UD-napištim is expected. Similar to the *Ballade of Early Rulers*, this omen source also lists Ziusudra in front of Huwawa (written as Humbaba); cf. c 2′–5′.

> A 6′–7′ [*šumma*(BE) *ina*] *amūti*(ba$_3$) *manzāzu*(ki.gub) *rēs*(saĝ)-*su* *u*$_3$ *qablā*$^?$ (murub$_4$)^{meš}-*šu*$_2$ *pa-aš*$_2$-*ṭa-ma* *išid*(suḫuš)-*su* *ki*-[*ma* ... KIMIN ... | *ša k*]*i-ma* *zi-su*$_3$-*ra* *balāṭa*(ti.la) *iš-te-u*$_2$-*ma* *ḫarrān*(kaskal) *zi-su*$_3$-*r*[*a* ...];
>
> c 2′–3′ [... *balāṭa iš-te*]-⌜*u*⌝-*ma* *ḫarrān*(kaskal) *z*[*i-su*$_3$-*ra* .. | ...] *ana* *māti*(kur)-*šu*$_2$ [...].
>
> [(If) in] the liver the top and the middle parts of the 'station' are 'effaced' and its base is like [..., it is an omen of Gilgameš, who] sought life like Zisudra and [made] the journey to Zisudra [...] to his land [...].

Miscellaneous Sources

At least from the Middle Babylonian and Assyrian periods onwards, the Akkadian name *ūta-na'ištim* began to be adapted according to zi-u$_4$-su$_3$-ra$_2$: UD (u$_4$) became the Sumerian equivalent of *ūta* (*u*$_2$-*ta*), on the one hand, and zi for *na'ištim, napištim*, or *napušte*, on the other. These adaptations can be seen in the Standard Babylonian version of the *Gilgameš Epic*: ^{m}UD-*napišti*(zi) *rūqi*, ^{m}UD-*napišti*(zi), or ^{m}UD-*napištim*(zi)^{tim}; the Akkadian versions of the *Instructions of Šuruppak*: ^{m}UD-*napu*[*šte*] for Ziusudra (Alster 1974: 121; Galter 2005: 281); the Neo-Assyrian copy of a group vocabulary (CT 18 30 iv 9): zi-sud$_3$-da = UD-*na-puš*$_2$-*te* (George 2003: 96); and the Late Babylonian text that goes together with 'The Babylonian Map of the World' (BM 92687 obv. 10′): [x x ^{m}] ⌜^{d}⌝UD-*napištim*(zi)^{tim} *šarru-kin u nūr*(zalag)-^{d}[*d*]*a-gan šar*$_3$ *bur-*⌜*ša-an*$^?$-*ḫa*⌝-*a*[*n-da*] '[... U]D-napištim, Sargon, and Nūr-[D]āgan the king of Buršaha[nda]' (Horowitz 1998: 36; George 2003: 152).

The Standard Babylonian Version of the Gilgameš Epic

This version of the Babylonian *Gilgameš Epic* probably represents the best example of the innovative amalgamation and adaptation of diverse traditions observed in this study. In addressing the legendary hero UD-napišti(zi)/Ūta-na'ištim the Distant from the Old Babylonian version as the 'son of Ubār-Tutu' (IX 6; X 208), the late version appears not only to identify UD-napišti(zi)/Ūta-na'ištim with Ziusudra, but also to base this identification on the chronographical source where Ziusudra is represented in genealogical relationship with Ubār-Tutu. The insertion of 'O man of Šuruppak, son of Ubār-Tutu' (XI 23) in the Flood story (compare OB *Atra-hasīs* III i 18–21; the

Sumerian Flood Story 154–5), which gives away the identity of the human recipient of Enki's instructions, further suggests that the author of the late version might have been familiar with the relevant passages in the *Instructions of Šuruppak*.

Interestingly, in IX 75, Gilgameš refers to UD-napišti as his forefather from whom he expected to receive the secret of eternal life: *ḫ*[*arrān*(kaskal)$^{?}$ (*ša*$_2$)] ^{m}UD-*napišti*(zi) *abi*(ad)-*ia* x [......] '[*I am seeking*] the [*road*] of my forefather, UD-napišti.' UD-napišti in this instance again represents Ziusudra as the last antediluvian ruler from the chronographical source. Such an attempt to connect one's lineage with an antediluvian ruler is not an isolated case. A bilingual inscription of king Nebuchadnezzar I (1125–1104 BC), entitled *The Seed of Kingship*,[85] from the Second Dynasty of Isin likewise ascribed to the king the remote descent from Enmeduranki, the king of Sippar. Enmeduranki was the ruler placed immediately before the last antediluvian dynasty in some chronographical traditions (W-B 444, W-B 62, UCBC 9-1819), but the last antediluvian king 'according to the Uruk List of Rulers and Sages, known from a manuscript dating to the Hellenistic period' (Beaulieu 2007: 6; see also Galter 2005: 291). The claim of Gilgameš's descent from UD-napišti/Ziusudra could have been based on a chronographical tradition in which Ziusudra and Gilgameš had long been established as an antediluvian ruler and a postdiluvian ruler respectively.

While UD-napišti is identified with the Flood hero Ziusudra in some instances, in other cases, especially Tablet XI where the Flood story is extensively quoted, it is the Flood hero who is identified with UD-napišti, or depicted like Gilgameš by the motif of seeking eternal life. For example, IX 76 (*balāṭa iš'u* 'he found life'), XI 7 (*balāṭa teš'u* 'you found life'), and XI 25 (*še'i napšāti*[zi]^{meš} 'seek life!') characterize the Flood hero as seeking or finding eternal life (compare OB VA + BM's characterization of Ūta-na'ištim the Distant),[86] which is similar to what was observed in the *Ballade of Early Rulers* and the omen apodoses (*balāṭa ište'ūma* 'he had sought eternal life') earlier.

The appearance of the Old Babylonian name of the Flood hero Atra-hasīs in the Flood story (XI 49,[87] 197) is surprising, given the author's attempts to

[85] See Lambert 1967: 126–38; Lambert 1974: 427–40; Frame 1995: 23–8; Foster 2005: 376–80.

[86] OB VA + BM uses *saḫāru* (i 8′, iii 2) to express the idea 'to seek, search for' and *watû* (i 8′, ii 10′, iii 2) to express the idea 'to find'. The Standard Babylonian version generally employs the same Akkadian verb *še'û* (IX 76; XI 7, 25) for both ideas, similar to the *Ballade of Early Rulers* 11, 21 in which the same Sumerian word kin is also used for both ideas. However, in SB *Gilgameš* XI 208, which clearly parallels OB VA + BM i 8′ and iii 2, one finds the author of the late version using *watû* for 'to find' and *bu''û* for 'to seek'.

[87] George (2003: 880) points out that 'The use of the epithet Atra-hasīs, "Exceeding-Wise," in this line is an indication, if one were needed, of the source of the Flood narrative in Gilgameš. From a literary point of view Ūta-napišti's self-reference in the third person does not sit well with the use of the first person in the rest of the narrative; it is perhaps an indication that the adaptation of the story was not carried out as expertly as it might have been.'

identify the Flood hero with UD-napišti as shown above. Tigay (1982: 216–17) takes this name as 'the giveaway' of the influence of the *Atra-hasīs Epic* on the late version of the *Gilgameš Epic*. Only aware of one single occurrence of this name in XI 197 at the time of his writing while the occurrence in XI 49 was not yet discovered,[88] Tigay was uncertain as to whether this exception to the general rule of using UD-napišti for the Flood hero in the epic is 'a slip or intentional' (1982: 217 n. 11). It is now clear that the occurrence of the name of Atra-hasīs is unlikely to be accidental, not just because it has occurred twice, but also because after a few lines following XI 197 the name UD-napišti is used again repeatedly.[89] The resumed use of the latter name is found at a critial juncture in the epic XI 203–6: the bestowal of eternal life upon the Flood hero and his wife and their settlement in a remote place by the gods after the Flood.

203 *ina pāna* ^{m}UD-*napišti*(zi) *amēlūtumma*
204 *eninnāma* ^{m}UD-*napišti*(zi) u *sinništa*(munus)*šu lū emû kīma ilī*(dingir)^{meš} *nâšīma*
205 *lū ašibma* ^{m}UD-*napišti*(zi) *ina rūqi ina pî nārāti*(id$_2$)^{meš}
206 *ilqû'innīma ina rūqi ina pî*(ka) *nārāti*(id$_2$)^{meš} *uštēšibu'inni*

203 'In the past UD-napišti was (one of) humankind.
204 but now UD-napišti and his woman shall be like us gods!
205 UD-napišti shall dwell far away, at the mouth of the rivers!'
206 They took me and settled me far away, at the mouth of the rivers.

The above lines regarding the closing episode of the Flood story are presumably adaptations of the parallel lines in the *Sumerian Flood Story* 256–61:

256 ti diĝir-gin$_7$ mu-un-na-šum$_2$-mu
257 zi da-ri$_2$ diĝir-gin$_7$ mu-un-<na>-ab-e$_{11}$-de$_3$
258 u$_4$-ba zi-u$_4$-su$_3$-ra$_2$ lugal-am$_3$
259 mu niĝ$_2$-gilim-ma numun nam-lu$_2$-ulu$_3$ uri$_3$ ak
260 kur-bal kur dilmun-na ki ^{d}utu e$_3$-še$_3$ mu-un-ti-eš
261 za-e$^{?}$ x [. . .] BA x-bi ti-eš x

256 They granted him life like a god.
257 They brought down to him eternal life, like a god.
258 At that time, Ziusudra, the king,

[88] The first half of XI 49, *ana bāb*(ka$_2$) *a-tar-ḫa-s*[*is*] 'to the gate of Atra-hasīs', is based on c$_1$ (VAT 11000), which was published by Maul (1999: 155–62).

[89] The name Atra-hasīs is used here probably because the author may have intended to convey that the Flood hero was exceeding in wisdom so as to be able to perceive the secret of the gods about the coming Flood catastrophe which was disclosed by Enki through a reed fence and a brick wall. Note the possible wordplay of *ḫissas* in XI 22 *kikkišu šimēma igāru ḫissas* 'Listen, O reed fence! Pay heed, O brick wall!' with the name Atra-hasīs. It is very likely that this episode is referred to as an aetiology of the name Atra-hasīs in the Standard Babylonian version of the *Gilgameš Epic* (see further discussion in Chen 2009 (Vol. II): 353–7).

259 who preserved the name of the animals and the seed of humankind,
260 they settled him in an overseas country in the land of Dilmun, where the sun rises.
261 . . .

The most obvious adaptation is the adding of the phrase *ina rūqi* 'far away' by the late version of the *Gilgameš Epic*. The word *rūqu* (distant, remote) is characteristic of the Babylonian *Gilgameš Epic*, which is used to describe not just the location of the legendary figure Ūta-na'ištim/UD-napišti but also the long journey Gilgameš had travelled in order to reach the legendary figure (especially in the late version as mentioned earier).[90] The notion that the Flood hero was settled at the mouth of the rivers seems to have come from the Babylonian *Gilgameš Epic* as well, as Gilgameš had to cross the ocean (OB VA + BM iii 24; SB *Gilgameš* X 82, 153, XI 293$^{?}$) or the river (X 106, 157) by boat in order to reach the legendary hero Ūta-na'ištim/UD-napišti the Distant.

In the light of these above adaptations of the Flood story by the Standard Babylonian version of the *Gilgameš Epic*, the change of the name of the Flood hero from Atra-hasīs to UD-napīšti clearly seems to have been motivated by the desire of the author of the late version to mark the transition of the Flood hero from being a mortal to becoming like a god. The transition also provides the aetiological occasion for the origin of the name UD-napišti the Distant.[91] The latter name was felicitously given by Enlil to the Flood hero as befitting the hero's newly gained status and settlement. The author could not have used Ziusudra (compare the omen apodoses mentioned earlier) as the previous name of the Flood hero—though it was already hinted at in XI 23—for the reason that Ziusudra was widely associated with eternal life, while Atra-hasīs was not.

As far as the representations of the Flood story and the Flood hero are concerned, the late version seems to have been substantially influenced by the *Death of Bilgames*. For example, the late version can be seen as broadly following the Sumerian composition in using the Flood story to provide aetiological explanations as to why Gilgameš, in spite of his illustrious career (Tablets I, II–VI) and his divine birth (Tablets I–II, X), had failed to obtain eternal life. However, it is only obvious that the late version quoted the Flood story (Tablet XI) more extensively than the Sumerian composition

[90] The notion that the Flood hero had a wife must be a late development. It is lacking in both the Old Babylonian version of the *Atra-hasīs Epic* and the *Sumerian Flood Story*, which follow the pattern of the Isin-Larsa royal hymns that employed the destruction-restoration rhetoric without any reference to the spouses of the rulers in question.

[91] See Galter (2005: 275) who writes: 'Als Utanapišti mit seiner Frau ewiges Leben erhält, wird auch sein Name geändert. Früher, als sterblicher Mensch, hieß er Atrahasis (XI 49, 197), nun nennt ihn Enlil Utanapišti (XI 203–205).'

did.[92] And contrary to the *Death of Bilgames* in which the Flood story was recounted by Enki, the Standard Babylonian version of the *Gilgameš Epic* represents the Flood story as being told by the Flood hero. Also at variance with the Sumerian composition in which the gods assembled concerning Gilgameš's fate, the late version represents the Flood hero as stating that no one would now assemble the gods for Gilgameš, presumably to decide whether he was to have eternal life (XI 207–8). The divergent representations of the Flood story in relation to Gilgameš's final destiny in the Sumerian composition and the Standard Babylonian version of the epic may have sprung from their conceptual differences: while the former holds the view that each individual's destiny was to be decided in the divine assembly, the latter follows the Old Babylonian *Gilgameš Epic* (OB VA + BM iii 3–5) that since human mortality had long been determined by the gods at the creation (X 319–22; George 2003: 507–8), the gods no longer had to assemble for such a matter again. They assembled for the case of the Flood hero only because of the extraordinary circumstance of the Flood. Thus, while eternal life was still proposed as a faint possibility for Gilgameš in the divine assembly according to the *Death of Bilgames*, no single thought of that was entertained in the Standard Babylonian version. The late version appears to be more emphatic than the Sumerian composition when it comes to the inescapable human fate of Gilgameš.

The most obvious example of the late version's adaptation of the *Death of Bilgames* is probably found in I 37–44:

37 *šīḫu* ^{d}GIŠ-*gim*$_{2}$-*maš gitmālu rašubbu*
38 *pētû nērebēti ša ḫursānī*
39 *ḫērû burī ša kišād*(gu$_{2}$) *šadî*(kur)^{i}
40 ⌜*ē*⌝*bir ayabba tâmati rapašti*(dagal)^{ti} *adi*(en) *ṣīt šamši*(^{d}utu.e$_{3}$)
41 *ḫā'iṭ kibrāti muštē'û balāṭi*
42 *kāšid dannūssu ana* ^{m}UD-*napišti*(zi) *rūqi*
43 *mutēr māḫāzī ana ašrīšunu ša uḫalliqu abūbu*
44 ⌜*mukīn*⌝ *parṣī ana nišī*(uĝ$_{3}$)^{meš} *apâti*

37 Gilgameš so tall, perfect and terrible,
38 who opened passes in the mountains;
39 who dug wells on the hill-flanks,
40 and crossed the ocean, the wide sea, as far as the sunrise;
41 who scoured the world-region ever searching for life,
42 and reached by his strength UD-napišti the Distant;
43 who restored the cult-centres that the Flood destroyed,
44 and established the proper rites for the human race!

[92] Though the Flood story found in the late version to a large degree follows that of the *Atra-hasīs Epic*, as indicated especially by the name of Atra-hasīs in XI 49, 197 and numerous other parallels between OB *Atra-hasīs* III and SB *Gilgameš* XI (Tigay 1982: 214–40), the ending of the story (XI 203–4; see also IX 76; XI 7) seems to be based on the *Sumerian Flood Story* or a similar tradition in which eternal life was granted to the Flood hero by Enlil.

While still retaining its original motif of seeking eternal life on the basis of Gilgameš's journey to Ūta-na'ištim the Distant in the Old Babylonian *Gilgameš Epic* (OB VA + BM), the meeting between Gilgameš and UD-napišti in the late version began to take on the character of the encounter between Gilgameš and Ziusudra as portrayed in the *Death of Bilgames*. The merging of the two originally separate traditions has resulted in a new conception of Gilgameš's journey in the late version: Gilgameš went out to seek eternal life for his personal salvation from death and its dread, but came back with the knowledge for the (re-)establishment of society and civilization, as an ideal ruler was expected to do (see also George 2003: 447).

This new conception of Gilgameš's journey exhibited in the review of Gilgameš's career is consonant with the unfolding of the plot in the rest of the late epic. In a well-connected sequence the epic narrates a series of events that led to the search for eternal life by Gilgameš. It started with the meeting of Gilgameš and Enkidu (Tablets I–II; compare OB II & III) to be followed immediately by their exploits for the establishment of eternal fame and personal glory (Tablets II–VI; compare OB III; *Bilgames and Huwawa A & B*; *Bilgames and the Bull of Heaven*). The exploits unfortunately resulted in the tragic sickness and death of Enkidu (Tablets VII–VIII; compare *Bilgames, Enkidu, and the Netherworld*). After that, Gilgameš became afraid of death and began to search for eternal life by trying to reach the long-lived legendary hero UD-napišti (previously Ūta-na'ištim in the Old Babylonian version) now identified as the Flood hero (Tablets IX–X; compare OB VA + BM). As Gilgameš finally arrived at the abode of the legendary hero, the latter reproached the former for having failed in his royal duties to his country and to the gods while wasting his energy and life in the hope of avoiding the inevitable (Tablet X; see George 2003: 504–6 for interpretation). The lesson of the unchangeable nature of human destiny was again stressed in the remaining part of the epic (Tablets XI–XII; cf. *Bilgames, Enkidu, and the Netherworld*).

From the above synopsis one can see that the author of the late version had inserted a lesson on royal duties (X 267–96) in the traditional plot of Gilgameš's journey to the legendary hero Ūta-na'ištim in search of eternal life. The lesson on royal duties was taught, most appropriately, by the Flood hero and the last antediluvian ruler, who represented ideal kingship for having contributed to the (re-)establishment of civilization and the survival of humankind and the divine world during the Flood. The author here had synthesized the two originally separate literary figures: Ūta-na'ištim the Distant from the Old Babylonian version of the *Gilgameš Epic*, and Ziusudra from the Sumerian Flood tradition (who was already absorbed in the *Death of Bilgames*), as he had done earlier in I 37–44. In addition, the two separate events from the *Death of Bilgames*, Gilgameš's journey to Ziusudra for the restoration of antediluvian civilization and his learning of the lesson on the inescapability of death, had been combined into one and made the climactic event in the Standard Babylonian version of the *Gilgameš Epic*. Thus the Flood hero, now called UD-napištim, carries both the function of transmitting to Gilgameš the antediluvian ideal of kingship in terms of cultic and civic duties, on the one hand, and the role of imparting to Gilgameš the lesson on human destiny, on the other.[93]

The late version also had reinterpreted the depictions of what Gilgameš had brought back from the Flood hero in the *Death of Bilgames* so that it now pertains not only to the 'technical' knowledge for the restoration of the proper rites (I 43–4) but also to the 'philosophical' knowledge of what ideal kingship means (see X 267–96), both of which must have been considered as lost or neglected in the frenzied pursuit of individual fulfilment and enjoyment as well as in the delusion of personal salvation from death and its dread.

The inserted lesson on the royal duties in the traditional plot in the epic suggests that the lesson on human destiny is delayed and relegated to a supporting role. These adaptations of the Old Babylonian version of the *Gilgameš Epic* are intended to accentuate the fact that in spite of his personal loss in his failure to obtain immortality through his meeting with UD-napišti, Gilgameš brought back vital information from the Flood hero for the restoration of the lost civilization.[94] The whole emphasis of the epic has now shifted from individual existence or fulfilment, the pursuit of which often characterizes the traditional depictions of Gilgameš's exploits, to a broader concern for civilization or society as a whole (see also George 2003: 504–6). This shift of emphasis may have resulted in the omission of the *carpe diem* advice (basically about staying content with one's mundane personal and family life) offered by the ale-wife to Gilgameš in OB VA + BM. That individualistic approach to life may have proved unsatisfactory to the author of the late version, for it had failed to address the significance of public welfare at large, without which individuals would be deprived of a secure environment vital for survival and growth.

Finally, the emphasis on Gilgameš's contribution to public welfare in spite of his personal failure to achieve immortality is further highlighted in the prologue (I 1–28) and epilogue (XI 322–8 // I 18–23) which frame the main body of the epic. It is no surprise that out of all Gilgameš's accomplishments, it was only his hard-won knowledge beneficial for public welfare and his public service in building the wall of Uruk that were most celebrated and regarded as immortal in the epic.[95]

[93] It is possible that both of these messages might have been considered in the late version of the epic as the antediluvian knowledge which Gilgameš brought back from the Flood hero (see [*u*]*bla ṭēma ša lām abūb*[*i*] in Tablet I 8; George 2003: 445).

[94] As opposed to the emphasis in the *Death of Bilgames* that, regardless of Gilgameš's partially divine birth and his grand achievements including the restoration of the lost civilization, he was not to escape death.

[95] Uruk was 'the archetypal Mesopotamian city' and the symbol of a civilized society (George 2003: 527). Its foundation is said to have been laid by the seven sages in the primeval era before the Flood (SB *Gilgameš* I 21; XI 326).

The exaltation of the ancient city Uruk in both the prologue and epilogue also signifies that what had enduring value did not lie somewhere far away (*rūqu*), but right at home in Gilgameš's own city. As valuable as it was, the city had been neglected due to his search for fame and immortality far afield. In the end, Gilgameš came to recognize Uruk's worth as he introduced the city to Ur-šanabi, the boatman of UD-napišti, apparently with pride (XI 322–8). Yet this recognition of the value of his home city would hardly have been possible had Gilgameš not been frustrated in his attempts to achieve immortality on his journey to a faraway place. Thus for the most part in the late version Gilgameš is not presented as an ideal king (Vanstiphout 2003: 12; 19 n. 45), but it was through his waywardness, striving, and disillusion that he came to learn wisdom with regard to the duties of kingship and the meaning of human existence.

Though the author of the late version was writing about Gilgameš, it is likely that he was using the epic as a vehicle for expressing his critical views on the political and social culture of his time. The choice of the legendary ruler Gilgameš may have been deliberate, comparable to the choice of Naram-Suen in *Curse Agade* and Solomon in *Qohelet*. Gilgameš was renowned for his surpassing heroic feats and exploits (I 17, 29, 45–6). If a king of his stature had failed to find eternal life, but had come to recognize the value of human society (especially the local community at home), why would anyone else try to make the same futile attempts and refuse to embrace the same value?

SOME OBSERVATIONS ON THE ANTEDILUVIAN SECTION OF THE CHRONOGRAPHICAL SOURCES AS A WHOLE

Having already examined the development of the last antediluvian dynasty in the chronographical sources, it will be important to take a look at the antediluvian section as a whole in the sources.

Identification of the Relevant Sources

Among the extant chronographical sources, the following texts have preserved the antediluvian section.[96]

[96] The lists of manuscript traditions with regard to the antediluvian section in this study are largely based on the *SKL* manuscript sources compiled by Edzard (1980–3: 77–8), Vincente (1995: 236–8), and Glassner (2004: 117–18, 126), together with the categorization of manuscripts with regard to the antediluvian section in Jacobsen (1939: 55–6). Vincente basically follows Edzard. Several manuscripts included by Edzard and Vincente are omitted by Glassner (2004: 57–8), such as W-B 62, IM 63095, Ni_2 and UCBC 9-1819, which Glassner treats as list fragments separate from the *SKL*.

Babyloniaca	See Verbrugghe and Wickersham (1996: 13–91). Date: 290 BC. Provenance: Babylon$^{?}$
The *Dynastic Chronicle*	Attested by the Neo-Assyrian copies, K 8532 + K 8533 + K 8534, which were initially considered by Jacobsen (1939: 11) as part of the manuscript tradition of *SKL* (K), but later became known as the *Dynastic Chronicle* (Grayson 1975: 139 f. and 285), with other fragments gradually being added: CT 46.5 = K 11624 + K 11261 (Lambert and Millard 1969: 17–18), K 12054 (Lambert 1973: 271–5), and BM 35572 + BM 40565 (Finkel 1980: 65–80). For the most recent edition, see Glassner (2004: 126–34). Date: Neo-Assyrian and Neo-Babylonian for the extant copies, but the original composition may go back to the Old Babylonian period as the incipit of the composition is found in an Old Babylonian catalogue (Jacobsen 1987: 145–50; Glassner 2004: 126). Provenance: Nineveh and Babylonia
IM 63095 (*SKL*)	Discovered by A. Goetze (still unpublished) and discussed in Finkelstein (1963: 39 n. 1; 45 n. 21; 47 n. 26). Date: early Old Babylonian. Provenance: Tell Harmal
MS 2855 (*SKL*)	Part of the Schøyen Collection. Published by Friberg (2007: 236–8). Date: probably from the early part of the Isin period. Provenance: unknown
Ni_2 = Ni 3195 (*SKL*)	Published by Kraus (1952: 31). Date: unknown. Provenance: Nippur
UCBC 9-1819 (*SKL*)	Published by Finkelstein (1963: 40) (the reverse side of the tablet). Date: no later than Samsu-iluna (1749–1712 BC). Provenance: Tutub (modern Iraqi village Khafaje)
W-B 62 (*SKL*)	Langdon (1923*b*: 256). Date: unknown. Provenance: unknown
W-B 444 (*SKL*)	Langdon (1923*a*: 8–21, 37–9), pls. I–IV. Date: no earlier than 1816 BC (Glassner 2004: 108). Provenance: Larsa$^{?}$

The condition of the texts preserved varies among the eight sources containing the antediluvian section. The original work of Berossos' *Babyloniaca* no longer exists. But the information regarding antediluvian history and the Flood story, which should be part of the first two books of *Babyloniaca*, may be extracted from ancient works from the first millennium AD that either quoted from or alluded to Berossos' books. *The Dynastic Chronicle*, also containing both mythological and chronographical materials in its antediluvian section, has been reconstructed from the Neo-Assyrian and Neo-Babylonian fragments. IM 63095 only has the end of the lines on each side of the tablet preserved, with the antediluvian section on the obverse and the first dynasty of Kiš on the reverse. MS 2855 (Plate 14) is a relatively small and fairly well-preserved tablet, with some damage in the upper and lower right-hand corners on the obverse. This source contains only the antediluvian section. Seriously damaged on the surface, the small Nippur tablet Ni$_2$ has only preserved five legible lines dealing with a few antediluvian rulers and their cities. UCBC 9-1819 has about seventeen lines for its antediluvian section on the reverse and the upper edge of the tablet. W-B 62 presents a full list that treats the antediluvian rulers (18 lines) exclusively with a few damaged lines.[97] W-B 444 is by far the most well-preserved and extensive of all extant sources. On this 'large rectangular clay prism inscribed with two columns on each side' (Langdon 1923*a*: 36), one finds not only 38 lines of the antediluvian section with two additional lines referring to the Flood, but also 337 lines of the postdiluvian section.

Apart from the above sources, it is fairly certain that the fragment P$_5$, another Old Babylonian source of *SKL*, must have been preceded by the antediluvian section in its original state.[98] Likewise, the Tell Leilān source of *SKL* originally should have contained the antediluvian section, with the relevant lines, about 26 in number, being unfortunately broken off in the constituent fragments (Vincente 1995: 244).

P$_5$	Poebel (1914*b*), PBS 5, 5. Date: the latter half of the First Dynasty of Babylon. Provenance: Nippur
TL	L 87–520a + 520b + 641 + 769 + 770 published by Vincente (1990: 8–9); Vincente (1995: 240–3, 244–6). Date: no later than Samsuiluna year 22. Provenance: Tell Leilān

[97] It is uncertain whether Ni$_2$ originally contained only the antediluvian section. Perhaps a school tablet, its scribe may have followed a more complete source like W-B 444 with both the antediluvian and postdiluvian sections, but may have only copied the original in part probably because of the limited space on the tablet. A similar situation may have applied to UCBC 9-1819, which also appears to be a school tablet. Support for the hypothesis that these two texts are copies of works with the postdiluvian section may be found in the fact that both Ni$_2$ and UCBC 9-1819 use the formula of transfer of kingship ba-gul 'was destroyed'. This formula is used only as part of the descriptions of the postdiluvian section in other sources of *SKL*, e.g. $P_2^?$ and Su$_2$ (Kraus 1952: 31; Finkelstein 1963: 39–41).

[98] See Jacobsen 1939: 56 n. 102; Edzard 1980–3: 78; Vincente 1995: 244; Glassner 2004: 108; contra Hallo 1963*b*: 54.

In addition, it is uncertain whether the antediluvian section was originally part of the following five sources of *SKL*.[99]

G	A fairly small fragment published by H. de Genouillac, PRAK II C 112. Date: the latter half of the First Dynasty of Babylon. Provenance: Kiš
$L_1 + N_1$	CBS 14220 published by Legrain (1922) PBS 13, 1; Ni 9712 a–c published by Kraus (1952: 35–8), also in Kramer (1952*b*: 19), fig. 9. Date: early Old Babylonian. Provenance: Nippur
P_6	CBS 15365 originally published by Poebel (1914*a*: 81), PBS 4/1, and was later re-identified and copied as N 1610 by Civil (1961: 80).[100] Date: early Old Babylonian[?]. Provenance: Nippur
Su_2	Fragment A published by Scheil (1934: 159–61). Date: the middle of the First Dynasty of Babylon. Provenance: Susa
$Su_3 + Su_4$	Fragments B and C published by Scheil (1934: 161–6). Date: the middle of the First Dynasty of Babylon. Provenance: Susa

The current study will primarily focus on the eight chronographical sources that have preserved the antediluvian section. First, some of the variations and patterns of stylistic and descriptive features in the antediluvian sections of these sources will be observed, on the basis of which some tentative conclusions on the historical development of these features will be drawn. Then, the factual data of the antediluvian sections, i.e. the order and number of antediluvian cities and kings, will be analysed.

Descriptive Formulae

Stylistic divergence and grouping can be observed in these sources. Though previous studies, especially that of Finkelstein (1963: 39–51), have noted some of the patterns in these antediluvian sources, it is important to present the data more systematically.

1 Formula for introducing the first ruler of each dynasty: (1) W-B 444: GN[ki] PN lugal mu X i_3-ak;[101] GN[ki] PN lugal-am_3 mu X i_3-ak 'In GN, PN was

[99] Concerning the uncertainty of inclusion of the antediluvian section in the following manuscripts, see Jacobsen (1939: 55–6) for P_6, L_1, Su_2, and Su_{3+4}; Kraus (1952: 32) for G, Su_2, and Su_{3+4}; Edzard (1980–3: 78) for $L_1 + N_1$, P_6, and Su_{3+4}; Vincente (1995: 244) for $L_1 + N_1$; Glassner (2004: 108) for Su_2.

[100] Civil (1961: 79) suggests that this fragment should be joined to the lower part of cols. x and xi of the same tablet as $L_1 + N_1$. But this suggestion has not been accepted by Edzard (1980–3: 78), Vincente (1995: 237), and Glassner (2004: 117).

[101] For the i_3-ak formula, compare L_1, L_2, N_1, P_2, P_3, P_4, P_6, Su_1, Su_2, Su_{3+4}, and G.

king and reigned X years'; GN^{ki} PN mu X i_3-ak 'In GN, PN reigned X years';[102] (2) MS 2855: PN lugal mu X i_3-ak 'PN was king and reigned X years'; (3) the *Dynastic Chronicle*: PN lugal-e mu X in-ak 'PN, the king, reigned X years'; GN^{ki} PN lugal-e mu X in-ak 'In GN, PN, the king, reigned X years';[103] (4) UCBC 9-1819: GN^{ki} PN mu X in-ak 'In GN, PN reigned X years';[104] (5) W-B 62 and Ni_2: no formula used

2 Formula for introducing single rulers: (1) W-B 444, MS 2855, and Ni_2: PN mu X i_3-ak 'PN reigned X years'; (2) the *Dynastic Chronicle*: PN lugal-e mu X in-ak 'PN, the king, reigned X years'; (3) UCBC 9-1819: PN mu X in-ak 'PN reigned X years'; (4) W-B 62: PN mu X 'PN, X years'

3 Formula for the summary of each dynasty: (1) W-B 444 and IM 63095 (compare P_2, P_6, L_1): X lugal mu-bi Y ib_2-ak 'X king(s) reigned Y years';[105] (2) the *Dynastic Chronicle*: X-am_3 lugal-e-ne bala GN^{ki} mu Y in-ak 'X kings, the dynastic cycle of GN: they reigned Y years'; 1 lugal-e bala GN^{ki} mu X in-ak '1 king, the dynastic cycle of GN: he reigned X years'; (3) W-B 62: X lugal GN^{ki} 'X kings in GN'; (4) MS 2855, UCBC 9-1819, and $Ni_2^?$ (compare *USKL*): no formula used

4 Formula for the change of dynasty: (1) W-B 444: GN_1^{ki} ba-šub nam-lugal-bi GN_2^{ki}-še ba-de_6 'GN_1 fell, kingship was taken to GN_2'; GN_1^{ki} ba-šub-be_2-en nam-lugal-bi GN_2^{ki}-še ba-de_6 'I will bring GN_1 to an end; kingship was taken to GN_2' (compare IM 63095);[106] GN_1 ba-šub nam-lugal-$še_3$ GN_2^{ki}-$še_3$ ba-de_6 'GN_1 fell, as for the kingship, it was taken to GN_2'; (2) the *Dynastic Chronicle*: GN_1^{ki} bala-bi ba-kur_2 nam-lugal-bi GN_2^{ki}-$še_3$ ba-nigin 'The dynastic cycle of GN_1 changed; its kingship went to GN_2'; (3) UCBC 9-1819: GN_1^{ki} ba-gul nam-lugal-bi GN_2^{ki} ba-tum_2 'GN_1 was destroyed; its kingship was taken to GN_2' (compare $P_2^?$, Su_2); (4) Ni_2: [eridu^{ki}] ba-gul mu [x x x r]a-kam$^{ki?}$-$še_3$ ba-tum_2 '[Eridu] was destroyed; . . . years;[107] . . . was taken to [La]rak'; and (5) W-B 62: no formula used

It may be significant that the above sources which either have preserved (IM 63095, Ni_2, UCBC 9-1819, W-B 62, W-B 444, and the *Dynastic Chronicle*) or

102 For IM 63095's use of the ergative -e after the name of the first ruler of a dynasty, see Finkelstein 1963: 45 n. 21.

103 For the in-ak formula, see IB = IB 1564 + 1565 (Wilcke 1987: 89–93), pls. 35–6; P_5; S; and TL.

104 The terminative -$še_3$ following UD.KIB.NUN^{ki} in UCBC 9-1819 line 10 may have been a scribal error resulting from vertical dittography in an earlier stage of textual transmission when the terminative was still used in the formula for the change of dynasty in the line above: UD.KIB.NUN^{ki}-$še_3$ ba-tum_2 (compare Ni_2).

105 IM 63095, according to Finkelstein (1963: 45 n. 21), uses i_3-ak throughout, even for the summary of each dynasty (compare Su_1, Su_2, Su_{3+4}, J), instead of the collective formula ib_2-ak used by W-B 444.

106 On the ba-šub formula, see Finkelstein (1963: 42, 45 n. 21).

107 The use of mu 'year' could be part of the formula for the summary of each dynasty, which usually precedes the formula for the change of dynasty in other chronographical sources.

are expected to have originally contained the antediluvian section (P_5 and TL) share the same Sumerian expression, mu X, 'X years', in the formula for introducing single rulers, regardless of the divergence in the finite verbs they employ. The same expression also occurs in source J of *SKL*, about which Jacobsen (1939: 12, 36, 56) expresses some doubt as to whether it originally contained the antediluvian section, and in the *USKL* and IB. All other manuscript traditions of *SKL* have the inverted order, X mu, for this expression (Jacobsen 1939: 42).

In addition to the above stylistic variations and patterns, the introductory and concluding formulae for the whole antediluvian section in W-B 444 distinguish this source from the other sources (except for the *Dynastic Chronicle* and possibly IM 63095): i 1 [nam]-lugal an-ta ⸢e$_{11}$⸣-de$_3$-a-ba 'When kingship descended from heaven'; i 39 a-ma-ru ⸢ba-ur$_3$⸣-«ra-ta» 'Then the Flood swept over.' W-B 444 further adds the stylistic and temporal formula related to the Flood to introduce the king list proper: i 40 eĝir a-ma-ru ba-ur$_3$-ra-ta 'After the Flood had swept over' (see also line 1 in the *Rulers of Lagaš*).[108]

The *Dynastic Chronicle* apparently has adopted and elaborated on the introductory formula from W-B 444. The adaptation is consistent with the mythological material the Chronicle includes regarding both the primeval history and the Flood story: i 8–9 [nam-lug]al-la an-ta e$_{11}$-de$_3$-eš-[a-ba]: [*ištu šarrūt*]*u ištu šamê ušēridā* | [nam-lu]gal-la an-ta e$_{11}$-de$_3$-eš-[a-ba]: [*ištu šarr*]*ūtu ištu šamê urda* 'When they lowered kingship from heaven, when kingship came down from heaven' (see also ii 10′–11′; Finkel 1980: 66–7).

It is likely that IM 63095 may have originally contained formulae similar to those found in W-B 444, especially the concluding formula for the antediluvian section and the introductory formula for the postdiluvian section.[109] IM 63095 may also have originally attached the antediluvian section to the king list proper (see Finkelstein 1963: 45 n. 21). But without a copy of the text available, it is difficult to judge how many lines of the antediluvian section the tablet could actually accommodate.

Ni$_2$ and UCBC 9-1819 could be partial copies of fuller versions of *SKL* with the postdiluvian section attached because of the stylistic formulae these two sources have adopted from the king list proper. But it is more likely that these two sources were originally independent of the king list proper, as it is fairly easy to see that both Ni$_2$ and UCBC 9-1819 have no introductory formulae as we find in W-B 444 i 1 and the *Dynastic Chronicle* i 8–9. UCBC

[108] As already noted in Chapter 2, the traditional introductory formula of *SKL*, nam-lugal an-ta e$_{11}$-de$_3$-a-ba 'When kingship had come down from heaven', is relegated to second place (W-B 444 i 41).

[109] Given that IM 63095 alone shares with W-B 444 the use of the same Sumerian verb -šub ('to fall, throw down, overthrow', etc.) for describing the change of dynasty.

9-1819 directly starts with the first antediluvian king: [. . . . . m]u$^{?}$ 36,000 in-ak '[. . .] reigned for 36,000 [ye]ars'. In Ni_2 the first 3 lines are missing. The first line may perhaps be reconstructed according to W-B 444 i 2 and the *Dynastic Chronicle* line 10 (BM 35572 + BM 40565; see Finkel 1980: 66): [eridu^{ki} nam-lugal-la] '[kingship was in Eridu]'. The second and third lines should deal with the names of the first two kings and their reigns as in the first two lines of UCBC 9-1819. Whether Ni_2 originally contained a concluding remark is impossible to judge now. Based on the traces of the last line of UCBC 9-1819, one at least knows that the tablet ends with the reign of an antediluvian king—thus the whole manuscript contains 'the bare list of the kings' (Finkelstein 1963: 43).[110]

Similar to UCBC 9-1819, W-B 62 starts with the first antediluvian king: a_2-lu-lim mu 67,200 -kam 'Alulim ruled 67,200 years', and ends with a summary of the antediluvian kings with reference to the Flood: [10] lugal [*pa*]-*nu* a-ma-ru '[Ten] kings before the Flood' (compare line 29 of the *Dynastic Chronicle*: 5 iri^{didli} 9 lugal-e-[ne mu . . . in-ak] 'Five cities; nine kings [reigned for . . . years]'). In spite of the possibility that *pānu* a-ma-ru might imply a section on the postdiluvian era, the whole composition of W-B 62 appears quite self-contained and may represent the only extant antediluvian king list tradition that has no postdiluvian list attached. The independent character of W-B 62 can also be derived from the above-analysed formulae this source uses, which finds almost no parallel among other king list traditions, except that it shares with Ni_2 no distinct formula for introducing the first ruler of a dynasty.

On the one hand, we have antediluvian king list traditions that exist apart from the king list proper and have no introductory formulae nam-lugal an-ta e_{11}-de_3-a-ba as seen especially in the case of W-B 62. On the other hand, there is the independent existence of the king list proper that starts with the introductory formula nam-lugal an-ta e_{11}-da-ba to be followed by the first dynasty of Kiš, see BT 14 + P_3 (Klein 2008) and *USKL* (Steinkeller 2003). On the basis of the evidence from these two groups of sources, it can be concluded that the antediluvian section and the postdiluvian section were indeed originally independent of each other and were joined together secondarily.[111] One can also conlude that the formula introducing the antediluvian section in W-B 444 i 1 was originally rooted in the king list proper as its introductory line and was only secondarily added to the antediluvian section when the section was prefixed to the king list proper. Once these two independent sections were

[110] The 26 missing lines in the first two columns of TL (Vincente 1995: 244), even given the more condensed style of this source, may just have enough room for all the antediluvian kings and the kings of Kiš before the first preserved line probably dealing with Kalibum, but not the introductory, concluding, and transitional notes as found in W-B 444.

[111] See Jacobsen 1939: 55–68, Kraus 1952: 31, and Finkelstein 1963: 44.

joined, the antediluvian section began to undergo a series of adaptations in accordance with the king list proper.[112]

But there is still uncertainty surrounding this process of adaptation. As Steinkeller (2003: 276) points out in his edition of *USKL*, so far the earliest *SKL* copy available, many of the structuring formulae and anecdotal notes found in the Old Babylonian copies of *SKL* were absent in the Ur-III copy. This suggests that the king list proper itself had gone through different stages of development, during which these formulae and notes were added gradually. Thus it is uncertain as to whether a particular formula or note in the antediluvian section was added or adapted by the scribe who joined the antediluvian section with the king list proper or at a later stage when the adaptation took place for both the antediluvian and postdiluvian sections after they had already been combined. It is also possible that certain formulae in the antediluvian section could have been influenced by the king list proper even with the two sections continuing to exist independently without being joined together in some traditions. This could be the case if Ni_2 and UCBC 9-1819, with some of their formulae evidently reflecting the influence of the postdiluvian section, are copies of independent antediluvian traditions such as W-B 62. But if Ni_2 and UCBC 9-1819 turn out to be copies of the king list traditions that had already combined both the antediluvian and postdiluvian sections such as W-B 444 and IM 63095, the formulae used by these two sources would seem to have developed under the influence of the king list traditions different from W-B 444.[113] For example, with regard to the formula for introducing single rulers, W-B 444, L_1, L_2, N_1, P_2, P_3, P_4, P_6, Su_1, Su_2, Su_3+$_4$, and G use i_3-ak 'N reigned X years'; while UCBC 9-1819, Ni_2, IM 63095, P_5, S, TL, and the *Dynastic Chronicle* use the in-ak verbal formula. Another example of divergence from W-B 444 can be found in the lack of the introductory heading in UCBC 9-1819 and Ni_2 in the antediluvian section.

While not knowing exactly when different stages of adaptation of the antediluvian section took place, at least one may roughly delineate what could have taken place during these stages on the basis of the antediluvian sources available and the parallel development of the king list proper as revealed especially by comparing the Ur-III copy with the Old Babylonian copies (Steinkeller 2003: 276).[114] The first stage of the antediluvian list tradition might have consisted of a simple list as reflected in W-B 62. At the second stage, different descriptive formulae were added for the summary of each dynasty,

[112] See Jacobsen 1939: 67–8; Galter 2005: 279.

[113] This is already reflected in Jacobsen's drawing of the genealogical relationship among the manuscript traditions of *SKL* (1939: 50, 55), in which W-B 444 and P_5, though both having joined the antediluvian and postdiluvian sections, sprouted from two separate textual branches.

[114] Of course, the development of each *SKL* source may not exactly follow the order sketched below.

the change of dynasty, and introducing single rulers and the first ruler of a dynasty. At the third stage, when the antediluvian and postdiluvian sections were joined, the introductory and concluding formulae for the antediluvian section and the new introductory formula (eĝir a-ma-ru ba-ur_3-«ra-ta» 'After the Flood had swept over') for the postdiluvian section were inserted and the different formulae were further adapted and correlated with those of the postdiluvian section (e.g. W-B 444). At the latest stage, the introductory section and the reference to the Flood were further expanded with the materials borrowed from various sources dealing with antediluvian tradition and the Flood story (e.g. the *Dynastic Chronicle* and *Babyloniaca*).[115] W-B 62 may represent the earliest antediluvian king list tradition because it lacks most of the formulae found in other texts, even any verbal form in describing the reign of rulers and the summary of each dynasty, which is present in all other *SKL* manuscript traditions. Keeping in mind the uncertainty regarding the relative dates of the antediluvian traditions, one may venture to propose a tentative chronological order of the antediluvian king list traditions represented by our manuscripts: W-B 62, UCBC 9-1819/Ni_2, MS 2855, W-B 444, IM 63095, the *Dynastic Chronicle*, and *Babyloniaca*.[116]

Factual Data

Stripping off most of the stylistic embellishments that were added secondarily and reducing the antediluvian section to its simple list, one may examine the basic information and order of antediluvian rulers and their dynastic cities, which, according to previous studies, show a considerable degree of fluidity. Finkelstein (1963: 50–1) explained this fluidity, or lack of a 'literary "consensus"', as being a result of the alleged scribal practice: when the scribes wrote these texts they mostly did so from memory, rather than strictly copying previous written sources. One of the chief examples Finkelstein (1963: 44) adduced in support of his theory is the unparalleled omission of Larak in UCBC 9-1819, even though its ruler Ensipazianna was included. Another possible example he

[115] Not every branch of the tradition had gone through all these stages. For example, while both Ni_2 and UCBC 9-1819 have the formula for the change of dynasty, the former lacks the formula for introducing the first king of each dynasty and the latter contains no introduction to the list. These variations make it difficult, if not impossible, to determine relative dates, if one only relies on the descriptive formulae as a criterion for tracing the process of evolution of the chronographical traditions.

[116] According to Finkelstein (1963: 45 n. 21), W-B 444 pre-dates IM 63095 because the former manuscript still used 'the older collective form ib_2-ak' in the formula for the summary of each dynasty, while the latter had already begun to use i_3-ak as in most of the exemplars of *SKL*. Also W-B 444's formula for the change of dynasty still had not fully shed the influence of its mythological source: ba-šub-be-en 'I will bring to an end'; compare ba-šub 'it was brought to an end' (IM 3195).

provided is the inversion of the order between Larak (usually the third antediluvian city) and Badtibira (usually the second antediluvian city) in Ni_2. In both of these cases, more so in the first, Finkelstein argued that the aberrant presentations 'must be explained as a memory lapse on the part of the scribe' instead of 'as evidence of some tradition' behind the texts in question.

But a further examination of UCBC 9-1819 and Ni_2 indicates that Finkelstein's study seems to have overlooked some of the crucial data in the texts which may point to a different interpretation. From the 'Comparative Chart of the Chronographical Sources Containing the Antediluvian Dynasties' (compare Finkelstein 1963: 45 and Friberg 2007: 240), one can see two important patterns which were first observed by Finkelstein: (1) Dumuzi almost always occupies the fifth position on the list (Finkelstein 1963: 49 n. 38), except in the account of Berossos in which Dumuzi occupies the sixth place, which can be explained by viewing Amenōn, the second king from Badtibira, as a mere duplicate of the first king in that city, Amelōn, which resulted in Dumuzi being pushed down to the sixth place in Berossos' list (Jacobsen 1939: 73 nn. 18, 22). (2) Badtibira, generally the second antediluvian city (except in Ni_2, the reason for which will be offered below), according to 'the normative tradition', has three kings (W-B 444, UCBC 9-1819, IM 63095; compare the *Dynastic Chronicle*), except in W-B 62, Ni_2, and *Babyloniaca* (Finkelstein 1963: 47). Why W-B 62 only assigns two kings, Dumuzi and Enmenluanna, has already been satisfactorily answered by Finkelstein (1963: 47). The anomalous numbers in Ni_2 (two kings) and *Babyloniaca* (five kings, in fact only four because of the doublet in the first two positions in Badtibira) will be explained below.

The significant datum Finkelstein has overlooked is that the same sequence, Ensipazianna followed by Dumuzi, occurs in both Ni_2 and UCBC 9-1819, which indicates that this sequence may reflect a genuine tradition behind these two sources. More specifically, this sequence may reflect a tradition that tended to put Ensipazianna, normally the only king from Larak, in front of Dumuzi, who, as mentioned above, almost always occupies the fifth place in the antediluvian king list traditions. Given that normally there are three kings in the dynasty of Badtibira, the placement of Ensipazianna right in front of Dumuzi makes one of the first two kings of Badtibira drop out. Thus one finds Enmegalanna being taken off the list in UCBC 9-1819 and Enmeluanna being omitted in Ni_2. Because Ensipazianna is the only king from Larak, his advancement in the list would naturally leave the dynasty of Larak, normally the third position of the antediluvian cities, unoccupied.

The insertion of Ensipazianna between Dumuzi and another Badtibira king also causes confusion with regard to the naming of the dynasty these three kings represent. UCBC 9-1819 and Ni_2 offer two different solutions to the above problems as a result of the promotion of Ensipazianna in the list. The former source opted to follow the traditional designation Badtibira for

A Comparative Chart of the Chronographical Sources Containing the Antediluvian Dynasties

MS 2855	W-B 444	W-B 62	UCBC 9-1819	Ni$_2$	The *Dynastic Chronicle*	*Babyloniaca*
ERIDU	ERIDU	HA.A^{ki}	ERIDU	[ERIDU]	[ERIDU]	BABYLON
Alulim	Alulim	Alulim	[Alulim]	[Alulim]	[Alulim]$^{?}$	Aloros
Elalgar	Alalgar	Alalgar	Alalgar	[Alagar]	[Alalgar]$^{?}$	Alaparos
		LARSA				
		[. . .]- kidunnu				
		[. . .]- alimma				
BADTIBIRA	BADTIBIRA	BADTIBIRA	BADTIBIRA	LARAK	[BADTIBIRA]	PAUTIBIBLON
Ammeluanna	Enmenluanna		Ammeluanna		[Enmeluanna]$^{?}$	Amelōn
						Amenōn
Enmegalanna	Enmengalanna			Enmegalanna	[Enm]egalanna	Amegalaros
			Ensipazianna	Ensipazianna		
				[BADTIBIRA]		
^{d}Dumuzi	^{d}Dumuzi	Dumuzi	^{d}Dumuzi	^{d}Dumuzi	Dumuzi	Daōnos
		Enmenluanna				
LARAK	LARAK	LARAK				
Ensipazianna	Ensipazianna	Ensipazianna				
SIPPAR	SIPPAR	SIPPAR	SIPPAR		SIPPAR	
Enmeduranna	Enmenduranna	Enmeduranna	Enmeduranki		Enmeduranki	Euedōrachos
					LARAK	LARAGCHOS
					Ensipazianna	Amempsinos
ŠURUPPAK	ŠURUPPAK	ŠURUPPAK	[ŠURUPPAK]		ŠURUPPAK	
Ubār-Tutu	Ubār-Tutu		[Ubār-Tutu]		Ubār-Tutu	Otiartes
		Man of Šuruppak, son of Ubār-Tutu				
		Ziusudra	[Ziusudra]$^{?}$		Ziusudra	Xisuthros
five cities, eight kings	five cities, eight kings	six cities, ten kings	four cities, eight$^{?}$ kings	five$^{?}$ cities, eight$^{?}$ kings	five cities, nine$^{?}$ kings	three cities, ten kings

the second antediluvian dynasty with the conventional number of kings. The ratio between two traditional Badtibira kings (Ammeluana/Enmeluanna and ^{d}Dumuzi) and one traditional Larak king (Ensipazianna) may have affected this decision. Once Ensipazianna became part of the Badtibira dynasty, his own dynastic city had no other king and thus had to be abandoned. Ni_2, however, chose another solution. The dynastic city represented by Enmegalanna and Ensipazianna is called Larak. The ratio between one traditional Badtibira king (Enmegalanna) and traditionally the only Larak king (Ensipazianna) may be conducive to this designation. But the solution in Ni_2 resulted in more violations of the traditional arrangement. Dumuzi now seems to be the only king representing the Badtibira dynasty, which is relegated to the third slot in the order of the antediluvian cities. The Larak dynasty is not only promoted to second place, but also contains one extra king!

The tradition behind Ni_2 and UCBC 9-1819 that puts Ensipazianna in front of Dumuzi reflects the fluidity of the dynasty of Larak in the antediluvian king list tradition. The fluidity can be further seen in *Babyloniaca* and the *Dynastic Chronicle*, in which Ensipazianna is placed after Enmeduranki, the only king from Sippar. In Berossos, the assignment of Enmeduranki in front of Ensipazianna from Larak made the former king no longer identified with Sippar and therefore resulted in one extra king in Badtibira.

With the above analysis of the variant traditions regarding the Larak dynasty, it becomes clear that MS 2855 and W-B 444 have basically preserved the 'original' or 'canonical' information and arrangement of the antediluvian king list, except that they did not include Ziusudra as the last antediluvian king. Apart from the insertion of the Larsa dynasty due to the 'local patriotism' of the scribe, which in turn resulted in the deduction of one king from the Badtibira Dynasty (Jacobsen 1939: 72 n. 17; Finkelstein 1963: 46), and the three-generation scheme for the last antediluvian dynasty, W-B 62 too has represented the 'original' or 'canonical' list faithfully. Thus we can reconstruct the original or canonical list as follows: (1) Eridu: Alulim, Alalgar; (2) Badtibira: Enmeluanna, Enmegalanna, Dumuzi; (3) Larak: Ensipazianna; (4) Sippar: Enmeduranki/Enmeduranna; and (5) Šuruppak: Ubār-Tutu, Ziusudra.[117] In total there are five antediluvian cities and nine kings, which correspond with the record in the *Dynastic Chronicle*. It is uncertain whether the above list represents the 'original' version, from which the variations such as those concerning Ensipazianna (Larak) deviated, or the 'canonical' version, which attempted to establish a consensus by putting Ensipazianna in a compromising position, after Dumuzi of Badtibira but before Enmeduranki of Sippar, between the representations of the two groups of variant traditions

[117] See Galter (2005: 279) who also arrives at the same reconstruction for the names and sequence of the antediluvian cities.

represented by UCBC 9-1819 and Ni_2 on the one hand, and *Babyloniaca* and the *Dynastic Chronicle* on the other.

SUMMARY

This chapter has investigated the development of divergent traditions regarding the names of the Flood hero and the last antediluvian rulers with their corresponding dynasties. Several compositions from the second half of the third millennium BC and the first quarter of the second millennium BC had contributed significantly to this development. One of these is the *Instructions of Šuruppak* from the Early Dynastic III period. The reason for the common use of this didactic source when constructing antediluvian history, especially with regard to the chronographical information about the last antediluvian dynasty, may be largely due to the antiquity of Šuruppak, modern-day Fara, in early Mesopotamian tradition (Krebernik 1998: 238–43). Šuruppak was generally regarded as the city in which the last antediluvian dynasty was based (W-B 444, W-B 62, and the *Dynastic Chronicle*). The *Atra-hasīs Epic*, however, does not mention Šuruppak. The only specific geographic site mentioned in the Babylonian epic is Ekur, Enlil's shrine in Nippur, which hints at the influence of the city laments on the epic (see Chapter 4). The utilization of the *Instructions of Šuruppak* by the Flood epic then should probably be explained in part by the shared wisdom character of the two compositions. The author of the epic seems to have been steeped in the didactic tradition. The fact that he chose to base the didactic episode in his work (OB *Atra-hasīs* III I 18–21) and the name of the Flood hero on the *Instructions of Šuruppak* suggests that he was well aware that this Sumerian didactic text had been used for the construction of antediluvian history.

The *SKL* likewise had been quite influential in the development of antediluvian traditions. Chronographically, it provided both the form and style with which the antediluvian traditions could begin to take shape as an extension of the king list proper into primeval history. Ideologically, the political doctrine of *SKL* asserted its influence in the way the antediluvian dynasties were conceived. In turn, this doctrine came to be anchored in the antediluvian period, especially in the event of the Flood which may have been used as the quintessential proof of dynastic discontinuity, so much so that even the last antediluvian ruler Ziusudra, otherwise described as the survivor of the Flood, may have been intentionally omitted in the *SKL* tradition represented by W-B 444 and MS 2855 (see also the *Rulers of Lagaš*). But such a view did not persist without being challenged. It was most vehemently opposed by the *Sumerian Flood Story* which in polemic fashion hailed the Flood hero Ziusudra as the only ruler in the antediluvian era.

The Isin-Larsa royal hymnic compositions from the early half of the Old Babylonian period had made equally significant contributions to the development of antediluvian traditions. Arguably, the concept of the antediluvian era and the corresponding literary expressions such as [*pa*]-*nu* a-ma-ru 'before the Flood' (W-B 62, line 18) or *ša lām abūbi* 'from before the Flood' (SB *Gilgameš* I 8) were developed on the basis of the stylistic and temporal formula eĝir a-ma-ru ur_3-ra-ta 'after the flood/Flood had swept over' from *Išme-Dagan A* and the *Instructions of Ur-Ninurta*. As a result of the projection of the catastrophe into the remote past, the royal agent of restoration who was granted eternal life in the royal hymns was transformed into the Flood hero and the last antediluvian ruler who had preserved antediluvian civilization and in turn received eternal life as a reward. It has been argued that the name Ziusudra for the Flood hero was first developed in the chronographical sources through this process. The emphasis on the royal contribution to the restoration of civilization to the Land in the Isin-Larsa royal hymnic compositions had not only influenced the development of antediluvian traditions but also the adaptation of the Gilgameš traditions, especially the Standard Babylonian version of the *Gilgameš Epic*'s critique of the individualistic attitude and the neglect of public welfare in the traditional portrayals of the king Gilgameš in seeking vain glory and elusive eternal life far away from home.

There are certain patterns that may be observed in the development of the Flood motif and antediluvian traditions. First, different literary traditions had exerted a mutual influence upon each other during the course of their evolution and transmission (see also Chen 2013). For example, the two-generation scheme of the last antediluvian dynasty in the chronographical sources was first developed on the basis of the Early Dynastic III versions of the *Instructions of Šuruppak*. This scheme was in turn used for the adaptation of the didactic composition during the Old Babylonian period. As a result, the three-generation genealogy was created and was subsequently adopted by the chronographical sources such as W-B 62. The same phenomenon of mutual influence can be seen in the interpenetration between the Ziusudra tradition and the Ūta-na'ištim tradition as they exchanged motifs with each other.

Assimilation of different traditions is yet another pattern which is frequently observed in the developmental process of the chronographical sources. It can also be detected in other sources such as the Old Babylonian version of the *Instructions of Šuruppak*, the *Ballade of Early Rulers*, the *Death of Bilgames*, the *Atra-hasīs Epic*, the *Sumerian Flood Story*, and the Standard Babylonian version of the *Gilgameš Epic*. This process involves not only joining traditions that were originally independent of each other, such as the mixing of the early rulers from the chronographical sources and the legendary figures from the Gilgameš tradition in the *Ballade of Early Rulers*, or the coalescence of the Ziusudra tradition and the Ūta-na'ištim tradition. It also involves merging those traditions that were parallel or even conflicting, as seen in the amalgamation of the two-generation genealogical scheme and the three-generation genealogical scheme for the last antediluvian dynasty in W-B 62 and the Standard Babylonian version of the *Gilgameš Epic*.

The above process of assimilation implies that the Flood and antediluvian traditions were developed gradually, often by accretion—though in some instances by attrition (e.g. the omission of Ziusudra in W-B 444). Antediluvian chronographical traditions, for example, must have first started off with some basic factual information: cities, rulers, and the number of years of their reigns (e.g. W-B 62). Then the descriptive and introductory formulae were added in accordance with those in the king list proper. Subsequently, the antediluvian section was joined with the king list proper with the introductory and concluding formulae inserted (e.g. W-B 444). At the later stages, parts of the Flood epic were incorporated (e.g. the *Dynastic Chronicle*; *Babyloniaca*). Of course, these elements did not grow in a linear genealogical fashion through a single tradition, but developed through cross-fertilization among divergent traditions.

Diverse motivations behind the development of the Flood and antediluvian traditions need also to be summarized. In many cases, motivations were clearly interpretive, as seen in the chronographical sources and the Old Babylonian version of the *Instructions of Šuruppak* which went their separate ways in interpreting the ambiguous opening lines of the Early Dynastic III versions of the *Instructions of Šuruppak*. While the ambiguity of this didactic composition was resolved in some of the later traditions (e.g. the clarification of the intellectual attributes by the Old Babylonian version of this composition), it was retained in others (e.g. the *Atra-hasīs Epic*). In many other cases, however, the development of the Flood and antediluvian traditions was ideologically motivated, to either reinforce or oppose a certain traditional political doctrine (e.g. W-B 444 vs. the *Sumerian Flood Story*), or to critically address the political, cultural, and social issues at hand (e.g. the Standard Babylonian version of the *Gilgameš Epic*).

Overall, the development of the Flood and antediluvian traditions from the Old Babylonian period on involved both involuntary sedimentation of the source materials produced as early as the Early Dynastic III period and the conscious selection, adaptation, and reorganization of traditions on the part of the ancient authors/scribes. Among them, the authors of the *Atra-hasīs Epic*, the W-B 444 version of *SKL*, the *Sumerian Flood Story*, the *Death of Bilgames*, the *Ballade of Early Rulers*, and the Standard Babylonian version of the *Gilgameš Epic* stand out both for their monumental contributions to the development of the Flood and antediluvian traditions and for their ability to ingeniously reshape tradition in attempts to engage in the political, religious, social, and cultural criticisms of their times.

4

The Flood Epic

Though the Sumerian compositions dealing with catastrophe have been available for decades, only a few scholars have taken note of the common conceptual and literary patterns between these compositions and the Flood epic. Apparently noticing the parallels between *LSU* 364–70 and the *Sumerian Flood Story* (CBS 10673 + CBS 10867) 158–60, Jacobsen (1981: 522 n. 14) attempted to restore lines 158–9 and 160 in the Flood story on the basis of *LSU* 364–5 and 369 respectively. Jacobsen also seems to have restored part of line 140 in the Flood story from *LSU* 147 on the basis of their similarities (Michalowski 1989: 84). A possible connection between the motif of human overpopulation as a cause of the divine decision to annihilate humankind at the beginning of *LW* and the same motif in the *Atra-hasīs Epic* is hinted at by Green (1984: 254). Furthermore, Postgate (1992: 295) notes, though only in passing, that the Babylonian Flood epic and the city laments share common themes or motifs in their depictions of catastrophe. Westenholz (1996: 198–200) also points out the common motifs of noise and the loss of intelligence in *Curse Agade* and the *Atra-hasīs Epic*, suggesting that the latter source has transformed the Sumerian motifs, mediated through the Old Babylonian version of the *Cuthean Legend of Naram-Suen*, to suit its own purpose. It is further hinted by Westenholz that the depiction of the primeval flood catastrophe is an expansion of the metaphorical portrayals of the flood catastrophe as seen in the earlier Sumerian and Akkadian compositions such as *Curse Agade* and the *Cuthean Legend of Naram-Suen*. Given that all these scholars only make brief and sporadic comparisons between the Sumerian compositions dealing with catastrophe and the Flood story or epic, a detailed and systematic comparison of the two traditions is called for. The following analysis will not only confirm the scholars' inklings about the intertextual and historical connections between the two traditions, but also demonstrate that the extent of the influence of the Sumerian compositions on the Flood epic is far greater than they suspected.

HISTORICAL BACKGROUND

With the disintegration of the Ur III dynasty, Sumer and Akkad fell into the hands of a number of regional powers (Isin, Larsa, Ešnunna, and Babylon), predominantly of Amorite origin. The early phase of this age in which the Amorites were to play so great a role was dominated by the Isin dynasty and its chief rival the Larsa dynasty. In an attempt to establish and consolidate their hegemony in the land, the Isin rulers adopted a number of traditional means of political legitimization. One was by appropriating the political ideology promulgated in the *SKL* to present themselves as the rightful inheritors of the Ur III dynasty (Michalowski 1983: 242–3; 1987: 57; 2005: 199). Another was by consciously imitating the royal hymns initiated primarily during the Ur III period.[1] In actual practice, the Isin rulers also modelled themselves on the traditional pattern of Mesopotamian rule by devoting themselves to the maintenance of different cults and temples as well as public works such as irrigation, as indicated in their year-names (Postgate 1992: 43–5) and royal inscriptions (Tinney 1996: 5). As in the Ur III period, the cult of Enlil in Nippur continued to receive special devotion and the city was granted preferential tax and military exemptions (Brisch 2007: 115) by the rulers of the Isin dynasty, because of the strategic role of Enlil as the chief deity in the Mesopotamian pantheon and Nippur as the religious centre in Sumer and Akkad. Several Isin rulers (e.g. Išbi-Erra, Šu-ilīšu, and Išme-Dagan) even called themselves sons of Enlil, and seem to have regarded their devotion to Enlil's cult in Nippur as fulfilling their filial piety.[2] 'With the reign of Išme-Dagan', Tinney (1996: 62) points out, 'the significance of Enlil and Nippur in the literary representation of royal ideology reached its zenith.'

Most importantly, however, much of the symbolic activity undertaken in ideology and in actual deeds was aimed at presenting the Isin rulers not just as the legitimate successors to the Ur III dynasty (Edzard 1957: 44–104) but also as the divinely chosen saviours who restored socio-economic and religious order and revived cities and temples that were destroyed by domestic turmoil and foreign invasions accompanying the fall of the Ur III dynasty and its aftermath. Some of the portrayals of destruction in the city laments or the Isin royal hymns are said to have been exaggerated as the collapse of the Ur-III dynasty may have been less dramatic and devastating (Michalowski 1989: 1–3, 6; Tinney 1996: 45, 83–4). Frayne's study (1998: 26–8) seems to suggest that the

[1] See Klein 1985: 7–38; 1990: 65–136; Tinney 1996: 63–80; Flückiger-Hawker 1999: 41–67; Brisch 2007: 19–31.

[2] Compare the construction and manipulation of mythical kinship by rulers during the Ur III period (see Wilcke 1989: 557–71; Woods 2012: 78–96).

destruction of the land or cities which the Isin rulers claimed to have restored may be intended to symbolize not so much the collapse of the Ur III dynasty as the negatively perceived rule of the Larsa dynasty, the chief rival of the Isin dynasty, in certain cities such as Nippur. As political rhetoric, these portrayals of catastrophe under the previous regime and restoration by the incumbent polity served to bolster the claims of epoch-making achievements by the Isin rulers, and maybe the competing claims by their rivals as well.

The state of development of the flood motif in Sumerian literature from the end of the Ur III period to the first half of the Isin-Larsa period reflects the transitional character of the time. No doubt, the conventional usage of the flood topos for adoration of the deities and rulers persisted in divine and royal hymns.[3] But contrasting with this hymnic praise of the gods and rulers are the city laments that employ, in an unprecedented fashion, dense and recurring storm or flood imagery in their dramatic depictions of and critical reflections on the destruction of different major cities and temples and even the whole Land of Sumer and Akkad. Instead of being a beneficiary of the mighty power of the gods, Sumer had become its victim, which can already be seen in several textual sources from the Ur III period.[4] Also, the destruction is often represented as an inversion of the motifs representing the establishment of civilization in the primeval era as found in many Sumerian mythological compositions and prologues. Thus the flood or storm, though in a figurative sense, became the means through which the established society or world was annihilated. Then, as the Isin rulers (possibly those of Larsa and Babylon as well, as suggested by Brisch 2007: 118) sought to legitimize their power by presenting themselves as the restorers of order and civilization, the emphasis in the usage of the flood motif began to shift from destruction to restoration. As a result, the hymnic mode of the flood motif resumes, yet with a different thrust, which is obviously the case in *Išme-Dagan A* and the *Instruction of Ur-Ninurta*, but already adumbrated in *LW* and *NL*, which used the destruction episode (the lament section) as preparation for the praise of Išme-Dagan as the divinely chosen agent of restoration (the hymnic section). It is this forging of a new political ideology through the process of literary transmutation, from the flood motif being used in divine and royal hymns to its use in lament literature and back to its use in divine and royal hymns, one might argue, that contributed decisively to the formation of the basic plot and the characterization of the protagonists of the Flood epic in the mid-Old Babylonian period.

[3] e.g. *Išme-Dagan S* 13; *Lipit-Eštar D* 47; *Būr-Suen A* 29–30; *Šu-ilīšu A* 1, 6, 47; *Iddin-Dagan D* 3, 10–15.

[4] e.g. *Year Name 22 of Ibbi-Suen*; see also *Year Name 14 of Ibbi-Suen* (Frayne 1997: 364–5).

THE CITY LAMENTS

The corpus of the city laments emerging from the Isin-Larsa period basically comprises five Sumerian literary texts, which may be listed in the following approximate order according to the tentative dates of their composition (Vanstiphout 1986: 9; Michalowski 1989: 5–6): *LSU, LU, LE/LW*, and *NL*. Among these texts, only *LSU, LU*, and *NL* are complete. All of the extant sources of these texts are from the Old Babylonian period, during which they became part of the school curriculum. These texts share some common poetic structuring features, *kirugu* 'song' and *gišgigal* 'antiphone'. Thematically, they are similar in some crucial respects (Green 1984: 253). Yet, the texts can vary, with each possessing distinct characteristics in style, structure, emphasis, and function (Green 1984: 253–4; Tinney 1996: 19–20).

The following study will examine how the city laments either as a whole or as individual compositions may have contributed to the development of the Flood epic. Furthermore, given that the city laments seem to interact closely with *Curse Agade* and *Ur-Namma A* and share some of the common topoi and motifs with these two Ur III compositions that also deal with catastrophic events and their effects,[5] it is necessary to examine the development of the Flood epic within the network of this group of Sumerian texts dealing with catastrophe from the Ur III period to the Isin-Larsa period.

THE CITY LAMENTS AND THE FLOOD EPIC

The following study will first analyse the city laments and the Flood epic in terms of their general conceptual patterns and literary motifs, and then move on to more detailed thematic and literary comparisons.

General Conceptual Patterns and Literary Motifs

To tackle the complex intertextual relationship between the city laments and the Flood epic, it is important to break the compositions down into major themes or motifs—the literary building blocks, so to speak—and examine them one by one contextually and comparatively. In this way, traces of intertextual connections otherwise buried in the flow of a piece of narrative or poetry gradually begin to come to light.

[5] See Cooper 1983: 20–6; Michalowski 1989: 8–9; Tinney 1996: 29–36; Flückiger-Hawker 1999: 85–91.

An Overview of the Depiction of Catastrophe in the City Laments

One of the main themes held in common among the city laments is their extensive depiction of destruction in Sumer. As Vanstiphout (1980: 85) points out, the depiction of destruction in the laments is 'complete, detailed and integrated'. Not only did the whole 'material' culture (houses, the palace, temples, roads, etc.) collapse, the 'immaterial' aspects of civilization—political, religious, and social institutions, and the arts and skills—were also disrupted. Disorder and injustice were running rampant. As far as the geographic range is concerned, the catastrophe annihilated the whole land of Sumer, including its major cities and their surrounding natural environment. In addition to the famine and drought that ravaged the land, there was indiscriminate mass killing of people, probably as a result of foreign invasion. Thus human beings, their civilization, and habitats were all reduced to naught. Vanstiphout calls the whole catastrophe depicted in the laments 'the death of an era' (1980: 83) or 'a great and universal mortality' (1980: 84). The mixed images of silence, darkness, burning, terror, and confusion that prevailed in the description of the city laments support these characterizations.

But the extent of destruction goes even further, for the effect of catastrophe reached even the divine realm. With their offerings being cut off as a result of the collapse of the state, economy, and transportation, their temples destroyed and desecrated by invaders, and their cultic personnel in exile, the gods were forced to abandon their patron cities. In *LSU, LU*, and *LE*, a great emphasis is put on the catastrophe being a tragedy for the gods. *LSU* in particular contains a long litany of the gods withdrawing from their cities and the goddesses wailing bitterly for their destroyed houses. The human king Ibbi-Suen, the last ruler of the Ur III dynasty, by comparison, is given much less attention (*LSU* 34–5, 104–6). The deities themselves were among the chief victims in the composition. They were portrayed as kings or queens of the cities (*LSU* 371; *LU* 85–94) who were even carried into exile and slavery (*LSU* 265, 271–80, 371–6; *LU* 307).

That the deities themselves were affected in the catastrophe signifies the ruthless character of destruction. Despite the groans of people as well as the bitter cries and earnest entreaties of the gods and goddesses in distress, An and Enlil, who were ultimately responsible for causing the catastrophe, would not relent (*LSU* 340–70; *LU* 144–68). Even those deities who were directly involved in bringing about the destruction had to suffer its consequences. Thus in the litany of the deities abandoning their cities in *kirugu* 2 of *LSU*, we find Enlil and his divine spouse Ninlil from Nippur (lines 139–42), Nintur from Adab (lines 144–8), Ninĝirsu and his divine spouse Bau from Ĝirsu (lines 159–62), Enki and his spouse Damgalnuna from Eridu (lines 243–50), and Inana from Unug (lines 150–4). In short, the calamity dramatically represented in the city laments is cosmic in scope and effect (see also *LU* 84–6), devastating the natural, human, and divine worlds alike.

The portrayal of destruction in the city laments in many respects echoes similar depictions in *Curse Agade* and *Ur-Namma A* from the Ur III period, except that the representations in the laments are more elaborate in style and form. Together these compositions dealing with catastrophe share many topoi and motifs in common that are in dialectical opposition to those found in the royal hymns and inscriptions which were used for the legitimization of kingship especially during the Ur III and Isin-Larsa periods. What are depicted as being destroyed by the flood or storm in a figurative sense are almost exactly the same as what were depicted as being constructed or achieved by the rulers who were praised in the hymns and inscriptions.[6]

Traditional motifs for legitimizing kingship in royal hymns and inscriptions[7]	vs.	Traditional motifs depicting destruction in literature on catastrophe
abundance		famine, drought, and economic disaster
care of and provision for the gods and their temples		abandoned and desecrated temples and cults
cultivation of rites		rites lost
divine assistance		divine alienation and hostility
expulsion of enemy troops		invasion of enemy troops
establishment of justice and order		injustice and disorder
maintenance of overland and riverine routes		dangerous travel and trading routes
establishment of irrigation, husbandry, and agriculture		disrupted irrigation, husbandry, and agriculture

Comparison with the Flood Epic

The Sumerian compositions dealing with catastrophe from the Ur III and Isin-Larsa periods constitute part of the literary and conceptual matrix in which the Flood epic was composed. A detailed comparative study of the two traditions will help shed light on some of the intriguing aspects of depiction of catastrophe in the Flood epic, which can be explained as the result of the epic's following the Sumerian antecedents. For example, in the Babylonian epic the

[6] The following comparative chart is in part based on the study of Flückiger-Hawker 1999: 28–58 concerning the traditional topoi, motifs, and formulae from the Early Dynastic III period to the Isin-Larsa period.

[7] It is important to note that the motifs for legitimizing kingship in royal hymns and inscriptions closely parallel the motifs dealing with the primeval time of origins in many Sumerian mythological texts or prologues.

Flood is represented as being instigated by Enlil and decided by the assembly of the gods who subsequently worked together to carry out the destruction. But in the end, it was Enlil and Anu who were blamed for causing the Flood.

That Enlil was chiefly responsible for bringing the destruction—often portrayed as storm-like—has been repeatedly affirmed in the Sumerian compositions: *Curse Agade* 1, 5, 57, 88, 99, 151, 157; *Ur-Namma A* 55, 200; *LSU* 72, 73, 75, 164–6, 260–1, 292, 296–9; *LU* 172–8, 180, 202, 408; *LW* 3.2–30; *NL* 28–9, 70–1, 95–108, 114. Likewise in the Flood epic, he is consistently represented as the instigator of destruction. Instead of listing numerous, well-known supporting references in the Flood epic, here it will suffice to direct our attention to Enki's response to the gods who asked him to create the Flood. Enki was approached for this task probably because he had been responsible for creating human beings to relieve the junior gods of labour. Enki replied to the gods that such a task was not his but Enlil's: *šipiršu ibašši it*[*ti* ^{d}*enlil*] 'That is the task of Enlil' (OB *Atra-hasīs* II vii 47).[8]

In *Ur-Namma A* 8–9, 207–8; *LSU* 21, 57, 365; *LU* 144–50, 159–60, 167–8; and *LW* 4.2–3, it was by the command of An and Enlil, the ultimate decision-makers, that destruction was relentlessly carried out. The same motif is seen in OB *Atra-hasīs* III v 39–43; the *Sumerian Flood Story* 159, 252, and 255.

Curse Agade 210, 222; *LSU* 364, 493–511; *LU* 151; and *LW* 1.5–8 (see also the restoration section in *NL* 237, 245) represent the destruction of the land and cities as a decision made by the divine assembly (pu-uḫ$_2$-ru-um), especially among the clique of the senior gods (An, Enlil, Enki, and Ninmah). OB *Atra-hasīs* II ii 11′, v 14–15, 28–9, vi 23–4; III iii 36–7, vi 7–8; the *Sumerian Flood Story* 143–4; and SB *Gilgameš* XI 14–19 contain a similar motif.

That the destruction took a corporate effort of the gods in *Curse Agade* 63–76, 210, 222; *LSU* 22–6, 58–64, 81–4, 103; *LU* 176, 179, 240; *LE* (the Nippur version) segm. C 1–25; and *LW* 1.7–11, 4.5–6 clearly has its counterparts in the Flood epic: OB *Atra-hasīs* II v 16–19, 30–2; vi 25–30. In the Flood episode, the image of different gods working together to bring about the final destruction, see OB *Atra-hasīs* II vii 48–53 *libtērū šū* [. . .] | ^{d}*šullat u* ^{d}[*ḫaniš*] | *lillikū ina* [*maḫri*] | *tarkullī* ^{d}*er*[*rakal linashsiḫ*] | *lilli*[*k* ^{d}*nin-urta*] *lir*[*di miḫra*] 'Let him [and . . .] choose, let Šullat and [Haniš] go [in front], let Errakal [tear up] the mooring poles, let [Ninurta] go and let [the weir] overflow'[9]

[8] This line may hark back to the reply of Bēlet-ilī when the gods requested that human beings be created: *ittīyāma lā natû ana epēši* | *itti enkīma ibašši šipru* 'It is not suitable for me to make (things). The task is Enki's' (OB *Atra-hasīs* I iv 200–1). The above two passages from the *Atra-hasīs Epic* suggest the epic might very well have originated in Eridu (Jacobsen 1981) as it seeks to portray Enki as the creator and preserver of the world and Enlil as the destroyer.

[9] The translation of OB Atra-hasīs II vii 52–3 'Let [Ninurta] go and make [the dykes] overflow' in Lambert and Millard (1969: 87) is apparently based on SB *Gilgameš XI* 103 *illak* ^{d}*nin-*⸢*urta*⸣ *miḫrī ušardi* 'Ninurta, going (by), made the weirs overflow' (George 2003: 708–9), where the Š-stem is used for the verb *redû* and the object of the verb is in the plural form *miḫrī*.

(// SB *Gilgameš* XI 99–103), in part echoes *Curse Agade* 74–5 ^{ĝeš}dimgul ku$_3$ im-du$_3$-du$_3$-a-bi | ^{d}en-ki-ke$_4$ abzu-a mi-ni-in-bu 'Enki tore out its well-anchored holy mooring pole in the *abzu*'.

The following analyses will further demonstrate how the Flood epic to a large degree simply followed the literary conventions and conceptual patterns of the Ur III and Isin-Larsa compositions in its portrayal of cataclysm. This is especially true when it comes to representing the scope and effect of catastrophe. Equally important in the task of tracing the transmission process of ideas and literary motifs, though, is the need to show that the author or redactors of the Flood epic not only extensively appropriated the previous Sumerian traditions dealing with catastrophe but also in some instances reinterpreted and reshaped them for their own purposes.

Though all have the tendency to depict the scope and effect of the catastrophe in cosmic proportions, the texts in question mostly restrict themselves to the Mesopotamian setting in the specific geographical references they give. *Curse Agade, Ur-Namma A*, and the city laments represent the disasters as having taken place within Sumer and Akkad, or in the land (kalam) of Sumer. The Flood epic is no exception, see the references to *mātum* = kalam (OB *Atra-hasīs* II i 2, 3; ii 8, 22); the Tigris and Euphrates (OB *Atra-hasīs* I i 25–6); the five antediluvian cities: Eridu, Badtibira, Larak, Sippar, Šuruppak (the *Sumerian Flood Story* 93–7); Ki-ur, the goddess Ninlil's shrine within Enlil's temple Ekur in Nippur (the *Sumerian Flood Story* 151); and Šurrupak, 'the [city that] is situated on the [banks] of the Euphrates' (SB *Gilgameš* XI 11–12). Of these geographical references, the Tigris and Euphrates are also the general setting in the city laments (see *LSU* 25, 38, 61, 94; *LW* 3.15). Eridu, Ki-ur, and Ekur are frequently mentioned in the city laments.

The above list of the antediluvian cities in the *Sumerian Flood Story* seems to have derived from the antediluvian chronographical traditions current in the Old Babylonian period (e.g. W-B 62 and W-B 444). But the idea of the major cities being destroyed altogether as depicted in the *Sumerian Flood Story* 156, 202 reflects the corresponding motif so prominently featuring in the city laments. The same idea is also present to a lesser degree in *Curse Agade* (primarily in the destruction of Agade and Ekur in Nippur, as well as other cities, see lines 168–71) and in *Ur-Namma A* 5.

The removal of kingship, which is a pivotal motif in *Curse Agade* 66–9, *Ur-Namma A, LSU* 17, 19, 28, 55, 99–100, 366–9, is also found in the *Sumerian Flood Story* 160 nam-lugal-bi bala-bi x [. . . . . .] 'its kingship, its reign. . . .'. The *Sumerian Flood Story* 158–9 seem to be verbatim quotations of *LSU* 364–5. Also line 160 of the Flood story was partially patterned after *LSU* 369 (nam-lugal-bi bala-bi ba-gid$_2$-e-de$_3$ ša$_3$ kuš$_2$-u$_3$-de$_3$ 'its kingship, its reign, has been so long that it has exhausted itself').

The disruption of the ecological system, agriculture, and husbandry likewise is shared by *Curse Agade* 123–4$^{?}$, 172–5; *Ur-Namma A* 24–5, 28–30; *LSU* 6–11,

42–51, 87–9, 129–32, 498–506; *LU* 265–74, 359–68; *LW* 2.14–17; OB *Atra-hasīs* II i 9–19, iv 1–9, v 16–17, 30–1, vi 13–14, 25–6; and the *Sumerian Flood Story* 253 (see also 49–50).

More specifically, damage to watercourses or canal systems crucial for irrigation and flood control, as well as transportation, which is explicitly mentioned in *Curse Agade* 264, *Ur-Namma* A 22–3, and *LSU* 127–8, 318–19, 322–9, must also be one of the dire consequences of catastrophe in the *Atra-hasīs Epic*. Such a consequence seems inevitable in the course of the gods' attempts to either reduce or entirely wipe out the human race which was created for the very purpose of substituting for the junior gods in maintaining the canal system. The significance of humankind building or maintaining the canal system is mentioned in both OB *Atra-hasīs* I vii 337–9 *allī marrī ibnû eš*[*rē*]*ti* | *īkī ibnû rabût*[*im*] | *bubūtiš nišī tîtiš* [*ilī*] 'With pickaxes and spades they built the shrines, they built the big canal banks, for the sustenance of the peoples, for the nourishment of [the gods]' and the *Sumerian Flood Story* 46, 99–100.

The outbreak of plague, which was the first attempt at destruction of the human race by the gods in OB *Atra-hasīs* I vii 337–viii 416, may find its parallels in the city laments. Vanstiphout (1980: 86–7) has suggested that some of the symptoms the people suffered in the calamity as described in *LU kirugu* 6 may be diagnosed as symptoms of an epidemic: 'apparent drunkenness generally and specifically connected with loss of control of the nervous system over the muscles' and 'the *bubo*'. To add to Vanstiphout's observations, one can further point to a possible allusion to plague: *LW* 1.25 unu^{ki}-ga teš$_2$-bi a-ba-a ib$_2$-ta-an-⌜gu$_7$$^{?}$⌝-[(x) x] gig a-ba-a in-[ga-x (x)] 'Who devoured all in Unug? Who . . . sickness too?' The Sumerian word gig '(to be) sick' in this line parallels the Akkadian term *murṣum* 'sickness, illness' in OB *Atra-hasīs* I vii 371.

Famine, drought, scarce resources and economic disasters, major aspects of the catastrophe as depicted in the Sumerian compositions (*Curse Agade* 121–4, 172–87, 233–4, 248–9; *Ur-Namma A* 27; *LSU* 60–1, 88–9, 102, 127–30, 196, 221, 251–3, 293–6, 303–17, 318–27, 389–91, 498–501; *LU* 227, 269–74; *LE* (the Nippur version) segm. C 17; and *NL* 105–6), are also prominent features in OB *Atra-hasīs* II i–iv. The episode in the *Atra-hasīs Epic* deals with the second attempt of Enlil to suppress human growth and noise by restraining rain and underground water in order to diminish agricultural yields. It is after this attempt being frustrated by Enki and his servant Atra-hasīs that Enlil resorted to the use of the Flood. More specifically, both *Curse Agade* 185–7 and the Neo-Assyrian recension of the *Atra-hasīs Epic* K 3399 + 3934 (S), rev. vi 11–15 portray cannibalism. In *Curse Agade* it was dogs that devoured people, while in the *Atra-hasīs Epic* it was people who devoured one another.

Carnage or destruction of human life is another common motif that binds the Flood epic together with the compositions dealing with catastrophe from the Ur III and Isin-Larsa periods: *Curse Agade* 192, 214, 217–18, 237–41; *LSU* 254, 301–2, 399–402; *LU* 164, 212–29, 249, 293, 341; *LW* 2a. 1–8, 4.25–7;

NL 70; OB *Atra-hasīs* II viii 34–5; III iii 37–54, iv 6; the *Sumerian Flood Story* 38–9, 157, 259; and SB *Gilgameš* XI 113, 122, 171. Furthermore, fish imagery is used in *LSU* 301, 407a and SB *Gilgmeš* XI 124 to portray the people being destroyed. And the Sumerian expression of utter destruction gul-gul in *LU* 139–41 uru$_2$-ĝu$_{10}$ gul-gul-lu-ba im-me-ne-eš-a-ba | uri$_2^{ki}$ gul-gul-lu-ba im-me-ne-eš-a-ba | uĝ$_3$-bi ug$_5$-ge-de$_3$ a$_2$ mu-un-aĝ$_2$-eš-a-ba 'when they had commanded the utter destruction of my city, when they had commanded the utter destruction of Ur, when they had ordered that its people be killed' (compare *LU* 161–3) is reflected in the Akkadian expression *gamertum* in OB *Atra-hasīs* II viii 34 *ilū iqbû gamert*[*am*] 'The gods commanded total destruction' (also OB *Atra-hasīs* III iii 37).

Human wailing and lament, a response to calamity in the Sumerian compositions (*Curse Agade* 195–204; *Ur-Namma A* 145–97; *LSU* 397–402, 479–81; *LU* 172–233; *LW* 2.1–10, 3.22, 12.24; and *NL* 38–43, 117–26), can be observed in the Neo-Assyrian recension of the *Atra-hasīs Epic* K 3399 + 3934 (S) rev. iv 23–6, where Atra-hasīs reported to Enki the suffering of the people as a result of the plague sent by Enlil: [*mā*] *bēl uttazzamā tanīšēti* | [*murṣ*]*īkunūma ekkal mātu* | [^{d}*e*]*a bēl uttazzamā tanīšēti* | [*murṣu*] *ša ilānīma ekkal mātu* 'Indeed, lord, the human race is groaning, your [disease] is consuming the land. Ea, lord, the human race is groaning, [the disease] of the gods is consuming the land.' The phrase *uttazzamā tanīšēti* 'the human race is groaning' (Dt Dur 3fpl of *nazāmu* 'to groan, growl') is reminiscent of the recurrent Sumerian phrase in *LU* 172–233 uĝ$_3$-e še am$_3$-ša$_4$ 'the people moan' (še ša$_4$ 'to moan, groan'). The Flood hero also wailed and cried for his fellow human beings; see the Neo-Babylonian recension of the *Atra-hasīs Epic*, Sippar SB V 60 *ūmešamma ibtanak(ki)* 'every day he would keep crying'; 82 *at*⌜*ta*⌝ *ya'u ša tabakkû* 'whoever you are, who is crying' (George and Al-Rawi 1996: 183).

In the midst of extermination of human lives and the destruction of their habitats and supporting institutions, other living creatures were not spared either, as seen in *Curse Agade* 219–20; *LSU* 7–8, 47–8, 131–2. In the Flood epic, this motif can be inferred from the fact that the Flood hero brought on board not only his family and possessions but also different species of animals; see OB *Atra-hasīs* III ii 29–37; and SB *Gilgameš* XI 27, 82–6. Both *NL* 253–8 and the *Sumerian Flood Story* 253 allude to the restoration of animals after the catastrophe.

Not only was the survival of the human race at stake, but also civilization as a whole, including different arts and skills, faced extinction. This can be seen in the depictions in *Curse Agade* 64, 70–1 (see also 29–39), *LSU* 1–55, 335–6, 435–8, and *LU* 265–74. In the Flood epic, this motif of civilization at risk can be derived from the fact that the Flood hero brought on board the artisans (see the Neo-Assyrian recension of the *Atra-hasīs Epic* DT 42, lines 7–9; SB *Gilgameš* XI 86), which was apparently aimed at the preservation of civilization.

The breakdown of the social order and its psychological repercussions, especially as related to familial ties, appears in *Curse Agade* 147–8, 190–2, 215–16,

237–41; *Ur-Namma A* 3, 5, 27; *LSU* 12–16, 93–7;[10] *LW* 1.22, 25; *NL* 18, 42–8, 103–4; and the Neo-Assyrian recension of the *Atra-hasīs Epic* K 3399 + 3934 (S), rev. v 18–24, vi 7–13. *Curse Agade* 215–16 lu$_2$ lu$_2$-u$_3$ zu-de$_3$ na-an-ni-in-pa$_3$-de$_3$ | šeš-e šeš-a-ni ĝeškim na-an-ni-in-e$_3$ 'May no one find his acquaintances there, may brother not recognize his brother!' finds its parallel with OB *Atra-hasīs* III iii 13–14 [*ul*] ⌜*ī*⌝ *mur aḫu aḫāšu* | [*ul*] *utēddû ina karāši* 'brother/one did not recognize his brother/the other, they couldn't recognize each other in the catastrophe' (// SB *Gilgameš* XI 112–13).

As mentioned above, the effects of the catastrophe are not restricted to the human sphere, but are extended into the divine sphere. The motifs of lamenting and distressed deities and their abandoning of their earthly abodes in the midst of the destruction are obviously held in common by *Curse Agade* 58–62; *Ur-Namma A* 8–19; *LSU* 115–62, 174–250, 271–80, 371–7; *LU* 1–37, 46, 62–3, 70–1, 76–168, 237–329; *LE* (the Nippur version) segm. A 11–14, segm. B 1, 3, 5–15, segm. C 26, 28, 30–6; *LE* (the Ur version) segm. B 1–6; OB *Atra-hasīs* III iii 25–54, iv 4–15; the *Sumerian Flood Story* 140–2 (see also 93–7); and SB *Gilgameš* XI 114–26.

Temple buildings, religious worship, and cultic services are portrayed as destroyed, neglected, or defiled in *Curse Agade* 77, 100–46; *Ur-Namma A* 52–3; *LSU* 151–3, 168–71, 183–4, 191–2, 204–5, 249–50, 324, 347–9, 408–48; *LU* 123–32, 241–9, 346–60; *LE* (the Nippur version) segm. A 43–7, 51–68, 87–99, segm. C 5–6, 11–12, 18; *LW* 30–1; and *NL* 53–61, 83–9. In the Flood epic, abandonment of religious worship or devotion to the patron gods or goddesses can be seen in the directives Enki gave to Atra-hasīs, *ē-t*[*a*]*plaḫā* ⌜*ī*⌝ *līkun* | *ē-tu*[*sa*]*lli'ā* [*i*]*štarkun* 'Do not reverence your gods, do not pray to your goddesses' (OB *Atra-hasīs* I vii 338–9; see also I viii 393–4, 405–6; II ii 9–10, 23–4). It is important to note that the abandonment of religious worship or devotion in the Flood epic is not a direct consequence of the destruction caused by the deities. Rather, it is a conscious measure taken by the human beings in reaction to the hostility of the gods.

The motif of sacred offerings affected by the catastrophe in *Curse Agade* 123–4, *Ur-Namma A* 52–3, 211; *LSU* 31, 102, 310–17, 325–6, 339, 343–4, 347, 435; *LU* 361–6; and *LE* (the Nippur version) segm. C 30–6 likewise finds its way into OB *Atra-hasīs* III iii 30–1, iv 15–22, v 30–7 (see also SB *Gilgameš* XI 161–3). The passages in the Flood epic vividly portray the gods as suffering from hunger and thirst because their human providers were destroyed by the Flood.

[10] The breakdown of familial relations may be extended to the divine realm in *LSU* 318–49, in which Nanna was unable to fulfil his filial piety to deliver the regular offerings to Enlil's shrine in Nippur because of the catastrophe caused by Enlil. As can be seen in *NL*, this motif was seized upon by Išme-Dagan, who viewed his restoration of the country and the offerings to Enlil in terms of his fulfilment of filial piety to his divine father Enlil.

It has been observed that the Flood epic shares many common motifs and topoi with *Curse Agade, Ur-Namma A*, and the city laments. Were there only a few similiarities between the Flood epic and the Sumerian compositions, one would be less confident about the historical connections between the two literary traditions because the Flood epic could have picked up these motifs or topoi through other sources. But with so many similarities and parallels, not only in terms of the general conceptual framework but also specific imagery (see further comparisons in the rest of the chapter) between the Flood epic and the Sumerian compositions, it seems rather implausible that these two traditions were unrelated historically. The earliest extant compositions of lamentation over catastrophe are *Curse Agade* and *Ur-Namma A* from the Ur III period (see also *Šulgi E* 74–151), and the origin of the repertoire of some of the common motifs and topoi may go back even further in time, 'which seems at home in a context of ritual lament' (Flückiger-Hawker 1999: 91; see also Löhnert 2011: 402–17 for the history and functions of laments). But the fact the city laments brought about an extensive development of these traditional literary expressions and in turn became a vital source of inspiration or a template for the portrayal of destruction in the Flood epic seems clear.

Means of Destruction

It has been noted in previous studies that u_4 'storm' is an image frequently used for depicting the means of destruction in the city laments. But the laments employ other meteorological images as well. The following study (see also Chapter 1) is intended to explore all the images used in the laments and then compare them with the means of destruction as depicted in the Flood epic.

Meteorological Images in the City Laments

a 'water': *LSU* 390; *LU* 317; *LE* (the Nippur version) segm. A 21

a maḫ e_3-a 'swelling flood wave': *LSU* 405; *LU* 183; *LW* segm. E 65, 97

a-ma-ru 'flood': *LSU* 76; *LU* 198

a-ma-ru $du_6^!$(ki) al-ak-e 'hoe-making flood': *LSU* 107; *LW* segm. E 13, 47

ĝiri$_3$-bal 'flooding': *LE* (the Nippur version) segm. C 4

i-zi 'wave(s)': *LSU* 456

im 'wind/storm': *LSU* 77, 258, 292; *LU* 128, 193; *NL* 101, 128, 273

im-ḫul 'destructive wind/storm': *LSU* 386α (variant); *LU* 178 (im-ḫul-im-ḫul 'destructive winds'), 183; *NL* 95

im-ḫul dal 'blowing destructive wind/storm': *LSU* 491

im ĝir$_2$ 'lightning storm/rain': *LSU* 159

lil$_2$ 'wind, ghost': *LU* 1–34, 347

mar-ru$_{10}$ 'tempest, flood (= a-ma-ru)': *LSU* 2, 113

muru$_9$ šeĝ$_3$-ĝa 'raining cloud, rainstorm': *LSU* 385; *NL* 67

šeĝ$_3$ 'rain': *LU* 128, 411

u$_2$-a e$_3$-a 'onrushing water/wave': *LSU* 257[11]

u$_{18}$-lu 'southwind, gale, storm, hurricane': *LSU* 214; *LE* (the Nippur version) segm. A 9, 10; *LU* 191; *LW* 4.15

u$_4$ 'storm': *LSU* 2, 70, 71, 80β (variant), 81, 113, 163, 171, 175, 176, 177, 225, 226, 236, 404 (variant), 483, 484, 485, 486, 487; *LU* 87, 88, 89, 90, 98, 109, 110, 111, 136, 138, 172, 176, 177, 182, 186, 198, 199, 200, 201, 202, 205, 225, 252, 326, 390, 393, 394, 397, 398, 400, 402, 403, 404, 405, 406, 407, 408, 409, 411, 413, 415; *LE* (the Nippur version) segm. A 20, 30, 33

u$_4$ gal 'great storm': *LSU* 108; *LU* 180, 181, 391

u$_4$ gig 'troublesome storm': *LSU* 59, 155, 483; *LU* 91, 196, 392

u$_4$ ḫul 'evil, destructive storm': *LSU* 207; *LU* 435

u$_4$ ḫul du$_3$-a 'evil-planting storm': *LE* (the Nippur version) segm. A 19; *LW* 3.6

u$_4$ ḫul-ĝal$_2$-e 'evil storm': *LU* 175

u$_4$ ḫuš 'furious storm': *LE* (the Nippur version) segm. A 7, 8

u$_4$ mer-mer 'raging storm': *LU* 187

u$_4$ šu ur$_3$-ur$_3$ 'sweeping storm': *LU* 197

u$_4$ te-eš du$_{11}$-ga 'roaring storm': *LE* (the Nippur version) segm. A 5

u$_4$ tur 'diminishing storm': *LU* 94, 100, 117

uru$_2$ 'flood': *LU* 98

From the above compilation of the meteorological terms used in the city laments, it is apparent that the storm (u$_4$) is most frequently used for the depiction of catastrophe. Even a cursory glance at the immediate contexts in which the term is used indicates that it may not be taken as referring to actual destruction caused by a storm. That battle, drought, and fire (*LSU* 171; *LU* 186, 187, 201, 394) were major aspects of the destruction of the land and cities would preclude a literal interpretation of the storm terminology. Neither do the representations of a storm as acting so deliberately as cutting the lock from the main gate of the temple or palace, dislodging its door (*LSU* 404 (variant); *LE* (the Nippur

[11] u$_2$-a here is for a-u$_2$ 'high water' (ePSD and ETCSL).

version) segm. A 33) and stacking the people in heaps (*LE* (the Nippur version) segm. A 34) suggest any genuinely literal portrayal of a storm catastrophe.

Overall, the term 'storm' is used abstractly, figuratively, and mythically, to signify something ominous (*LSU* 59), relentless,[12] ineluctable (*LSU* 108, 404), unfathomable (*LSU* 163), lamentable,[13] evil or wicked,[14] debilitating (*LU* 94, 100, 117), fearsome (*LU* 98, 391), raging (*LU* 187), violent (*LSU* 155), furious (*LE* segm. A 7, 8), indiscriminate,[15] hatefully ordered (*LU* 202, 326, 408), but above all, destructive.[16] As a 'recurrent image',[17] the storm sets the tone and creates a particular type of ambience with the above negative attributes.

The storm image, however, is seldom marked morphologically with the equative postposition -gin$_7$.[18] In the majority of cases the term serves as the subject of a sentence.[19] While it is not always clear as to what exactly the storm signifies,[20] in several instances it is safe to infer from the immediate context that this meteorological term refers to invading foreigners: the Gutians (*LSU* 70, 71) or the Elamites.[21] The Sumerian expression u$_4$ ḫul-du$_3$-a 'evil-planting storm' in *LW* 3.6 clearly refers to the countenance of the flood monster (see also 3.3).

What is unmistakable, though, is that the storm imagery is intimately associated with Enlil more than any other deity: *LSU* depicts him as one who 'blew an evil storm' (line 59), 'sent down Gutium from the mountains' (line 75, in conjunction with the storm in lines 70, 71), 'brought down the Elamites, the enemy, from the highlands' (line 166), and handed the city Lagaš to the Elamites symbolized by the storm.[22] His word was 'an attacking storm' (line 163). In *LU*, it was also Enlil who 'called the storm',[23] 'issued directions to the evil storm' (line 175), and entrusted it to kin-gal-u$_4$-da, the keeper of the storm (line 176). The storm was ordered by Enlil in hatred.[24] In *LW* 3.2–3, it was again Enlil who invoked the flood monster.

[12] *LSU* 70, 71, 81; *LU* 110, 111, 196.

[13] *LU* 87, 90, 117, 172, 175, 180, 181.

[14] *LSU* 59, 207, 483; *LU* 91, 175, 392, 435; *LE* (the Nippur version) segm. A 19; *LW* 3.6.

[15] *LU* 400, 402–6; *LE* (the Nippur version) segm. A 20.

[16] *LSU* 2, 80β, 113, 155, 163, 171, 175, 176, 177, 225, 226, 484, 485; *LU* 98, 136, 138, 182, 198, 199, 200, 252, 390, 393; *LE* (the Nippur version) segm. A 30.

[17] For the study of 'recurrent image' in Sumerian literature, see Black 1998: 55–6, 156–9.

[18] Only in *LSU* 108, 171, 427.

[19] *LSU* 2, 70, 71, 80β, 81, 113, 155, 207, 225, 226, 404, 483, 484, 485, 486, 487; *LU* 87, 90, 136, 181, 182, 197, 198, 199, 200, 201, 202, 205, 390, 392, 393, 394, 397, 398, 400, 402, 403, 404, 405, 406, 407, 408, 409, 411; *LE* (the Nippur version) segm. A 5, 7, 8, 19, 20, 30, 33.

[20] *LSU* 2, 59, 113, 155, 207, 225, 226, 237, 427; *LU* 87, 88, 89, 90, 91, 94, 98, 100, 110, 111, 117, 136, 138, 172, 175, 176, 177, 180, 181, 182, 186, 187, 196, 197, 198, 199, 200, 201, 202, 205, 225, 252, 326, 390, 391, 392, 393, 394, 397, 398, 400, 402, 403, 404, 405, 406, 407, 408, 409, 411, 413, 415, 435; *LE* (the Nippur version) segm. A 5, 7, 8, 19, 20, 30, 33.

[21] *LSU* 163[?], 171, 175, 176, 177.

[22] *LSU* 171, 175, 176, 177.

[23] *LU* 172; see also 177, 181.

[24] *LU* 202, 408; see also 326.

The usage of the rest of the meteorological terms in the city laments, in most cases, does not genuinely represent the whole destruction as achieved by the means of destructive weather conditions either, certainly not a watery disaster, partly due to the images of fire, drought, and war invoked in the depiction of the catastrophe. In the majority of cases, like u_4 'storm', these terms are used abstractly, figuratively, and mythically. lil_2 'wind, ghost' at the beginning of *LU* 1–34, for example, is parallel to u_4 'storm' used as an abstract concept of total destruction announced in the first *kirugu* in *LSU* 1, 113, except that lil_2 is monotonously repeated 34 times in *LU*. Some of these meteorological terms signify the unstoppable arrival of the invading barbarians: the Gutians (*LSU* 76), the Elamites sent by Enlil,[25] and Subir.[26] They also refer to hunger;[27] the complete and relentless destruction of houses, cities, temples, and the land;[28] Enlil's terrifying, darkened heart (*LSU* 456); the densely flying barbed arrows of the enemy that covered the outer side of the besieged city Ur (*LSU* 385); the blood of the victims splashed by their enemies on the ground (*NL* 67); the fore-runner of the invading Gutians (*LSU* 77); that which carried away the possessions of Nippur (*NL* 101, 173); and that which silenced Eridu (*LE* (the Nippur version) segm. A 9, 10). More frequently than u_4 'storm', the figurative construction of these images is marked morphologically with the equative postposition -gin_7,[29] or by the enclitic copula -am_3 (*NL* 95).[30] Mythically, a-ma-ru $du_6^!$(ki) al-ak-e 'the hoe-making flood' in *LW* 4.4 is the epithet of the flood monster. Furthermore, *LSU* 292; *LU* 178, 191, 193; *LE* (the Nippur version) segm. C 4; *LW* 3.3; and *NL* 95 point to Enlil as chief instigator of mass destruction. Often these meteorological images work in clusters and combine mythical and figurative meanings to create an inimical, fearsome atmosphere and a psychological effect of paralysis. The image of the unstoppable arrival of the invading enemy hordes is coupled with the images of drought, famine, social disorder, mass slaughter, burning, the destruction of cities and temples, and the departure of patron deities from major cities (Plate 15).[31]

According to the above analyses of the meteorological images, the catastrophe portrayed in the city laments does not seem to have been carried out by a large-scale storm or flooding. The laments also contain other representations of the outbreak of water-related disasters: *LSU* 89 $buru_{14}$ išin-bi-a mu-un-su-su ^{d}ašnan i_3-tur-re 'the crop was drowning while it was still on the stalk, (the

[25] *LSU* 257, 258?, 405.

[26] *LE* (the Nippur version) segm. A 21; *LW* 4.22, 5.20.

[27] *LSU* 390 $ša_3$-ĝar-e iri^{ki} a-gin_7 ba-e-si 'Hunger filled the city like water.'

[28] *LSU* 107, 159, 386α, 491; *LU* 183, 197, 198, 317; *NL* 95, 128.

[29] *LSU* 2, 67, 113, 257, 258, 385, 390, 405, 456, 491; *LU* 98, 183, 411; *LE* (the Nippur version) segm. A 9, 10, 21; *LW* 4.22, 5.20; NL 67.

[30] For the enclitic copula used as equivalent to the equative postposition -gin_7 in descriptions and comparisons, see Thomsen 2001: 109, 276.

[31] For the study of 'image clusters' in Sumerian literature, see Black 1998: 110–15.

yield of) the grain diminished'; *LW* 2.17 ḪAR SUḪ$_3$ a-ša$_3$-ga a ba-ab-ĝar iri sug-ge$_4$ ba-ab-⌜gu$_7$⌝ '. . . It drenched the fields with water; it swallowed the city into a swamp.' To what extent these representations should be regarded as literal is difficult to judge. It is possible that these too are literary topoi similar to the well-known metaphor of a swamp that swallows everything (sug-ge gu$_7$) in Sumerian literature (see *LU* 132, 231, and 279).

The meteorological terms examined above, in their figurative and mythical sense, were used as literary topoi similar to those used in the hymnic compositions whose earliest attestations go back to the Early Dynastic III period. Some of the meteorological terms found in the city laments have already been seen in the *Stele of the Vultures*, the *Temple Hymns*, *Inana and Ebih*, and *Gudea Cylinders A* & *B*: a e$_3$-a 'swelling water', a-ma-ru 'flood', im-ḫul 'destructive wind or storm', u$_{18}$-lu 'southwind, storm, hurricane', u$_4$ 'storm', u$_4$ du$_7$ du$_7$ 'a goring storm', u$_4$ gal 'a great storm' (see Chapter 1). Like the earlier Sumerian compositions, the city laments employ these terms to convey the gods' invincible will or power (*LSU* 57). The city laments further share in common with the earlier Sumerian compositions the association of the meteorological images with animal imagery,[32] battle scenes,[33] and mythical monsters.[34]

Also following the earlier literary conventions is the fact that in the city laments some of the meteorological terms are mutually explicatory and can be used interchangeably. This can be seen in the following cases of u$_4$ 'storm' and a-ma-ru/mar-ru$_{10}$ 'flood': *LSU* 2 and 113 u$_4$-de$_3$ mar-ru$_{10}$-gin$_7$ teš$_2$-bi i$_3$-gu$_7$-e 'the storm devours all like a flood/tempest'; *LSU* 107–8 a-ma-ru du$_6^!$(ki) al-ak-e šu im-ur$_3$-ur$_3$-re | u$_4$ gal-gin$_7$ ki-a ur$_5$ mi-ni-ib-ša$_4$ a-ba-a ba-ra-e$_3$ 'the hoe-making flood was sweeping away everything. Like a great storm it roared over the earth—who could escape it?'[35] The usage of the meteorological images in clusters and recurrent fashion in the city laments is another indication of the laments following the earlier Sumerian literary tradition (e.g. the *Temple Hymns*).

Unlike the earlier Sumerian hymnic tradition, which of course continued to flourish, the city laments employ the meteorological images neither for the praise of the awe-inspiring attributes of the gods nor for the flattering of the rulers.[36] In many respects, as already noted earlier, the city laments represent a

[32] e.g. *LU* 205; *Temple Hymns* 297; *Gudea Cylinder B* ix 21–2.

[33] e.g. *LSU* 377–88; *LW* 4.8–31, 5.2–34; *Stele of the Vultures*, obv. x 4; *Inana and Ebih* 131–7.

[34] e.g. *LW* 3.3–17; *Gudea Cylinder A* iv 14–21.

[35] e.g. *Stele of the Vultures*, obv. x 3–4 umma^{ki}-a im-ḫul-im-ma-gin$_7$ | a-MAR mu-ni-tak$_4$ 'Like the destructive winds, he unleashed$^?$ a flood in Umma.'

[36] *LSU* 427 u$_4$-gin$_7$ kur-kur-ra im-si-a an-usan an-na-gin$_7$ ba-e-du$_3$ 'Like a storm that filled the lands, it was built there like twilight in the heavens', which refers to the temple of Nanna E-kiš-nu-ĝal in Ur, is an exception. This hymnic line (see also *Gudea Cylinder A* xxv 1, 9) describes the glory of the temple before its destruction.

dramatic reversal of the traditional royal ideology exhibited in royal hymns and inscriptions. In the traditional hymnic compositions, the gods or the rulers are depicted as directing the destructive power of inclement weather phenomena to pound the enemy lands or the recalcitrant mountainous regions.[37] Overall, the manifestations of the mighty power of the gods were deemed essentially beneficial for Sumer.[38] By contrast, the city laments depict the enemy hordes as coming to destroy Sumer and Akkad like a storm or flood at the behest of the gods of Sumer turning hostile towards the Land.[39] In *kirugu* 5 of *LSU*, the author is calling for a return to 'normalcy' established or aspired to in the royal hymns:

> O bitter storm, retreat O storm, storm return to your home! O storm that destroys cities, retreat O storm, storm return to your home! O storm that destroys temples, retreat O storm, storm return to your home! Indeed, the storm that blew on Sumer, blew on the foreign lands. Indeed, the storm that blew on the Land, blew on the foreign lands. It has blown on Tidnum, it has blown on the foreign lands. It has blown on Gutium, it has blown on the foreign lands. It has blown on Anšan, it has blown on the foreign lands. It levels Anšan like a blowing evil wind. Famine has overwhelmed the evildoer—may (those) people submit. (*LSU* 483–92)

No doubt, the city laments' use of the meteorological topoi for the depiction of the destruction of Sumer and Akkad has its antecedents. At least from the Ur III period, in the Sumerian literary-historical and historical compositions of catastrophe, a-ma-ru 'flood'[40] and u$_{4}$ te-eš du$_{11}$ 'the roaring storm'[41] were used to portray the destruction of Sumer and Akkad by the gods. In *Ur-Namma A* 49, where the text describes the destitution of Ur-Namma's widow, the broken line has ki-nu$_{2}$ nitadam-a-⌜ni$^{?}$ ba$^{?}$⌝-[x (x)] ⌜x x⌝ u$_{18}$-lu-da ba-da-dul 'His spouse . . . resting place . . . was smothered by the southwind/storm.' This passage parallels *LE* (the Nippur version) segm. A 9–10 za-pa-aĝ$_{2}$-bi niĝ$_{2}$-me-ĝar u$_{18}$-lu-gin$_{7}$ ba-⌜e-dul⌝ [uĝ$_{3}$-bi . . .] | eridu^{ki} niĝ$_{2}$-me-ĝar u$_{18}$-lu-gin$_{7}$ ba-e-dul uĝ$_{3}$-⌜bi⌝ [. . .] 'Its [the city's] voice was smothered with silence as by the southwind/storm, [its people . . .]; Eridu was smothered with silence as by the southwind/storm, its people. . . .'[42]

[37] e.g. *Stele of the Vultures*, obv. x 1–4; *Temple Hymns* 142, 255, 433–5; *Inana and Ebih* 130–7; CBS 11553 (a royal hymn to Šulgi) (Sjöberg 2005: 291–300) obv. 13–15; *Šū-Suen* D 6, 36; *Būr-Suen* A 29–30.

[38] e.g. *Ur-Ninurta F* segm. A 1–9, segm. B 1–10.

[39] e.g. *LSU* 70, 71, 76, 163$^{?}$, 166, 171, 175–7, 257, 258$^{?}$, 405; *LE* (the Nippur version) segm. A 21; *LW* 4.22, 5.20.

[40] *Curse Agade* 150; *Year Name 22 of Ibbi-Suen*; see also *LSU* 76, 107; *LU* 198; *LW* 3.3, 4.4.

[41] *Curse Agade* 149; see also *LE* (the Nippur version) segm. A 7, 8.

[42] Flückiger-Hawker (1999: 90) has already noted the parallel between *Ur-Namma A 49* and *LE* (the Nippur version) segm. A 9–10.

Antecedent traditions from both the hymnic compositions as well as the Ur III compositions dealing with catastrophe had influenced the city laments in the use of meteorological imagery. However, judging from the list of the meteorological terms as compiled earlier in this section, it is not difficult to see that the city laments developed these topoi into much more elaborate forms. Furthermore, the meaning of these terms has become much more abstract in the laments. Most important for the development of the Flood epic is the fact that meteorological imagery was employed in such a high degree of density and frequency in the city laments that these topoi of storm and flood for the first time in Mesopotamian literary history began to affect the structure of a literary composition.[43] Furthermore, the destruction by the storm or flood in a figurative and mythical sense is depicted in the city laments (already in *Curse Agade* and *Year Name of Ibbi-Suen* 22 from the Ur III period) as an inversion of the motifs concerning the creation or cultural establishments as found in the Sumerian mythological texts dealing with the primeval era (see Chapter 2). Arguably, this unprecedented literary development served as a crucial impetus behind the development of the primeval flood catastrophe motif and its dramatization in the Flood epic. The author of the epic may have been inspired by the pervasive imagery of destructive storm or flood in the literary representation of the demise of the Ur III period and its aftermath in the city laments. The following comparison will show how the Flood epic, though overall having adopted a literal representation of weather catastrophe, to a certain extent still contains some traces of the figurative and mythical tradition.

Comparison with the Flood Epic

Different versions and recensions of the Flood epic are prone to use clusters of meteorological images (especially the Neo-Assyrian recension of the *Atra-hasīs Epic* BM 98977 + 99231 (U) and SB *Gilgameš* XI), and seem to have drawn from the similar stock of meteorological terms as found in the figurative tradition. The relevant Akkadian terms (with their Sumerian equivalents following ePSD) used in the Flood epic include:

abūbu 'Flood' (// a-ma-ru; uru$_2$ 'flood'): OB *Atra-hasīs* II vii 44, 46, III i 37, iii 11, 15, 20, 53, iv 25, v 42, vi 21, viii 9, 18; SB *Gilgameš* XI 14, 110, 114, 129, 131, 170, 184, 188, 190, 192, 194

amurru 'west wind' (// mar-ru$_{10}$ 'west wind'): the Neo-Assyrian recension of the *Atra-hasīs Epic* BM 98977 + 99231 (U) rev. 6, 10

[43] Regarding the density of imagery in a Sumerian composition as an analytical criterion, see Black (1998: 115–18). See Black (1998: 159) also for his discussion on 'structural' or 'dramatic' imagery.

iltānu 'northwind': the Neo-Assyrian recension of the *Atra-hasīs Epic* BM 98977 + 99231 (U) rev. 6

imḫullu 'destructive wind, storm' (// im-ḫul 'destructive wind, storm'): the Neo-Assyrian recension of the *Atra-hasīs Epic* BM 98977 + 99231 (U) rev. 8

meḫû 'storm, tornado' (// u_{18}-lu 'southwind; gale; storm; hurricane'): OB *Atra-hasīs* III iii 5, vi 25; SB *Gilgameš* XI 109, 129, 131

rādu 'rainstorm, cloudburst' (// âĝar$_5$; âĝar$_6$ 'rainshower, downpour'): OB *Atra-hasīs* III vi 25

siqsiqqu 'gale, storm-wind' (// mar-ru$_{10}$ 'storm-wind; tempest'$^?$): the Neo-Assyrian recension of the *Atra-hasīs Epic* BM 98977 + 99231 (U) rev. 7

šadû 'east wind' (// kur 'east wind'): the Neo-Assyrian recension of the *Atra-hasīs Epic* BM 98977 + 99231 (U) rev. 6; SB *Gilgameš* XI 110

šāru 'wind' (// im 'rain, storm'): OB *Atra-hasīs* III ii 54, iii 16, v 30 (*šārī* 'winds'); SB *Gilgameš* XI 129; the Neo-Assyrian recension of the *Atra-hasīs Epic* BM 98977 + 99231 (U) rev. 4, 5 (*šār erbetti* 'four winds'), 8 (*šārū* 'winds')

šūtu 'southwind' (// u_{18}-lu 'southwind; gale; storm; hurricane'): the Neo-Assyrian recension of the *Atra-hasīs Epic* BM 98977 + 99231 (U) rev. 6, 9

Except for the expressions 'the four winds', 'east wind', 'northwind', and 'west wind', which could have been additions in the epic to complement 'southwind', the rest of the terms in their Sumerian counterparts are commonly used in the figurative tradition represented by the Sumerian hymnic compositions and the texts dealing with catastrophe as already examined.

The following meteorological terms are employed in the *Sumerian Flood Story* (CBS 10673 + CBS 10867):

a gal 'mighty water, waves': line 205

a-ma-ru 'flood': lines 137, 156, 202, 204

^{im}si-si-ig 'gale(s)': line 201

im-ḫul 'destructive wind': lines 205, 201 (im-ḫul-im-ḫul 'destructive winds')

The Sumerian words a-ma-ru and im-ḫul or im-ḫul-im-ḫul have been encountered in the figurative tradition as examined in the previous sections. The verb which the *Sumerian Flood Story* chooses for a-ma-ru is ur$_3$ 'to drag; to sweep away': DAG$^?$-me-a a-ma-ru ugu-kab-⌜du$_{11}$⌝-[ga . . .] ba-⌜ur$_3$⌝ [. . .] 'the Flood will sweep over the capitals, on all the . . .' (line 156); a-ma-ru ugu-kab-du$_{11}$-ga ba-an-da-ur$_3$-e 'the Flood swept over the capitals' (line 202); a-ma-ru kalam-ma ba-ur$_3$-ra-ta 'after the Flood had swept over the land' (line 204). The same verb has also been used with a-ma-ru in the city laments: *LSU* 107 a-ma-ru du$_6^!$(ki) al-ak-e šu im-ur$_3$-ur$_3$-re 'the hoe-making flood was sweeping away everything'. It has also been used with u_4 'storm': *LU* 197 u_4 šu ur_3-ur_3-re kalam i_3-ur_4-ur_4-re 'the sweeping storm was making the Land shake'. As shown in other parts of this study, the particular expression a-ma-ru kalam-ma ba-ur_3-ra-ta 'after the Flood had swept over the land' in line 203 of the *Sumerian Flood Story* derived from lines 39–40 of W-B 444: a-ma-ru ba-ur_3-«ra-ta» | eĝir a-ma-ru ba-ur_3-ra-ta 'Then the Flood swept over. After the Flood had swept over. . . .'

Of course, it is insufficient to rely on the criterion of shared meteorological terms or images alone for establishing the historical relationship between the Flood epic and the figurative tradition in the earlier Sumerian hymns and the compositions dealing with catastrophe, which must not have been the only compositions that employed these stock expressions or images. At least, the use of a-ma-ru in conjunction with the verb ur_3 does not occur exclusively in the city laments and the *Sumerian Flood Story*.[44] But correlated with other criteria, e.g. conceptual, structural, and stylistic, as well as the manner in which these meteorological terms are used, which either have been discussed above or are to be demonstrated below, the sharing of similar meteorological terms or images between the Flood epic and the figurative tradition does strengthen the argument for their intertextual and historical relationship.

If the authors of the Flood epic had indeed relied on the figurative tradition, especially the city laments, for their depictions of the flood or weather catastrophe, the adaptation process could have been done quite easily. As mentioned earlier, the meteorological images in the city laments are not always marked morphologically; they could have been read literally once taken out of context and expanded into a dramatic story of the primeval flood catastrophe, as suggested by Westenholz (1996: 198–200). A strong argument in support of this theory of the Flood epic growing out of the figurative tradition is that there are still traces left in the epic that betray the figurative background of its depiction of catastrophe and its usage of the flood and other meteorological terms.[45]

One clear piece of evidence of the figurative usage of weather imagery is found in the Neo-Assyrian recension of the *Atra-hasīs Epic* K 3399 + 3934 (S) rev. iv 11–12 [*kīm*]*a meḫ̮ê liziqāšinātīma* | [*mur*]*ṣu di'u šuruppû asakku* 'Like a tornado, let disease, sickness, plague, and pestilence blow upon them (the people)' (compare the fulfilment in lines 15–16). The context is that Enlil, being disturbed by the noise the people were making, commanded Namtar, the deity of plague, to diminish their noise, an episode which corresponds to the first destruction cycle in OB *Atra-hasīs* I vii 337–viii 416. This section of Enlil's command of the plague happens to be broken in the Old Babylonian version.

[44] See *Šulgi S* 4 [a-m]a-ru-gin$_7$ ur_4-ur_4-ra-am (with ur_4 for ur_3; Sjöberg 2005: 299); also *Angim* 73–5.

[45] This is a phenomenon which has also been observed by Westenholz (1996: 197); Streck (1999: 59, 106, 113, 132, 211).

The Late Assyrian recension may have preserved the original reading with slight deviations from the extant Old Babylonian version. The section iv 13–14 can be considered as an addition resulting from the attempts of the scribe(s) of the Late Assyrian recension to supply the fulfilment of the command, and iv 15–16 as a result of the repetitive style often characteristic of the late recensions.

OB *Atra-hasī* I vii	**The Neo-Assyrian recension K 3399 + 3934 (S) rev. iv**	
360 . . . *šu-r* [*u-up-pu-u*$_2$ *li-ib-*⸢*ši*⸣	9	[*qi-b*]*a-ma šu-ru-pu-u lib-ši*
361 . . .] x x-*ši-n*[*a*] x x x	10	[*li-š*]*ak-li-ṣi ri-gim-ši-na nam-tar*
362 x [. . . . . .] x x x [. . .]	11	[*ki-m*]*a me-ḫe-e li-zi-qa-ši-na-ti-ma*
363 *li*-x [. . .	12	[*mur*]-*ṣu di-ʾu šu-ru-pu-u a-sa-ku*
	13	[*iq-b*]*u-ma šu-ru-pu-u ib-ši*
	14	[*u*$_2$]-*riš*$^{ri\text{-}iš}$ *i-ṣi ri-gim-ši-na nam-tar*
	15	[*ki-m*]*a me-ḫe-e i-zi-qa-ši-na-ti-ma*
	16	[*mur*]-*ṣu di-ʾu šu-ru-pu-u a-sa-ku*
360 '. . .] let there be plague	9	'Command that there be plague,
361 . . .] thei[r]	10	let Namtar diminish their noise.
362 . [. . . . . .]. . .[. . .]	11	Like a tornado, let disease, sickness,
363 . . [. . .'	12	plague, and pestilence blow upon them.'
	13	They commanded and there was plague,
	14	. . . Namtar diminished their noise.[46]
	15	Like a tornado, disease, sickness,
	16	plague, and pestilence blew upon them.

u$_{18}$-lu 'southwind, gale, storm, hurricane', the Sumerian equivalent of *mehû*, is used in a similar way in *LE* (the Nippur version) segm. A 9–10, which describes the silencing of the city of Eridu: za-pa-aĝ$_2$-bi niĝ$_2$-me-ĝar u$_{18}$-lu-gin$_7$ ba-e-dul [uĝ$_3$-bi . . .] | eridu^{ki} niĝ$_2$-me-ĝar u$_{18}$-lu-gin$_7$ ba-e-dul uĝ$_3$-bi [. . .]. 'Its [the city's] voice was smothered with silence as by a southwind/storm. [Its people . . .]; Eridu was smothered with silence as by a southwind/storm. Its people. . . .'. In both the Sumerian and Akkadian texts, the figures of speech are marked morphologically, with the equative morpheme -gin$_7$ in *LE* and the preposition *kīma* in the Flood

[46] The two words [*u*$_2$]-*riš*$^{ri\text{-}iš}$ *i-ṣi* are difficult on this line. The rendering of the line is that of Lambert and Millard (1969: 107; followed by Foster 2005: 271). For the first word, Lambert and Millard (1969: 165) suggest *erēšu* 'ask' or 'plant' or *râšu* 'rejoice'. It seems that *erēšum* 'to ask; to request, wish for' in the intensive stem D is to be preferred in the context, thus normalizing [*u*]*rriš*. But the identification of the subject is difficult. For the second word, Lambert and Millard propose *wiāṣum* or *êṣum* 'to be(come) too little, small', pointing out, however, that the D or Š-stem is expected for the rendering 'diminish' rather than the G-stem in the current form of the verb.

epic. The intertextual relationship between the Flood epic and the city laments is further strengthened by the fact that they share the motif of plague according to our earlier comparison of the general motifs regarding destruction.

Further evidence of the metaphorical and mythical background of the Flood epic can be seen in the association of the Flood with the images of animals, mythical monsters, and battle. Streck (1999: 59) has already noted that the figurative depiction of the Flood in the image of a bull can be found in OB *Atra-hasīs* III iii 15–17 [*abūb*]*u kīma lî išabbu* | [*kīma p*]*arî nā'eri* | [x x (x)*ni*]*m šāru* '[The Flood] bellowed like a bull, [like] a whining wild ass the winds [howled].' The animal imagery with which the flood is often associated in the Sumerian traditions is that of a lion (e.g. *Gudea Cylinder A* iv 18–19; B ix 21–2). But the juxtaposition of the flood imagery and the bull and ram can be found in *Šū-Suen D* 2–4 ^{d}nin-urta x ⸢mar⸣-ru$_{10}$ ug gal šen-šen-na ru-ru-gu$_{2}$ | a$_{2}$-ĝal$_{2}$ uĝ$_{3}$ erim$_{2}$ x-⸢RA⸣.SU uru$_{2}$ gul-lu a$_{2}$-dam saḫar-re-eš gi$_{4}$ | ^{d}nin-urta am gal gu$_{4}$-si-AŠ bad$_{3}$ gal ⸢ŠU.KAD$_{4}$-ŠU.KAD$_{4}$⸣-e 'Ninurta … flood/tempest, great lion, fierce opponent in battle! Mighty one, who … the enemy peoples, destroyer of cities, who turns the settlements into dust! Ninurta, great wild bull, a battering ram who … great walls!'

The association between the Flood and a mythical monster is alluded to in OB *Atra-hasīs* II vii 44–7 where Enki responded to the gods when they tried to bind him with an oath in order to bring about the Flood: *abūbu ša taqabb*[*âninni*] | *mannu šū anāku* [*ul īde*] | *anākūma ullada* [*abūba*] | *šipiršu ibašši it*[*ti* ^{d}*enlil*] 'the Flood that you are commanding [me], who is it/he? I [do not know]. Am I to give birth to [a Flood]? That is the task of Enlil.' Lambert and Millard (1969: 158) are puzzled by the *mannu* used to refer to the Flood when they write: 'It is not clear why the personal interrogative is used, unless perhaps Enki is represented as pretending to take *abūbu* as a personal name.' *ullada* (G Dur. 1 cs of *walādu* 'to give birth', with the ventive) suggests that the Flood is referred to here by Enki as a personal being.[47] The same Akkadian verb *walādu* is used in the Neo-Assyrian recension of the *Atra-hasīs Epic* K 3399 + 3934 (S) obv. iii 18 in the establishment of the birth ritual of human beings *akkī ālittu ulladūma* 'and when the pregnant woman gives birth'. In *LW* 3.3, the flood monster is described as a-ma-ru du$_{6}^{!}$(ki) al-ak-e 'a hoe-making flood'. According to *kirugu* 1 and *kirugu* 3 of the same composition it had different fearsome bodily features (if the descriptions refer to the same monster) and was given birth by An and Enlil (*LW* 1.9 an ^{d}en-lil$_{2}$-bi ba-an-u$_{3}$-tu-uš-[a …]-gin$_{7}$ e-ne ba-si$_{3}$ 'When An and Enlil had given birth to it, that one resembled$^{?}$ …'). It was later called upon by Enlil to destroy the land (segm. E 11–27).

More specifically, the depiction of the flood monster in the image of the Anzu bird in *LW* 3.7–10 ĝeš-nu$_{11}$-bi nim ĝir$_{2}$-re anzu^{mušen}-gin$_{7}$ igi ⸢su$_{3}$⸣-ud-bi bar-re-dam | gu$_{3}$-bi mir-mir-ra-am$_{3}$ izi bar$_{7}$-a kur-re su$_{3}$-su$_{3}$-u$_{3}$-dam | eme-bi

[47] Kilmer (1996: 127–39; 2006: 211) views the *abūbu* in the *Atra-hasīs Epic* as a monster being created.

ga-an-ze$_2$-er-ra-am$_3$ u$_3$-dub$_2$ šeg$_3$-ĝe$_{26}$ kalam-ma dar-re-dam | a$_2$-bi anzu^{mušen} maḫ dub$_3$ bad-re$_6$ niĝ$_2$-nam nu-e$_3$-am$_3$ 'Its glint (of its eyes) shall be lightning that flashes far like the Anzu bird. Its voice shall rage—a blazing fire that extends as far as the Netherworld. Its tongue shall be a flame, raining embers, that sunders the Land. Its wings (lit. arms) shall be the majestic Anzu bird that nothing can escape when it spreads wide its knees' (see also *Gudea Cylinder A* iv 18–19) finds its parallel in OB *Atra-hasīs* III iii 7–12 [*anzû ina ṣ*]*uprīšu* | [*ušarriṭ*] *šamā'ī* | [. . . . . . *m*]*ātam* | [*kīma karpati r*]*igimša iḫpi* . . . '[Anzu with] his talons [rent] the heavens. [He . . .] the land and shattered its noise [like a pot].'[48] The animal imagery of the parallel lines in SB *Gilgameš* XI 106–8 is different: *ša* ^{d}*adad šuḫarras* ⸢*su*⸣ *ibā'u šamê* | [*mi*]*mma namru ana* ⸢*da*⸣ ['*u*]*m*[*mat*] *uttēru* | [*irḫ*]*iṣ māta*(kur) *kīma*(gin$_7$) *alp*[*i*(gu$_4$) . . .] x *iḫp*[*īša*] 'The still calm of the storm god passed across the sky, all that was bright was turned into gloom. Like an ox [he] trampled the land, he smashed [it like a pot].'

The association of the meteorological images with the battle scene, which is prevalent in the figurative tradition,[49] can be observed in the monologue of the divine narrator (the mother goddess$^{?}$, as suggested by Lambert and Millard 1969: 165) at the end of OB *Atra-hasīs* III viii 12–13 *têretiš*[*ka*] | *ušabši qa*[*bla*] 'At [your] decree I set battle in motion', which apparently alludes to the Flood. Westenholz (1996: 197; see also Streck 1999: 113) notes that this passage follows the figurative tradition in which the images of *qablu*(*m*) 'battle' and *abūbu*/a-ma-ru 'flood/Flood' are 'inextricably intertwined', that is, as battle can be likened to the flood, so can the flood be likened to battle. Both Westenholz and Streck further view SB *Gilgameš* XI 122 *ana ḫulluq nišīya qabla aqbīma* '(How) I (Bēlet-ilī) declared a war to destroy my people' as a parallel to OB *Atra-hasīs* III viii 13. As observed by Streck (1999: 59; 106–7), the same figurative association between battle and the flood/Flood also occurs in OB *Atra-hasīs* III iii 12 [. . . . . . *ittaṣâ*] *abūbu* [*kīma qabl*]*i* ⸢*e*⸣*li nišī ibā' kašūšu* '[. . .] the Flood [set out], the cataclysm passed over the peoples [like a battle]'; SB *Gilgameš* XI 110–11 *ḫanṭiš izīqamma* x[. . .]*ši šadâ*(kur)^{a} ⸢*a*⸣[*būbu*$^{?}$] | *kīma qabli eli*(ugu) *nišī*(uĝ$_3$)^{meš} *uba''û* [*kašūšu*] 'Quickly it blew and the [Flood . . .] the east wind, like a battle [the cataclysm] passed$^{!}$ over the peoples';[50] and XI

[48] The name of Anzu is partially preserved in the Neo-Assyrian recension BM 98977 + 99231 (U) rev. 16–17: [*anz*]*û ina ṣuprīšu šamê* ⸢*u*⸣[*šarriṭ*] | [x x *m*]*āta kīma karpati milikša isp*[*uḫ*] 'Anzu with his talons [rent] the heavens; [he. . .] the land like a pot, he scattered its counsel.'

[49] e.g. *Curse Agade* 100–19, 155–9; *LSU* 75–6, 166, 377–88; *LU* 210–24, 243–5; *LW* 4.8–31, 5.2–34.

[50] Normalization and rendering of *ka-šu-šu* are based on George 2003: 711. Alternatively, one may follow the rendering 'die *kašūšu*-Waffe' by Streck (1999: 59). The word *kašūšu* may either refer to a divine weapon of Nergal or serve as a designation of catastrophe (CDA 153). The rendering 'its might' by Lambert and Millard (1969: 95) is based on *kaššu* 'massive, strong' (of flood waters) with the possessive suffix -*šu*.

131 *te*$^{?}$*-riq*$^{?}$ *šu-u*$_2$ *a-bu-bu qab-la* 'it was relenting, the Deluge, in respect of battle' (so MS J_1; George 2003: 711 n. 26).

The battle motif is also featured in the OB *Atra-hasīs Epic* and its recensions in which the Akkadian word *qablum* 'battle, conflict' occurs repeatedly,[51] together with *tāḫāzum* 'battle, combat';[52] *tuqumtum* 'battle';[53] *mitḫuṣum* 'fight, combat'.[54] These bellicose scenes pertain to the attack on Enlil's temple Ekur by the rebellious Igigi (compare the attack on Ekur by Naram-Suen in *Curse Agade*).

Aside from the above parallels, the Sumerian compositions dealing with catastrophe from the Ur III and Isin-Larsa periods further share with the Flood epic similar depictions of the ominous atmosphere of catastrophe. The notion that the occasion is characterized by darkness or night as an ominous sign is found in the depictions of catastrophe in both traditions: *Ur-Namma A* 14; *LSU* 80A, 82, 214; *LU* 190; *LE* (the Nippur version) segm. A 22–3; *NL* 202, 293; OB *Atra-hasīs* III iii 13$^{?}$, 18; the *Sumerian Flood Story* 206; SB *Gilgameš* XI 107, 112–13, 134.

Furthermore, the image of fire or burning in the destruction of the land or cities in the Sumerian compositions (*Curse Agade* 131; *LSU* 79, 159, 168, 171; *LU* 187–8, 192, 201, 227, 239–40, 259–60, 377; *LE* (the Ur version) segm. A 8; *LW* 3.8–9, 71, 91) is also reflected in SB *Gilgameš* XI 104–5 ^{d}*anunnakkī iššû dipārāti* | *ina namrīrīšunu uḫammaṭū mātum* 'The Anunnaki bore torches aloft, setting the land aglow with their brilliance.' The description here in the *Gilgameš Epic* obviously is metaphorical, to symbolize the lightning that boded the coming storm.

The above comparisons show that in terms of the use of meteorological images in figurative and mythical associations and the portrayal of the overall atmosphere of catastrophe, different versions or recensions of the Flood epic exhibit a close relationship with the Sumerian figurative tradition, especially the city laments. Is it possible that it was the Flood epic that had existed before the city laments and had influenced the laments in their use of weather imagery for depicting catastrophe? One of the arguments against such a possibility is that the city laments have a stronger tie with the previous figurative tradition, while the Flood epic has begun to part with that tradition and moved toward a literal and chronographical representation of the flood as the catastrophic event that ended the primeval era.

If the Flood epic came after the city laments, what could have triggered the use of weather catastrophe imagery in such an unprecedented degree of high

[51] OB *Atra-hasīs* I ii 62, 83, 110; iii 128, 131, 140, 143.

[52] OB *Atra-hasīs* I ii 62; iii 129, 141.

[53] OB *Atra-hasīs* I iii 130, 142, 146, 160.

[54] Sippar SB II 38, 50.

density and frequency in the laments in the first place? One can only speculate that there might indeed have been a serious storm or flood that exacerbated the already precarious situation in the final days of the Ur III dynasty, if the storm catastrophe referred to in *Year Name 22 of Ibbi-Isin* is to be taken literally to some degree (Civil 1987: 28). This alleged event might subsequently have been represented, in a highly literary fashion, as the means of destruction of that whole era in the city laments. Whatever historical factors might have been represented with regard to the composition of the city laments, one can be reasonably certain, on the basis of the preceding as well as ensuing comparisons, that the literary development of the city laments, more than any other extant early Mesopotamian compositions, had served as a reservoir of conceptual and literary sources from which the author(s) of the Flood epic drew inspiration for the portrayal of destruction.

Cause of Destruction

Scholars have long debated the cause of destruction of the human race by the gods in the Flood epic.[55] Was the destruction provoked by some human faults or sins? Or was it a result of sheer divine caprice? There are no simple answers to these questions because of the variables and ambiguities embedded in the texts of the Flood epic. By delving into the representations of the cause of destruction in the Sumerian compositions dealing with catastrophe from the Ur III and Isin-Larsa periods, one may see that some of the variables and ambiguities in the Flood epic were simply inherited from the earlier compositions that had grappled with the issue of the cause of destruction at least a couple of centuries before the emergence of the epic in the mid-Old Babylonian period.

Grappling with the Cause of Destruction in the City Laments

The destruction of the Land of Sumer, cities, temples, and human life led to questioning the cause of destruction in the city laments.[56] Such a terrible tragedy signifies divine hostility, specifically of Enlil, towards Sumer.[57] But in the light of the professed innocence and righteousness (zi) of the victims,[58] what could have motivated the divine hostility or curse? It is stated in *NL* 73–5: uĝ₃ saĝ ge₆-ga us₂ zi bi₂-ib-dab₅-ba | a-na ib₂-ak a-na im-ḫa-lam-ma-bi-še₃ | u₃-mu-un-bi ib₂-ta-ib₂ saĝ-ki-a mu-un-DU 'What had the black-headed people,

---

[55] For a brief overview, see Shehata 2001: 14.
[56] *LSU* 240–2, 341–2; *LU* 324–5; *LW* 1.19; *NL* 81, 83, 92, 144.
[57] *LU* 202, 326, 408; *LE* (the Nippur version) segm. C 4.
[58] *LU* 41, 42, 66, 67, 73, 118, 121, 318, 372; *NL* 72.

who had taken a true path, done, what had they forsaken, that their lord [Enlil] has become enraged with them and *walked in anger*?' (Tinney 1996: 103).[59] Likewise, *LSU* 66, 163, and 457 pronounce the fate of Sumer and Ur as unfathomable. The image of indiscriminate destruction further reinforces the enigmatic character of destruction.[60]

What makes the situation even more perplexing is that in the midst of this catastrophe, not even the gods, including those who participated in deciding on or carrying out the destruction, were spared. Neither did the bitter laments and earnest entreaties of Nanna/Suen (*LSU*) and Ningal (*LU*) make An and Enlil relent. As already pointed out in our overview of the laments, *LSU, LU* and *LE* in particular focus on the devastating effect of catastrophe on the gods themselves. The laments present long litanies of the withdrawing gods and wailing goddesses. Most enigmatic of all is probably the devastation of the cult and shrine of Enlil, the instigator of the destruction, in Nippur. In *kirugu* 3 of *LSU*, the focus of the text shifts from the destruction of other cities to the destruction of Ur, the city of Nanna/Suen (the son of Enlil) as well as the capital of the Ur III dynasty. The city was presumably an important source of provision for the cult of Enlil in Nippur, as indicated both in a literary composition entitled *Nanna-Suen's Journey to Nippur* and in historical sources (Tinney 1996: 58–60). Due to the drought that drained the watercourse crucial for transportation, the lack of cultic personnel to carry out the sacred rites, and the depletion of natural resources and cultivated goods, no more food offerings could be delivered from Ur to Nippur (*LSU* 303–39). In his first supplication to his father Enlil (*LSU* 341–9), Nanna bemoaned:

> O father who begot me, why have you turned away from my city which was built[?] for you? O Enlil, why have you turned away from my Ur which was built[?] for you? The boat with first-fruit offerings no longer brings first-fruit offerings to the father who begot him. Your food offerings can no longer be brought to Enlil in Nippur. The *en* priests of the countryside and city have been carried off by phantoms. Ur, like a city raked by a hoe, is to be counted as a ruin-mound. The Ki-ur, Enlil's resting place, has become a haunted shrine. O Enlil, gaze upon your city, an empty wasteland. Gaze upon your city Nippur, an empty wasteland. . . .

The above poignant words of appeal seem to have penetrated to the heart of the theological issues which the authors and their generation were grappling with: why would the gods act in such a self-destructive, unconstrained, and

[59] According to Tinney (1996: 145), 'The expression sag-ki-a DU is difficult. It would seem reasonable, given the context, to connect it with sag-ki . . . gíd = *nekelmû*, "to frown, look with disfavor upon." Although no such connection can be documented, one might entertain the possibility that the expression is here elliptical for sag-ki-gíd-a DU and posit a basic meaning "to go in anger" or "to (take a) stand in anger, of disfavor." It is not clear whether sag-ki-DU-ḫa-az in *MSL SS* 1:12 vii 16′ is relevant here.'

[60] *LSU* 110–11; *LU* 400, 402–6; *LE* (the Nippur version) segm. A 20; *NL* 28, 66.

seemingly irrational way in the calamity they caused in Sumer? Evidently, the authors of the laments had sought to understand the plight that befell Sumer by elevating it to a divine or theological level. But the outcomes of this theological exploration did not turn out to be satisfying.

When their efforts to understand the cause of the catastrophe on a moralistic, theological—essentially rationalistic—level had been deemed unsuccessful, the authors of the laments turned to the ultimate explanatory avenues: fate and divine sovereignty. For example, one finds the author of *LSU* resorting to both explanations in Enlil's replies to Nanna's first and second entreaties in *kirugu* 4.

> Oh Nanna, the noble son . . . why do you concern yourself with crying? The judgment uttered by the assembly cannot be reversed. The pronouncement of An and Enlil knows no overturning. Ur was indeed given kingship (but) it was not given an eternal reign. From time immemorial, since the land was founded, until the people multiplied, who had ever seen a reign of kingship that would take precedence (for ever)? The reign of its kingship had been long indeed but had to exhaust itself. O my Nanna, do not exert yourself in vain, abandon your city. (*LSU* 363–70)

> My son, the city built for you in joy and prosperity was given to you as your reign. Destroying the city, overthrowing its great wall and battlements: all this too is part of that reign . . . the black, black days of the reign that has been your lot. (*LSU* 461–3)

Both replies of Enlil suggest that the author sought recourse to a deterministic and naturalistic view: that is just the way things are, as they have always been. Note also the legal tone in the first reply of Enlil: di-til-la inim pu-uḫ$_2$-rum-ma-ka šu gi$_4$-gi$_4$ nu-ĝal$_2$ | inim du$_{11}$-ga an ^{d}en-lil$_2$-la$_2$-ka šu bal-e nu-zu 'The judgment uttered by the assembly cannot be reversed. The pronouncement of An and Enlil knows no overturning' (*LSU* 364–5). These two authoritarian statements find resonance three times in *kirugu* 1 (*LSU* 21, 56, 57) where the divine intention to destroy Sumer and its capital Ur is first announced, further reinforcing the deterministic interpretation with divine sanction. What is peculiar about the deterministic and authoritarian perspectives in *LSU* is that they are applied not as much to human as to divine kingship (Tinney 1996: 35), which implies that even the gods are not immune to the effect of the relentless shift of fortune and the unbending command of An and Enlil.

There exist considerable variations among the laments. *LU*, for example, chose to highlight the unremitting decision of An and Enlil, who refused to grant respite to Ur until it was utterly destroyed, even when its patron goddess Ningal made supplication to them twice (*LU* 136–68). In *LSU* 460–74, by comparison, Enlil relented when his son Nanna approached him the second time.

Though still holding on to an authoritarian perspective (*LW* 4.2–3), *LW* seems to postulate an alternative explanation in the broken section of *kirugu* 1: that the destruction might have been triggered by the increase of human population who might have disturbed the repose of the gods with 'the excessive human activity or noise' (Green 1984: 254, 277). The motif of overpopulation may be expressed in segm. A 1–6:

> [. . .] x ĝar-ra re šu gur-bi [x] x-⸢dam⸣ [. . .] ⸢(x) an$^{?}$ ki⸣-ke$_4$ me-bi [x] x ⸢nu$_2$⸣ [. . .] x E NE ba-ab-ra [. . .] lu$_2$ ti diĝir-re-e-[ne-gin$_7$] a-na me bi$_2$-ib$_2$-tab [. . .]-bi-ta ĝalga su$_3$-e [mi-ni-in]-si$_3$-ge$_5$-eš-a [. . .] diĝir-re-e-ne-ke$_4$ ša$_3$ x [(. . .)] mu-un-gu$_7$
>
> The . . . which had developed—its wiping clean$^{?}$ was to be [accomplished$^{?}$]. The . . . of heaven and earth put their divine powers . . . sleep$^{?}$. . . . mortal man multiplied$^{?}$ (to become) as numerous$^{?}$ as the gods. When together$^{?}$ . . . had achieved a momentous decision, the . . . of the gods. . . .

In the same *kirugu*, segm. B 3 also seems to deal with the expansion of human population: [. . .]-ni saĝ a-na-aš ba-ab-su$_3$ [uĝ$_3$ saĝ ge$_6$-ga] a-ab-a in-lu-lu-un 'Why was . . . expanded? Who made [the black-headed people] so numerous?' But this particular line and the rest of segm. B are not part of the major manuscript CBS 3762 (Green 1984: 255–6). If overpopulation indeed proves to be represented as a cause of the gods' decision to destroy the human race in *LW*, which is exactly what the *Atra-hasīs Epic* portrays, one is still left with the question as to whether such a motif is originally created by the author of this lament or borrowed from elsewhere, perhaps from the Babylonian Flood epic during the course of transmission of this lament. It is also possible that both *LW* and the *Atra-hasīs Epic* might have borrowed the motif from another source.

The attempts of the city laments to understand the cause of destruction must be viewed within the continuum of the Sumerian tradition. With regard to the moralistic perspective, Cooper (1983: 29) has observed that royal inscriptions and hymns 'from earliest time' had tended to draw a 'causal link' between the behaviour of rulers and the fate that befell them. However, the literary-historical tradition does not always draw such a link. While regarding the destruction of Agade as a consequence of Naram-Suen's sacrilegious attack on Enlil's shrine in Nippur, *Curse Agade* (at least at the beginning of the text) still seems to attribute the initial decision of the downfall of Agade to a deterministic and authoritarian cause (Cooper 1983: 30; Steinkeller 2003: 285), against which Naram-Suen rebelled after his seven-year humble entreaty and lament had brought about no change in the divine decision. Finding no fault in Ur-Namma, who proved truthful (zi) to both the gods and his people,[61] the author of *Ur-Namma A* concluded that the tragic fate that befell the king and his family must be the result of divine caprice, treachery, and unfaithfulness,[62]

[61] *Ur-Namma A* 6–7, 18, 21, 155, 202.
[62] *Ur-Namma A* 8–9, 58, 156–65, 208–10.

especially that of An and Enlil, whose unremitting and unchecked authority aroused strong resentment in the text. The city laments, in general, like *Ur-Namma A*, emphasize the truthfulness (zi) of the victim,[63] in this case, the suffering cities and people of Sumer, and their undeserved fate which was caused by the gods.

Rejecting the moral explanation taught in *Curse Agade, LSU* chose to represent the destruction of Ur and its divine kingship as the result of fate (Cooper 1983: 29; Michalowski 1989: 9). This deterministic view in *LSU*, as well as its more latent manifestation in *Curse Agade*, resonates with the fundamental tenet of the political ideology of *SKL* (Michalowski 1983: 237–48; 1989: 6) already attested in the Ur III period and probably current as early as the Sargonic period (Steinkeller 2003: 283–4). Although the laments had basically followed *Curse Agade* and *Ur-Namma A* in their reflections on the cause of catastrophe, they went further than the Ur III compositions in exposing the irrationality of the unconstrained exercise of divine authority and power. Such irrationality is dramatically and abstractly represented by the laments' frequent use of catastrophic weather imagery. For the laments, both the means and cause of destruction are unfathomable (e.g. *LSU* 66–8, 163).

Comparison with the Flood Epic

The comparative task in this section involves first reviewing the sequence of events in the Flood epic represented by the Old Babylonian version of the *Atra-hasīs Epic* and then examining how the pivotal motif of noise (*rigmu* 'voice, cry, noise' and *ḫubūru* 'bustle, clamour') is used throughout the epic. The epic starts with a conflict within the divine realm: the labouring gang rebelling against those who ruled over them. Tension began to build up as the rebels surrounded the residence of Enlil, the counsellor of the gods. At the urgent call of Enlil, the great Anunnaki convened in order to resolve the conflict. They arrived at the solution that one god among the rebels be slaughtered and human beings be created out of the slaughtered god's flesh and blood to be mixed with clay. The toil which the gods of the labouring gang had to perform would then be transferred to the humans, thus relieving the gods and granting them freedom.

When first implemented, the solution seemed to work out well. But then it led to another crisis: the growth of the human population created too much noise which disturbed the sleep of Enlil. To suppress the human growth, Enlil commanded plague through the plague god Namtar. But Atra-hasīs, the human protagonist in the epic, sought help from his patron deity Enki. Enki instructed his servant to command heralds to loudly proclaim to human beings

[63] *LU* 41, 42, 66, 67, 73, 118, 121, 318, 372; see also *NL* 72.

that they revere or worship not their gods or goddesses, but turn their devotion to Namtar, presumably in order to bribe him to stop the plague. Enki's instructions did help to stop the plague. As human growth resumed, so did the noise that disturbed Enlil's sleep. Then Enlil commanded drought and famine through the storm god Adad and the goddess Nisaba who was responsible for produce. In response, Atra-hasīs was given by Enki a solution similar to that in the first round of attack. Thus human beings kept thriving upon their recovery from the second round of destruction. Finally Enlil seems to have discovered how his attempts to stop human growth had failed. Enki was bound by an oath not to help his human creatures in another attempt at destruction through drought and famine commanded by Enlil (II iii 7–8).[64] This time, Enlil involved more gods in the destruction: Anu and Adad to guard the upper region so that no rain would descend; Enlil himself to guard the earth, presumably so that food supply would be cut off; and Enki presumably to guard the underground

[64] Reading after Moran (1987: 251); see also Shehata (2001: 108); Foster (2005: 243). The third destruction cycle is preserved more fully in the late recensions: K 3399 + 3934 (S) rev. iv 37–vi 28 and Sippar SB V 43–117; see also BE 39099 (x) rev. i 1–7. In the Neo-Assyrian recension K 3399 + 3934 (S) rev. iv 37–vi 28, the second and third destruction cycles are conflated. There are obviously variations between the Old Babylonian version and the Late Assyrian and Babylonian recensions. Here it is relevant to mention that the motif of binding Enki with an oath by Enlil is rather problematic in the manuscript tradition of the epic. In the Old Babylonian version, clear indications of Enki being bound by an oath occur in II vii 42–3, that is, after the failure of the third cycle of destruction and right before the sending of the Flood. A passage concerning oath-taking at the beginning of the third cycle, OB *Atra-hasīs* II iii (D) 7–10 [x] x-*a i-li ta-mi-ma* | [x x] *i-ša-ak-ka-na i-na šu-na-a-ti* | [. . .] ^{d}*en-ki ta-mi-ma* | [. . .]-x-*ak-ka-na i-na šu-na-a-ti* has engendered different interpretations (for a concise summary, see Shehata 2001: 108). According to Lambert and Millard (1969: 77), these lines deal with Atra-hasīs' invoking Enki through an oath: 'He (Atra-hasīs) swore by [. . .] of the god, giving [attention] to dreams. He swore by [. . .] of Enki, giving [attention] to dreams.' But Moran (1987: 251) viewed these lines as conveying Enki being bound by an oath, a view which is adopted by Foster (2005: 243), who provides the following renderings: 'My god [would speak to] me, but he is under oath, he will [inform] (me) in dreams. Enki [would speak to] me, but he is under oath, he will [inform] (me) in dreams.' It is interesting, as pointed out by Shehata (2001: 108), that these lines are missing in the corresponding lines in Sippar SB V 62–3 and another Neo-Babylonian recension BE 39099 (x) rev. i 15–16. Instead, in Sippar SB V 3–4 and the Neo-Assyrian recension Q rev. 11′–12′, the gods began to swear an oath at the beginning of the second destruction cycle, according to Enki's words to Atra-hasīs. BE 39099 (x) rev. ii 46–8 describes that Enlil led the gods to take an oath to bring the Flood at the end of the third destruction cycle, similar to OB *Atra-hasīs* II vii 42–3. The synopsis of the epic above follows Moran's interpretation, primarily because the mentioning of Enki under oath at the junction of OB *Atra-hasīs* II iii 7–10 is crucial for explaining why in the third destruction cycle, unlike in the first two, Enki's communication with Atra-hasīs was interrupted and became indirect. Even when Enki did send a passage through his monsters to Atra-hasīs, it was very brief, restrained, and vague (see Sippar SB V 100, 102). The placement of the motif of oath-taking among the gods at the beginning of the third destruction cycle also explains why the motif of Enki instructing Atra-hasīs to command the people to counter Enlil's hostilities, which has occurred in the previous two cycles of destruction, is missing in the third cycle. It is difficult to know whether the oath-taking episode referred to in Sippar SB V 62–3 and Q rev. 11′–12′ should be considered equivalent to OB *Atra-hasīs* II iii 7–10 as interpreted by Moran, or to a passage at the beginning of OB *Atra-hasīs* II ii which is lost due to the lacuna.

water (Apsû), including the seas (II v 16–21, 30–5, vi 25–30). Once again, Enki succeeded in rescuing his human creatures by a trick, as indicated in the Neo-Babylonian recension BE 39099 (x) rev. ii 16–27, 32–43. Furious because of Enki's opposition, Enlil again? bound Enki by an oath as he set out to launch the final and complete destruction of humankind by the Flood. However, Enki still managed to inform his protégé of the coming destruction and helped him survive the Flood by instructing him to build a boat.

The motif of noise plays a pivotal role in the epic because it functions to bind all the constituent events in a cause-and-effect sequence. This is done mostly through the author's play on the Akkadian word *rigmu* 'voice, cry, noise', which is used to refer to different kinds of noise in the story. Such wordplay is an ingenious way for the author to connect and progress from one episode to another (Moran 1987: 245–55; Foster 2005: 236 n. 4). Its first occurrence in the epic represents the war cry (*rigmu*) made by the rebel gods who surrounded Enlil's house Ekur (I ii 77). Distressed by the rebellion, Enlil wished to leave his post and urged Anu to find a substitute for him (OB *Atra-hasīs* I iv 172–3; reading after Foster 2005: 227, 234). But Anu in reply expressed his sympathy with the rebels who protested concerning the burden of their task: 'What do we denounce them for? Their forced labour was heavy, [their misery too much]. [Every day] ... [The outcry was] loud, [we could] hear the clamour (*rigmu*)' (I iv 176–9). When the mother goddess Nintu (or Bēlet-ilī) finished creating humankind at the request of the gods, she announced: 'I have imposed your drudgery on man. You have bestowed? clamour (*rigmu*) upon humankind' (OB *Atra-hasīs* I v 241–2; see also II vii 31–82), which may allude to the heartbeat of human beings (OB *Atra-hasīs* I v 241 *aḫriātiš ūmī uppa i nišme* '(So that) in future days may we hear the drum').[65]

When the growing human race began to pose a problem for the gods, it is said: '[The land had grown numerous], the people had increased, the [land] was bellowing [like a bull]. The god was disturbed with [their uproar (*rigmu*)]. [Enlil heard] their clamour (*rigmu*). [He said to] the great gods: "The clamour (*rigmu*) of humankind [has become too burdensome to me], I am losing sleep [in their uproar (*ḫubūru*)]"' (OB *Atra-hasīs* I vii 353–9; see also the Neo-Babylonian recension Sippar SB V 44–50). According to this passage, *rigmu* and *ḫubūru* are used interchangeably. In his command for Namtar to attack humankind with plague, Enlil stated that his intention was to diminish human noise (*rigmu*).[66] In his instructions to his servant Atra-hasīs who sought help for humanity suffering because of the plague Enlil sent, Enki said: '[Command]:

[65] For the interpretation of the drumbeat as the heartbeat of human beings in this passage, see Kilmer 1972: 162–6.

[66] This episode is lost in the incomplete Old Babylonian version, but preserved in the Neo-Assyrian recension K 3399 + 3934 (S) rev. iv 10, 14.

"Let heralds proclaim, let them raise a loud clamour (*ri-*[*ig*]*-ma li-*[*še*]*-eb-bu-*⸢*u*⸣) in the land: 'Do not reverence your (own) gods, do not pray to your (own) goddess, seek the door of Namtar, bring a baked (loaf) before it. May the flour offering please him, may he be shamed by the gift and withdraw his hand'"' (OB *Atra-hasīs* I vii 376–83; see also K 3399 + 3934 (S) rev. iv 30–6). The instructions were passed on by Atra-hasīs to the elders (OB *Atra-hasīs* I 391–8) who in turn carried out the orders (OB *Atra-hasīs* I 403–10). The incomplete lines in OB *Atra-hasīs* I viii 412–13 seem to deal with the departure of the plague and the return of clamour.

In the following two cycles of destruction, the same motif of the noise created by the growing human population that disturbed Enlil reappears almost word for word.[67] So are the motifs of Enki using similar strategies to aid human beings to counter Enlil's hostile attacks[68] and the resumption of human growth and noise[69] repeated, except for the change of the name of the god (Adad, the storm god) to whom human beings were to redirect their devotion. It is worth noting again that Enki's instructions to Atra-hasīs are missing in the third cycle of destruction presumably because Enki was bound by an oath not to save humankind.

Finally, in the Flood episode, *rigmu* is applied to the noise made by the storm god Adad who was roaring in the clouds, an indication of the coming storm which prompted Atra-hasīs to seal the entrance of his boat: OB *Atra-hasīs* III ii 48–51 *ūmu išnû pānūšu* | *ištagna* ^{d}*adad ina erpēti* | *ila išmû rigimšu* | [*k*]*upru babil ipeḫ̮ḫi bābšu* 'The appearance of the weather changed, Adad roared in the clouds. The god (Adad), they heard his voice. Pitch was brought (to him) so that he could close his door.'[70] In the storm, the noise (*rigmu*) of the land was shattered like a pot by the Anzu bird immediately before the Flood arrived (OB *Atra-hasīs* III iii 7–10). The Flood was said to bellow like a bull (OB *Atra-hasīs* III iii 15 [*abūb*]*u kīma lî išabbu*) with a noise (OB *Atra-hasīs* III iii 23 *rigim a*[*būb*]*i* 'the noise of the Flood') that even frightened the gods.[71] The same

[67] Cycle two: OB *Atra-hasīs* II i 2–8 (see also the Neo-Assyrian recension K 3399 + 3934 (S) rev. iv 38–41); cycle three: lost in the incomplete Old Babylonian version, but preserved in the Neo-Babylonian recension SB V 44–50 and another Neo-Babylonian recension BE 39099 (x) rev. i 2–3.

[68] Cycle two: OB *Atra-hasīs* II ii 6–15, 21–9.

[69] Cycle two: OB *Atra-hasīs* II ii 34–5 (see also the Neo-Babylonian recension Sippar SB V 39–40); cycle three: hinted at as a result of Enki's rescue; OB *Atra-hasīs* II v 19–21, 32–5, vi 27–30; the Neo-Babylonian recension BE 39099 (x) rev. ii 2–43.

[70] The word *ila* in III ii 50 is treated as a conjunction 'as soon as' in Lambert and Millard (1969: 93, 160). The rendering provided above follows Foster's (2005: 249), which is based on Jiménez-Zamudio (1996: 133–6).

[71] The reading of OB *Atra-hasīs* III iii 24 [*li-ib*]*-bi i-li uš-ta-*⸢*ka-ad*⸣ follows von Soden (1994: 640), which is supported by the Neo-Assyrian recension 98977 + 99231 (U) rev. 20–1 and SB *Gilgameš* XI 116 in meaning.

bovine image is used to describe the land or the people when they disturbed Enlil's sleep earlier in the epic (OB *Atra-hasīs* I vii 353–9; see also the Neo-Babylonian recension Sippar SB V 44–50), as also observed by Streck 1999: 59. In the mother goddess Mami/Nintu's self-deprecatory speech and her lament for the destruction of her human creatures, the word *rigmu* supposedly represents the noise of human groaning and the sound of the mother goddess's crying: *ana ramānīya u pagrīy[a]* | *ina ṣērīyāma rigimšina ešme* | *elēnūya kīma zubbī* | *īwû lillidū* | *u anāku kī ašābi* | *ina bīt dimmati šaḫurru rigmī* 'Unto my own self and my body, in my backbone I heard their (the people's) cry (or the sound of screaming)! (My) offspring have become like flies above me! And as for me, how to dwell in the house of grief, (while) my voice is deathly silent (loss of voice due to excessive crying)?' (OB *Atra-hasīs* III iii 42–7).[72]

From the above listing of all the occurrences of the word *rigmu* or *ḫubūru* in the Flood epic one can see how the topos of noise is used strategically to create a logical connection and progression between different episodes of the Flood epic, which is more obvious in the Old Babylonian version than in the late recensions. Here it is important to recapitulate the storyline more concisely: the hard toil the senior gods imposed on the junior gods led to the latter group's noise of groaning and grumbling, which in turn led the labouring gang to make the noise of defiance and rebellion outside the door of Enlil's residence. To resolve the crisis, human beings were created and the task of labour was transferred to them; so was the noise, which foreshadows the coming crisis. As the growing human population made too much noise, Enlil was disturbed in his repose. To put down the noise, Enlil sent plague to stem the rapid and boisterous human growth. To counter Enlil's attack, Enki instructed Atra-hasīs to command heralds to make a loud call for human beings to shift their devotion from their patron deities to the deities responsible for the plague in order to ward off the attack. As the attack was lifted, human beings recovered; so did their disturbing noise to Enlil. Such confrontation was repeated two or more times in the epic, until at last the frustrated Enlil decided to send the Flood to wipe out the entire human race once and for all. The noises of the destructive agents, Adad, Anzu, and the Flood, even frightening the gods, smothered the

[72] The rendering of these lines is literal; compare 'As a result of my own choice, and to my own hurt I have listened to their noise. My offspring—cut off from me—have become like flies! And as for me, like the occupant of a house of lamentation my cry has died away' by Lambert and Millard (1969: 95); 'Of my own accord, from myself alone, to my own charge have I heard (my people's) clamour! [My] offspring—with no help from me—have become like flies. And as for me, how to dwell in (this) abode of grief, my clamour fallen silent?' by Foster (2005: 250). The more literal rendering adopted in this study is preferred on account of the poignancy it creates in the context. *šaḫurru* (*ša-ḫu-ur-ru*) is problematic, given the normal writing *šuḫarruru* 'to become dazed, still, numb with fear; to abate, subside' (CAD Š III 203); 'to be deathly still' (CDA 380). Compare *šaḫurrat* (*ša-ḫu-ur-ra-at*) in OB *Atra-hasīs* II iii 15; *šuḫurrat* (*šu-ḫu-rat*) in the Neo-Assyrian recension of the epic K 3399 + 3934 (S) rev. v 33 (Lambert and Millard 1969: 112–13).

human noise of vitality and replaced it with the human noise of groaning and the noise of the mother goddess's cry (even that died away because of the excess of the goddess's grief), an indication of the human race's destruction.

The use of the motif of noise in the Flood epic seems to be its author's ingenious (re-)interpretation of the cause of destruction as well as his reorganization of the sequence of events in the Sumerian compositions dealing with catastrophe. In the Sumerian compositions often the destroyed land, cities, and human victims, once vigorous and dignified,[73] were portrayed as being silenced, on the one hand,[74] and filled with the noise of the destructive agents,[75] the cries, screaming, and moaning of the human victims[76] and the laments of the goddesses, on the other. It is interesting to note that both the Flood epic and the Sumerian compositions dealing with catastrophe employ the bovine image to illustrate the former vitality of the destroyed land or city.[77] More specifically, *LSU* 315 a e_2 gu_4-gin_7 gu_3 bi_2-ib_2-du_{11}-ga-a 'the house (Ur) which used to bellow like a bull' can be viewed as a close parallel to OB *Atra-hasīs* I vii 353; II i 3 *mātum kīma lî išabbu* 'the land was bellowing like a bull'.

From the portrayals in the Sumerian compositions dealing with catastrophe that the destroyed land and cities had once bellowed like a bull but were then silenced, the author of the Flood epic may have deduced that the noise made by the land and cities had been the cause of divine displeasure and the ensuing destruction. Likewise, he may have inferred from the obstruction of human growth due to mass slaughter during the catastrophe, the destruction of Adab 'the city whose lady fashions living beings, who promotes birthing' (*NL* 218), or the promises and blessings of human growth by Enlil after the catastrophe (*LSU* 516; *NL* 320) in the Sumerian compositions that overpopulation may have contributed to the catastrophe and connected this with the motif of noise.

Not only does the author of the *Atra-hasīs Epic* seem to have derived the causes of catastrophe from the results of destruction as portrayed in the Sumerian materials, he also seems to have consciously transformed some of the effects of destruction as found in the Sumerian compositions into causes. For example, as already suggested by Westenholz (1996: 198–200), the loss of sleep among divine and human victims as a result of catastrophe in the Sumerian compositions[78] may have been transformed into Enlil's insomnia

[73] *Curse Agade* 3, 79–81; *Ur-Namma A* 45, 170–1; *LSU* 52, 54, 259, 315; *LW 5.10*, 5.17–18.

[74] *Curse Agade* 185, 255, 263; *Ur-Namma A* 44, 185; *LSU* 59, 315; *LU* 86, 199; *LE* (the Nippur version) segm. A 9–10; *LW* 2.20; *NL* 85, 193; cf. SB *Gilgameš* XI 106, 134.

[75] *Curse Agade* 149; *LE* (the Nippur version) segm. A 7; *LW* 1.14, 2.28.

[76] *LW* 5.2–3; *LU* 172–96.

[77] The Akkadian word *lû* 'bull' is found in OB *Atra-hasīs* I vii 354; II i 3 (see also the Neo-Babylonian recension Sippar SB V 45). The Sumerian word gu_4 'bull, ox, cattle' is found in *Curse Agade* 3, 80; *Ur-Namma A* 171; *LSU* 315; *LW* 5.10. The Sumerian word am 'wild bull' is found in *Curse Agade* 79; *Ur-Namma A* 170; *LSU* 52, 259; *LW* 5.17.

[78] e.g. *Ur-Namma A* 20; *LU* 99–100; *LW* 3.23–4. Sleeplessness in *Curse Agade* 24, 260, however, is 'a sign of eager industriousness' (Cooper 1983: 238).

due to human activities which led the deity to bring about a series of attempts to reduce and eventually wipe out the human race in the Flood epic.[79] However, as mentioned earlier, the divine insomnia as a cause of catastrophe may also be seen in *LW* 1.2$^{?}$ (Green 1984: 277).

By the same token, the loss of umuš[80] and dim$_2$-ma,[81] which is a frequently used topos in the Sumerian compositions dealing with catastrophe, may have been converted into the cause of destruction. These two Sumerian words are often semantically related in Sumerian literature and can be synonymous 'thought, planning, instruction' (ePSD). They clearly carry the connotation of sound mental order in the context of *NL* 47–8 a$_2$-e$_3$ lu$_2$-e$_3$-da umuš-bi nu-zu-gin$_7$ | [uĝ$_3$] ⌜ba⌝-sag$_3$ dim$_2$-ma-bi ba-suḫ$_3$ 'like the foster-children of an ecstatic no longer knowing their (own) intelligence, [the people] were smitten, their minds thrown into disorder (or "became confused").' The words seem to refer to divine endowments, like ĝeštu$_2$ 'reason, understanding, wisdom'.[82] The word umuš also appears to be related to or based on divine counsel.[83]

In the Flood epic, Enlil and Anu were accused by the mother goddess of lacking counsel in their decision to annihilate the human race with the Flood: OB *Atra-hasīs* III v 39–43 *êša anu illikam* | *bēl ṭēmi* | ^{d}*enlil iṭḫi'a an qutrinni* | *ša lā imtalkūma iškunū abūba* | *nišī ikmisū ana karāši* 'where has Anu, the chief decision-maker, gone? Has Enlil drawn nigh the incense? They, who did not deliberate, brought about the Flood, and consigned the peoples to destruction?'[84] What the author of the Flood epic seems to have done is ascribe the loss of rationality or good counsel in human victims, as a result of the distressed situation created by catastrophe,[85] to the lack of rationality and good counsel

[79] See OB *Atra-hasīs* I 352–9, II i 1–8; the Neo-Assyrian recension K3399 + 3934 (S) rev. iv 1–8, 40–1; the Neo-Babylonian recensions BE 39099 rev. i 2–3 and Sippar SB V 45–6, 49–50. In Sippar SB the motif of Enlil's attempts to suppress human population growth seems to be more obvious, particularly in V 42.

[80] *Curse Agade* 148; *Ur-Namma A* 27; *LW* 1.22; *NL* 18, 47, 104.

[81] *Curse Agade* 147; *LW* 1.22; *NL* 48, 103.

[82] See *NL* 216–17 eridu^{ki} ša$_3$-bi ĝeštu$_2$ i-i umuš zi ḫal-ḫa-la-da | ĝarza maḫ-bi nu-ḫa-lam-me-da inim-bi im-de$_6$-am$_3$ 'Of Eridu, its heart sending forth wisdom, so that good sense be allotted, they (Enlil and Ninlil) brought the news that its magnificent rites would not be forgotten.'

[83] See *NL* 18–19 uru$_2$ ša$_3$-bi umuš ba-ra-pa$_3$-da | ^{d}a-nun-na-ke$_4$-ne na ba-an-deg$_x$(RI)-ge-eš-am$_3$ 'the city's heart no longer revealed any (sign) of intelligence there where the Anuna used to give advice!'

[84] See OB *Atra-hasīs* III iii 53–4; SB *Gilgameš* XI 170, 184. The verb *imtalkū* can be either G perfect or Gt preterite (preferable) of 3rd mp. *malākum*, which is rendered 'They, who did not consider' by Lambert and Millard (1969: 99); compare the rendering of the parallel line in SB *Gilgameš* XI 170 by George (2003: 715) *aššu lā imtalkūma iškunu abūbu* 'because he lacked counsel and caused the Deluge'. The adverbial rendering of the whole line in OB *Atra-hasīs* III v 42 by Foster (2005: 2501), 'They who irrationally brought about the flood', helps bring out another nuance of this Akkadian word in this context, which is especially meaningful for our current comparison of the Flood epic with the Sumerian compositions dealing with catastrophe.

[85] Which is also found in the Flood epic; see the Neo-Assyrian recension BM 98977 + 99231 (U) rev. 15–16 [*anz*]*û ina ṣuprīšu šamê* ⌜*u*⌝ [*šarriṭ*] | [x x *m*]*āta kīma karpati milikša isp*[*uḫ*] '[Anz]u with his talon [rent] the heavens, [He . . .] the land like a pot, he scattered its counsel.'

in the very gods who were supposed to be the possessors of these qualities. Note that Enlil is called the *mālikum* 'adviser, counsellor' of the gods in OB *Atra-hasīs* I i 8. Anu's epithet *bēl ṭēmi* in OB *Atra-hasīs* III v 42 (quoted earlier), in the light of the goddess's trenchant remarks about the loss of rationality by Anu and Enlil, seems to be another satirical twist of the Sumerian motif in critique of the gods by the Flood epic. The Akkadian term *ṭēmum* 'thought, planning, understanding' is lexically equivalent to dim_2-ma and umuš (ePSD), two terms related to human intelligence which was depicted as lost due to catastrophe in the Sumerian compositions. In this respect, the Flood epic represented by *Atra-hasīs* has shifted its emphasis from the effect of catastrophe on humans to its divine cause (see Westenholz 1996: 198–9).

However, the critique on the irrationality of divine decisions or actions in the Flood epic is but a further development of what had already begun in the Sumerian compositions dealing with catastrophe. The irrationality of the gods is vividly conveyed in both the Sumerian compositions[86] and the Flood epic by the motif of divine food or sacred offerings being interrupted or totally cut off in catastrophe. Following the Sumerian antecedents, the Flood epic continued with the theological critique that the gods only jeopardized their own livelihood in destroying their human sources of support, while further adding a satirical scene of the gods suffering severe hunger and thirst upon the destruction of their human subjects. The satirical depiction is especially clear in OB *Atra-hasīs* III v 34–5 where the gods swarmed to feast on the offerings made by Atra-hasīs immediately after the Flood: [*īṣinū il*]*ū erēša* | [*kīma zubb*]*ī elu niqî paḫrū* '[The gods sniffed] the smell, they were gathered [like flies] over the offering.'[87] This motif of divine hunger and thirst forms a meaningful parallel with the earlier instances of drought and famine which human beings suffered as a result of the gods' punitive actions in Tablets I and II of the Old Babylonian version of the *Atra-hasīs Epic*.[88] The parallel suggests that if the gods pushed the limits too far in their hostilities towards their human subjects they would suffer the same fate as their human subjects did.

Blatant injustice, particularly when it comes to the indiscriminate annihilation of life, which is frequently portrayed in the Sumerian compositions dealing with catastrophe,[89] has also been confronted on a theological level in both

[86] e.g. *Ur-Namma A*, the Nippur version 211 // the Susa version, segm. D 18; the Nippur version 158; *Ur-Namma* C 103.

[87] This satirical portrayal in the *Atra-hasīs Epic*, according to Tigay (1982: 224–6), has been toned down in SB *Gilgameš* XI 161–3 *ilū īṣinū irīša* | *ilū īṣinū irīša ṭāba* | *ilū kīma zumbē eli bēl niqî iptaḫrū* 'The gods smelled the savour, the gods smelled the sweet savour, the gods gathered like flies over the sacrifice' for theological reasons.

[88] See especially OB *Atra-hasīs* II iv 1–18.

[89] *Curse Agade* 190–2; *LSU* 110–11, 439; *LU* 230; *LW* A.2, *LW* 3.18–30; *NL* 261.

the Sumerian compositions dealing with catastrophe and the Flood epic.[90] In *Ur-Namma A, LU*, and the Flood epic it was either a goddess (Inana, Ningal, Nintu/Bēlet-ilī) or a god (Enki) who uttered complaints against the ultimate decision-makers Enlil and Anu. In the Flood epic, human beings were not as innocent as they were represented in the city laments because of their active engagement in confrontation with Enlil and the hostile gods. The critique on divine injustice in the Flood epic focuses not so much on the incomprehensibility of catastrophe as in the laments, but rather on the Flood as a disproportionate penalty.

The Flood epic's (re-)interpretation of the cause of destruction signifies that it might have reorganized the events or aspects of destruction portrayed in the Sumerian compositions dealing with catastrophe. While the Sumerian compositions freely mix catastrophic weather imagery with plague, drought, famine, and other images of destruction, the Flood epic is much more schematic in its presentation, consistently using the topoi of noise and human growth to structure the events of destruction in a progression which culminated in Enlil's final unleashing of the Flood.

However, this does not mean that the city laments totally lack structure for the events they describe. Besides the thematic structures Green (1984: 253–4) has observed in the city laments (most obviously, for example, destruction and restoration) that a couple of laments represent the destruction as having taken place in two phases, marked by the Sumerian temporal expression 2-kam-ma-še$_3$ 'for the second time', or 'again': *LSU* 260–1 ^{d}en-lil$_2$-le lu$_2$ nam tar-tar-re-de$_3$ a-na [bi$_2$-in-ak-a-ba] | 2-kam-ma-še$_3$ elam^{ki} lu$_2$-kur$_2$-ra kur-ta [ba-ra-e$_3$] 'This is what Enlil, who determines destinies, did: for the second time he sent down the Elamites, the enemy, from the mountains' (see also *LSU* 163–6; *LE* (the Nippur version) segm. A 30). In *LU* 151 (see also 136–50, 151–68), the goddess Ningal also appealed to the divine assembly twice for them to relent. But both times An and Enlil refused to change their decision.

Nonetheless, even with these structural features found in the city laments, some of which could have inspired the author of the Flood epic to represent catastrophe in cycles, the rigorous pursuit of logical organization of the events of destruction in the *Atra-hasīs Epic* is remarkable by comparison. Part of the reason for this difference might be that the laments followed the metaphorical tradition closely and tended to use compound images of destruction to convey devastating effects. The Flood epic, on the other hand, in its literal representation of catastrophe, had to differentiate images of destruction and stage them in series, though there are still vestiges of mixed images (e.g. flood, fire, and battle) that can be observed in the epic.

[90] *Ur-Namma A* 7–9, 18, 21, 58, 155–65, 202; *LSU* 223, 493; *LU* 41–2, 66–7, 73, 118, 121, 124–5, 202, 318, 324–6, 408; OB *Atra-hasīs* III iii 39–40, 53–4, iv 42–3, vi 25–6; SB *Gilgameš* XI 170, 184–95.

Interestingly, when it comes to the logical organization of events, *Atra-hasīs* may have more in common with *Curse Agade* than with the city laments. *Curse Agade* starts with Enlil's shift of his favour from Kiš and Uruk to Agade. Later when Agade too was abandoned by Enlil, its king Naram-Suen first sought to change Enlil's decision by petition. When that attempt had failed, Naram-Suen rebelled and tried to alter the divine decision by force through attacking Enlil's shrine in Ekur, which in turn triggered a series of catastrophes in Sumer and eventually led to the cursing and destruction of Agade by the gods.[91] In the *Atra-hasīs Epic*, one also finds that it was the confrontation between the human subjects and Enlil that intensified the crisis and drove it step by step to the gods' final decision to destroy humankind completely.

The *Sumerian Flood Story*, another version of the Flood epic dated later than the *Atra-hasīs Epic* but still from the Old Babylonian period, contains at least two cycles of destruction. The first cycle is lost in the lacuna of col. i (about thirty-six lines missing), but is alluded to in the remaining section of the same column. The second cycle, which is also partially damaged in cols. iii–v, deals with the Flood. The events that led to the Flood are now lost in the lacuna in col. iii (about thirty-four lines missing). But judging from the passage in col. iv where the epic closely parallels *LSU* 364–70 (Plate 16), it seems that the cause of the Flood may have been represented quite differently from that which is found in the *Atra-hasīs Epic*.

LSU	***The Sumerian Flood Story* (CBS 10673 + CBS 10867)**
364 di-til-la inim pu-uḫ$_2$-ru-um-ma-ka šu gi$_4$-gi$_4$ nu-ĝal$_2$	158 di-til-la inim pu-uḫ$_2$-ru-[um . . . . . .]
365 inim du$_{11}$-ga an ^{d}en-lil$_2$-la$_2$-ka šu bal-e nu-zu	159 inim du$_{11}$-ga an ^{d}en-[lil$_2$-la$_2$-ka . . .]
366 uri$_5^{ki}$-ma nam-lugal ḫa-ba-šum$_2$ bala da-ri$_2$ la-ba-an-šum$_2$	
367 u$_4$ ul kalam ki ĝar-ra-ta za$_3$ uĝ$_3$ lu-a-še$_3$	
368 bala nam-lugal-la saĝ-bi-še$_3$ e$_3$-a a-ba-a igi im-mi-in-du$_8$-a	
369 nam-lugal-bi bala-bi ba-gid$_2$-e-de$_3$ ša$_3$ kuš$_2$-u$_3$-de$_3$	160 nam-lugal-bi bala-bi ba-[. . . . .]
370 ^{d}nanna-ĝu$_{10}$ na-an-kuš$_2$-kuš$_2$-u$_3$-de$_3$ iri^{ki}-zu e$_3$-bar-ra-ab	161 ⸢e-na⸣-eš$_2$ [. . . . .]

[91] As noted in the textual commentary on *Curse Agade* in Chen 2009 (Vol. 2): 86, the text contains an episode of immediate retaliation by Enlil which was inserted by a later scribe or scribes.

364 The verdict, the word of the divine assembly cannot be reversed.	158 The verdict, the word of the divine assembly . . .
365 The pronouncement by An and Enlil knows no overturning.	159 The pronouncement by An and Enlil . . .
366 Ur was indeed given kingship (but) it was not given an eternal reign.	
367 From time immemorial, since the land was founded, until people multiplied,	
368 Who has ever seen a reign of kingship that would take precedence (for ever)?	
369 Its kingship, its reign had been long indeed but had to exhaust itself.	160 Its/their kingship, its/their reign . . .
370 O my Nanna, do not exert yourself in vain, abandon your city.	161 Now . . .

From the above comparison it should be easy to see that the *Sumerian Flood Story* follows *LSU* at least in part. Jacobsen (1981: 522 n. 14) apparently noticed the close connections between the two texts as he attempted to restore lines 158–9 and 160 in the Flood Story on the basis of *LSU* 364–5 and 369 respectively. The fact that the author of the *Sumerian Flood Story* chose to follow this particular passage from *LSU* in constructing Enki's instructions to his protégé Ziusudra (as quoted above) just before the coming flood is revealing. The passage in *LSU* was meant to communicate the inexorable divine decision behind the fatalistic destruction of Sumer and Ur through the flood-like catastrophe. The parallel lines in the *Sumerian Flood Story* likewise refer to the same unchangeable divine decree that aimed to annihilate the capitals and kingship by the Flood. By alluding to the authoritarian and deterministic perspective of *LSU*, the *Sumerian Flood Story* does not seem to identify with the strictly logical presentation of the cause of catastrophe in *Atra-hasīs*. Yet differently from *LSU*, the *Sumerian Flood Story* portrays that despite divine opposition, kingship, idealized in the person of the Flood hero Ziusudra from the antediluvian era,[92] would not succumb to fate, but was to persist as it had survived the Flood, the worst catastrophe in recorded history.

The above comparison shows that the intertextual connections between the Sumerian compositions dealing with catastrophe and the Flood epic are manifold. Attending to these connections would not only aid our reconstruction of

[92] Note the emphasis on the significance of kingship in lines 88–9 and on Ziusudra's royal identity in lines 145, 209, 211, 254, 258.

the historical development of the Flood epic, but also help unravel some of the puzzling features such as the repeated use of the motif of noise, whose significance would otherwise be difficult to grasp. As the authors of the Flood epic or story continued to grapple with the cause of catastrophe in the same vein as their predecessors, they manipulated and transformed the traditional materials in order to represent the catastrophic events in new forms, according to new understandings, and for new purposes. One major distinction between the city laments and the *Atra-hasīs Epic* is that while the former group of texts generally finds the catastrophe inexplicable, the Flood epic traces the cause of catastrophe in a logical sequence of events from the initial conflict within the divine community at the beginning of the epic to Enlil's final dispatching of the Flood (Moran 1987: 245–55; Wilcke 1999: 70). For this reason, any attempt to pinpoint one single cause of the catastrophe without considering the cause-and-effect chain in the epic will never be sufficient. It is also important to be aware of the variables within different versions of the Flood epic. The *Sumerian Flood Story* differs from the *Atra-hasīs Epic* when representing the cause of catastrophe, which reflects a deliberate choice of the author of the Flood story to follow the authoritarian explanation found in *LSU* so that he might eventually repudiate the *SKL* ideology and prove the tenacity of kingship.

Petition and Restoration

Petitions for relief or clemency persistently punctuate the city laments. Though time and again rejected by An and Enlil, petitions did come to realization towards the end of each lament. The following study is intended to demonstrate that many patterns with regard to petition and restoration in the laments may have influenced the composition of the Flood epic. Most importantly, the portrayal or characterization of the Flood hero as a literary figure in the epic seems to have grown out of this influence.

Petition and Restoration in the City Laments

Petitions in the city laments take different forms. Laments may be considered as a form of petition (Flückiger-Hawker 1999: 87–8). They were meant to arouse a sense of pity and compassion for the devastated victims on the part of the deities causing the destruction, in the hope that the deities would relent. Many references to divine or human mourning in the laments may serve this purpose.[93] Incantations or prayers too may be viewed as supplications.[94]

[93] *LSU kirugu* 2; *LU kirugus* 5–7; *LW* 12.24.
[94] *LSU* 483–518; *LU* 381–6, 411–16.

Petitions can also take the form of interrogatives that draw attention to the unfathomable or unjust cause, the severity or extent, as well as the prolonged and thus unbearable duration, of catastrophe,[95] so that the divine decision may be re-evaluated and the duration of destruction shortened (*NL* 150–3). But the city laments do contain formal petitions in which the chief deities were directly approached and implored to intervene.[96]

In terms of the parties involved in petitions, often it was a god or goddess, suffering great losses in the catastrophe, who appealed to An, Enlil, and the divine assembly. Petitions were also offered to the deities suffering the calamity so that they might be comforted and return to their abandoned cities.[97] Sometimes it was human subjects, speaking in the voice of the narrator, who petitioned An and/or Enlil on behalf of a distraught deity[98] or a grief-stricken city or temple (*NL* 68–75). *LW* 12.24–7 and *NL* 305–7 explicitly mention Išme-Dagan, the most illustrious ruler of the Isin dynasty, as one who interceded for the destroyed cities, though royal petitions may also be tacitly alluded to in other laments (Tinney 1996: 23–4).[99]

In most cases, efforts at repeated supplication proved futile because An and Enlil refused to budge in their inimical decision. The rejected deities, and the Anunna gods (*LSU* 377), eventually had to evacuate the cities and go into exile as the storm or flood-like destruction moved in and completely annihilated the cities and the land.[100] *LSU*, *LU*, and *LE* paint a picture of the unremitting and malicious gods An and Enlil, on the one hand, and the compassionate yet powerless deities (Nanna, Ningal, and Enki) of the attacked cities, on the other. Occasionally in *LU*, because the patron goddess could do nothing to help her suffering city, she too was perceived as having deserted Ur and acted hostilely to it.[101] However, in spite of her forced desertion of her city or her momentary antagonism towards her people, Ningal lamented bitterly for her destroyed city and people (*LU* 251–329).

[95] *NL* 1–41, 74, 79–83, 90, 92, 143, 144, 179, 181; *LE* (the Nippur version) segm. C 28, 30, 31; *LW* 1.15–27.

[96] *LSU* 340–56, 449–58; *LU* 144–8, 151–8.

[97] *LU* 341–86; *LE* (the Nippur version) segm. C 45–52.

[98] *LU* 378–86; *LE* (the Nippur version) segm. C 49.

[99] *LSU* 517; *LU* 430–1; *LE* (the Nippur version) segm. C 50–2.

[100] *LSU* 371–448; *LU* 161–249.

[101] E.g. *LU* 254 ama ^{d}nin-gal uru$_2$-ni lu$_2$-erim$_2$-gin$_7$ bar-ta ba-da-gub 'Mother Ningal, like an enemy, stands outside her city'; *LU* 373–7 nin-ĝu$_{10}$ e$_2$-ta e$_3$-a ḫe$_2$-me-en uru$_2$-ta ba-ra-e$_3$-me-en | en$_3$-še$_3$-am$_3$ uru$_2$-za lu$_2$-erim$_2$-gin$_7$ bar-ta ba-e-da-gub | ama ^{d}nin-gal uru$_2$-zu lu$_2$-erim$_2$-gin$_7$ gaba-za ba-e-de$_3$-sa$_2$ | nin uru$_2$-ni ki aĝ$_2$ ḫe$_2$-me-en-na uru$_2$-zu-ta ba-e-ni-tag | kalam-ma-ni-še$_3$ kuš$_2$-u$_3$ ḫe$_2$-me-en-na za-e mu-e-tag 'My lady, you are one who has left the house, you are one who has left the city. How long will you stand aside from your city like an enemy? Mother Ningal, you *confronted* your city like an enemy! Although you are a lady who loves her city, you *rejected* your city. Although you are (a lady) who cares for her land, you *rejected* (it).'

Eventually, after the complete annihilation of the people, the cities, the land, and, indeed, the entire civilization, destruction seems to have subsided and restoration commenced. Again, considerable variations exist in the representations of restoration among the laments. In *LSU*, restoration arrived as Enlil responded positively to Nanna's second supplication. Much about the restoration is expressed in Enlil's blessing or promise to Nanna, as well as incantations or prayers in the closing section of the text, though a few passages do describe the fulfilment of restoration (*LSU* 475–7A, 486–92). In *LU* and *LE*, no divine petition succeeded, and restoration seems to be only hinted at in the incantation or prayer offered in the voice of the narrator on behalf of Ningal, Nanna, and Enki.

Only *LW* and *NL* explicitly mention the Isin ruler Išme-Dagan as playing a vital role in the fulfilment of restoration. *NL*, in particular, was structured in such a way as to build up anticipation for deliverance, by repeatedly stressing the long-suffering of the city Nippur and the land of Sumer prior to the deliverance through Išme-Dagan.[102] Išme-Dagan was regarded as one whose supplications and prayers successfully placated Enlil,[103] even when the deities had failed in other laments (e.g. Nanna in *LSU*), probably because of the Isin ruler's allegedly close familial relationship with Enlil. Because of him, not only had Enlil become merciful (*NL* 297), but also the Anunna gods as a whole had turned from being hostile to being beneficent (*NL* 245, 265–8). Moreover, Išme-Dagan was portrayed as a divinely chosen agent for the restoration of the cities, the land, and civilization.[104]

The restoration described in the city laments can be characterized as a dramatic reversal of the effects of destruction (Tinney 1996: 44–5), most of which have been discussed earlier:

Motifs of destruction	**Motifs of restoration**
departure of the gods	return of the gods (*NL* 160, 197–8, 210; *LSU* 475–7)
destruction of temples	rebuilding of temples (*NL* 163–6)
lost and desecrated rites	restored rites (*NL* 167–77, 217, 277–80, 299–300)
disrupted cultic worship	resumed cultic worship (*NL* 304–14; *LW* 12.7–9, 14–19)
lament	removal of lament (*NL* 182–3, 195)
divine hatred and hostility	divine compassion and favour (*NL* 184, 190–1)

[102] *NL* 31, 36, 37, 80, 94, 100, 112, 119, 179.
[103] *LW* 12.6–19; *NL* 304–14.
[104] *NL* 163–70, 201–35, 261, 275–82, 297–303.

silence	return of vitality and festivity (*NL* 193–4)
darkness	sunlight (*NL* 201–2, 292–3)
disrupted food supply in the temple	abundant food supply in the temple (*NL* 205, 281–2, 302; *LW* 12.10–13)
famine	abundant supply in the Land (*LSU* 466, 468, 500–1)
drought	water supply (*LSU* 498–500)
loss of intelligence and good sense	return of intelligence and good sense (*NL* 216)
dispersion of the people	return of the people to safe dwellings (*NL* 215)
Sumer and Akkad destroyed	Sumer and Akkad restored (*NL* 214)
major cities destroyed	major cities restored (*NL* 220–35; *LSU* 469)
suppression of growth of the people and the land	restoration of growth of the people and the land (*NL* 219, 251; *LSU* 509, 512, 516)
devastated agriculture and husbandry	restoration of agriculture and husbandry (*NL* 253–8; *LSU* 505)
lack of justice	re-establishment of justice (*NL* 261; *LSU* 493–4)
destruction of temples and temple property	restoration of temples and temple property (*NL* 272–4)
destruction of social order	re-establishment of social order (*NL* 284–91)
foreign invasion	foreign submission (*LSU* 471, 492)
destruction of Sumer	destruction of enemy lands (*LSU* 483–91)
cursing	blessing (*LSU* 464–74)
destruction of kingship	long life and reign for the king and his dynasty (*NL* 236–7, 314; *LSU* 507)
unchanged fate of destruction	unchanged fate of prosperity (*NL* 284; *LW* 12.28–38; *LSU* 493–511)

These schematic and formulaic descriptions of destruction and restoration, most elaborate in *NL*, are characteristic of hymnic compositions, especially royal hymns such as *Išme-Dagan A* and *Ur-Ninurta A*. Thus Tinney (1996: 23–5) defines *NL* this way: 'with its first half rooted in lamentations, and its second half distinctly hymnic in character'. This particular literary form attests to the destruction-restoration ideology that sought to present the Isin rulers as the divinely chosen saviours who rescued Sumer and its major cities from disorder and chaos. Such ideology stresses the symbiotic relationship between the cult in Nippur, especially that of Enlil, and the Isin dynasty. As the Isin rulers devoted themselves to the renovation of, and provision for, Nippur as the cultic centre in the Land, the city, its cultic personnel, and scribal school would reciprocate by helping legitimize and blessing the Isin rulers (*NL* 236–7, 314–18).

Given the fact that there were several competing regimes after the disintegration of the Ur III dynasty in Sumer and Akkad, one would expect that the Isin rulers would not be the only ones who invoked the destruction-restoration ideology for the legitimation and consolidation of their power.[105] It remains uncertain whether the tacit allusions to the unspecified royal figures in *LSU* 517; *LU* 430–1; *LE* (the Nippur version) segm. C 50–2 refer to the Isin rulers. Green (1978: 128–30), for example, suggests that *LE* could have been composed under the sponsorship of either the Isin ruler Išme-Dagan or the Larsa ruler Nur-Adad, though the former case is more likely.

With the restoration, the mode of the city laments shifts to hymnic praises dedicated not only to royal figures but also to deities.[106] The images of the chief deities being praised for their beneficent kingship and majesty contrast sharply with the images of their malicious, irrational exercise of authority and power in the lament section of the compositions. The pitiful images of the deities such as Nanna (*LSU*) and Inana (*LW*) who stood powerless in the face of the destruction of their cities and temples too were changed into images of glory.

There exist many parallels between the city laments and the Ur III compositions dealing with catastrophe, such as *Curse Agade* and *Ur-Namma A*, with regard to representations of petition and restoration. In *Curse Agade*, Naram-Suen too made supplications to the gods by putting on mourning clothes for seven years after he had been informed of the bleak prospects of Agade. Twice had Naram-Suen performed extispicy (lines 94–7) regarding the temple project, similar to the two petitions made by Nanna in *LSU* and by Ningal in *LU*. Inana, the patron goddess of the Akkad dynasty, was not of much help but gave in to the gods' plan to destroy Agade (lines 57–65). In the rest of *Curse Agade*, it is Nippur and Enlil's shrine Ekur, rather than Agade, that should be regarded as a parallel to the destroyed cities and temples in the city laments. Ekur was devastated by Naram-Suen's blasphemous attack. Towards the end of the text, Enlil himself rebuilt his shrine, but on a smaller scale than before (lines 193–4). Agade, on the other hand, was treated in a similar way to the countries of the enemy that attacked Sumer at the end of *LSU*, repaid with a more severe destruction than that which Naram-Suen had caused in Nippur.

In *Ur-Namma A*, the mother goddess Ninmah and the king's divine mother Ninsumun lamented over Ur-Namma's fate; so did several other deities such as Enki, Nanna, and Utu (lines 11–14). The king apparently made supplications for himself, but was rejected (lines 52–5). In the Netherworld, Ur-Namma

[105] See royal compositions from Larsa: *Gungunum A* segm. B 5; *Suen-iddinam E* 46; *Suen-iqīšam A* 51–6; *Rīm-Suen E* 72–84.

[106] *LSU* 464–73, 475–7, 514; *LU* 437; *LW* 12.1–5; *NL* 247–59, 319–22.

lamented over his fate and that of his spouse, rancorously complaining against the deities for repaying his faithful service to them with an evil end. Even those deities who expressed pity for him at the beginning of the text are deemed in Ur-Namma's criticism to have abandoned him and his wife (lines 166–86). Only after the intervention of Ur-Namma's divine spouse Inanna was the deceased king's fate ameliorated. In the style of a royal hymn, Ur-Namma was commemorated for his civic achievements (lines 222–31).

The destruction-restoration rhetoric apparently did not start with the city laments, but is already observable in the Ur III period, as in *Year Name 22 of Ibbi-Suen* (see also *Šulgi E* 174 ff. and *Amar-Suen A*). If Flückiger-Hawker (1999: 66–7) is correct in her reading of *Ur-Namma C* 57–9 (see also *Išme-Dagan A* 118–23), such rhetoric can be traced even further back, as early as the time of the first ruler of the Ur III dynasty, *c.*2112–2095 BC, or even earlier (see *Enanatum I E1.9.4.2; Ukg E1.9.9.1; Gudea Cylinders A* & *B*).

The city laments, however, differ from *Curse Agade* and *Ur-Namma A* in several major respects. Most obviously, regardless of their unabated questioning of the rational basis of divine decisions, the laments contain neither human nor divine defiance against the supreme decrees of the great gods. The authority of An and Enlil, though resented in the laments, was still accepted. By contrast, *Curse Agade* and *Ur-Namma A* contain human or divine attempts to challenge and alter the fates assigned by the great gods. It might be in response to the defiant spirit in *Curse Agade* and *Ur-Namma A* that the city laments reaffirm that divine decisions were immutable, unless An and Enlil decided, rather than were forced, to change their minds. Even if there was room for petition, the success of petition still depended on the status of the petitioner—only Enlil's divine son Nanna and human son Išme-Dagan were qualified. The fact that *LSU* repeatedly emphasizes the sole responsibility of Enlil in causing the devastation in the Land of Sumer also seems to respond to the notion in *Curse Agade* that Naram-Suen could arrogate to himself such unearthly power.[107] Moreover, as Cooper (1983: 20–1) has already pointed out, in constrast to the laments, *Curse Agade* portrays the city as being permanently doomed with no hope for restoration, a justifiable punishment given Naram-Suen's sacrilegious act. Overall, the laments (except for a few references in *LW* that suggest the growth of human population as a cause of catastrophe) tend to avoid presenting human provocations, probably, in some instances, in order to confront divine injustice more strongly.

In the following comparison we shall see that the Flood epic in many ways follows the formulae of petition and restoration in the city laments. The distinctive features in *Curse Agade* and *Ur-Namma A* likewise find their parallels in the epic.

[107] *LSU* 72, 73, 75, 164–6, 260–1, 292, 296–9.

Comparison with the Flood Epic

Petition in the Flood epic is primarily expressed as offered by Atra-hasīs to his lord Enki. The types of Atra-hasīs's petition on behalf of the people include inquiring about the duration of the plague,[108] lamenting,[109] the incubation of dreams,[110] and direct supplications.[111] All of these can find parallels in the city laments, except for communication through dreams, which is seen in *Curse Agade* 83–7 where the downfall of Agade was conveyed to Naram-Suen.

The extended laments of the mother goddess Nintu in the midst of and immediately after the Flood (OB *Atra-hasīs* III iii 28–iv 18; v 46–vi 4) resonate particularly with the prolonged laments of Ningal in the midst of or after the total destruction of Ur in *LU* 246–329. Nintu's regret for her compliance with the gods' destructive plan in the epic (OB *Atra-hasīs* III iii 36–43) may mirror Ningal's being conceived as having joined in the destruction of Ur regardless of her compassion for her city and people in *LU*. Furthermore, Nintu's diatribes against the wilful and irrational decision of Anu and Enlil (OB *Atra-hasīs* III iii 51–4, v 39–43) correspond with Inana's rebuke of Anu and Enlil in *Ur-Namma A* 207–10 for their erratic revoking of the established rules. More specifically, the mother goddess's barring of Enlil from partaking of the offerings provided by the Flood hero (SB *Gilgameš* XI 168–71), and in fact the entire motif of the gods suffering from hunger and thirst as a result of the destruction of the human race, are reminiscent of the motif of the deities' abundant supply being cut short which is referred to in Inana's rebuke of An and Enlil in *Ur-Namma A* 211.

Restoration in the Flood epic likewise is portrayed by way of inverting the effects of destruction, as in the Sumerian compositions dealing with catastrophe:

Motifs of destruction	**Motifs of restoration**
suppression of human growth and destruction of humankind	expansion of the land and population growth; survival of the human race (OB *Atra-hasīs* II i 2, III vi 9–10; the *Sumerian Flood Story* 259)
diminishing of food supply and water	abundant food supply and water (OB *Atra-hasīs* II ii 30–4, v 20)
divine hunger and thirst	offerings to the gods (OB *Atra-hasīs* III v 30–5; the *Sumerian Flood Story* 211)
darkness	sunlight (the *Sumerian Flood Story* 206; SB *Gilgameš* XI 137)
overthrowing of kingship	bestowal of life like a god on the king Ziusudra (the *Sumerian Flood Story* 256)

108 OB *Atra-hasīs* I vii 370–1 *adi māmī ib-*[. . .] | *murṣa immidūniāti a*[*na dāri*] 'How long . . . ? Will they impose disease on us [for ever]?'

109 OB *Atra-hasīs* II iii 4, 14.

110 OB *Atra-hasīs* II iii 5, 8, 10.

111 The Neo-Assyrian recension K 3399 + 3934 (S) rev. iv 23–8.

Most important is the correspondence between the portrayals of the human agent of petition and restoration in the Flood epic and those in the city laments. First of all, the royal identity of the agent of restoration, implicitly or explicitly expressed in the city laments, is often either hinted at or openly acknowledged at least in different versions of the Flood epic. In the *Atra-hasīs Epic*, there is no indication of the royal identity of the Flood hero. Instead, in several instances he is referred to as *ardīšu* 'his [Enki's] servant' (OB *Atra-hasīs* I vii 373, III i 16).[112] But the royal identity of Atra-hasīs might have been hinted at in the commanding status of Atra-hasīs and his role as intermediary between Enki and the people.[113] However, in the *Sumerian Flood Story* the royal status of the Flood hero is repeatedly affirmed,[114] due to the Flood story's emphasis on kingship (as in *LSU*). Though not directly calling the Flood hero a king, SB *Gilgameš* XI seems to depict him as a royal figure coming from the city Šuruppak (XI 11, 23), the last antediluvian city according to certain chronographical traditions,[115] and as the son of Ubār-Tutu (XI 23), an antediluvian king according to W-B 444 and W-B 62 and Berossos' account. In addition, the Flood hero's royal status is expressed, as also observed by Galter 2005: 275, obliquely in SB *Gilgameš* XI 95–6 *ana pēḫî ša* ^{ĝeš}*eleppi*(ma$_2$) ^{m}*puzur-*^{d}*enlil*(kur.gal) $^{\text{lu}}{}_2$*malāḫi*(ma.laḫ$_4$) | *ēkalla*(e$_2$.gal) *attadin adi būšēšu* 'To the man who sealed the boat, the shipwright Puzur-Enlil, I have given the palace with all its goods.'

Both the city laments and the Flood epic characterize the royal agent of restoration as pious or humble: *LW* 12.22–3 ⸢lu$_2$⸣ sun$_5$-na ĝiri$_3$-zu mu-un-dab$_5$-ba | ni$_2$-tuku nam-maḫ-zu mu-un-zu-a 'as a humble man who has grasped your (Inana's) feet, as a pious one who has experienced your exaltedness'; *NL* 276 ^{d}iš-me-^{d}da-gan šita u$_4$-da gub ḫul$_2$ ni$_2$-tuku-ni-ra 'To Išme-Dagan, the priest, who daily serves, the joyous, his pious one'; *NL* 310 sun$_5$-na

[112] See also the Neo-Assyrian recension K 3399 + 3934 (S) v 27. iv 17; v 27: [*bēl t*]*ašīmti* ^{m}*atra-ḫasīs amēlu* 'the sagacious one, the man Atra-hasīs'.

[113] Lambert and Millard (1969: 20–1) argue that it is unlikely that the Old Babylonian version of the *Atra-hasīs Epic* contains a reference to the antediluvian kings in the lost lines 307–51, because the epic uses a different chronological system from that used in the king lists. The scholars further suggest that the *Atra-hasīs Epic* represents a separate antediluvian history in which Atra-hasīs is the only king reigning during the whole antediluvian period. If this is true, the antediluvian tradition in the *Atra-hasīs Epic* seems to agree with the representation of the Flood hero as the only antediluvian ruler in the *Sumerian Flood Story*. Finkelstein (1963: 48) and Davila (1995: 204–5), on the other hand, argue for the non-royal identity of Atra-hasīs. But Finkelstein also notes that the epithet of Atra-hasīs, *amēlu*, equivalent to the Sumerian determinative $^{\text{lu}}{}_2$, may 'represent some honorific such as "the noble, the lordly, etc." which is exactly as it is used in the salutational phraseology of the Old Babylonian letters'. Such an honorific is used in the epic presumably in order to convey Atra-hasīs's high social status in his community because of his exceptional wisdom.

[114] The *Sumerian Flood Story* 145, 209, 211, 254, 258.

[115] See W-B 62, W-B 444, UCBC 9-1819; and the *Dynastic Chronicle*.

šita-ba ki la$_2$-a-ne$_2$-eš$_2$ ĝiri$_3$-ba si$_3$-ga-ne$_2$-eš$_2$ 'Because the humble one prostrated himself (in supplication) in his devotions, because he served there'; the *Sumerian Flood Story* 147 nam-sun$_5$-na inim si$_3$-si$_3$-ge ni$_2$ te-ga$_2$ [. . .]. 'with humility (and) well-chosen words, in reverence' (after Civil 1969: 143).[116] The agent of restoration who is portrayed as offering laments, prayers, and supplications to the deities can be found in both the Sumerian compositions dealing with catastrophe and the Flood epic.[117] The agent also provided food and drink for the deities.[118] That the sacred rites were restored through the royal figure, which may be seen in *NL* 167–70, 275–80, 299–301, can be deduced from the Flood hero's priestly function in the *Sumerian Flood Story* 145–50 (see also SB *Gilgameš* XI 157–60). In other words, the emphasis on the priestly function of the king Ziusudra who survived the Flood may suggest that the rites embodied in him must also have been preserved.

The blessing of the royal agent by Enlil and An is another common motif in the city laments and the Flood epic. More specifically, the notion that an extended life or reign was granted to the royal figure of restoration can be observed in *LSU* 507 e$_2$-gal-la zi su$_3$-ud ĝal$_2$ [u$_3$-tu] <an-ne$_2$ nam-kur$_2$-re> 'that there shall be long life in the palace—may An not change it'; *LW* 12.33 lu$_2$ iri-bi nam-ti niĝ$_2$ du$_{10}$-ge 'Man and this city! Life and well-being!'; *NL* 314 nam-nun-na mu su$_3$-su$_3$-ra$_2$-ni e-ne-er in-na-an-du$_{11}$-ga-am$_3$ 'His dominion of years made long, to him (Išme-Dagan) he (Enlil) promised'; the Middle Babylonian recension of the *Atra-hasīs Epic* from Ras Shamra Ugaritica v. 167 = RS 22.421 rev. 1–4 [. . .] x *ilāni*^{m}[^{eš}] *ba-l[a-ṭa$_2$ . . .]* [x x (x)] | x-*ta aššat-ka* x [. . .] | [x] x-*a tuk-la-at u$_3$* x [. . .] | *ki-i ilāni*^{meš} *ba-la-ṭa$_2$ lu-u$_2$* [. . .] '[. . .]. the gods life [. . .] [. . .] . . your wife. [. . .] [. .]. help and. [. . .] Life like the gods [you will] indeed [possess]'; the *Sumerian Flood Story* 256–7 ti diĝir-gin$_7$ mu-un-na-sum-mu | zi da-ri$_2$ diĝir-gin$_7$ mu-un-<na>-ab-e$_{11}$-de$_3$ 'they granted him life like a god, they brought down to him eternal life like (that of) a god'; SB *Gilgameš* XI 203–4 *ina pāna* ^{m}UD-*napišti*(zi) *amēlūtumma* | *eninnāma* ^{m}UD-*napišti*(zi) *u sinništa*(munus)*šu lū emû kīma ilī*(dingir)^{meš} *nâšīma* 'In the past UD-napišti was (one of) humankind, but now UD-napišti and his woman shall be like us gods'; and the Neo-Babylonian/Achaemenid fragment of the *Atra-hasīs Epic* MMA 86.11.378A rev. v 18–19 *m[ār-ka ašš]at-ka u mārat-ka ta-kal-ti lib$_3$-bi-[ka* x x] | [*lu*]-⸢*u$_2$*⸣ *šu-mat-ma it-ti ilāni ba-la-ṭu* x [x (x)] '[Your] son, your wife, your daughter, [your] friends?

116 For references to lu$_2$ sun$_5$-na, see also *LE* (the Nippur version) segm. C 50; *LU* 421.

117 *LW* 12.7–8, 24; *NL* 177, 304–11; OB *Atra-hasīs* I vii 370–1, II iii 4, 14; the *Sumerian Flood Story* 147–50, 210, 255; SB *Gilgameš* XI 138–9.

118 *LW* 12.9–13; *NL* 173, 275–82; OB *Atra-hasīs* III v 30–6; the *Sumerian Flood Story* 211–17.

(lit. the trust of [your] heart) [. . .], you shall be made like a god and [receive] (eternal) life!'[119]

As argued in our discussion on the Ziusudra tradition in Chapter 3, this notion of the divine endowment of extended life or reign on a royal personage, which appears ubiquitously as a topos in royal hymns and inscriptions, may constitute the chief motivation for creating the literary figure Ziusudra (zi-u_4-su_3-ra_2, probably meaning 'life of distant/prolonged days') as the Flood hero and an antediluvian ruler during the Old Babylonian period. The motif of granting eternal life to the Flood hero seems to be absent in the Old Babylonian version of the *Atra-hasīs Epic*, partly because the Babylonian epic followed the tradition that human mortality was only instituted after the Flood. This implies that Atra-hasīs and those who were from the antediluvian era and survived the Flood with him in the life-saving boat, unlike those born in the postdiluvian era, were already capable of living forever as long as the gods allowed them. As pointed out by George (2003: 507–8), the same idea that death was only instituted after the Flood can be observed in the *Death of Bilgames* (the Mê-Turan version) 76–7, 166–7. This conception of death differs from the tradition that human mortality started from the creation as seen in the Babylonian *Gilgameš Epic*: OB VA + BM iii 1–5; SB *Gilgameš* X 319–22.

Another reason for the motif of granting eternal life to be missing in the Old Babylonian version of the *Atra-hasīs Epic* may have to do with the Babylonian epic's emphasis on the persistence of the human race rather than the immortality of an individual, especially a royal hero. While *LSU*, the Isin royal hymnic compositions, the W-B 444 version of *SKL*, and the *Sumerian Flood Story* use the catastrophe or the Flood as the aetiological foundation for their doctrines of kingship, the *Atra-hasīs Epic* uses the Flood for a different aetiological purpose: to account for the human condition in general. The lacuna in OB *Atra-hasīs* III vi 28–39 does not seem likely to contain this motif. Rather, it may contain part of Enki's rebuke of Enlil as found in SB *Gilgameš* XI 188–98.

That the motif of Enlil granting eternal life to the Flood hero figures in the Neo-Babylonian/Achaemenid copy of the *Atra-hasīs Epic*, MMA 86.11.378A, Plates 59, 60, rev. v 15–23, seems to be a result of the influence from the Sumerian traditions about Ziusudra and the Standard Babylonian version of

[119] See '[Your] son, your wife, your daughter, ... [. . .]. You will become like a god; [you will receive] life' by Lambert (2005: 200). The above reading follows Lambert, except that the current author reconstructs the sign *ka* after *lib*$_3$*-bi* in line 18. The word *šu-mat-ma* in line 19, according to Lambert, is based on the Š-stem of *emû/ewûm* 'to become'; compare *lū emû kīma ilī nâšīma* 'they shall be like us gods!' in SB *Gilgameš* XI 204. The form *šūmâtma*, supposedly the predicative 2ms, appears irregular, as *šūmâtāma* is expected. The preposition following this word may also be problematic, as already noted by Lambert: '*emû/šūmû* is normally construed with *iš* or *kīma/kî*, rarely with *ana*. One could add *itti* to this list on the basis of this passage, but there is a possibility that a phonetic sign KI at some point in the transmission was misunderstood and rendered as *itti*.'

the *Gilgameš Epic*. In MMA 86.11.378A, Plates 59, 60, rev. v 17 *at-t[a-ma]* ^{I}*zi-su*$_3$*-ud-ra lu-u*$_2$ UD-*napištim*^{tim} [*šum*$_3$*-ka*] 'You are Zisudra, let [your name] be UD-*napištim*', the name Zisudra is that of the Flood hero from the Sumerian antediluvian tradition (as reflected in the *Sumerian Flood Story* and the W-B 62 version of *SKL*), and the name UD-napištim is that of the legendary hero in the Babylonian *Gilgameš Epic*. The use of these names, instead of Atra-hasīs, for the Flood hero, and the insertion of the motif of the Flood hero receiving eternal life attest to the convergence of the Babylonian Flood epic, the Sumerian antediluvian tradition, and the Babylonian Gilgameš tradition. The above passage in MMA 86.11.378A betrays the attempt of the redactor of this recension to use the Flood story as an aetiological account for the shift from the name Ziusudra to UD-napištim. A similar syncretistic attempt can also be observed in SB *Gilgameš* XI 197–204, where the name of the Flood hero is switched from Atra-hasīs to UD-napištim. As the Flood story was incorporated into the Babylonian *Gilgameš Epic*, the main figures in the two traditions had to be syncretized or harmonized, not just their names, but also their characterizations and the literary motifs associated with them (see discussion in Chapter 3).

Returning to our comparison of the Sumerian compositions dealing with catastrophe and the Flood epic, the hymnic ending of *NL* 319–22 'On the day for decreeing fates, every part of Sumer and Akkad, among the black-headed people flocking like sheep, among their well-tended people, they will praise forever the majesty of the Great Mountain Nunamnir (Enlil), *enkar* weapon of heaven and earth! It is his awe-inspiring way!' runs parallel to the doxology in OB *Atra-hasīs* III viii 11–18 'You, the counsellor of the [great] gods, at [your] decree I set bat[tle] in motion. For your praise let the Igigi hear this song and extol your greatness to one another. I have sung of the Flood to all the peoples. Hear it!' The epithet of Enlil in *NL*, enkar an ki-ke$_4$ '*enkar* weapon of heaven and earth', may be related to the flood weapon, as found in the divine hymn *Inana and Ebih* 2–6.

Despite the above similarities between the city laments and the Flood epic, the Flood epic had gone its own way in representing petition and restoration. But even in the instances where the Flood epic differs from the city laments, it seems rather clear that the author of the epic was still working on the basis of the city laments, reformulating or reorganizing the materials in the laments in order to present a new dramatized version of the catastrophe. For example, instead of presenting restoration only at the end of the composition, the *Atra-hasīs Epic* was constructed with several cycles of destruction, appeal, and restoration. Yet it is exactly the restoration towards the end of each cycle that precipitated a renewed and more grievous round of destruction. Here again the author of the Flood epic may have aimed at pursuing a logical sequence of events which finally led to Enlil's desperate attempt to completely destroy the human race by the Flood. In so doing, the author of the epic also extended the role of the human agent of restoration, which only comes at the end of the city laments (except for *NL*), into the main section of the composition. As a result, the Flood hero is depicted as performing not only the role of the human royal agent of restoration but also the role of the petitioning god or goddess in the city laments. In line with this thinking, the Flood hero's departure from his city or land in the Flood episode may also be seen as equivalent to the deities' abandonment of their cities before the arrival of the final destruction.[120]

Cycles of destruction-restoration can also be observed in the *Sumerian Flood Story*, but with a presentation significantly different from that which is found in the *Atra-hasīs Epic*. This particular version of the Flood story emphasizes that after the initial destruction of the human race (col. i) civilization was established by an anonymous deity, possibly Enki (whose name must be mentioned in the lacuna). According to Jacobsen (1981: 516), the introduction of this composition follows the typical presentation of those Sumerian texts dealing with the mythical origin of humankind. When first created by the gods, human beings were barbarous, naked, and vulnerable (e.g. the *Debate between Grain and Sheep*, obv. i 3–6), living a primitive life without arts and crafts, especially those skills necessary for securing their well-being through the establishment of irrigation and agriculture. Nor were religious rites, temples, and cities in place. Above all, human beings did not have kingship,[121] the essential institution by which everything else in a civilized life was organized. The *Sumerian Flood Story* is basically about the pivotal role of kingship in the establishment of civilization and the human race prior to the Flood and in the preservation of civilization and the human race during the Flood. It glorifies the kingship personified and idealized in the Flood hero Ziusudra who not only embodied the essence of civilization (lines 88–9) but also preserved the seed of humankind at the time of destruction, for which he was granted eternal life that befitted his name (lines 256–9).[122]

[120] Note that OB *Atra-hasīs* III ii 45–7 *irrub u uṣṣi* | *ul uššab ul ikammis* | *ḫepīma libbāšu imâ' martam* 'But he was in and out: he could not sit, could not crouch. For his heart was broken and he was vomiting gall' represent the Flood hero in ways similar to what one may find in *LU* 246–329 (especially line 294 ⸢me⸣-le-e-a me-a tuš-u_3-de_3 me-a gub-bu-de_3-en 'Woe is me! Where can I sit, where can I stand?'), where the text portrays the agitation of the goddess Ningal abandoning her city to destruction.

[121] See the fragment of the Sumerian mythological composition UET 6.61, lines 1–17 (partially restored), as referred to by Jacobsen (1981: 516).

[122] These lines in the *Sumerian Flood Story* indicate an aetiological motive. A similar motive can be observed in SB *Gilgameš* XI 196–7 *anāku ul aptâ pirišti ilī rabûti* | *atra-ḫasīs šunata ušabrīšumma pirišti ilī išme* 'I did not myself disclose the great gods' secret; I let Atra-hasīs see a dream and so he heard the gods' secret', where the author or redactor of the *Gilgameš Epic* attempted to explain the origin of the previous name of the Flood hero as Atra-hasīs ('one exceeding in wisdom') by emphasizing his extraordinary wisdom in discerning the secret of the gods about the coming Flood catastrophe which was only disclosed to him obliquely and cryptically by Enki through a dream.

The manner in which restoration was achieved in the *Atra-hasīs Epic* clearly seems to indicate an ingenious and satirical spin the author of the epic gave to the common motif of the interruption of divine offerings during the catastrophe in the city laments. While the laments only exposed the irrationality of the self-destructive behaviour of the gods, the Flood epic went further in exploiting this motif at the expense of the gods. The interruption of cultic worship and offerings to the deities in the laments appears to have been reinterpreted in the Flood epic as the people's deliberate withdrawal of devotion from these hostile and unhelpful deities. Instead, as a form of bribery, they redirected offerings to the gods in charge of plague and weather. Having received the gifts from the people, the gods were ashamed and stopped their destructive works. The epic's portrayals of the gods suffering dire hunger and thirst in the midst of the Flood also show how much the gods depended on their human servants. It may have been for this very reason that Enlil came to his senses and allowed Atra-hasīs and those with him to live after the Flood. Thus food and drink offerings, symbols of the gods' reliance on human beings, were manipulated in the epic to accomplish what the distraught gods or goddesses had often failed to do with their tears and supplications in the city laments.

The above perception of the human and divine relationships provides a means of manipulation through cultic offerings to keep the gods' hostility in check. Such cultic manipulation was carried out in actual practice, as indicated by a quotation of the *Atra-hasīs Epic* in a report presented by a Babylonian incantation priest to a Neo-Assyrian king as advice on drought:

K 761 1–5 (Lambert and Millard 1969: 27–8)
[(*ša*) ᵈ*ad*]*adma ši'a bābšu bili up*[*untu*] | ⸢*a*⸣*na qudumīšu lillikšumma ma*[*šḫ̮ātu*] | *nīqu ina šērēti imbaru liš*[*aznin*] | *eqlu kī šarrāqūtu māmū lišš*[*i*] | *kī zunnu ina māt akkadî*ᵏⁱ *īteqiru annâ e*[*pša*]

Seek the door of Adad, bring meal in front of it. May the offering of sesame-meal be pleasing to him. May he rain down a mist in the morning, so that the field will furtively bear water. When rain has become scarce in the land of Akkad, do this.

The perception of the human and divine relationships also gives the reader a sense of assurance that the gods could not afford to bring about another catastrophe such as the Flood, as the destinies of the gods and humankind were interwoven. This close affinity between the gods and humankind is hinted at with the wordplay between *ilū* and *awīlum* in the opening line of the epic *inūma ilū awīlum* 'when gods were (like) men' (OB *Atra-hasīs* I i 1);[123] in the creation of human beings *ilumma u awīlum libtalilū* | *puḫ̮ur ina ṭiṭṭi* 'That god

[123] For the metaphorical interpretation of this opening line, see Lambert and Millard 1969: 43, 146; Westenholz 1996: 188; Foster 2005: 229.

and human may be mixed together in the clay' (OB *Atra-hasīs* I iv 212–13); and in the name of the god Aw-ila who was slaughtered for the creation of humankind (OB *Atra-hasīs* I vii 223).[124] In the city laments, however, the hope that the catastrophe would never return was totally dependent on the good will of the gods who were much less connected with human beings.[125]

The Flood epic also differs from the city laments in terms of representing restoration as a result of the opposition between Enki and Enlil. One may speculate that such opposition reflects competition between Nippur and Eridu at the time of composition of the epic, whose author came from and represented Eridu (Jacobsen 1939: 60; 1981: 513). In addition, the Sumerian compositions dealing with contests, especially those between Enki and other deities, such as *Enki and Ninmah*, or *Inana and Enki*, could also have been sources of inspiration for the author of the Flood epic in this regard.[126] The prevalent belief that Enki was responsible for the creation and preservation of humankind (e.g. *Ur-Ninurta B* 33) in contrast with the notion in Sumerian literature that Enlil was often responsible for causing catastrophe may also have contributed to the conception of rivalry between the two gods in the Flood epic.

Lastly, different from the final restoration in the city laments, the *Atra-hasīs Epic* presents a compromise between Enlil and Enki after the Flood (OB *Atra-hasīs* III vi 43–vii 11). Though the human race was allowed to persist, several constraints were imposed to keep human population and noise under control (Lambert and Millard 1969: 13). These constraints include the institution of infant mortality, the prohibition of childbirth for several types of women, and death as the ultimate fate of all human beings (Foster 2005: 228), as opposed to the uninhibited growth promised in the city laments.[127] The establishment of these constraints after the Flood in the *Atra-hasīs Epic* links with the overall presentation of the epic, especially the logical sequence that leads one event after another to the final, complete destruction. If the vicious cycle was to be broken and the final catastrophe was to be prevented, the restoration of the human race, uninhibited in the first three destruction-restoration cycles in the epic, must be kept within bounds by the imposition of some constraints. Furthermore, the institution of these constraints was motivated by the aetiological interest of the author of the epic to explain the human condition.[128]

[124] See George and Al-Rawi 1996: 150; Alster 2002: 35–40; George 2003: 453; Foster 2005: 231, 236.

[125] See *LSU* 483–511; *LU* 408–16.

[126] As also suggested by Jacobsen 1981: 513–15; Horowitz 1998: 142–3, particularly n. 48; and Shehata 2001: 6 n. 23.

[127] See *LSU* 512–13, 516; *NL* 318, 320.

[128] The same aetiological motive also lies behind the entire composition that sought to present a mythological and dramatic story of how the primeval flood catastrophe came about.

The above analyses show that the Flood epic in many instances has adopted certain motifs and structural patterns from the Sumerian compositions dealing with catastrophe when representing petition and restoration. Meanwhile, the epic has also transformed considerably some of the materials found in the Sumerian compositions in order to make them fit its own organizing principle, i.e. the logical sequencing of events. One of the interesting results of this adaptation process is that the Flood hero now plays both the role of the pleading deities and the role of the royal agent of petition and restoration in the city laments. The multifaceted representation of the Flood hero has also incorporated the defiant character as seen in Naram-Suen in *Curse Agade* and the subservient character of the divine agent of restoration in the laments and the Isin-Larsa royal hymnic compositions (e.g. *Išme-Dagan A*, the *Instructions of Ur-Ninurta*). The Flood epic seems to have further manipulated the common motif of disrupted cultic offerings during the catastrophe in the laments in its critique of the traditional conceptions of the gods. Wilful in their malice towards their human subjects, their power was not as absolute as it appeared, and could be harnessed because of their dependence on human beings for subsistence. Innovative utilization of traditional materials can also be observed in the *Sumerian Flood Story*, principally in its manipulation of the imagery of the flood catastrophe to serve a political ideology dialectically different from that which is found in *LSU* and the *SKL* tradition.

SUMMARY

Previous comparative and historical studies of Mesopotamian traditions related to the Flood often tended to restrict their scope of research to the Flood episode of the *Atra-hasīs Epic*. By analysing the Flood epic as a whole that starts with several cycles of destruction and restoration and culminates in the Flood, the above study argues that the Sumerian compositions dealing with catastrophe, especially the city laments, constitute the main sources of inspiration for the composition of the Flood epic in terms of its depictions of destruction and restoration. Only in one case, the representation of overpopulation as a cause of catastrophe in *LW kirugu* 1 (1.1–8), is there uncertainty as to whether it was *LW* that had led to the same motif in *Atra-hasīs* or the other way round. It is also possible that both texts may have followed a common tradition.

Discovery of the origin of the Flood epic in this quarter of Mesopotamian literature may seem unexpected at first. But it should not be totally surprising if one considers the fact that both the laments and the Flood epic belong to the same literary category that treats catastrophe as 'the death of an era' (Vanstiphout 1980: 83). The intertextual relationship between the Sumerian compositions dealing with catastrophe and the Flood epic demonstrates many important continuities as well as changes in the political, religious, and literary traditions from the Ur III (possibly even earlier) and Isin-Larsa periods.[129] Investigating the development of the Flood epic in the context of these traditions helps us see how the epic was composed as a continuation of some of the conceptual and literary patterns or templates in the Ur III and Isin-Larsa periods. Such investigation also guides us in discerning the literary innovations the authors or redactors of different versions and recensions of the Flood epic had achieved—often in the process of their adapting the traditional materials—and the factors or principles which might have motivated the authors or redactors to produce those distinctive features characterizing their particular versions or recensions.

Two salient examples of the innovative character of the *Atra-hasīs Epic* are the rigorously pursued logical sequence of the events of catastrophe and the manipulation of the traditional motif of interrupted cultic offerings. The use of flood or storm catastrophe by the author of the *Sumerian Flood Story* to exalt kingship, a function of flood or storm imagery which is dialectically different from what is found in *LSU*, is equally noteworthy. The differences in purpose and in choice of the traditional materials between the two versions of the Flood epic—the *Atra-hasīs Epic* is more closely related to *LU* while the *Sumerian Flood Story* owes more to *LSU*—also suggest that they represent different attempts, approximately in the mid- and late Old Babylonian period, to convert the imagery of storm or flood catastrophe as found in the city laments for depicting the demise of the Ur III dynasty into a literal and aetiological representation with a dramatic plot. This is clearly an example of what Hallo (1975: 190) called 'to recast recent history into cosmological terms (myth)'.[130]

While the Flood epic may have reflected the socio-economic tensions at the time of its composition (Shehata 2001: 6), the political and religious atmosphere in the Old Babylonian period was also conducive to expressing a critical attitude towards religion as found in the Flood epic. Religious censorship seems to have been relaxed considerably, with the political establishment beginning to gain an upper hand (Postgate 1992: 300). What could have only been tolerated in the didactic literature as a critique of royal hubris (*Curse Agade*) and in extreme circumstances such as the tragic, premature death of a pious king (*Ur-Namma A*), or expressed in a restrained manner (as in the city laments), could now be explored more elaborately. The confrontation of divine flaws and the chastening of the unworthy gods were openly expressed in the religious sentiment of the general population in prayers as well as literature

[129] For political, religious, and literary continuities and changes between the Ur III and Isin-Larsa periods, see also Cooper 1983; Michalowski 1983, 1989; Klein 1985, 1990; Tinney 1996; Flückiger-Hawker 1999; and Brisch 2007.

[130] Hallo (1975: 190–1) also observes that most of the Mesopotamian aetiological myths of origins came from the Old Babylonian period, with a few from earlier dates.

(see Lambert 1960: 10–12). In royal propaganda represented by the *Sumerian Flood Story*, kingship was exalted at the expense of the gods whose authority and power, formerly portrayed as relentless and unchallenged, were now viewed as having failed to achieve their intended goal (though already reflected in *Year Name 22 of Ibbi-Suen*).

Conclusion

With the aim of tracing the historical development of the Flood motif and its historiographical and mythological representations, this book has examined various types of textual evidence from the Early Dynastic III period to the end of the first millennium BC, with a particular focus on the Old Babylonian period. Chapter 1 starts with orthographic and semantic analyses of flood terminology, and concludes that the specialized meaning 'the primeval flood catastrophe' for both the Sumerian term a-ma-ru and the Akkadian term *abūbu* only occurred from the Old Babylonian period onwards as far as the extant textual evidence is concerned. The ensuing analyses of the usage of flood terminology indicate that the flood terms were used chiefly in a figurative and mythical sense in the textual sources. The usage of a-ma-ru and *abūbu* in the specialized sense 'the primeval flood catastrophe' seems to have grown out of the figurative and mythical usage during the Old Babylonian period. This hypothesis can be supported by the fact that the usage of the flood term *abūbu* in the Old Babylonian version of the *Atra-hasīs Epic* and the Standard Babylonian version of the *Gilgameš Epic* (Tablet XI) still retain some of the same features as found in figurative and mythical usage. Yet, in the meantime, the usage of *abūbu* in the Babylonian Flood epic has made a clear departure from the traditional usage of flood terminology, both linguistically and conceptually.

Chapter 2 traces the emergence of the Flood motif in the broader literary-historical context of representations of the primeval time of origins. It is observed that both in terms of temporal conceptions and stylistic features, the motif emerged as an innovation during the Old Babylonian period in the literary traditions related to the primeval time of origins. The rise of the motif may have to do, at least partly, with the ideological and temporal manipulation of the demise of the Ur III dynasty and the restoration brought about by the Isin rulers, such as Išme-Dagan and Ur-Ninurta.

Chapter 3 investigates the development of divergent traditions related to antediluvian dynasties. It is observed that the interpretive history of the *Instructions of Šuruppak* and the ideological and chronographical framework of *SKL* were decisive for the formation of antediluvian traditions. The chapter also uncovers some of the major conceptual and literary mechanisms and processes through which antediluvian traditions were produced.

Chapter 4 compares the mythological compositions related to the Flood, principally the *Atra-hasīs Epic* and the *Sumerian Flood Story*, with the Sumerian compositions dealing with catastrophe, especially the city laments. It is shown that the former group of compositions follow many of the conceptual and literary patterns of the latter when representing destruction and restoration and characterizing the protagonists. At the same time, the comparisons also reveal some of the major conceptual and literary innovations brought about by the *Atra-hasis Epic* and the *Sumerian Flood Story*.

Thus, by approaching the relevant textual evidence from various angles, it is argued that Mesopotamian traditions related to the Flood only emerged from the Old Babylonian period onwards. Judging from this study, the traditions of the Flood as a primeval event in Mesopotamian cultural history belong to the type of '"Traditions" which appear or claim to be old' but 'are often quite recent in origin and sometimes invented' (Hobsbawm 1983: 1). Though based on the *realia* of the hydrological conditions of lower Mesopotamia, the Flood motif and its literary dramatizations (e.g. the plot and cast of the Flood story or epic) and chronographical constructions are largely intellectual and cultural constructs (already noted by King 1918: 102) forged in particular socio-political contexts. Similar phenomena of 'inventing tradition' in ancient Mesopotamia and in other cultures and times have already been observed by different scholars (e.g. Hobsbawm and Ranger 1983; Van Seters 1989: 49–61; Brisch 2007; Trevor-Roper 2008).

Mesopotamian Flood traditions as cultural products of their times attest to the power of creativity of ancient authors or scribes who tried to make sense of reality and respond to the ideological, social, and intellectual issues at hand. Despite their ideological functions, the motivations behind these traditions were not entirely self-serving manipulations and unfounded speculations. Time and time again one finds in many of these traditions a moral vision that aimed to promote the preservation and restoration of society, civilization, and the wider world; profound understandings of the human condition and destiny; penetrating observations of both *la longue durée* and *histoire événementielle* of natural and social history; and serious but lively theological and philosophical discourses. While these traditions may not be suitable sources for extracting reliable scientific information about the prehistoric events they intended to recount, they are extremely valuable for studying how the ancient Mesopotamians arrived at their understanding of prehistory in relation to more recent history. The process through which the ancient authors or scribes achieved historical consciousness with regard to early world history was often inseparable from whatever contemporary issues confronted them. The fact that these traditions continue to exert their influence beyond the rise of critical thinking, the separation of historical facts from legends and myths during the

Classical and Hellenistic periods,[1] and even the Age of Enlightenment in human understanding of the origins and early phases of the world proves that they have achieved a permanent and canonical status in the world's cultural heritage and memory. Arguably, such status of Mesopotamian Flood traditions was secured once they were connected with biblical and Hellenistic traditions.

Hallo (1990: 194–9) was certainly right when he regarded the development of Mesopotamian flood traditions as one of the best illustrations for the study of linguistic, literary, political, and religious history of the ancient Near East. By examining the textual evidence primarily from the Early Dynastic III period to the Old Babylonian period within the broader lexicological, literary, conceptual, and social contexts, this study has demonstrated that the development of the flood traditions involves various involuntary and conscious human factors. The development also bears witness to continuities and changes in Mesopotamian scholarship (e.g. linguistics, literary production, historiography), politics, and religion.

With ample textual evidence in diverse genres coming from different historical periods, the flood traditions are well suited for the study of literary history. This book has followed Hallo's suggestion (1962: 13–26) to trace different stages of the literary growth of a number of relevant literary compositions (with a particular focus on the *Atra-hasīs Epic*): from the conception of the Flood motif, to the development of diverse antediluvian traditions, to the composition of the Babylonian Flood epic, and finally to the adaptation of the Flood epic and different antediluvian traditions in the Standard Babylonian version of the *Gilgameš Epic*.[2] Special attention has been given to how the growth and interaction of various major strands of Mesopotamian traditions contributed to the emergence and development of the Flood traditions. These traditions include the flood topos and other meteorological topoi as often found in divine and royal hymnic compositions, literary representations of the primeval time of origins in mythological compositions and prologues, the *Instructions of Šuruppak*, the *SKL*, and the Sumerian and Babylonian compositions related to Gilgameš (see Chen 2013).

According to the above study, the Flood motif and its literary and historiographical representations as found in the W-B 444 version of *SKL* and the *Atra-hasīs Epic* are the results of several stages of development (figurative tradition, mythologization, historicization, and the convergence of traditions)

[1] Critical thinking and the separation of historical facts from legends and myths can already be observed in traditions such as the *Ballade of Early Rulers* from the Old Babylonian period.

[2] To a large extent, tracing this developmental process is not unlike tracing the evolutionary process of biological species by Darwin as shown in *On the Origin of Species*. Both cultural history and natural history share certain features in common, such as variation, adaptation, and hybridism. See Jacobsen 1939; Kramer 1944*b*; Hallo 1962; Tigay 1982; Dalley 1999; and George 2003 for applying the evolutionary perspective to the study of Mesopotamian literary history.

which, though culminating in the Old Babylonian period, had started in earlier literary periods in Sumerian traditions.[3] While much of the detailed process of the development still remains elusive, the extant textual sources have provided important evidence for our understanding of the key conceptual and literary steps in the process.[4] Future discoveries of new cuneiform sources will undoubtedly further clarify the origin of these conceptual and literary phenomena.[5] They may help fill some missing gaps in the historical framework this book has proposed for the development of the Flood motif, and reveal more variations and patterns during the evolution of the motif, thus making the framework more complete and accurate.

One needs to bear in mind, however, that it is not by trying to search for the still earlier textual evidence or *Vorlage* alone that we shall be able to unravel the literary-historical issues surrounding Mesopotamian Flood traditions. The origin of these conceptual and literary phenomena may not lie in single textual exemplars, but rather in the complex process of conceptual and literary developments, in which the composition and transmission histories of relevant literary traditions are closely intertwined.[6] It is by attending to this process, which involves tackling various interrelated conceptual and literary issues in multiple textual sources coming from different historical periods, that the contours of the origin of these phenomena may begin to surface.

Though this book has tackled the main areas of development of Sumerian and Babylonian Flood traditions, certain historical issues require further investigation. One is whether the Flood motif was based on the primeval storm motif used for the depiction of the union of heaven and earth as seen in the *Barton Cylinder*. Whether the development of the motif was connected with the watery origin in Babylonian cosmogony (Lambert 1975) also calls for investigation.[7] Another tantalizing issue has to do with the origin of the Flood story which is represented as the climactic episode of the *Atra-hasīs Epic*. Though the story appears to be an integral part of the Babylonian epic (Alster 2005: 33

[3] See also discussion in van Dijk 1964: 16–34; 1983: 33; Lambert and Millard 1969: 20; Van Seters 1989: 53–4; Hallo 1990: 195–9; 1991: 173; Glassner 2004: 109; Liverani 2005: 235; Chen 2012: 161–2.

[4] Written documents from ancient Mesopotamia are very much like fossil records in palaeobiology. Our collections and studies of both written documents from ancient Mesopotamia and fossil records in palaeobiology have reached such a level that in some cases they do not merely attest to the existence of certain literary phenomena or biological species, but reveal the evolution of these phenomena or biological species, i.e. how they originated and evolved in relation to preexisting and ensuing literary phenomena or biological species.

[5] It is especially hoped that Rubio's forthcoming publication of Sumerian literary texts from the Ur III period and Lambert's publication (2013) on Mesopotamian creation myths may shed new light on the issue. Perspectives and findings of comparative mythology (e.g. Witzel 2010, 2013) may also be valuable.

[6] For a similar emphasis on the conceptual and literary process of Mesopotamian literary phenomena, see Tinney 1996: 7–8 and George 2003: 106.

[7] The current author is indebted to Professor Andrew George for this suggestion.

n. 9)—which may have influenced the depictions of the Flood in the *Sumerian Flood Story* and the allusions to the Flood in the *Death of Bilgames*—it is possible that the story might have existed earlier than the Babylonian epic and was absorbed by the epic. As noted earlier, the Babylonian epic has adopted and woven together several traditional stories. Furthermore, the development of school curricula in various scribal centres, especially from the Ur III period to the Old Babylonian period, is an important topic which has not been dealt with in this book. As illustrated by the recent study of Koppen (2011: 140–66), detailed research on the topic will undoubtedly shed new light on how the composition and transmission of antediluvian traditions and the Flood epic were affected by the literary corpora available to the scribes and their professional background and religious involvement during the Old Babylonian period. Other than the above issues, the historical development of the tradition about the sages in relation to the Flood (see Lenzi 2008) has not been examined in this book because it is a late development in Mesopotamian intellectual and literary history. The tradition about the sages, as already noted by Lambert and Millard (1969: 19), 'is a tradition not specifically related to the great flood, but only secondarily and in some cases synchronized with it' (see also Hallo 1970: 62).

This book is by no means definitive on the study of Mesopotamian flood traditions. As stated in the Introduction, it focuses primarily on the textual sources from the Early Dynastic III to the Old Babylonian periods in order to trace the emergence and early development of the Flood motif and its historiographical and literary representations. But numerous cuneiform sources related to the flood traditions can be found from the Kassite period to the Hellenistic period towards the end of the first millennium BC. It is the author's hope that the references about the textual sources from the post-Old Babylonian period as collected in Appendix IV in Chen (2009 (Vol. 2)) will facilitate further research on the post-Old Babylonian development of the flood traditions. Even the development of the flood traditions already investigated extensively in the current research should be re-examined in the light of new textual evidence and new methodologies.

To close this study, it is appropriate to quote a felicitous remark of George Smith in *The Chaldean Account of Genesis* (1876: 301), which speaks eloquently of what the present author wishes to express as a personal reflection on what has been propounded in this book:

> I never lose sight myself of the fact, that . . . both in the decipherment of the broken fragments and in the various theories I have projected respecting them, I have changed my own opinions many times, and I have no doubt that any accession of new material would change again my views respecting the parts affected by it. These theories and conclusions, however, although not always correct, have, on their way, assisted the inquiry, and have led to the more accurate knowledge of the texts; for certainly in cuneiform matters we have often had to advance through error to truth.

Bibliography

Abusch, T. 1993. Gilgamesh's Request and Siduri's Denial, Part II: An Analysis and Interpretation of an Old Babylonian Fragment about Mourning and Celebration. *ANES* 22: 3–17.

Adams, R. McC. 1981. *Heartland of Cities*. Chicago: University of Chicago Press.

Alster, Bendt 1974. *The Instructions of Suruppak*. Mesopotamia. CSA 2. Copenhagen: Akademisk Forlag.

—— 1976*a*. Early Patterns in Mesopotamian Literature. In B. L. Eichler *et al.* eds., *Kramer Anniversary Volume: Cuneiform Studies in Honor of Samuel Noah Kramer*, 13–24. Neukirchen-Vluyn: Neukirchener Verlag.

—— 1976*b*. On the Early Sumerian Literature Tradition. *JCS* 28: 109–26.

—— 1990. The Sumerian Poem of Early Rulers and Related Poems. *OLP* 21: 5–25.

—— 1992. Interaction of Oral and Written Poetry in Early Mesopotamian Literature. In M. E. Vogelzang and H. L. J. Vanstiphout, eds., *Mesopotamian Epic Literature: Oral or Aural?* 23–70. Lewiston, NY: Edwin Mellen Press.

—— 2002. *ilū awīlum: we-e i-la*, 'Gods: Men' versus 'Man: God': Punning and the Reversal of Patterns in the Atrahasis Epic. In Tzvi Abush, ed., *Riches Hidden in Secret Places: Ancient Near Eastern Studies in Memory of Thorkild Jacobsen*, 35–40. Winona Lake, Ind.: Eisenbrauns.

—— 2005. *Wisdom of Ancient Sumer*. Bethesda, Md.: CDL Press.

—— 2008. Scribes, Sages, and Seers in Ancient Mesopotamia. In Leo G. Perdue, ed., *Scribes, Sages, and Seers: The Sages in the Eastern Mediterranean World*, 46–63. Göttingen: Vandenhoeck & Ruprecht.

Alster, Bendt, and Jeyes, U. 1986. A Sumerian Poem about Early Rulers. *ASJ* 8: 1–11.

Alster, Bendt, and Vanstiphout, Herman 1987. Lahar and Ashnan: Presentation and Analysis of a Sumerian Disputation. *ASJ* 9: 1–43.

Alster, Bendt, and Westenholz, Aege 1994. The Barton Cylinder. *ASJ* 16: 15–46.

Annus, Amar 2002. *The God Ninurta in the Mythology and Royal Ideology of Ancient Mesopotamia*. SAAS 14. Helsinki: NATCP, University of Helsinki.

Arnaud, Daniel 2007. *Corpus des textes de bibliothèque de Ras Shamra-Ougarit (1936–2000) en sumérien, babylonien et assyrien*. Sabadell-Barcelona: Editorial Ausa.

Beaulieu, Paul-Alain 2007. The Social and Intellectual Setting of Babylonian Wisdom Literature. In R. J. Clifford, ed., *Wisdom Literature in Mesopotamia and Israel*, 3–19. SBL Symposium Series 36. Atlanta, Ga.: SBL.

Berlin, Adele 1979. *Enmerkar and Ensuhkešdanna: A Sumerian Narrative Poem*. OPBF 2. Philadelphia: University of Pennsylvania Museum.

Biggs, Robert 1966. The Abū Ṣalābīkh Tablets: A Preliminary Survey. *JCS* 20: 73–88.

—— 1971. An Archaic Sumerian Version of the Kesh Temple Hymn from Tell Abū Ṣalābīkh. *ZA* 61: 193–207.

—— 1974. *Inscriptions from Tell Abū Ṣalābīkh*. OIP 99. Chicago: University of Chicago Press.

Black, Jeremy 1992. Some Structural Features of Sumerian Narrative Poetry. In M. E. Vogelzang and H. L. J. Vanstiphout, eds., *Mesopotamian Epic Literature: Oral or Aural?* 71–101. Lewiston, NY: Edwin Mellen Press.

—— 1998. *Reading Sumerian Poetry*. London: Athlone Press.

Borger, Rykle 1956. *Die Inschriften Asarhaddons Königs von Assyrien. AfO* 9. Osnabrück: Biblio-Verlag.

—— 2003. *Mesopotamisches Zeichenlexikon*. AOAT 305. Münster: Ugarit-Verlag.

Brisch, Nicole Maria 2007. *Tradition and the Poetics of Innovation: Sumerian Court Literature of the Larsa Dynasty (c. 2003–1763 BCE)*. AOAT 339. Münster: Ugarit-Verlag.

Buringh, P. 1957. Living Conditions in the Lower Mesopotamian Plain in Ancient Times. *Sumer* 13: 30–46.

Castellino, G. R. 1957. Les Origines de la civilisation selon les textes bibliques et les textes cunéiformes. In George W. Anderson, ed., *Congress Volume: Strasbourg 1956*, 116–37. VTSup 4. Leiden: Brill.

Cathcart, Kevin J. 1997. The Age of Decipherment: The Old Testament and the Ancient Near East in the Nineteenth Century. In J. A. Emerton, ed., *Congress Volume: Cambridge 1995*, 81–95. VTSup 66. Leiden: Brill.

Cavigneaux, Antoine 2000. La Fin de Gilgameš, Enkidu et les Enfers d'après les manuscrits d'Ur et de Meturan. *Iraq* 62: 1–19.

Cavigneaux, Antoine, and Al-Rawi, F. N. H. 2000. *Gilgameš et la mort. Textes de Tell Haddad VI: avec un appendice sur les textes funéraires sumériens*. CM 19. Groningen: Styx.

Charpin, Dominique 2010. *Reading and Writing in Babylon*. Trans. Jane Marie Todd. Cambridge, Mass.: Harvard University Press.

Chen, Y. S. 2009. *The Emergence and Development of Sumerian and Babylonian Traditions Related to the Primeval Flood Catastrophe from the Old Babylonian Period*. 2 vols. D.Phil. thesis, University of Oxford.

—— 2012. The Flood Motif as a Stylistic and Temporal Device in Sumerian Literary Traditions. *JANER* 12: 158–89.

—— 2013. Major Literary Traditions Involved in the Making of Mesopotamian Flood Traditions. In Jason M. Silverman, ed., *Opening Heaven's Floodgates: The Genesis Flood Narrative, Its Contexts and Reception*, 141–90. Piscataway, NJ: Gorgias.

Civil, Miguel 1961. Texts and Fragments. *JCS* 15: 79–80.

—— 1969. The Sumerian Flood Story. In W. G. Lambert and A. R. Millard, *Atra-ḫasīs: The Babylonian Story of the Flood*, 138–45, 167–72. Oxford: Clarendon Press.

—— 1984. Notes on the 'Instructions of Šuruppak'. *JNES* 43: 281–98.

—— 1987. Ibbi-Suen, Year 22. *NABU* 49: 27–8.

Civil, M., and Biggs, R. D. 1966. Notes sur des Textes Sumériens Archaïques. *RA* 60: 1–16.

Clay, A. T. 1922. *A Hebrew Deluge Story in Cuneiform and other Epic Fragments in the Pierpont Morgan Library*. YOR 5, 3. New Haven, CT: Yale University Press.

Clifford, R. J. 1994. *Creation Accounts in the Ancient Near East and the Bible*. Washington, DC: CBAA.

Cohen, Mark E. 1988. *The Canonical Lamentations of Ancient Mesopotamia*. 2 vols. Potomac, Md.: CDL Press.

Cole, Steven 1994. Marsh Formation in the Borsippa Region and the Course of the Lower Euphrates. *JNES* 53: 81–109.

Cole, Steven, and Gasche, Hermann 1999. Levees, Floods, and the River Network of Northern Babylonia: 2000–1500 BC and 1000–500 BC—A Preliminary Report. In Johannes Renger, ed., *Babylon: Focus mesopotamischer Geschichte, Wiege früher Gelehrsamkeit, Mythos in der Moderne*, 87–110. CDOG 2. Saarbrücken: Saarbrücker, Druckerei und Verlag.

Cooper, Jerrold S. 1978. *The Return of Ninurta to Nippur*. AnOr 52. Rome: Pontificium Institutum Biblicum.

—— 1983. *The Curse of Agade*. Baltimore, Md.: Johns Hopkins University Press.

—— 1992. Babbling on: Recovering Mesopotamian Orality. In M. E. Vogelzhang and H. L. J. Vanstiphout, eds., *Mesopotamian Epic Literature: Oral or Aural?* 103–22. Lewiston, NY: Edwin Mellen Press.

Dahl, Jacob L. 2007. *The Ruling Family of Ur III Umma: A Prosopographical Analysis of an Elite Family in Southern Iraq 4000 Years Ago*. Leiden: Nederlands Instituut voor het Nabije Oosten.

Dalley, Stephanie 1999. Authorship, Variation and Canonicity in Gilgamesh and other Ancient Texts. *Interaction* 2: 31–47.

—— 2005. The Language of Destruction and its Interpretation. *BadM* 36: 275–85.

Darwin, Charles 1859. *On the Origin of Species*. London: John Murray.

Davila, James R. 1995. The Flood Hero as King and Priest. *JNES* 54: 199–214.

De Maaijer, Remco, and Jagersma, Bram 1997–8. Review of Åke W. Sjöberg, ed., *The Sumerian Dictionary of the University Museum of the University of Pennsylvania*. *AfO* 44–5: 277–88.

Dietrich, Manfried 1995. *ina ūmī ullûti* 'An jenen (fernen) Tagen': Ein sumerisches kosmogonisches Mythologem in babylonischer Tradition. In Manfried Dietrich and Oswald Loretz, eds., *Vom Alten Orient zum Alten Testament: Festschrift für Wolfram Freiherrn von Soden zum 85. Geburtstag am 19. Juni 1993*, 57–72. Neukirchen-Vluyn: Neukirchener Verlag.

Dijk, J. J. A. van 1962. Die Tontafeln aus dem rēš-Heiligtum. *UVB* 18: 43–60.

—— 1964. Le Motif cosmique dans la pensée sumérienne. *ActOr* 28: 1–59.

—— 1976. *Cuneiform Texts: Texts of Varying Content*. TIM IX. Leiden: Brill.

—— 1983. *LUGAL UD ME-LÁM-bi NIR-ĜÁL: Le Récit épique et didactique des Travaux de Ninurta, du Déluge et de la Nouvelle Création*. Leiden: Brill.

Driver, G. R., and Miles, John C. eds. 1955. *The Babylonian Laws, Vol. II*. Oxford: Clarendon Press.

Dundes, Alan, ed. 1988. *The Flood Myth*. Berkeley: University of California Press.

Durand, J. M. 1988. *Archives épistolaires de Mari* 1, 1. ARM 26, 1. Paris: Éditions Recherche sur les Civilisations.

Eco, Umberto 1986. *Semiotics and the Philosophy of Language*. Bloomington, Ind.: University of Indiana.

Edzard, D. O. 1957. *Die zweite Zwischenzeit Babyloniens*. Wiesbaden: Harrassowitz.

—— 1980–3. Königslisten und Chroniken. *RLA* 6: 77–86.

—— 1997. *Gudea and his Dynasty*. RIM 3/1. Toronto: University of Toronto Press.

—— 2003. *Sumerian Grammar*. Handbook of Oriental Studies 71. Leiden: Brill.

Eichler, Barry L. 1993. mar-URU$_5$: Tempest in a Deluge. In Mark E. Cohen, D. C. Snell and D. B. Weisberg, eds., *The Tablet and the Scroll: Near Eastern Studies in Honor of William W. Hallo*, 90–4. Bethesda, Md.: CDL Press.

Falkenstein, A. 1949. *Grammatik der Sprache Gudeas von Lagaš*. I Schrift- und Formenlehre. AnOr 29. Rome: Pontificium Institutum Biblicum.

—— 1951. Zur Chronologie der sumerischen Literatur. *RAI* 2: 12–30.

Faraone, Christopher A., and Lincoln, Bruce 2012. Imagined Beginnings: The Poetics and Politics of Cosmogonic Discourse in the Ancient World. *ARG* 1: 3–13.

Ferrara, A. J. 1995. Topoi and Stock-Strophes in Sumerian Literary Tradition: Some Observations, Part I. *JNES* 54: 81–117.

—— 2006. A Hodgepodge of Snippets: Some Thoughts on Narrative Now and Then. In Piotr Michalowski and Niek Veldhuis, eds., *Approaches to Sumerian Literature: Studies in Honour of Stip (H. L. J. Vanstiphout)*, 47–66. Leiden: Brill.

Finkel, Irving S. 1980. Bilingual Chronicle Fragments. *JCS* 32: 65–80.

Finkelstein, J. J. 1963. The Antediluvian Kings: A University of California Tablet. *JCS* 17: 39–51.

Flückiger-Hawker, Esther 1999. *Urnamma of Ur in Sumerian Literary Tradition*. OBO 166. Göttingen: Vandenhoeck & Ruprecht.

Foster, Benjamin R. 2005. *Before the Muses: An Anthology of Akkadian Literature*. 3rd edn. Bethesda, Md.: CDL Press.

Frame, Grant 1995. *Rulers of Babylonia from the Second Dynasty of Isin to the End of Assyrian Domination (1157–612 B.C.)*. RIMB 2. Toronto: University of Toronto Press.

Frayne, Douglas R. 1997. *Ur III Period (2112–2004 BC)*. RIME 3/2. Toronto: University of Toronto Press.

—— 1998. New Light on the Reign of Išme-Dagan. *ZA* 88: 6–44.

Friberg, Jöran 2007. *A Remarkable Collection of Babylonian Mathematical Texts: Manuscripts in the Schøyen Collection*. Cuneiform Texts I. SSHMP. New York: Springer.

Gadd, C. J., and Kramer, S. N. 1966. *Literary and Religious Texts*. UET 6/2. London: Trustees of the British Museum and the Trustees of the University of Pennsylvania Museum.

Galter, Hannes D. 2005. *Ša lām abūbi*: Die Zeit vor der großen Flut in der mesopotamischen Überlieferung. In Robert Rollinger, ed., *Von Sumer bis Homer: Festschrift für Manfred Schretter zum 60. Geburtstag am 25. Februar 2004*, 269–301. Münster: Ugarit-Verlag.

George, Andrew 2003. *The Babylonian Gilgamesh Epic: Introduction, Critical Edition and Cuneiform Texts*. 2 vols. Oxford: Oxford University Press.

—— 2007. The Gilgameš epic at Ugarit. *AuOr* 25: 237–54.

—— 2009. *Babylonian Literary Texts in the Schøyen Collection*. CUSAS 10. Bethesda, Md.: CDL Press.

George, A. R., and Al-Rawi, F. N. H. 1996. Tablets from the Sippar Library VI. Atra-hasīs. *Iraq* 58: 147–90.

Glassner, Jean-Jacques 2004. *Mesopotamian Chronicles*. Atlanta, Ga.: SBL.

Gomi, T. 1984. On the Critical Economic Situation at Ur Early in the Reign of Ibbisin. *JCS* 36: 211–42.

Grayson, A. K. 1975. *Assyrian and Babylonian Chronicles*. Locus Valley, NY: J.J. Augustin Publisher.

—— 1991. *Assyrian Rulers of the Early First Millennium B.C. I (1114–859 B.C.)*. RIMA 1. Toronto: University of Toronto Press.

Green, M. W. 1978. The Eridu Lament. *JCS* 30: 127–67.

—— 1984. The Uruk Lament. *JAOS* 104: 253–79.

Guillaume, Philippe. 2003. Sifting the Debris: Calendars and Chronologies of the Flood Narrative. In Jason M. Silverman, ed., *Opening Heaven's Floodgates: The Genesis Flood Narrative, Its Contexts and Reception*, 55–82. Piscataway, NJ: Gorgias.

Hallo, W. W. 1962. New Viewpoints on Cuneiform Literature. *IEJ* 12: 13–26.

—— 1963*a*. On the Antiquity of Sumerian Literature. *JAOS* 83: 167–76.

—— 1963*b*. Beginning and End of the Sumerian King List in the Nippur Recension. *JCS* 17: 52–7.

—— 1970. Antediluvian Cities. *JCS* 23: 57–67.

—— 1975. Toward a History of Sumerian Literature. In S. J. Lieberman, ed., *Sumerian Studies in Honor of Thorkild Jacobsen on his Seventieth Birthday June 7, 1974*, 181–203. AS 20. Chicago: University of Chicago Press.

—— 1990. The Limits of Skepticism. *JAOS* 110: 187–99.

—— 1991. Information from before the Flood: Antediluvian Notes from Babylonia and Israel. *Maarav* 7: 173–81.

Heimpel, Wolfgang 1968. *Tierbilder in der sumerischen Literatur*. Studia Pohl 2. Rome: Pontificium Institutum Biblicum.

Hobsbawm, Eric J. 1983. Introduction: Inventing Traditions. In Eric J. Hobsbawm and Terence O. Ranger, eds., *The Invention of Tradition*, 1–14. Cambridge: Cambridge University Press.

Hobsbawm, Eric J., and Ranger, Terence O. eds. 1983. *The Invention of Tradition*. Cambridge: Cambridge University Press.

Hoffner, H. 1976. Enki's Command to Atra-hasis. In Barry L. Eichler *et al.* eds., *Kramer Anniversary Volume: Cuneiform Studies in Honor of Samuel Noah Kramer*, 241–5. AOAT 25. Neukirchen-Vluyn: Neukirchener Verlag.

Horowitz, Wayne 1998. *Mesopotamian Cosmic Geography*. Winona Lake, Ind.: Eisenbrauns.

Huehnergard, John 2005. *A Grammar of Akkadian*. 2nd ed. Harvard Semitic Museum Studies 45. Winona Lake, Ind.: Eisenbrauns.

Hurdle, Jon 2012. A Museum Full of Antiquities Embraces Modernity. *The New York Times*, 4 December.

Jacobsen, Thorkild 1939. *The Sumerian King List*. AS 11. Chicago: University of Chicago Press.

—— 1946. Sumerian Mythology: A Review Article. *JNES* 5: 128–52.

—— 1953. The Reign of Ibbī-Suen. *JCS* 7: 36–47.

—— 1980. Death in Mesopotamia (Abstract). In *Death in Mesopotamia*, ed. Bendt Alster, 19–23. Copenhagen: Akademisk Forlag.

—— 1981. The Eridu Genesis. *JBL* 100: 513–29.

—— 1987. *The Harps That Once. . . . Sumerian Poetry in Translation*. New Haven, Conn.: Yale University Press.

Jacobus, Helen R. 2013. Flood Calendars and Birds of the Ark in the Dead Sea Scrolls (4Q252 and 4Q254a), Septuagint, and Ancient Near Eastern Texts. In Jason M. Silverman, ed., *Opening Heaven's Floodgates: The Genesis Flood Narrative, Its Contexts and Reception*, 83–114. Piscataway, NJ: Gorgias.

Jiménez-Zamudio, Rafael 1996. Acusativo del todo y de la parte, una peculiaridad sintáctica en *Atramhasis* III 2: 50 (version paleobabilonia). *AuOr* 14: 133–6.

Katz, Dina 2007. Enki and Ninhursaĝa, Part One: The Story of Dilmun. *BiOr* 64: 568–89.

—— 2008. Enki and Ninhursaĝa, Part Two: The Story of Enki and Ninhursaĝa. *BiOr* 65: 320–41.

Keetman, Jan 2008. Der Kampf im Haustor. Eine der Schlüsselszenen zum Verständnis des Gilgameš-Epos. *JNES* 67: 161–73.

Kennedy, Maev 2010. Relic reveals Noah's ark was circular. *The Guardian*, 1 January.

Kilmer, A. D. 1972. The Mesopotamian Concept of Overpopulation and its Solution as Reflected in the Mythology. *Or.* 41: 160–77.

—— 1996. Fugal Features of Atrahasīs: The Birth Theme. In M. E. Vogelzang and H. L. J. Vanstiphout, eds., *Mesopotamian Poetic Language: Sumerian and Akkadian*, 127–39. CM 6. Groningen: Styx.

—— 2006. Visualizing Text: Schematic Patterns in Akkadian Poetry. In Ann K. Guinan *et al.* eds., *If a Man Builds a Joyful House: Assyriological Studies in Honor of Erle Verdun Leichty*, 209–21. Leiden: Brill.

King, L. W. 1918. *Legends of Babylon and Egypt in Relation to Hebrew Tradition.* The Schweich Lectures 1916. London: British Academy.

Klein, Jacob 1976. Šulgi and Gilgameš: Two Brother-Peers (Šulgi O). In B. L. Eichler, *et al.* eds., *Kramer Anniversary Volume: Cuneiform Studies in Honor of Samuel Noah Kramer*, 271–92. AOAT 25. Neukirchen-Vluyn: Neukirchener Verlag; Kevelaer: Butzon & Bercker.

—— 1981. *Three Šulgi Hymns: Sumerian Royal Hymns Glorifying King Šulgi of Ur.* Bar-Ilan Studies in Near Eastern Languages and Culture, Publications of the Bar-Ilan University Institute of Assyriology. Ramat-Gan, Israel: Bar-Ilan University Press.

—— 1985. Šulgi and Išme-Dagan: Runners in the Service of the Gods (*SRT* 13). *Beer-Sheva* 2: 7–38.

—— 1990. Šulgi and Išme-Dagan: Originality and Dependence in Sumerian Royal Hymnology. In Jacob Klein and A. Skaist, eds., *Bar-Ilan Studies in Assyriology: Dedicated to Pinhas Artzi*, 65–136. Ramat Gan: Bar-Ilan University Press.

—— 1991. A New Nippur Duplicate of the Sumerian Kinglist in the Brockmon Collection, University of Haifa. In P. Michalowski *et al.* eds., *Velles Paraules: Ancient Near Eastern Studies in Honor of Miguel Civil on the Occasion of his Sixty-Fifth Birthday*, 123–9. AuOr 9. Sabadell (Barcelona), Spain: Editorial Ausa.

—— 1997. The God Martu in Sumerian Literature. In I. L. Finkel and M. J. Geller, eds., *Sumerian Gods and their Representations*, 99–116. CM 7. Groningen: Styx.

—— 2008. The Brockmon Collection Duplicate of the Sumerian Kinglist (BT 14). In Piotr Michalowski, ed., *On the Third Dynasty of Ur: Studies in Honor of Marcel Sigrist*, 77–91. Boston: ASOR.

Komoróczy, G. 1975. Akkadian Epic Poetry and its Sumerian Sources. *ActAnt* 23: 40–63.

Koppen, Frans van 2011. The Scribe of the Flood Story and his Circle. In Karen Radner and Eleanor Robson, eds., *The Oxford Handbook of Cuneiform Culture*, 140–66. Oxford: Oxford University Press.

Kramer, Samuel N. 1944*a*. *Sumerian Literary Texts from Nippur in the Museum of the Ancient Orient at Istanbul.* AASOR 23. New Haven, Conn.: ASOR.

—— 1944*b*. The Epic of Gilgameš and its Sumerian Sources. *JAOS* 64: 7–23.
—— 1947. Gilgameš and the Land of the Living. *JCS* 1: 3–46.
—— 1952*a*. *Enmerkar and the Lord of Aratta: A Sumerian Epic Tale of Iraq and Iran*. Philadelphia: University of Pennsylvania Museum.
—— 1952*b*. A Fulbright in Turkey. *UMB* 17/2: 3–56.
—— 1980. Inanna and the *Numun*-plant: A New Sumerian Myth. In Ruth Adler *et al.* eds., *The Bible World: Essays in Honor of Cyrus H. Gordon*, 87–97. New York: KTAV Publishing House.
Kraus, F. R. 1952. Zur Liste der älteren Könige von Babylonien. *ZA* 50: 29–60.
Krebernik, Manfred 1998. Die Texte aus Fāra und Tell Abū Ṣalābīh. In P. Attinger and M. Wäfler, eds., *Mesopotamien: Späturuk-Zeit und Frühdynastische Zeit*, 237–430. OBO 160/1. Göttingen: Vandenhoeck & Ruprecht.
Lambert, M. 1961. La Littérature sumérienne à propos d'ouvrages récents. *RA* 55: 181–4.
Lambert, W. G. 1960. *Babylonian Wisdom Literature*. Oxford: Clarendon Press.
—— 1965. A New Look at the Babylonian Background of Genesis. *JTS* 16: 287–300.
—— 1967. Enmeduranki and Related Matters. *JCS* 21: 126–38.
—— 1973. A New Fragment from a List of Antediluvian Kings and Marduk's Chariot. In M. A. Beek *et al.* eds., *Symbolae biblicae et mesopotamicae: Francisco Mario Theodoro de Liagre Böhl dedicatae*, 271–80. Leiden: Brill.
—— 1974. The Seed of Kingship. In Paul Garelli, ed., *Le Palais et la royauté*, 427–40. CRRA 19. Paris: Geuthner.
—— 1975. The Cosmology of Sumer and Babylon. In Carmen Blacker and Michael Loewe, eds., *Ancient Cosmologies*, 42–65. London: George Allen & Unwin Ltd.
—— 2005. Atra-ḫasīs. In Ira Spar and W. G. Lambert, eds., *Cuneiform Texts in the Metropolitan Museum of Art II: Literary and Scholastic Texts of the First Millennium B.C.*, 195–201. New York: Metropolitan Museum of Art.
—— 2013. *Babylonian Creation Myths*. MC 16. Winona Lake, Ind.: Eisenbrauns.
Lambert, W. G., and Millard, A. 1965. *Babylonian Literary Texts*. CT 46. London: Trustees of the British Museum.
—— 1969. *Atra-ḫasīs: The Babylonian Story of the Flood, with the Sumerian Flood Story by M. Civil*. Oxford: Clarendon Press.
Langdon, S. 1915. *Sumerian Epic of Paradise, the Flood and the Fall of Man*. PBS X 1. Philadelphia: University of Pennsylvania Museum.
—— 1917. *Sumerian Liturgical Texts*. PBS X 2. Philadelphia: University of Pennsylvania Museum.
—— 1923*a*. *Historical Inscriptions, Containing Principally the Chronological Prism, W-B. 444*. OECT II. The Weld-Blundell Collection II. Oxford: Oxford University Press.
—— 1923*b*. The Chaldean Kings before the Flood. *JRAS*: 251–9.
Legrain, Leon 1922. *Historical Fragments*. PBS XIII. Philadelphia: University of Pennsylvania Museum.
Lenzi, Alan 2008. *Secrecy and the Gods: Secret Knowledge in Ancient Mesopotamia and Biblical Israel*. SAAS 19. Helsinki: NATCP, Helsinki University.
Lewis, Jack P. 1992. Flood. In David N. Freedman, ed., *The Anchor Bible Dictionary*, Vol. 2, 798–803. New York: Doubleday.

Liverani, Mario 2005. *Israel's History and the History of Israel*. Trans. Chiara Peri and Philip R. Davies. London: Equinox.

Livingstone, Alasdair 1986. *Mystical and Mythological Explanatory Works of Assyrian and Babylonian Scholars*. Oxford: Clarendon Press.

Löhnert, Anne 2011. Manipulating the Gods: Lamenting in Context. In Karen Radner and Eleanor Robson, eds., *The Oxford Handbook of Cuneiform Culture*, 402–17. Oxford: Oxford University Press.

Luckenbill, D. D. 1924. *The Annals of Sennacherib*. OIP II. Chicago: University of Chicago Press.

Machinist, Peter 1976. Literature as Politics: The Tukulti-Ninurta Epic and the Bible. *CBQ* 38: 455–82.

——1983a. Rest and Violence in the Poem of Erra. *JAOS* 103: 221–26.

——1983b. Assyria and Its Image in the First Isaiah. *JAOS* 103: 719–37.

——1986. On Self-Consciousness in Mesopotamia. In S. N. Eisenstadt, ed., *The Origins and Diversity of Axial Age Civilizations*, 183–202. Albany: SUNY Press.

——1993. Assyrians on Assyria in the First Millennium B.C. In K. Raaflaub, ed., *Anfange politischen Denkens in der Antike*, 77–104. Schriften des Historischen Kollegs, Kolloquien 24. Munich: Oldenbourg.

——1994. Outsiders or Insiders: The Biblical View of Emergent Israel and Its Contexts. In L. J. Silberstein and R. L. Cohn, eds., *The Other in Jewish Thought and History*, 35–60. Constructions of Jewish History and Identity. New York: New York University Press.

——1995a. Fate, Miqreh, and Reason: Reflections on Qohelet and Biblical Thought. In Ziony Zevit, Seymour Gitin, and Michael Sokoloff, eds., *Solving Riddles and Tying Knots: Biblical, Epigraphic, and Semitic Studies in Honor of Jonas C. Greenfield*, 159–75. Winona Lake: Eisenbrauns.

——1995b. The Transfer of Kingship: A Divine Turning. In A. B. Beck, A. H. Bartelt, C. A. Franke, and P. R. Raabe, eds., *Fortunate the Eyes That See: Essays in Honor of David Noel Freedman in Celebration of His Seventieth Birthday*, 105–20. Grand Rapids: Eerdmans.

——1995c. The Fall of Assyria in Comparative Ancient Perspective. In S. Parpola and R. M. Whiting, eds., *Assyria 1995: Proceedings of the 10th Anniversary Symposium of the Neo-Assyrian Text Corpus Project, Helsinki, September* 7–11, 1995, 179–95. Helsinki: NATCP.

——2003. The Voice of the Historian in the Ancient Near Eastern and Mediterranean World. *Interpretation* 57: 117–37.

——2005. Order and Disorder: Some Mesopotamian Reflections. In Shaul Shaked, ed., *Genesis and Regeneration*, 31–61. Jerusalem: Israel Academy of Sciences and Humanities.

Mallowan, M. E. L. 1964. Noah's Flood Reconsidered. *Iraq* 26: 62–82.

Matouš, L. 1960. Les Rapports entre la version sumérienne et la version akkadienne de l'épopée de Gilgameš. In P. Garelli, ed., *Gilgameš et sa légende*, 83–94. CRRA 7. Paris: Librairie C. Klincksieck.

Maul, S. M. 1999. Wer baute die babylonische Arche? Ein neues Fragment der mesopotamischen Sintfluterzählung aus Assur. *MDOG* 131: 155–62.
Michalowski, Piotr 1983. History as Charter: Some Observations on the Sumerian King List. *JAOS* 103: 237–48.
——1987. Charisma and Control: On Continuity and Change in Early Mesopotamian Bureaucratic Systems. In R. D. Biggs and M. Gibson, eds., *The Organization of Power: Aspects of Bureaucracy in the Ancient Near East*, 55–68. Chicago: University of Chicago Press.
——1989. *The Lamentation over the Destruction of Sumer and Ur*. Winona Lake, Ind.: Eisenbrauns.
—— 1991. Negation as Description: The Metaphor of Everyday Life in Early Mesopotamian Literature. *AuOr* (Fs. M. Civil) 9: 131–6.
——1995. Sumerian Literature: An Overview. In Jack M. Sasson, ed., *Civilizations of the Ancient Near East*, Vol. IV, 2279–91. New York: Scribner.
——2000 (publ. 2005). The Life and Death of the Sumerian Language in Comparative Perspective. *ASJ* 22: 177–202.
——2005. Literary Works from the Court of King Ishbi-Erra of Isin. In Yitschak Sefati *et al.* eds., *'An Experienced Scribe Who Neglects Nothing': Ancient Near Eastern Studies in Honor of Jacob Klein*, 199–212. Bethesda, Md.: CDL.
——2010. Maybe Epic: The Origins and Receptions of Sumerian Heroic Poetry. In David Konstan and Kurt A. Raaflaub, eds., *Epic & History*, 7–25. Oxford: Wiley-Blackwell.
——2011. *The Correspondence of the Kings of Ur: An Epistolary History of an Ancient Mesopotamian Kingdom*. Winona Lake, Ind.: Eisenbrauns.
Milstein, Sara J. 2010. *Reworking Ancient Texts: Revision through Introduction in Biblical and Mesopotamian Literature*. Ph.D. dissertation, New York University.
Mittermayer, Catherine 2009. *Enmerkara und der Herr von Arata. Ein ungleicher Wettstreit*. OBO 239. Fribourg: Academic Press; Göttingen: Vandenhoeck & Ruprecht.
Moran, William 1987. Some Considerations of Form and Interpretation in Atra-hasīs. In F. Rochberg-Halton, ed., *Language, Literature, and History. Philological and Historical Studies Presented to Erica Reiner*, 245–55. AOS 67. New Haven, CT: AOS.
Parpola, Simo 1993. *Letters from Assyrian and Babylonian Scholars*. SAA 10. Helsinki: University of Helsinki.
Poebel, Arno 1914*a*. *Historical Texts*. PBS IV 1. Philadelphia: University of Pennsylvania Museum.
—— 1914*b*. *Historical and Grammatical Texts*. PBS V. Philadelphia: University of Pennsylvania Museum.
Postgate, J. N. 1992. *Early Mesopotamia: Society and Economy at the Dawn of History*. New York: Routledge.
Ravn, O. E. 1955. Selected Passages in Enuma eliš and Gilgameš. *ActOr* 22: 28–54.
Reiner, Erica 1984. *Damqam-īnim* revisited. *StOr* 55 (Memoriae Jussi Aro dedicata): 177–82.
Robson, E. 2001. The Tablet House: A Scribal School in Old Babylonian Nippur. *RA* 95: 39–66.
——2002. More than Metrology: Mathematics Education in an Old Babylonian Scribal School. In J. M. Steele and A. Imhausen, eds., *Under One Sky: Mathematics and Astronomy in the Ancient Near East*, 325–65. AOAT 297. Münster: Ugarit-Verlag.

—— 2011. The Production and Dissemination of Scholarly Knowledge. In Karen Radner and Eleanor Robson, eds., *The Oxford Handbook of Cuneiform Culture*, 557–76. Oxford: Oxford University Press.

Römer, W. H. Ph. 1965. *Sumerishe 'Königshymnen' der Isin- zeit*. DMOA 13. Leiden: Brill.

Rubio, Gonzalo (forthcoming). *Sumerian Literary Texts from the Ur III Period*. Winona Lake, Ind.: Eisenbrauns.

Sallaberger, Walther 2007. From Urban Culture to Nomadism: A History of Upper Mesopotamia in the Late Third Millennium. In Catherine Kuzucuoğlu and Catherine Marro, eds., *Sociétés humaines et changement climatique à la fin du troisième millénaire: Une crise a- t- elle eu lieu en Haute Mésopotamie? Actes due Colloque de Lyon, 5–8 décembre 2005*, 417–56. Paris: De Boccard.

Samet, Nili 2009. *The Lamentation over the Destruction of Ur: A Revised Edition*. Ph.D. thesis, Bar-Ilan University.

Sauren, H. 1993. Nammu and Enki. In M. E. Cohen *et al.* eds., *The Tablet and the Scroll: Near Eastern Studies in Honor of William W. Hallo*, 198–208. Bethesda, Md.: CDL Press.

Scheil, V. 1898. Un fragment d'un nouveau récit babylonien du déluge, de l'époque du roi Ammizadouga. *RB* 7: 5–9.

——1934. Listes susiennes des dynasties de Sumer-Accad. *RA* 31: 147–66.

Shehata, Dahlia 2001. *Annotierte Bibliographie zum altbabylonishen Atramhasīs-Mythos Inūma ilū awīlum*. GAAL 3. Göttingen: der Universität Göttingen.

Sigrist, Marcel, and Damerow, Peter, eds. 1991. *Mesopotamian Yearnames: NeoSumerian and Old Babylonian Date Formulae*. Vol. 1. Preprint version. Potomac, Md.: CDL Press.

Sjöberg, Åke W. 2002. In the Beginning. In Tzvi Abusch, ed., *Riches Hidden in Secret Places: Ancient Near Eastern Studies in Memory of Thorkild Jacobsen*, 229–47. Winona Lake, Ind.: Eisenbrauns.

——2005. A New Shulgi Hymn. In Yitschak Sefati *et al.* eds., *'An Experienced Scribe Who Neglects Nothing': Ancient Near Eastern Studies in Honor of Jacob Klein*, 291–300. Bethesda, Md.: CDL.

Smith, George 1873. The Chaldean Account of the Deluge. *TSBA* 2: 213–34.

——1876. *The Chaldean Account of Genesis*. London: Sampson Low, Marston, Searle, and Rivington.

Soden, Wolfram von 1960. Status-rectus Formen vor dem Genitiv im Akkadischen und die sogenannte uneigentliche Annexion im Arabischen. *JNES* 19: 163–71.

——1994. Der altbabylonische Atramchasis-Mythos. In Otto Kaiser, ed., *Weisheitstexte, Mythen und Epen*, 612–45. TUAT III/4. Gütersloh: Gütersloher Verlagshaus.

Sollberger, E. 1967. The Rulers of Lagaš. *JCS* 21: 279–91.

Steiner, G. 1996. Huwawa und sein 'Bergland' in der sumerischen Tradition. *ASJ* 18: 187–215.

Steinkeller, Piotr 2003. An Ur III Manuscript of the Sumerian King List. In Walther Sallaberger *et al.* eds., *Literatur, Politik und Recht in Mesopotamien: Festschrift für Claus Wilcke*, 267–92. OBC 14. Wiesbaden: Harrassowitz.

Streck, Michael 1999. *Die Bildersprache der akkadischen Epik*. AOAT 264. Münster: Ugarit-Verlag.

——2002. Die Prologe der sumerischen Epen. *Or.* 71: 189–266.

Thomsen, Marie-Louise 2001. *The Sumerian Language: An Introduction to Its History and Grammatical Structure.* Mesopotamia. CSA 10. 3rd edn. (1984) Copenhagen: Akademisk Forlag.

Thureau-Dangin, F. 1912. *Une relation de la huitième champagne de Sargon (714 av. J. - C.).* Paris: Librairie Paul Geuthner.

Tigay, Jeffrey 1982. *The Evolution of the Gilgamesh Epic.* Philadelphia: University of Pennsylvania Press.

—— 1985. *Empirical Models for Biblical Criticism.* Philadelphia: University of Pennsylvania Press.

Tinney, Steve 1996. *The Nippur Lament: Royal Rhetoric and Divine Legitimation in the Reign of Išme-Dagan of Isin (1953–1935 B.C.).* OPSNKF 16. Philadelphia: University of Pennsylvania Museum.

——1999. On the Curricular Settings of Sumerian Literature. *Iraq* 61: 159–72.

——2011. Tablets of Schools and Scholars: A Portrait of the Old Babylonian Corpus. In Karen Radner and Eleanor Robson, eds., *The Oxford Handbook of Cuneiform Culture*, 577–96. Oxford: Oxford University Press.

Trevor-Roper, H. 2008. *The Invention of Scotland: Myth and History.* New Haven: Yale University Press.

Van De Mieroop, Marc 2004. *A History of the Ancient Near East.* Oxford: Blackwell.

—— (forthcoming). The Mesopotamians and their Past. In J. Wiesehöfer, ed., *Periodisierung und Epochenbewusstsein in der antiken Geschichtsschreibung.* Oriens et Occidens. Stuttgart.

Van Seters, J. 1989. Myth and History: The Problem of Origins. In Albert de Pury, ed., *Historie et conscience historique dans les civilisations du Proche- Orient ancien*, 49–61. Leuven: Peeters.

Vanstiphout, H. L. J. 1980. The Death of an Era: The Great Mortality in the Sumerian City Laments. In Bendt Alster, ed., *Death in Mesopotamia*, 83–9. Copenhagen: Akademisk Forlag.

——1986. Some Thoughts on Genre in Mesopotamian Literature. In K. Hecker *et al.* eds., *Keilschriftliche Literatur*, 1–11. Berlin: Reimer Verlag.

——1997. The Disputation between Bird and Fish. In William W. Hallo, ed., *The Context of Scripture I: Canonical Compositions from the Biblical World*, 581–4. Leiden: Brill.

——2003. *Epics of Sumerian Kings: The Matter of Aratta.* Atlanta, Ga.: SBL.

Veldhuis, Niek 1997. *Elementary Education at Nippur. The List of Trees and Wooden Objects.* Ph.D. dissertation, University of Groningen.

——2001. The Solution of the Dream: A New Interpretation of Bilgames' Dream. *JCS* 53: 133–48.

——2004. *Religion, Literature, and Scholarship: The Sumerian Composition Nanše and the Birds, with a Catalogue of Sumerian Bird Names.* Leiden: Brill.

Verbrugghe, Gerald P., and Wickersham, John M. 1996. *Berossos and Manetho, Introduced and Translated: Native Traditions in Ancient Mesopotamia and Egypt.* Ann Arbor: University of Michigan Press.

Verhoeven, Kris. 1998. Geomorphological Research in the Mesopotamian Flood Plain. In Hermann Gasche and Michel Tanret eds., *Changing Watercourses in Babylonia: Towards a Reconstruction of the Ancient Environment in Lower Mesopotamia*, Vol. 1,

159–245. Mesopotamian History and Environment II. University of Ghent and the Oriental Institute of the University of Chicago, 1998.

Vincente, Claudine-Adrienne 1990. Tell Leilān Recension of the Sumerian King List. *NABU* 11: 8–9.

——1995. The Tell Leilān Recension of the Sumerian King List. *ZA* 85: 234–70.

Vogelzang, M. E., and Vanstiphout, H. L. J., eds. 1992. *Mesopotamian Epic Literature: Oral or Aural?* Lewiston, NY: Edwin Mellen Press.

Westenholz, Joan Goodnick 1992. Metaphorical Language in the Poetry of Love in the Ancient Near East. In D. Charpin and F. Joannès, eds., *La Circulation des biens, des personnes et des idées dans le Proche- Orient ancien*, 381–7. CRRA 38. Paris: Éditions Recherche sur les Civilisations.

—— 1996. Symbolic Language in Akkadian Narrative Poetry: The Metaphorical Relationship between Poetical Images and the Real World. In M. E. Vogelzang and H. L. J. Vanstiphout, eds., *Mesopotamian Poetic Language: Sumerian and Akkadian*, 183–206. CM 6. Groningen: Styx.

——1997. *Legends of the Kings of Akkade: The Texts*. Winona Lake, Ind.: Eisenbrauns.

Wilcke, Claus 1975. Formale Gesichtspunkte in der sumerischen Literatur. In Stephen J. Lieberman, ed., *Sumerological Studies in Honor of Thorkild Jacobsen on his Seventieth Birthday June 7, 1974*, 205–316. AS 20. Chicago: University of Chicago Press.

——1977. Die Anfänge der akkadischen Epen. *ZA* 67: 153–216.

——1978. Philologische Bemerkungen zum Rat des Šuruppag. *ZA* 68: 202–32.

——1987. Die Inschriftenfunde der 7. und 8. Kampagnen (1983 und 1984). In Barthel Hrouda, ed., *Isin-Ishan Bahriyat III: Die Ergebnisse der Ausgrabungen 1983–1984*, 89–93. München: BAW.

—— 1989. Genealogical and Geographical Thought in the Sumerian King List. In H. Behrens *et al.* eds., *Dumu-E$_2$-DUB-BA-A: Studies in Honor of Äke W. Sjöberg*, 557–71. OPKF 11. Philadelphia: University of Pennsylvania Museum.

—— 1999. Weltuntergang als Anfang: theologische, anthropologische, politisch-historische und ästhetische Ebenen der Interpretation der Sintflutgeschichte im babylonischen Atram-hasīs-Epos. In Adam Jones, ed., *Weltende: Beiträge zur Kultur- und Religionswissenschaft*, 63–112. Wiesbaden: Harrassowitz.

Witzel, Michael 2010. Pan-Gaean Flood Myths: Gondwana Myths—and Beyond. In Wim M. J. van Binsbergen and Eric Venbrux, eds., *New Perspectives on Myth. Proceedings of the Second Annual Conference of the International Association for Comparative Mythology, Ravenstein (the Netherlands), 19–21 August, 2008*, 225–42. PIP-TraCS 5. Haarlem, the Netherlands: Shikanda.

——2013. *The Origins of the World's Mythologies*. Oxford: Oxford University Press.

Woods, Christopher 2012. Sons of the Sun: The Mythological Foundations of the First Dynasty of Uruk. *JANER* 12: 78–96.

Index

NAMES OF DEITIES AND OTHER MYTHICAL FIGURES

NAMES OF HUMAN BEINGS

Alulim (Alulu?) 188, 192–3
Amegalaros 192; *see also* Enmegalanna; Enmengalanna
Amelōn 191–2; *see also* Enmenluanna
Amempsinos 141, 192; *see also* Ensipazianna
Amenōn 191–2; *see also* Enmenluanna
Ammisaduqa 3
Ashurbanipal 1
Atra-hasīs 54, 115–18, 120, 129–31, 153, 156–8, 163, 176–8, 205–7, 225–9, 232, 242–6, 248

Bilgames 10, 74, 107, 166; *see also* Gilgameš

Damiq-ilišu 5
Daōnos 192; *see also* Dumuzi (the Shepherd)
Dumuzi (the Shepherd) 45, 57, 86, 110–12, 114, 126, 191–3

Eanatum 42, 47, 55
En-hedu-ana 59
Enkidu 159, 164–5, 167–8, 172–3, 180
Enmeduranki (Enmeduranna, Enmenduranna) 150, 172, 176, 192–3
Enmegalanna (Enmengalanna) 191–3
Enmenluanna (Ammeluanna) 191–2
Enmerkar 68, 108–11, 122
Ensipazianna 141, 190–3
Etana 68, 173–4
Euedōrachos 192; *see also* Enmeduranki

Gilgameš 68, 74–6, 91, 103, 106–8, 122, 127, 149–50, 158–9, 161–82, 195, 246, 255
Gudea 37, 39, 42, 106

Hammurabi 38, 40, 44

Ibbi-Suen 47, 62, 96–8, 125, 201
Išbi-Erra 198
Išme-Dagan 37, 44, 46, 51—2, 55, 57, 62, 97, 101, 125, 149, 198–9, 237–8, 240–1, 243–4, 253

Naram-Suen 46, 68, 94–5, 182, 220, 224–4, 240–2, 250
Nebuchadnezzar I 150, 176
Nūr-Dāgan 171

Otiartes 130, 141–3, 150, 192; *see also* Ubār-Tutu

Puzur-Enlil 243

Samsu-iluna 141, 183
Sargon 170–1, 175
Šar-ur 37, 39, 42, 45, 53
Šiduri 11, 170
Šu-ilīšu 198
Šulgi 16, 27–8, 35, 44–6, 49, 51–4, 56–7, 62, 74–6, 122
Sursunabu 11, 170; *see also* Ur-šanabi
Šū-Suen 27, 35, 39, 40, 42, 44

Ubār-Tutu 9, 102, 130, 135–45, 150, 153–6, 175, 192–3, 243
UD-napišti 10, 160, 162, 175, 181, 246
Ur-Namma 7, 45, 62, 73–4, 76, 213, 224, 240–1
Ur-Ninurta 33, 46, 62, 99, 101, 103, 122, 127, 253
Ur-šanabi 11, 170
UR_2.AŠ 8–9, 132–8, 142–5, 153
Ūta-na'ištim 10–11, 129, 158–62, 166, 169–76, 178, 180, 195

Xisuthros 129–30, 141–3, 150–1, 192; *see also* Ziusudra

Ziusudra (Zisudra) 5, 8–11, 62, 102, 107, 119–20, 129–31, 135–7, 139–47, 149–55, 157–8, 161–2, 165–7, 169–78, 180, 192–6, 235, 242, 244–7

GEOGRAPHICAL NAMES

Abū Ṣalābīkh 8, 13, 102, 132, 138, 142–3
Adab 8–9, 102, 132–8, 142–3, 145, 154, 157, 201, 230
Agade 94–5, 204, 224, 234, 240, 242
Akkad 36, 43, 50–1, 57–8, 60, 75, 94, 170–1, 198–9, 204, 213, 239–40, 246, 248
Anšan 213

Babylon 183–5, 198–9
Babylonia 151
Badtibira 110, 191–3, 204

Dilmun 5, 80–3, 108–9, 119, 170, 177–8

Eridu 40, 44–5, 51, 53–4, 79–80, 85, 109, 123, 126, 151, 186, 188, 192–3, 201, 204, 211, 213, 217, 249
Ešnunna 198

Gutium 45, 210, 213

SUBJECTS AND CONCEPTS

linguistic, literary, political, and religious history of the ancient Near East 13, 255
Mesopotamian cultural 106, 254, 255 n. 2
Mesopotamian cultural and literary 3
Mesopotamian intellectual and literary 257
Mesopotamian political 77
natural 255 n. 2
natural and social 254
normal or normal course of 122, 126
political 77, 106
political and cultural 106
prehistory 254
recent or recent course of 122, 251, 254
recorded 235
Roman 17
transition from the nineteenth to eighteenth century B.C. 5
world 3,
see also antediluvian history; interpretive history; literary history; primeval history
human beings/humankind 44, 88–9, 248
birth ritual of 218
creation of 83–4, 90, 115–19, 203, 225, 229, 247–8
black-headed people 105, 119, 148, 224, 246
connection with the gods 249
destroyed 53, 201, 206
existence 116
granted grain and sheep by the gods for their sustenance 89
having no kingship 247
heart-beat of 227
helped by Enki to counter Enlil's hostile attacks 228
instructed by Enki not to revere their gods or to pray to their goddesses 207, 225–6, 228–9
instructed by Enki to bribe the storm god for relieving drought 116
not innocent 233
not to have immortality after the Flood 107–8
overpopulation 197, 224, 230, 250
population growth and control 115, 163, 226, 231 n. 79, 242, 249
preservation during the Flood 105
providing subsistence for the gods 250
recovered after catastrophe 229
suffering famine and drought 232
ultimate fate of 249
human condition 90, 105–6, 118, 245, 249, 254
human provocations 241
hunger:
and thirst of gods 207, 232, 242, 248
of human beings 116, 211 and n. 27
hydrological condition(s) 1, 64, 254
hymns 16, 40, 61, 121, 124, 202, 213, 216, 224
divine 2, 17, 61, 65, 96, 174 n. 84, 199, 246
royal 2, 16–17, 27–8, 35, 37, 49, 51, 54, 56–7, 61, 65, 69, 73–6, 96, 98, 101, 121, 124, 147, 160, 169 n. 74, 171, 174 n. 84, 178 n. 90, 195, 198–9, 202, 213, 239, 241, 245
hymnic compositions 16, 96, 147, 171, 195, 212–15, 239, 245, 250, 255
hymnic ending 246
hymnic mode 199
hymnic praise 199, 240
hymnic section 102, 199
hymnic tradition 212
hypothesis 25, 161, 184 n. 97, 253

identity 34–5, 120, 130, 139, 144, 145, 153, 155, 176, 235 n. 92, 243
ideological responses 123, 125, 127
ideology:
political 6, 77, 94, 96, 101, 104, 118, 120, 145, 146–8, 152, 198–9, 213, 225, 236, 239–40, 250
religious 72
royal 101
see also destruction-restoration ideology
image(s):
abstract 59
compound 233
concrete 50–9
mixed 60, 201, 233
recurrent 210
see also flood image
image clusters 50, 60–1, 211 n. 31
imagery 19, 24–6, 72, 206, 208, 210, 212, 214, 216, 218–19, 220, 225, 233, 250–1
density of 50, 214 n. 43
form of 34–46
frequency of 26, 50
historical development of 26
poetic 72
structural or dramatic 214 n. 43
Sumerian and Akkadian 26, 34
see also animal imagery; flood imagery; meteorological imagery
immortality 108, 165, 170 n. 76, 245
see also Atra-hasīs; Flood hero; Gilgameš; Ūta-na'ištim/UD-napišti; Ziusudra
incantation 2, 236, 238, 248

SELECTIVE QUOTATIONS OR CITATIONS OF MODERN SCHOLARSHIP

SUMERIAN AND AKKADIAN TEXTS QUOTED

Middle Babylonian Version
Neo-Assyrian Recensions

SUMERIAN WORDS DISCUSSED

a-ma-ru 27–8
a-ma-ru$_{12}$ 28
a-ma$_2$-ru 28
a-ma$_2$-uru$_5$ 28
a-MAR 26
a-mar-uru$_5$ 288

dim$_2$-ma 231–2

e-ma-ru 28
e$_2$-mar-uru$_5$ 21, 28–31

ĝeštu$_2$ 132, 157 and n. 39, 231

lu$_2$ ti-la 165–7, 172, 174

ma$_2$-uru$_5$ 21, 28
mar-TE 29
mar-uru$_5$ 21, 28

SU.KUR.LAM 130

Ubār-Tutu 135, 137
umuš 231–2
UR$_2$.AŠ 137–8, 142
uru$_2$ (URU×UD) 30
uru$_5$ 30
uru$_{18}$ (URU×A) 30

zi-u$_4$-su$_3$-ra$_2$ 158–82

AKKADIAN WORDS DISCUSSED

Printed and bound by CPI Group (UK) Ltd, Croydon, CR0 4YY